I'M READY FOR MY
MOVIE CONTRACT

I'M READY FOR MY MOVIE CONTRACT

a  GET FUZZY collection by darby conley

Andrews McMeel
Publishing, LLC

Kansas City

Get Fuzzy is distributed internationally by United Feature Syndicate, Inc..

07 08 09 10 11 BBG 10 9 8 7 6 5 4 3 2 1

ISBN-13: 978-0-7407-6922-1
ISBN-10: 0-7407-6922-7

Library of Congress Control Number: 2007925931

Get Fuzzy can be viewed on the Internet at

www.comics.com/getfuzzy.

Other Books by Darby Conley

The Dog Is Not a Toy (House Rule #4)

Fuzzy Logic: Get Fuzzy 2

Groovitude: A Get Fuzzy Treasury

The Get Fuzzy Experience: Are You Bucksperienced

I Would Have Bought You a Cat, But . . .

Blueprint for Disaster

Bucky Katt's Big Book of Fun

Say Cheesy

Scrum Bums

Treasuries

Groovitude: A Get Fuzzy Treasury

Bucky Katt's Big Book of Fun

Loserpalooza

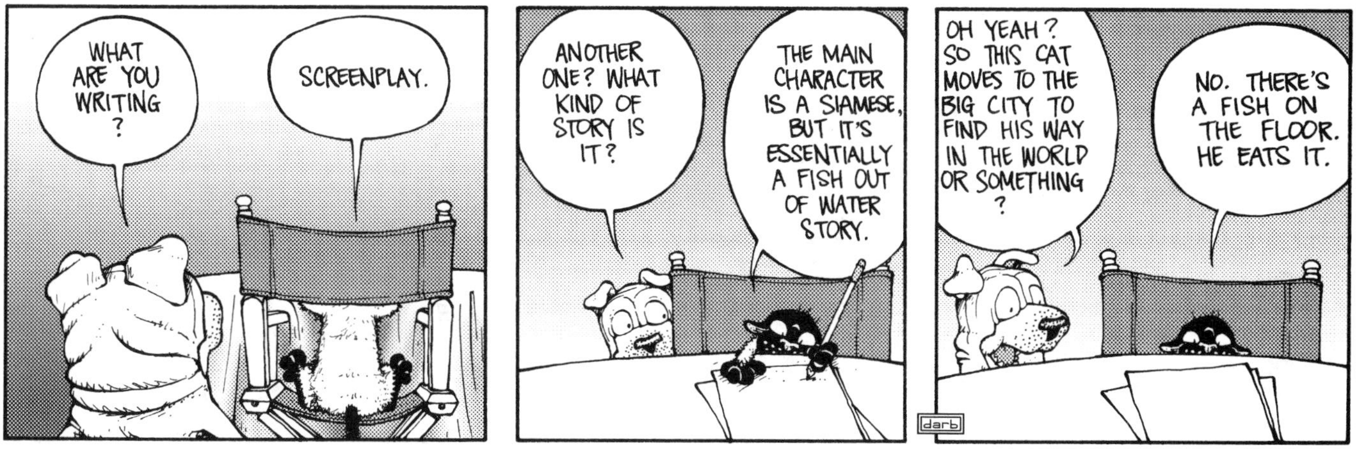
WHAT ARE YOU WRITING ?
SCREENPLAY.
ANOTHER ONE? WHAT KIND OF STORY IS IT?
THE MAIN CHARACTER IS A SIAMESE, BUT IT'S ESSENTIALLY A FISH OUT OF WATER STORY.
OH YEAH? SO THIS CAT MOVES TO THE BIG CITY TO FIND HIS WAY IN THE WORLD OR SOMETHING ?
NO. THERE'S A FISH ON THE FLOOR. HE EATS IT.
darb

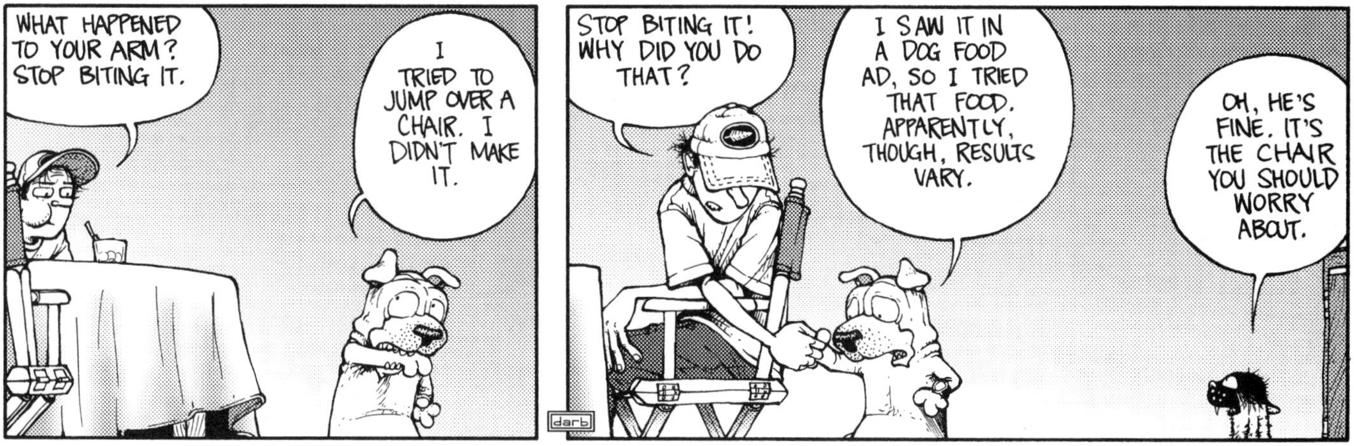
WHAT HAPPENED TO YOUR ARM? STOP BITING IT.
I TRIED TO JUMP OVER A CHAIR. I DIDN'T MAKE IT.
STOP BITING IT! WHY DID YOU DO THAT?
I SAW IT IN A DOG FOOD AD, SO I TRIED THAT FOOD. APPARENTLY, THOUGH, RESULTS VARY.
OH, HE'S FINE. IT'S THE CHAIR YOU SHOULD WORRY ABOUT.
darb

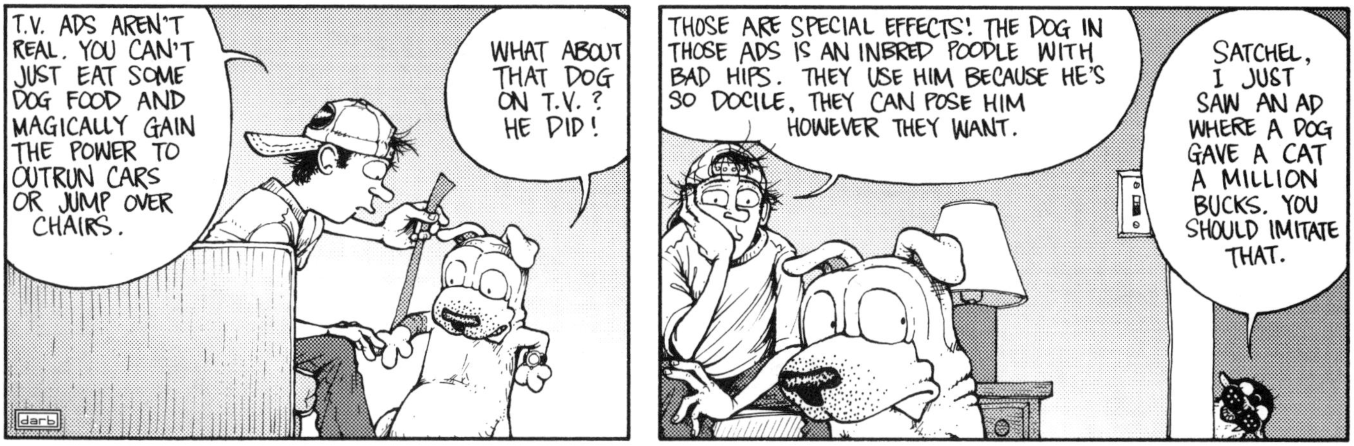
T.V. ADS AREN'T REAL. YOU CAN'T JUST EAT SOME DOG FOOD AND MAGICALLY GAIN THE POWER TO OUTRUN CARS OR JUMP OVER CHAIRS.
WHAT ABOUT THAT DOG ON T.V.? HE DID!
THOSE ARE SPECIAL EFFECTS! THE DOG IN THOSE ADS IS AN INBRED POODLE WITH BAD HIPS. THEY USE HIM BECAUSE HE'S SO DOCILE, THEY CAN POSE HIM HOWEVER THEY WANT.
SATCHEL, I JUST SAW AN AD WHERE A DOG GAVE A CAT A MILLION BUCKS. YOU SHOULD IMITATE THAT.
darb

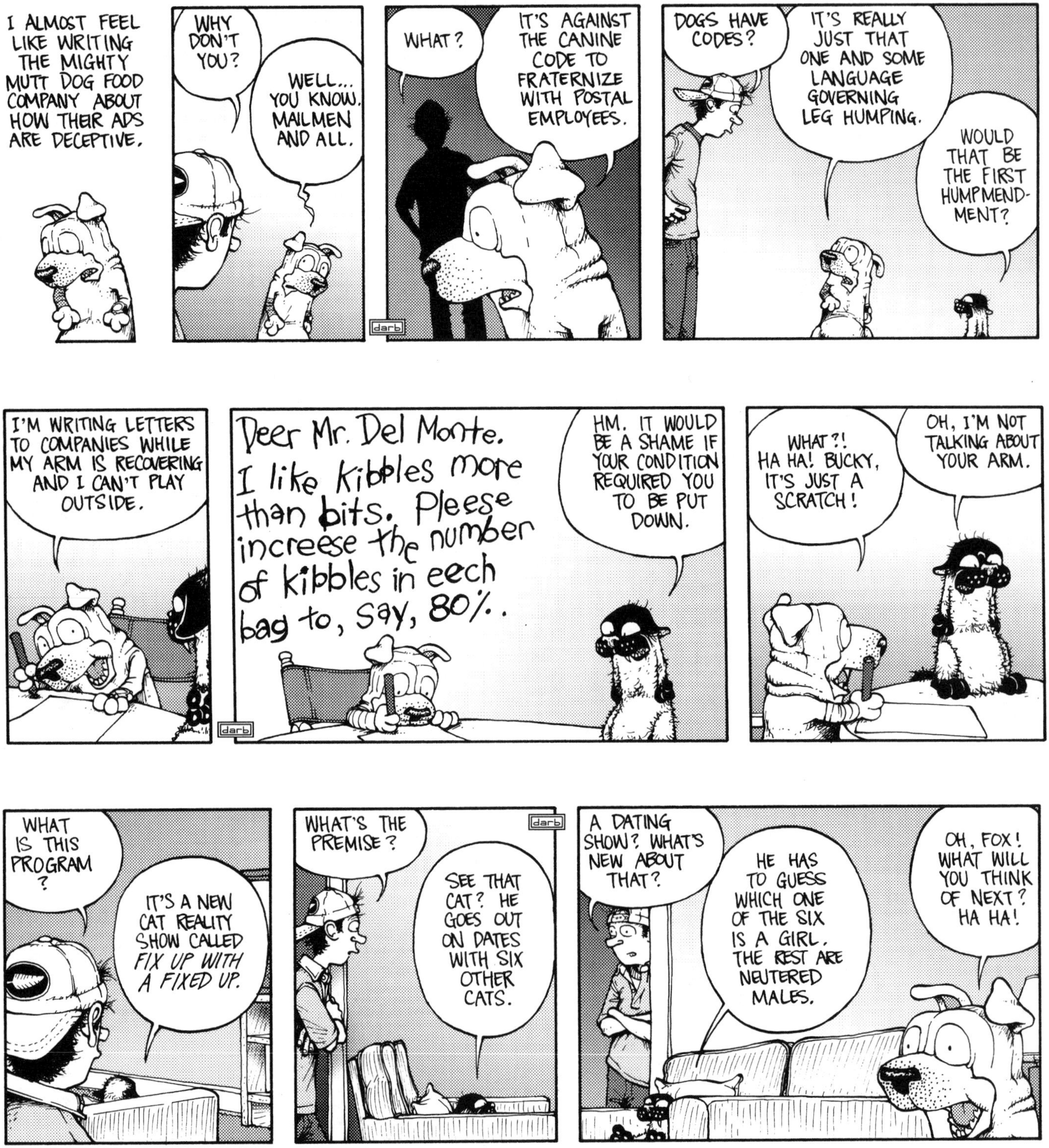
I ALMOST FEEL LIKE WRITING THE MIGHTY MUTT DOG FOOD COMPANY ABOUT HOW THEIR ADS ARE DECEPTIVE.
WHY DON'T YOU?
WELL... YOU KNOW. MAILMEN AND ALL.
darb
WHAT?
IT'S AGAINST THE CANINE CODE TO FRATERNIZE WITH POSTAL EMPLOYEES.
DOGS HAVE CODES?
IT'S REALLY JUST THAT ONE AND SOME LANGUAGE GOVERNING LEG HUMPING.
WOULD THAT BE THE FIRST HUMPMENDMENT?
I'M WRITING LETTERS TO COMPANIES WHILE MY ARM IS RECOVERING AND I CAN'T PLAY OUTSIDE.
darb
Deer Mr. Del Monte.
I like kibbles more than bits. Pleese increese the number of kibbles in eech bag to, say, 80%..
HM. IT WOULD BE A SHAME IF YOUR CONDITION REQUIRED YOU TO BE PUT DOWN.
WHAT?! HA HA! BUCKY, IT'S JUST A SCRATCH!
OH, I'M NOT TALKING ABOUT YOUR ARM.
WHAT IS THIS PROGRAM?
IT'S A NEW CAT REALITY SHOW CALLED FIX UP WITH A FIXED UP.
WHAT'S THE PREMISE?
darb
SEE THAT CAT? HE GOES OUT ON DATES WITH SIX OTHER CATS.
A DATING SHOW? WHAT'S NEW ABOUT THAT?
HE HAS TO GUESS WHICH ONE OF THE SIX IS A GIRL. THE REST ARE NEUTERED MALES.
OH, FOX! WHAT WILL YOU THINK OF NEXT? HA HA!

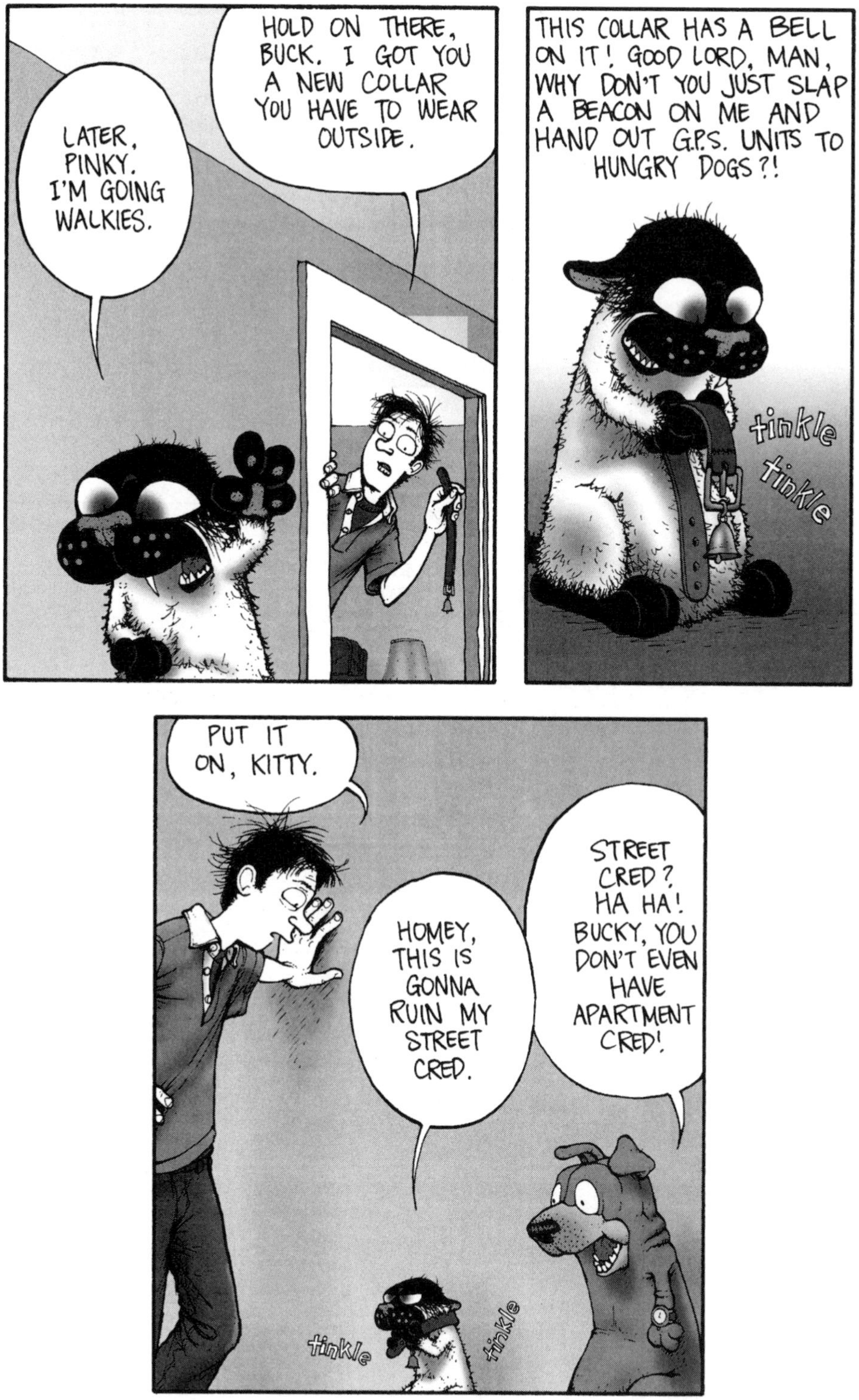
LATER, PINKY. I'M GOING WALKIES.
HOLD ON THERE, BUCK. I GOT YOU A NEW COLLAR YOU HAVE TO WEAR OUTSIDE.
THIS COLLAR HAS A BELL ON IT! GOOD LORD, MAN, WHY DON'T YOU JUST SLAP A BEACON ON ME AND HAND OUT G.P.S. UNITS TO HUNGRY DOGS?!
tinkle
tinkle
PUT IT ON, KITTY.
HOMEY, THIS IS GONNA RUIN MY STREET CRED.
STREET CRED? HA HA! BUCKY, YOU DON'T EVEN HAVE APARTMENT CRED!
tinkle
tinkle

I CAN'T BELIEVE THAT DOG FOOD COMPANY CAN RUN ADS OF DOGS JUMPING OVER CARS AND STUFF... IT'S DECEPTIVE ADVERTISING!

I CAN'T BELIEVE YOU IMITATED IT.

THEY SHOULD HAVE TO RUN A DISCLAIMER BEFORE THEIR ADS SAYING *DON'T TRY THIS AT HOME.*

WHO KNEW MIGHTY MUTT DOG FOOD ADS WERE THE "JACKASS" OF DOG T.V.?

I HAVE HALF A MIND TO WRITE THEM A LETTER.

SO DO IT. YOUR HALF-MIND NEVER GOT IN YOUR WAY BEFORE.

Deer Mighty Mutt Dog Fud, I seen yer tv ad and ate yer fud hoping to get the sooper powerz the dog in yer ad got, but I perceevd no gain in sooper powerz. I got hert.

SATCHEL! STOP BITING YOUR ARM!

Perhaps in foocher, yoo shood considr showing the sad consiquensez of such over exooberance in yer ads.

SO I WROTE A LETTER TO MIGHTY MUTT ABOUT THEIR DECEPTIVE ADVERTISING.

ISN'T THAT BREAKING THE STUPID ANTI-MAILMAN CODE DOGS HAVE?

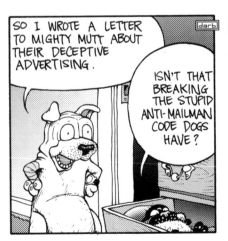

NO, SEE, ROBBO IS MAILING IT FOR ME.

AH, A LOOPHOLE. YOU'RE A SCAB.

I'M NOT HOLDING MY BREATH FOR A RESPONSE, THOUGH! **HA HA HA HA!**

OOF. YOU COULD HOLD IT FOR ME, IF YOU DON'T MIND.

10

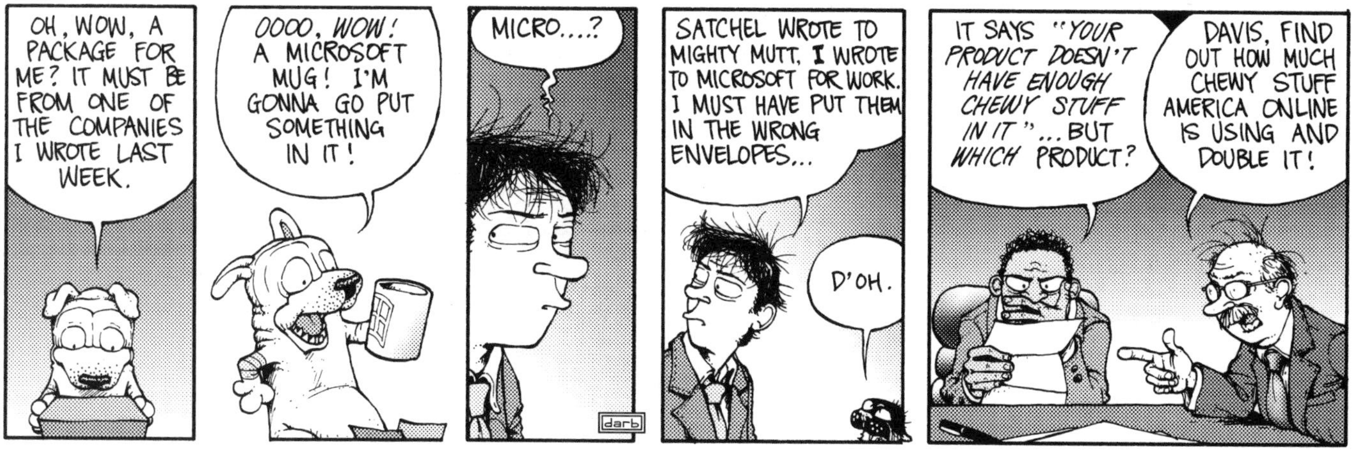
OH, WOW, A PACKAGE FOR ME? IT MUST BE FROM ONE OF THE COMPANIES I WROTE LAST WEEK.
OOOO, WOW! A MICROSOFT MUG! I'M GONNA GO PUT SOMETHING IN IT!
MICRO....?
darb
SATCHEL WROTE TO MIGHTY MUTT. I WROTE TO MICROSOFT FOR WORK. I MUST HAVE PUT THEM IN THE WRONG ENVELOPES...
D'OH.
IT SAYS "YOUR PRODUCT DOESN'T HAVE ENOUGH CHEWY STUFF IN IT"... BUT WHICH PRODUCT?
DAVIS, FIND OUT HOW MUCH CHEWY STUFF AMERICA ONLINE IS USING AND DOUBLE IT!

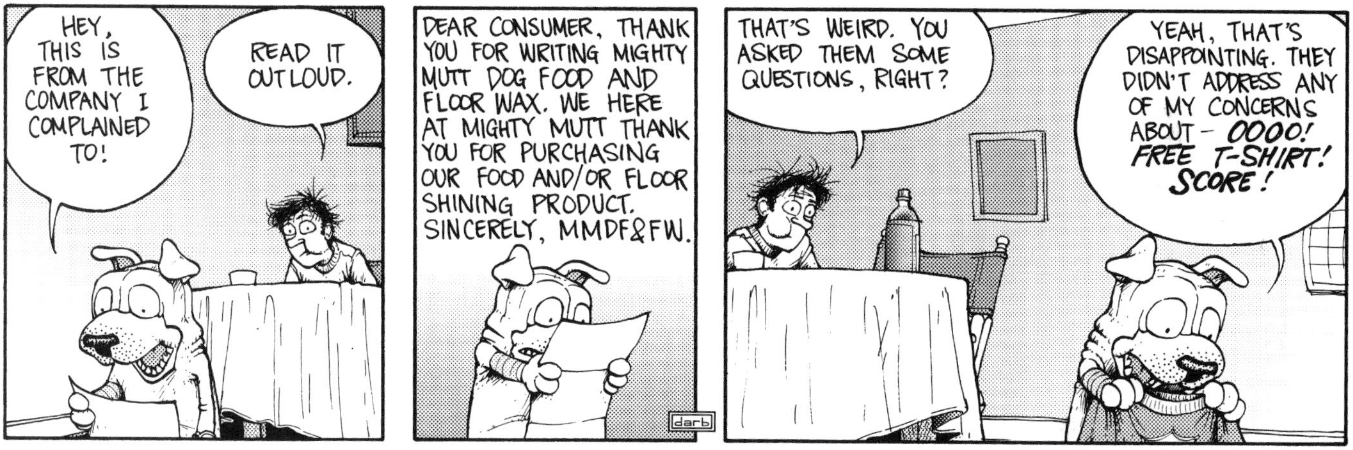
HEY, THIS IS FROM THE COMPANY I COMPLAINED TO!
READ IT OUTLOUD.
DEAR CONSUMER, THANK YOU FOR WRITING MIGHTY MUTT DOG FOOD AND FLOOR WAX. WE HERE AT MIGHTY MUTT THANK YOU FOR PURCHASING OUR FOOD AND/OR FLOOR SHINING PRODUCT. SINCERELY, MMDF&FW.
darb
THAT'S WEIRD. YOU ASKED THEM SOME QUESTIONS, RIGHT?
YEAH, THAT'S DISAPPOINTING. THEY DIDN'T ADDRESS ANY OF MY CONCERNS ABOUT - OOOO! FREE T-SHIRT! SCORE!

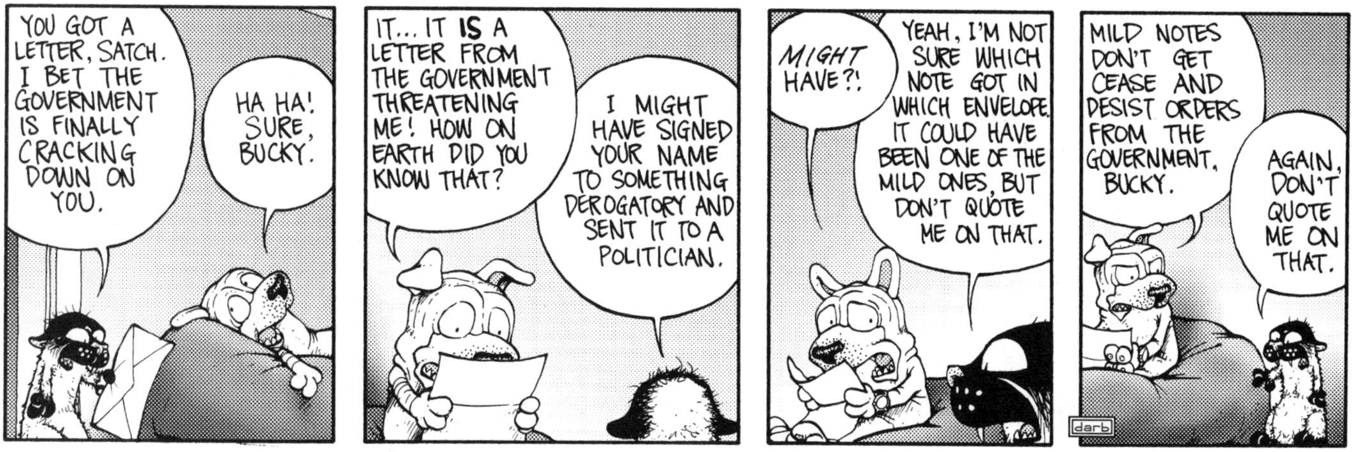
YOU GOT A LETTER, SATCH. I BET THE GOVERNMENT IS FINALLY CRACKING DOWN ON YOU.
HA HA! SURE, BUCKY.
IT... IT IS A LETTER FROM THE GOVERNMENT THREATENING ME! HOW ON EARTH DID YOU KNOW THAT?
I MIGHT HAVE SIGNED YOUR NAME TO SOMETHING DEROGATORY AND SENT IT TO A POLITICIAN.
MIGHT HAVE?!
YEAH, I'M NOT SURE WHICH NOTE GOT IN WHICH ENVELOPE. IT COULD HAVE BEEN ONE OF THE MILD ONES, BUT DON'T QUOTE ME ON THAT.
darb
MILD NOTES DON'T GET CEASE AND DESIST ORDERS FROM THE GOVERNMENT, BUCKY.
AGAIN, DON'T QUOTE ME ON THAT.

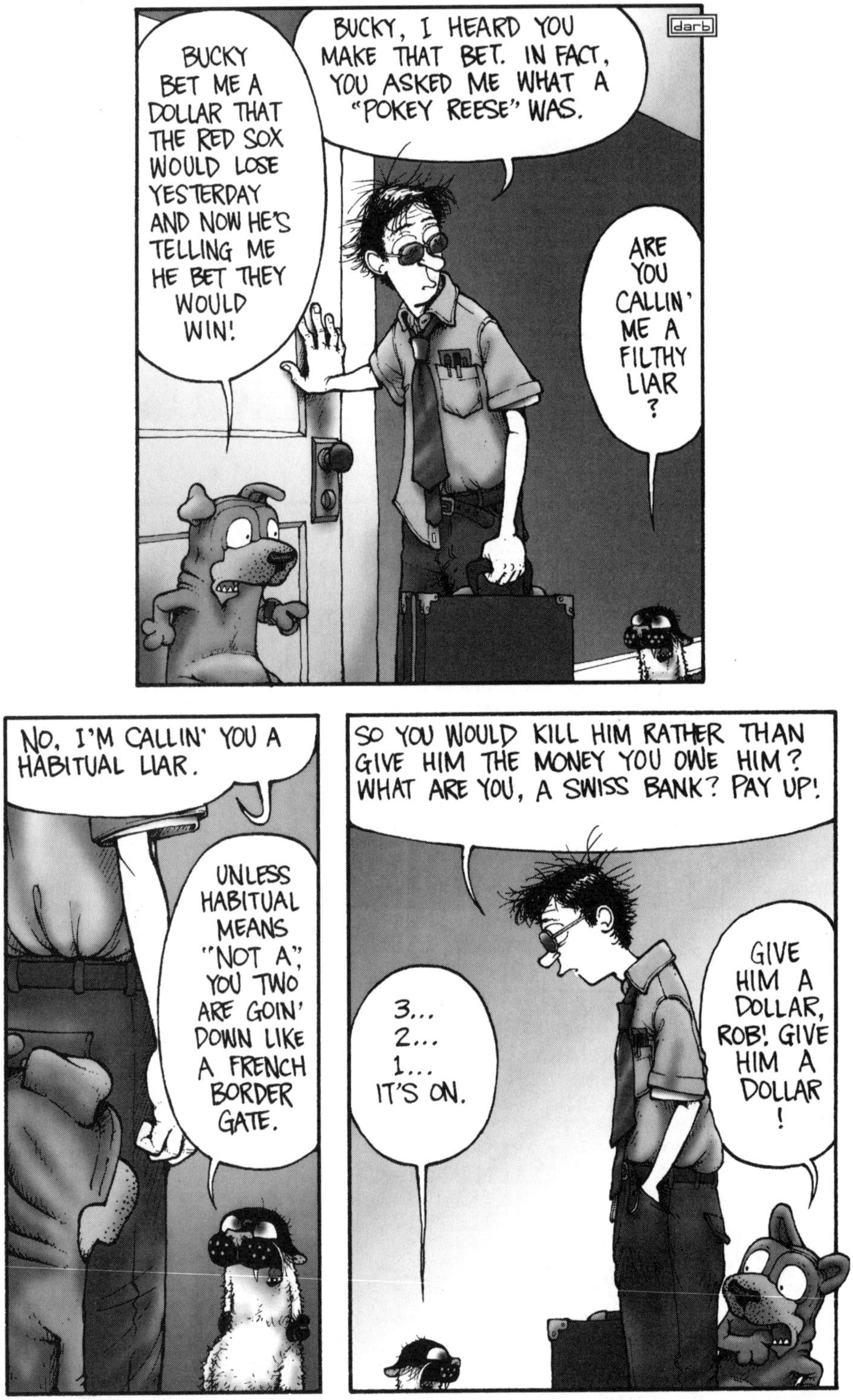
darb
BUCKY BET ME A DOLLAR THAT THE RED SOX WOULD LOSE YESTERDAY AND NOW HE'S TELLING ME HE BET THEY WOULD WIN!
BUCKY, I HEARD YOU MAKE THAT BET. IN FACT, YOU ASKED ME WHAT A "POKEY REESE" WAS.
ARE YOU CALLIN' ME A FILTHY LIAR?
NO, I'M CALLIN' YOU A HABITUAL LIAR.
UNLESS HABITUAL MEANS "NOT A", YOU TWO ARE GOIN' DOWN LIKE A FRENCH BORDER GATE.
SO YOU WOULD KILL HIM RATHER THAN GIVE HIM THE MONEY YOU OWE HIM? WHAT ARE YOU, A SWISS BANK? PAY UP!
3... 2... 1... IT'S ON.
GIVE HIM A DOLLAR, ROB! GIVE HIM A DOLLAR!

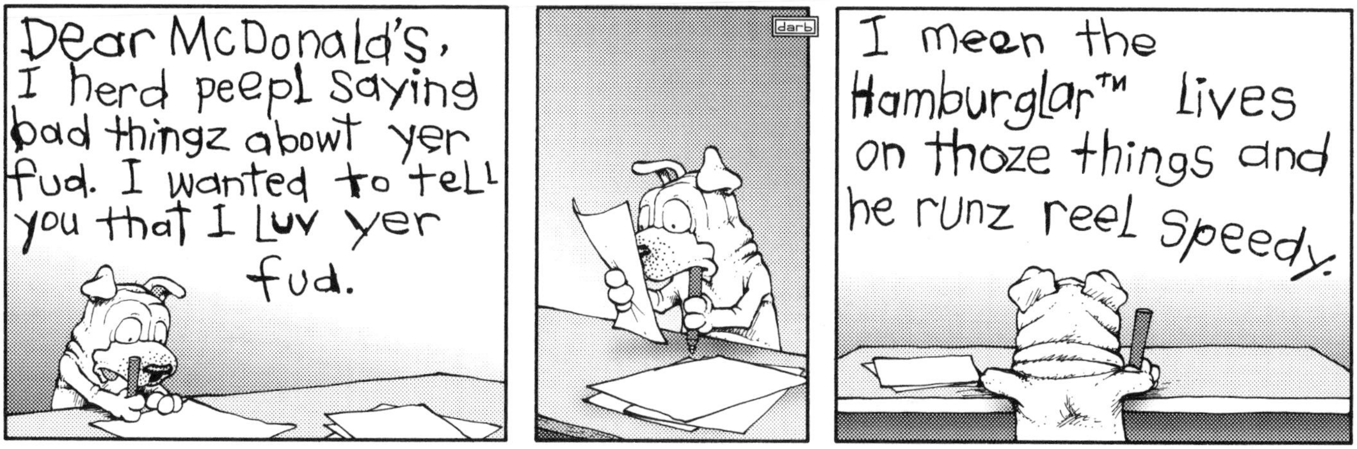
Dear McDonald's, I herd peepl saying bad thingz abowt yer fud. I wanted to tell you that I luv yer fud.
darb
I meen the Hamburglar™ lives on thoze things and he runz reel speedy.

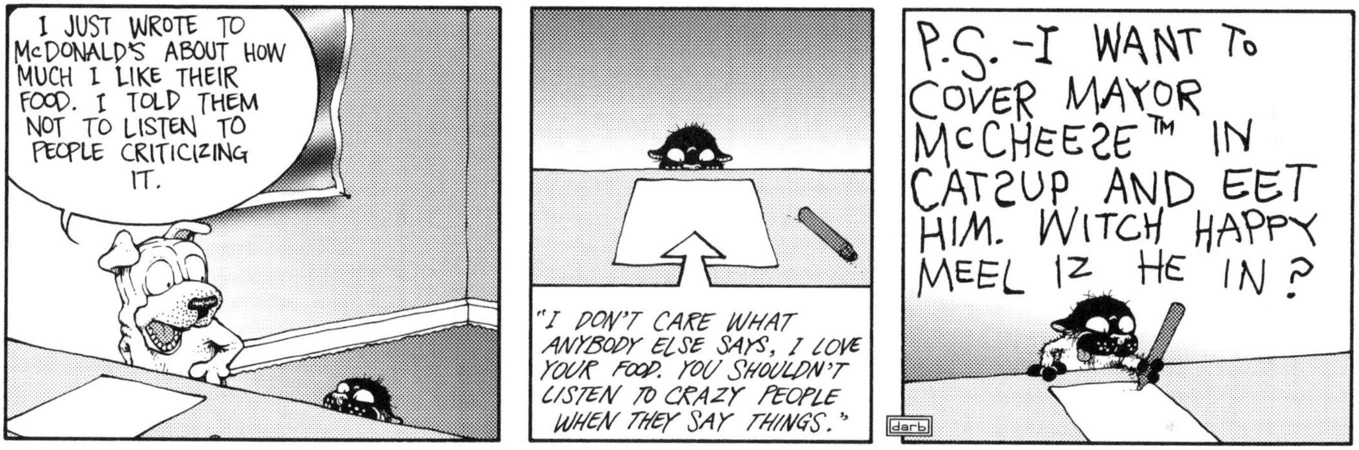
I JUST WROTE TO McDONALD'S ABOUT HOW MUCH I LIKE THEIR FOOD. I TOLD THEM NOT TO LISTEN TO PEOPLE CRITICIZING IT.
"I DON'T CARE WHAT ANYBODY ELSE SAYS, I LOVE YOUR FOOD. YOU SHOULDN'T LISTEN TO CRAZY PEOPLE WHEN THEY SAY THINGS."
darb
P.S.-I WANT TO COVER MAYOR McCHEEZE™ IN CATZUP AND EET HIM. WITCH HAPPY MEEL IZ HE IN?

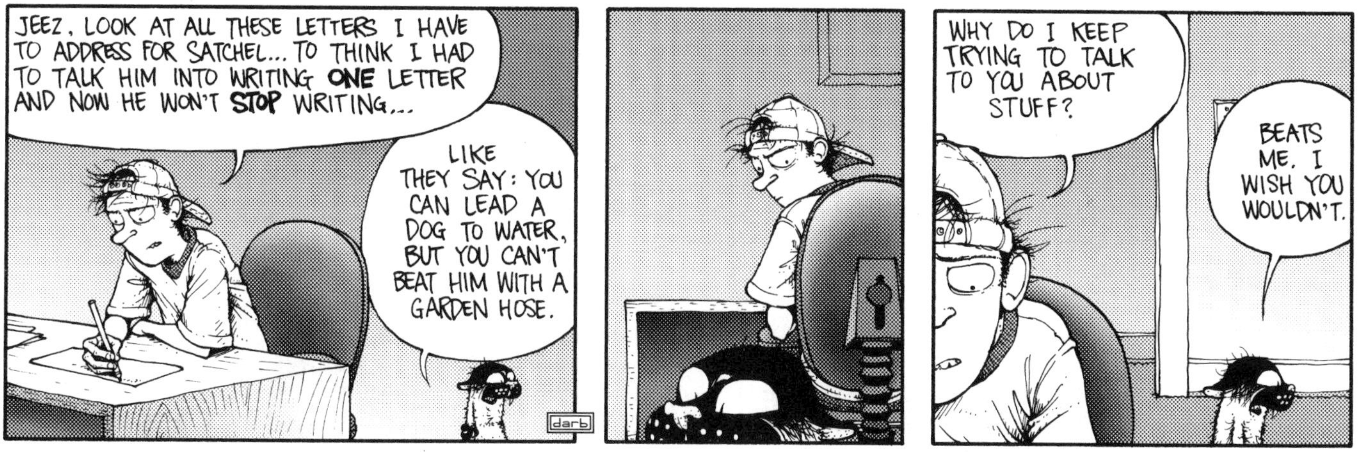
JEEZ, LOOK AT ALL THESE LETTERS I HAVE TO ADDRESS FOR SATCHEL... TO THINK I HAD TO TALK HIM INTO WRITING ONE LETTER AND NOW HE WON'T STOP WRITING...
LIKE THEY SAY: YOU CAN LEAD A DOG TO WATER, BUT YOU CAN'T BEAT HIM WITH A GARDEN HOSE.
darb
WHY DO I KEEP TRYING TO TALK TO YOU ABOUT STUFF?
BEATS ME. I WISH YOU WOULDN'T.

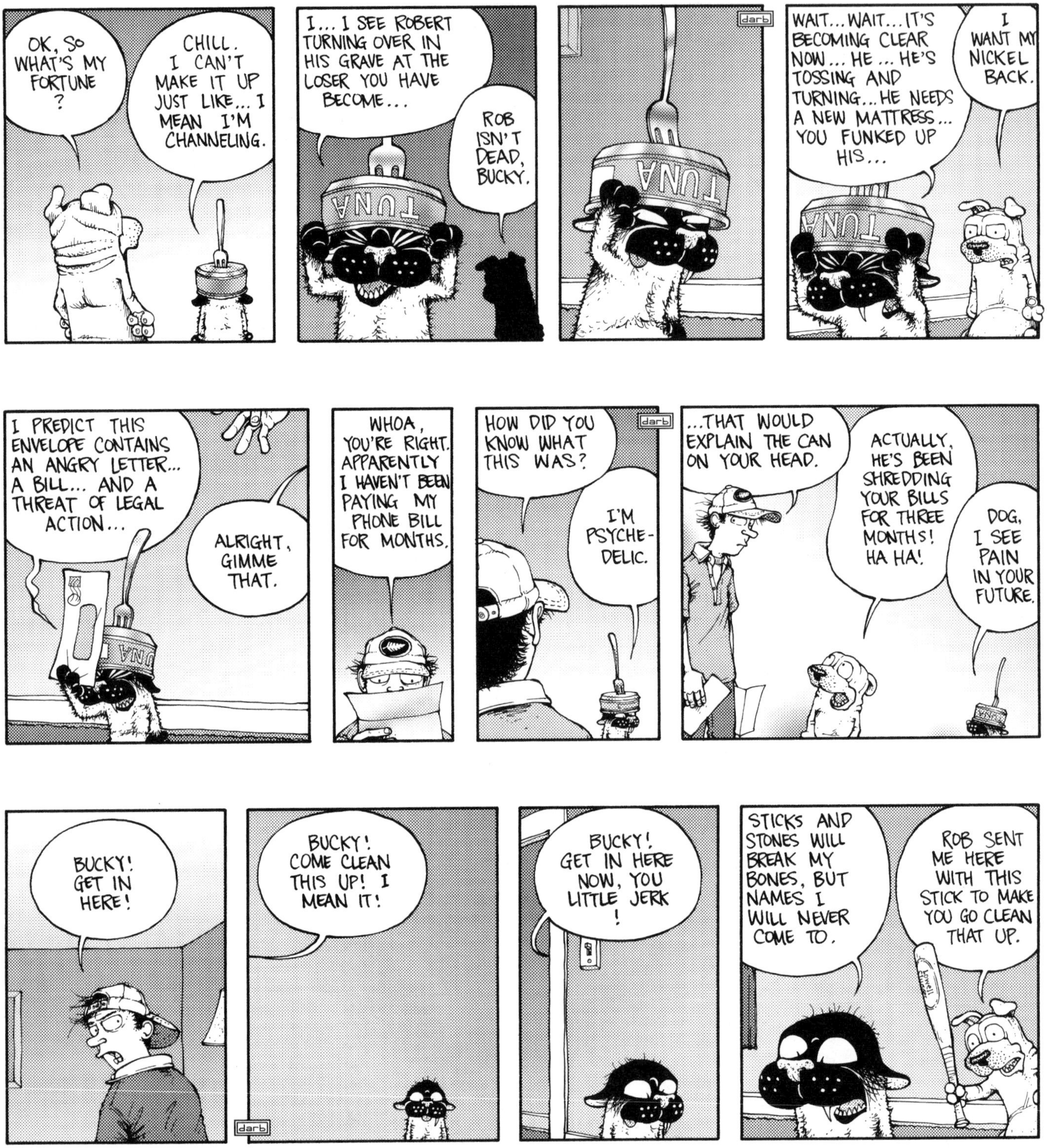
OK, SO WHAT'S MY FORTUNE ?
CHILL. I CAN'T MAKE IT UP JUST LIKE... I MEAN I'M CHANNELING.
I... I SEE ROBERT TURNING OVER IN HIS GRAVE AT THE LOSER YOU HAVE BECOME...
ROB ISN'T DEAD, BUCKY.
TUNA
darb
WAIT... WAIT... IT'S BECOMING CLEAR NOW... HE... HE'S TOSSING AND TURNING... HE NEEDS A NEW MATTRESS... YOU FUNKED UP HIS...
I WANT MY NICKEL BACK.
I PREDICT THIS ENVELOPE CONTAINS AN ANGRY LETTER... A BILL... AND A THREAT OF LEGAL ACTION...
ALRIGHT, GIMME THAT.
WHOA, YOU'RE RIGHT. APPARENTLY I HAVEN'T BEEN PAYING MY PHONE BILL FOR MONTHS.
HOW DID YOU KNOW WHAT THIS WAS?
I'M PSYCHE-DELIC.
...THAT WOULD EXPLAIN THE CAN ON YOUR HEAD.
ACTUALLY, HE'S BEEN SHREDDING YOUR BILLS FOR THREE MONTHS! HA HA!
DOG, I SEE PAIN IN YOUR FUTURE.
BUCKY! GET IN HERE!
BUCKY! COME CLEAN THIS UP! I MEAN IT!
BUCKY! GET IN HERE NOW, YOU LITTLE JERK !
STICKS AND STONES WILL BREAK MY BONES, BUT NAMES I WILL NEVER COME TO.
ROB SENT ME HERE WITH THIS STICK TO MAKE YOU GO CLEAN THAT UP.

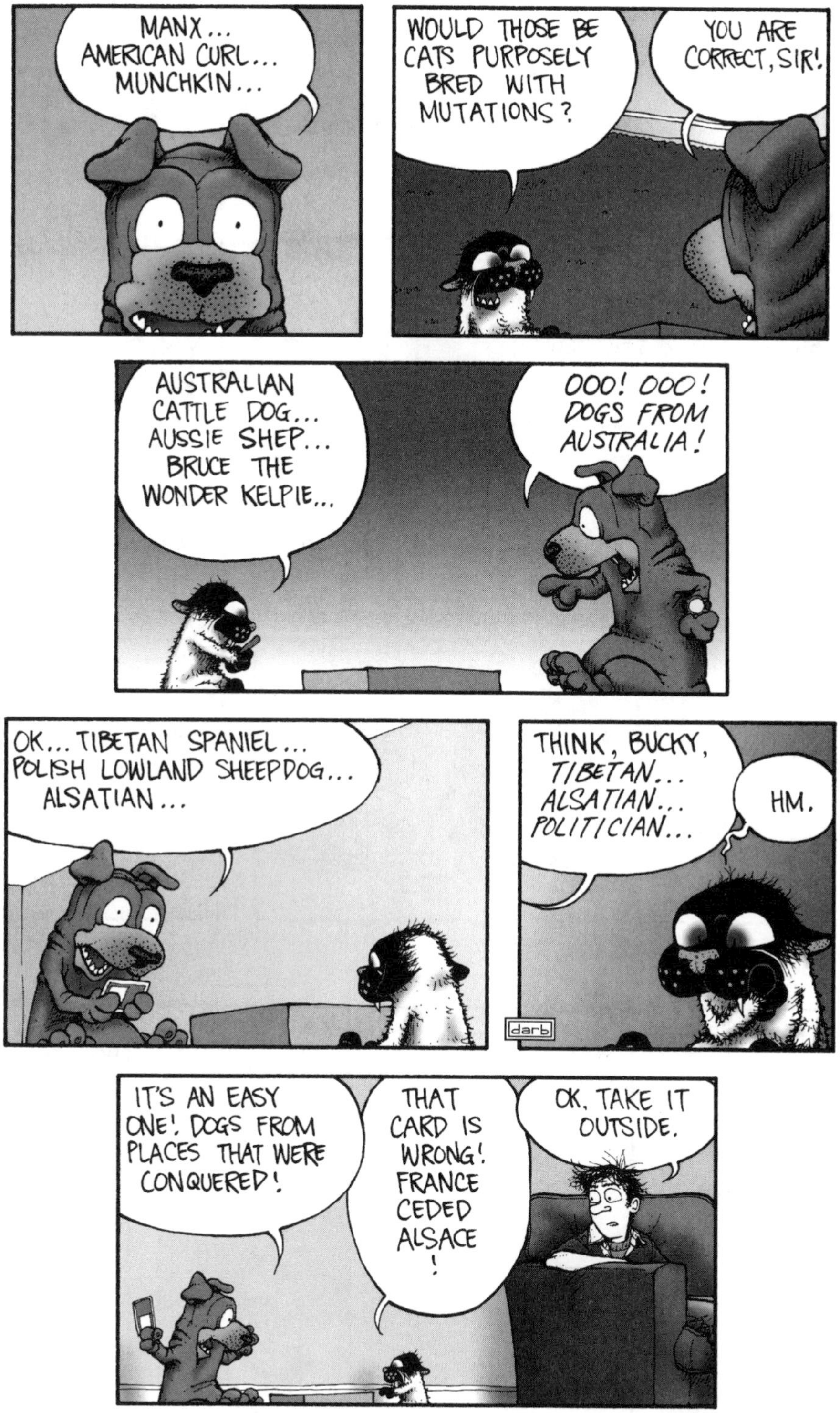
MANX... AMERICAN CURL... MUNCHKIN...
WOULD THOSE BE CATS PURPOSELY BRED WITH MUTATIONS?
YOU ARE CORRECT, SIR!
AUSTRALIAN CATTLE DOG... AUSSIE SHEP... BRUCE THE WONDER KELPIE...
OOO! OOO! DOGS FROM AUSTRALIA!
OK... TIBETAN SPANIEL... POLISH LOWLAND SHEEPDOG... ALSATIAN...
THINK, BUCKY, TIBETAN... ALSATIAN... POLITICIAN...
HM.
darb
IT'S AN EASY ONE! DOGS FROM PLACES THAT WERE CONQUERED!
THAT CARD IS WRONG! FRANCE CEDED ALSACE!
OK. TAKE IT OUTSIDE.

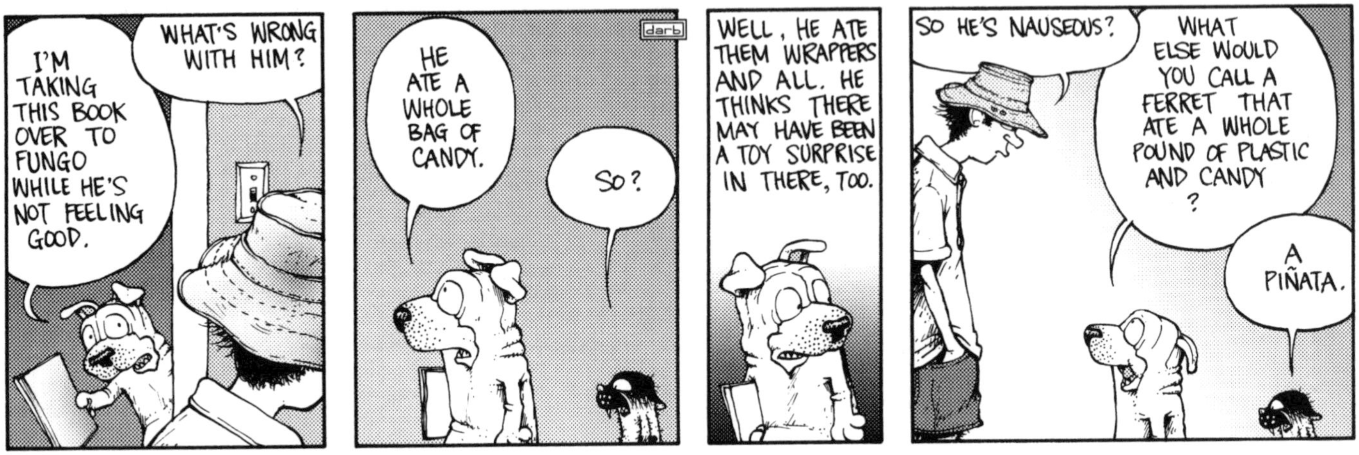
I'M TAKING THIS BOOK OVER TO FUNGO WHILE HE'S NOT FEELING GOOD.
WHAT'S WRONG WITH HIM?
HE ATE A WHOLE BAG OF CANDY.
SO?
WELL, HE ATE THEM WRAPPERS AND ALL. HE THINKS THERE MAY HAVE BEEN A TOY SURPRISE IN THERE, TOO.
SO HE'S NAUSEOUS?
WHAT ELSE WOULD YOU CALL A FERRET THAT ATE A WHOLE POUND OF PLASTIC AND CANDY?
A PIÑATA.

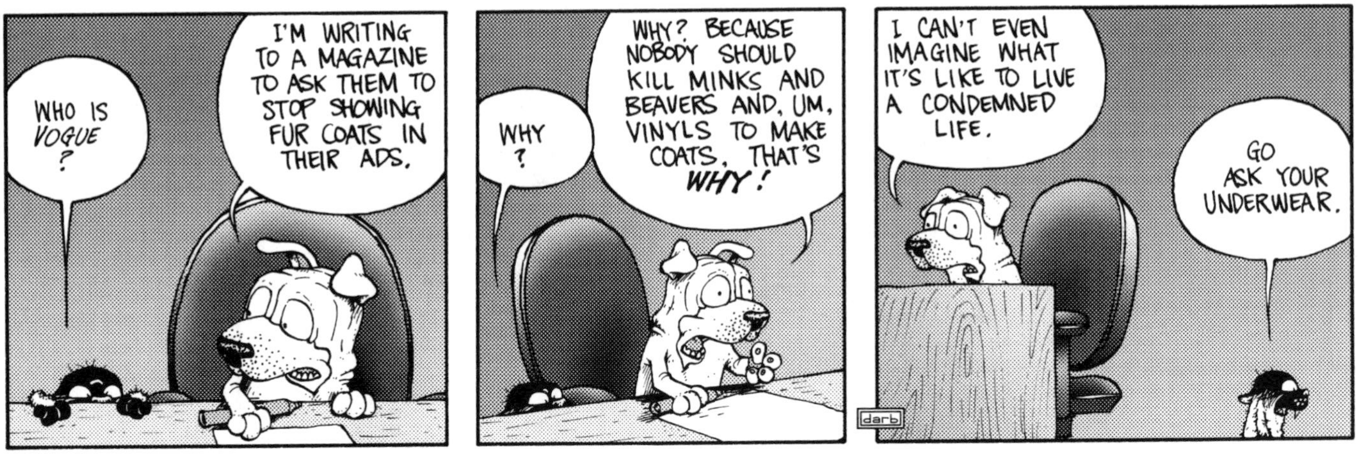
I'M WRITING TO A MAGAZINE TO ASK THEM TO STOP SHOWING FUR COATS IN THEIR ADS.
WHO IS *VOGUE*?
WHY?
WHY? BECAUSE NOBODY SHOULD KILL MINKS AND BEAVERS AND, UM, VINYLS TO MAKE COATS, THAT'S ***WHY!***
I CAN'T EVEN IMAGINE WHAT IT'S LIKE TO LIVE A CONDEMNED LIFE.
GO ASK YOUR UNDERWEAR.

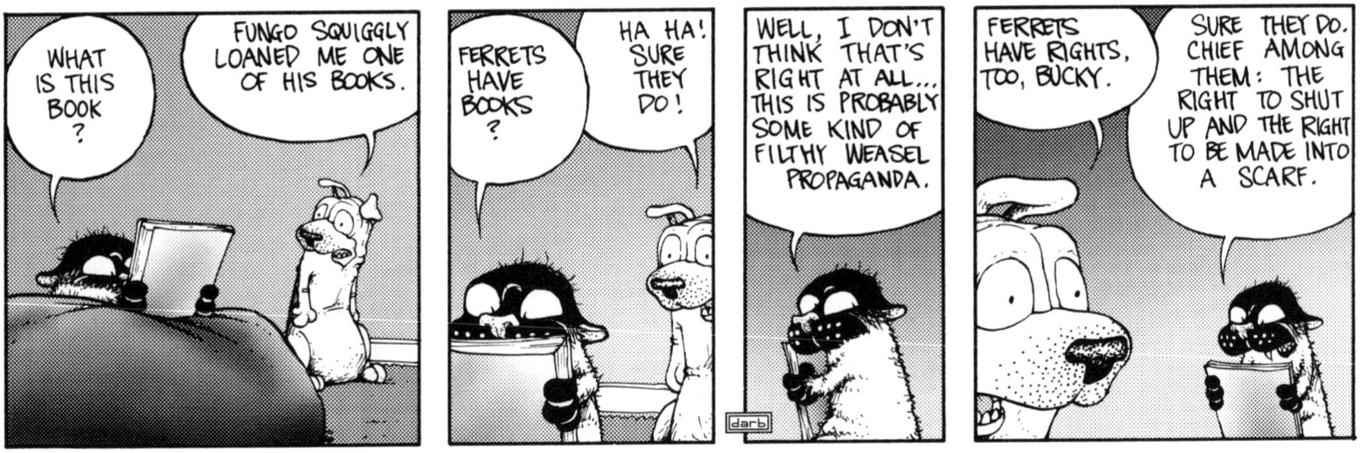
WHAT IS THIS BOOK?
FUNGO SQUIGGLY LOANED ME ONE OF HIS BOOKS.
FERRETS HAVE BOOKS?
HA HA! SURE THEY DO!
WELL, I DON'T THINK THAT'S RIGHT AT ALL... THIS IS PROBABLY SOME KIND OF FILTHY WEASEL PROPAGANDA.
FERRETS HAVE RIGHTS, TOO, BUCKY.
SURE THEY DO. CHIEF AMONG THEM: THE RIGHT TO SHUT UP AND THE RIGHT TO BE MADE INTO A SCARF.

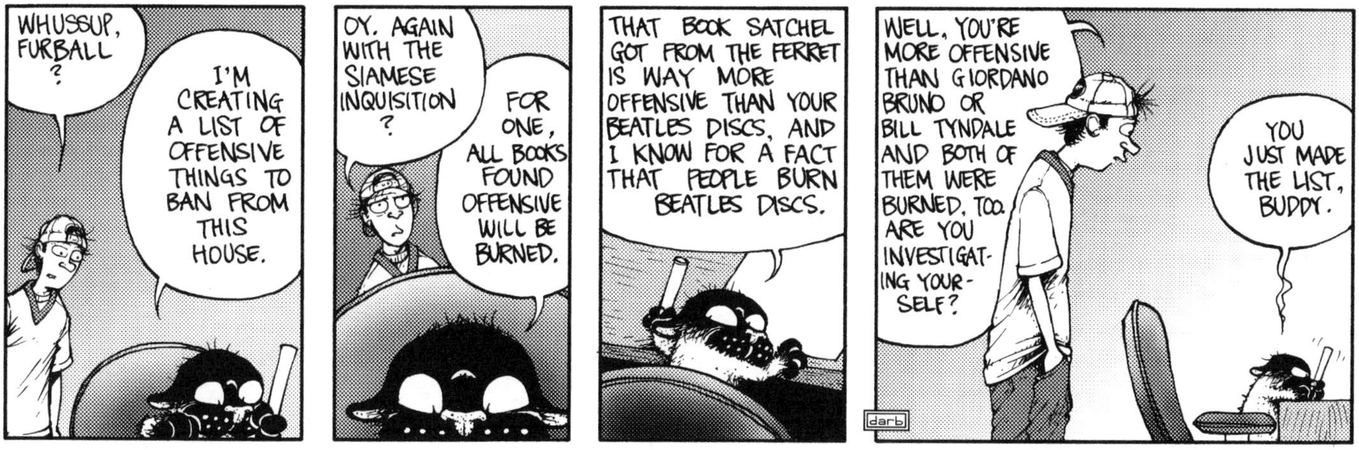
WHUSSUP, FURBALL ?
I'M CREATING A LIST OF OFFENSIVE THINGS TO BAN FROM THIS HOUSE.
OY. AGAIN WITH THE SIAMESE INQUISITION ?
FOR ONE, ALL BOOKS FOUND OFFENSIVE WILL BE BURNED.
THAT BOOK SATCHEL GOT FROM THE FERRET IS WAY MORE OFFENSIVE THAN YOUR BEATLES DISCS, AND I KNOW FOR A FACT THAT PEOPLE BURN BEATLES DISCS.
WELL, YOU'RE MORE OFFENSIVE THAN GIORDANO BRUNO OR BILL TYNDALE AND BOTH OF THEM WERE BURNED, TOO. ARE YOU INVESTIGATING YOURSELF?
YOU JUST MADE THE LIST, BUDDY.
darb

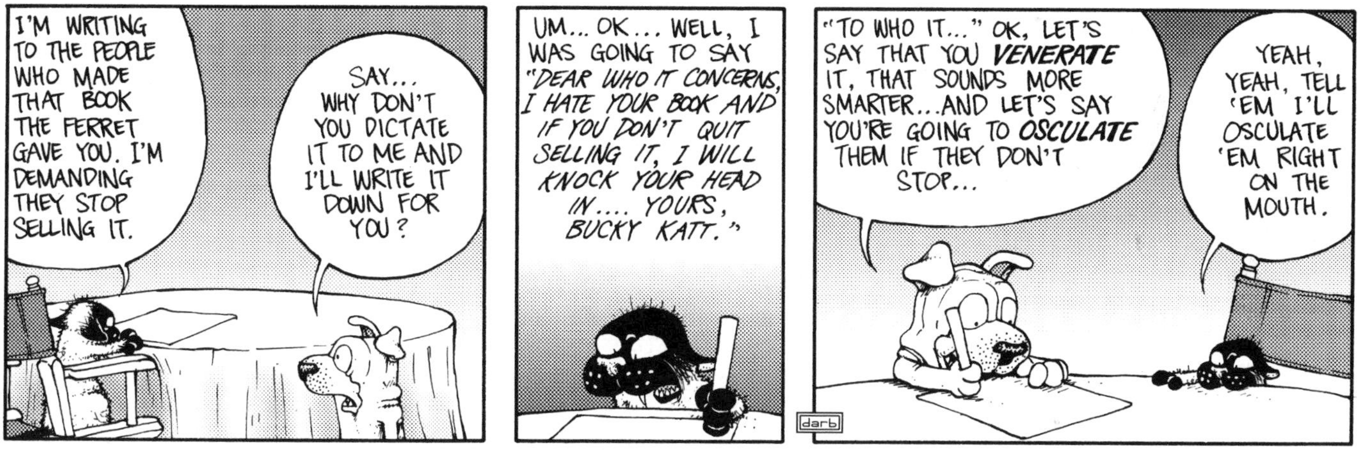
I'M WRITING TO THE PEOPLE WHO MADE THAT BOOK THE FERRET GAVE YOU. I'M DEMANDING THEY STOP SELLING IT.
SAY... WHY DON'T YOU DICTATE IT TO ME AND I'LL WRITE IT DOWN FOR YOU ?
UM... OK... WELL, I WAS GOING TO SAY *"DEAR WHO IT CONCERNS, I HATE YOUR BOOK AND IF YOU DON'T QUIT SELLING IT, I WILL KNOCK YOUR HEAD IN.... YOURS, BUCKY KATT."*
"TO WHO IT..." OK, LET'S SAY THAT YOU ***VENERATE*** IT, THAT SOUNDS MORE SMARTER...AND LET'S SAY YOU'RE GOING TO ***OSCULATE*** THEM IF THEY DON'T STOP...
YEAH, YEAH, TELL 'EM I'LL OSCULATE 'EM RIGHT ON THE MOUTH.
darb

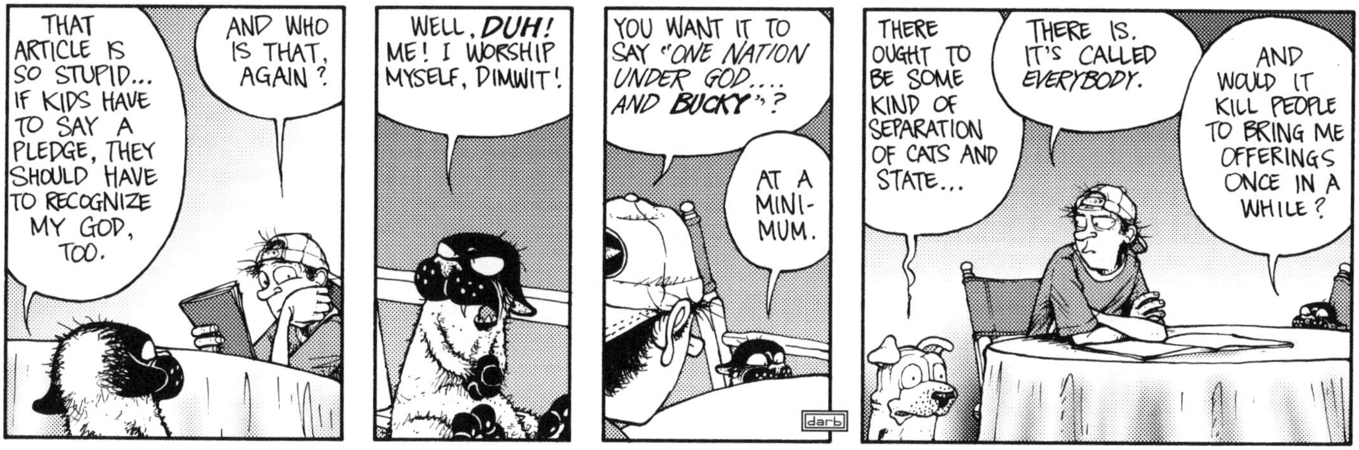
THAT ARTICLE IS SO STUPID... IF KIDS HAVE TO SAY A PLEDGE, THEY SHOULD HAVE TO RECOGNIZE MY GOD, TOO.
AND WHO IS THAT, AGAIN ?
WELL, ***DUH!*** ME! I WORSHIP MYSELF, DIMWIT!
YOU WANT IT TO SAY *"ONE NATION UNDER GOD.... AND **BUCKY**"* ?
AT A MINIMUM.
darb
THERE OUGHT TO BE SOME KIND OF SEPARATION OF CATS AND STATE...
THERE IS. IT'S CALLED *EVERYBODY*.
AND WOULD IT KILL PEOPLE TO BRING ME OFFERINGS ONCE IN A WHILE ?

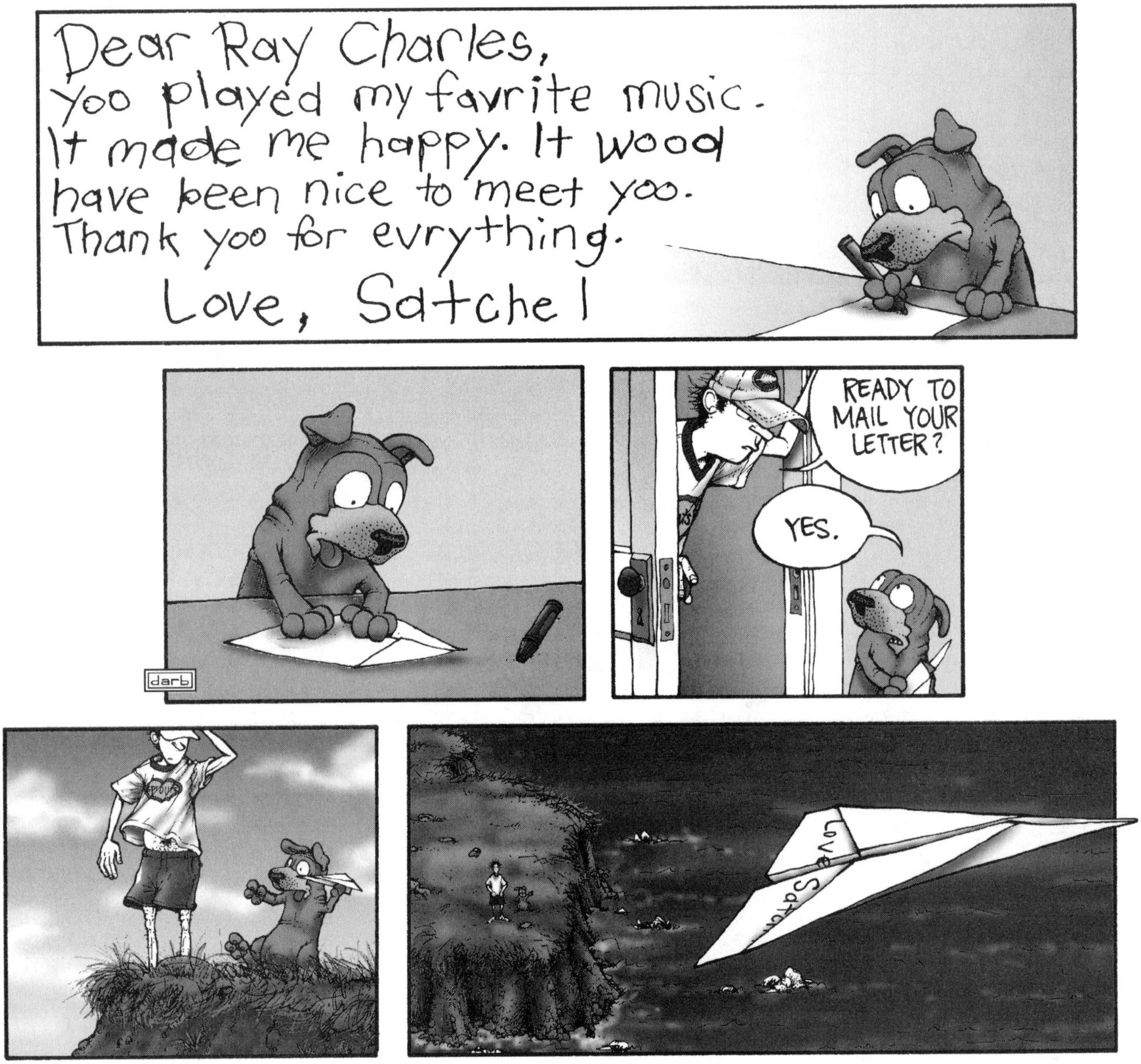
Dear Ray Charles,
yoo played my favrite music.
It made me happy. It wood
have been nice to meet yoo.
Thank yoo for evrything.
Love, Satchel
darb
READY TO MAIL YOUR LETTER?
YES.
Love Satch

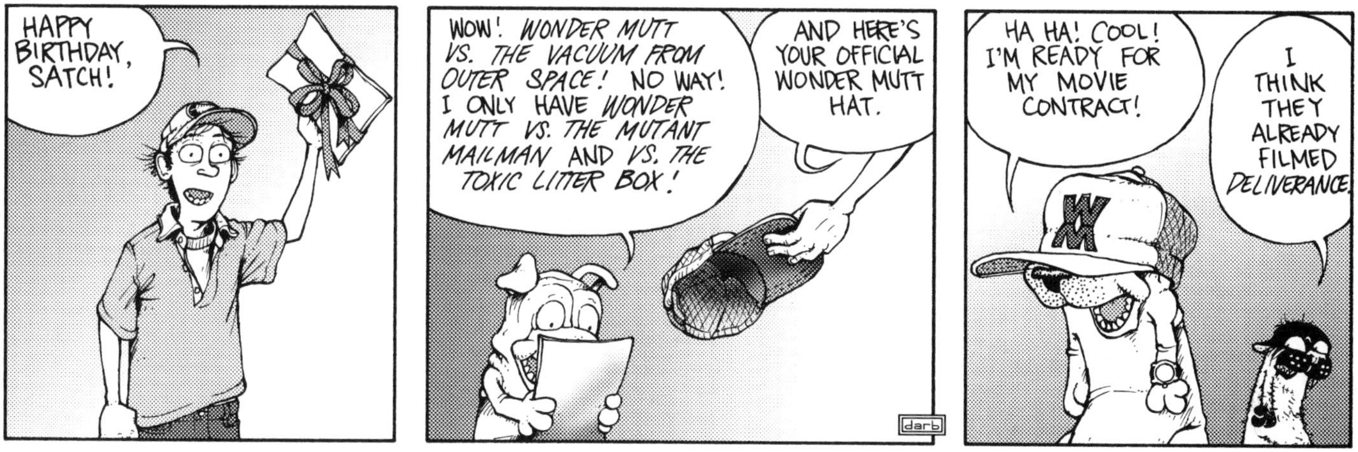
HAPPY BIRTHDAY, SATCH!
WOW! WONDER MUTT VS. THE VACUUM FROM OUTER SPACE! NO WAY! I ONLY HAVE WONDER MUTT VS. THE MUTANT MAILMAN AND VS. THE TOXIC LITTER BOX!
AND HERE'S YOUR OFFICIAL WONDER MUTT HAT.
HA HA! COOL! I'M READY FOR MY MOVIE CONTRACT!
I THINK THEY ALREADY FILMED DELIVERANCE.

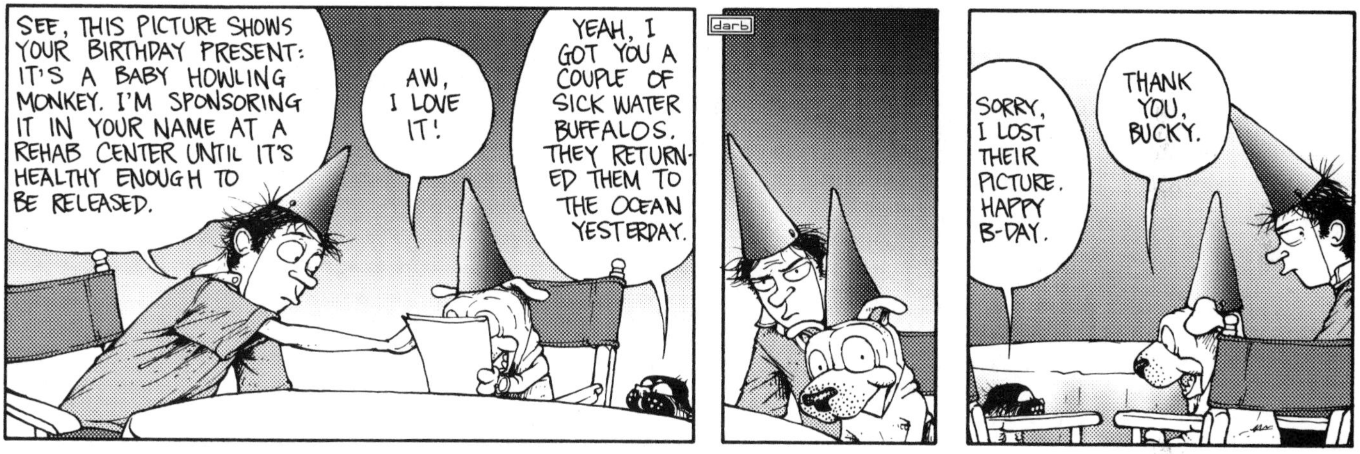
SEE, THIS PICTURE SHOWS YOUR BIRTHDAY PRESENT: IT'S A BABY HOWLING MONKEY. I'M SPONSORING IT IN YOUR NAME AT A REHAB CENTER UNTIL IT'S HEALTHY ENOUGH TO BE RELEASED.
AW, I LOVE IT!
YEAH, I GOT YOU A COUPLE OF SICK WATER BUFFALOS. THEY RETURNED THEM TO THE OCEAN YESTERDAY.
SORRY, I LOST THEIR PICTURE. HAPPY B-DAY.
THANK YOU, BUCKY.

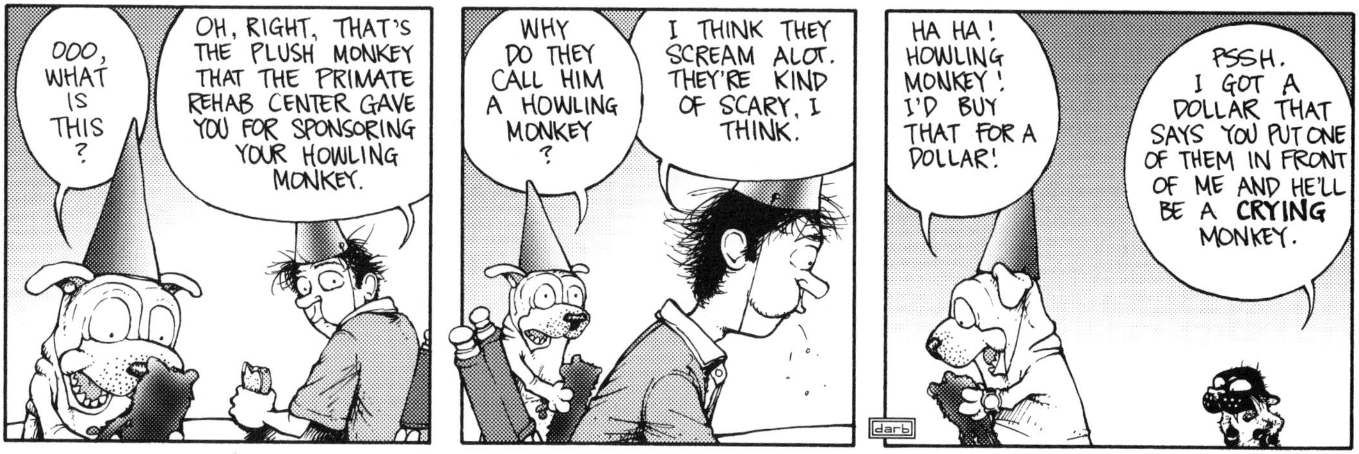
OOO, WHAT IS THIS?
OH, RIGHT, THAT'S THE PLUSH MONKEY THAT THE PRIMATE REHAB CENTER GAVE YOU FOR SPONSORING YOUR HOWLING MONKEY.
WHY DO THEY CALL HIM A HOWLING MONKEY?
I THINK THEY SCREAM ALOT. THEY'RE KIND OF SCARY, I THINK.
HA HA! HOWLING MONKEY! I'D BUY THAT FOR A DOLLAR!
PSSH. I GOT A DOLLAR THAT SAYS YOU PUT ONE OF THEM IN FRONT OF ME AND HE'LL BE A CRYING MONKEY.

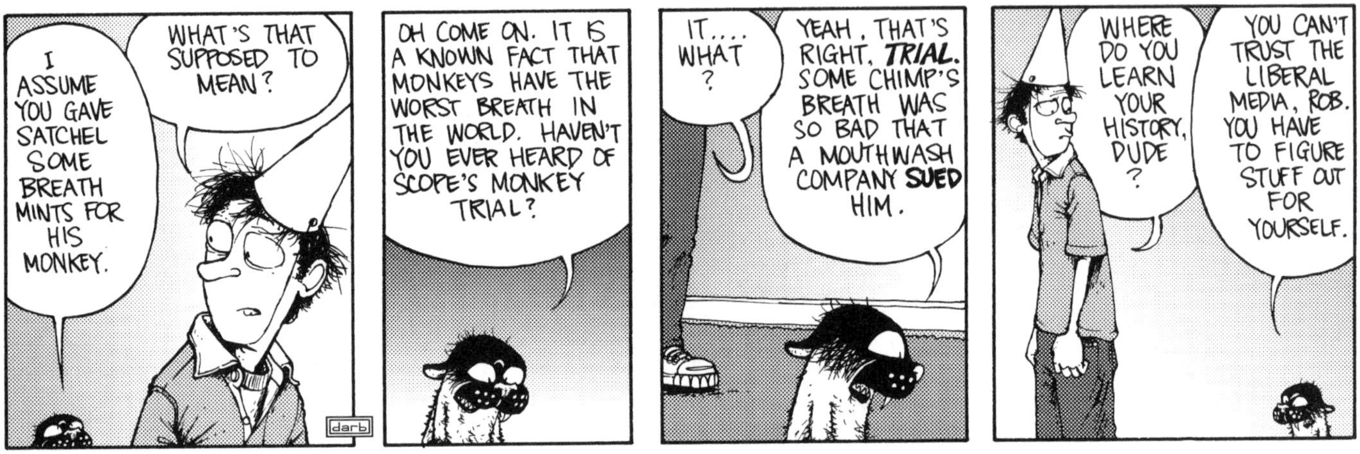
I ASSUME YOU GAVE SATCHEL SOME BREATH MINTS FOR HIS MONKEY.
WHAT'S THAT SUPPOSED TO MEAN?
OH COME ON. IT IS A KNOWN FACT THAT MONKEYS HAVE THE WORST BREATH IN THE WORLD. HAVEN'T YOU EVER HEARD OF SCOPE'S MONKEY TRIAL?
IT.... WHAT?
YEAH, THAT'S RIGHT, ***TRIAL.*** SOME CHIMP'S BREATH WAS SO BAD THAT A MOUTHWASH COMPANY **SUED** HIM.
WHERE DO YOU LEARN YOUR HISTORY, DUDE?
YOU CAN'T TRUST THE LIBERAL MEDIA, ROB. YOU HAVE TO FIGURE STUFF OUT FOR YOURSELF.
darb

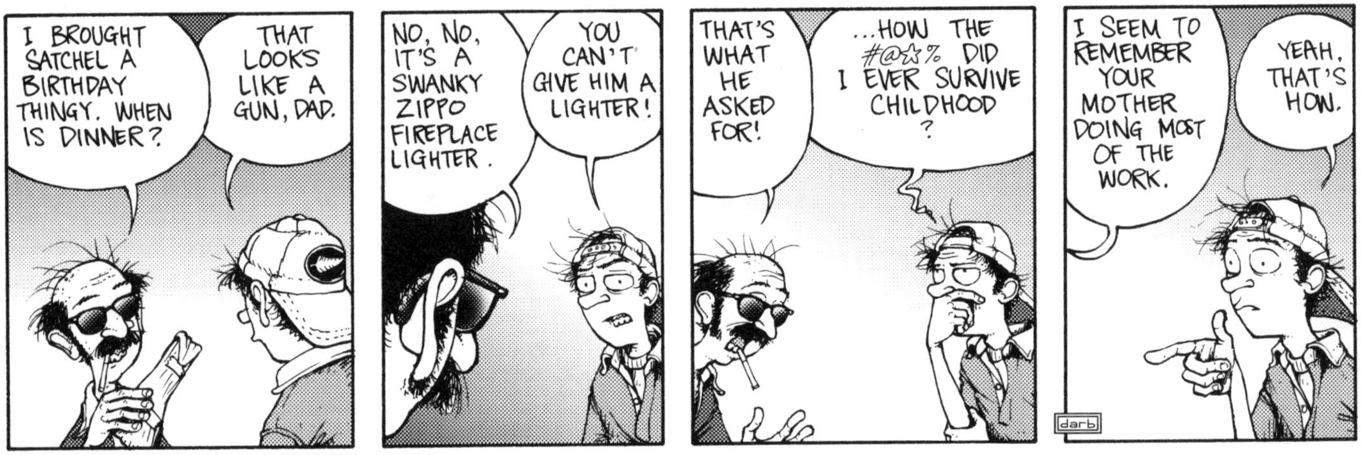
I BROUGHT SATCHEL A BIRTHDAY THINGY. WHEN IS DINNER?
THAT LOOKS LIKE A GUN, DAD.
NO, NO, IT'S A SWANKY ZIPPO FIREPLACE LIGHTER.
YOU CAN'T GIVE HIM A LIGHTER!
THAT'S WHAT HE ASKED FOR!
...HOW THE #@☆% DID I EVER SURVIVE CHILDHOOD?
I SEEM TO REMEMBER YOUR MOTHER DOING MOST OF THE WORK.
YEAH. THAT'S HOW.
darb

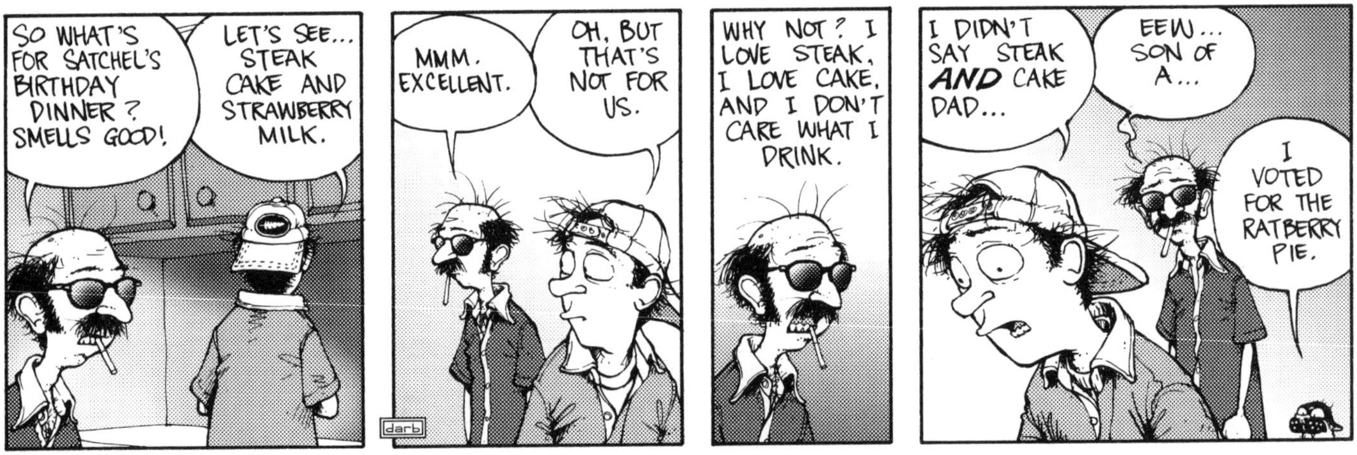
SO WHAT'S FOR SATCHEL'S BIRTHDAY DINNER? SMELLS GOOD!
LET'S SEE... STEAK CAKE AND STRAWBERRY MILK.
MMM. EXCELLENT.
OH, BUT THAT'S NOT FOR US.
darb
WHY NOT? I LOVE STEAK, I LOVE CAKE, AND I DON'T CARE WHAT I DRINK.
I DIDN'T SAY STEAK ***AND*** CAKE DAD...
EEW... SON OF A...
I VOTED FOR THE RATBERRY PIE.

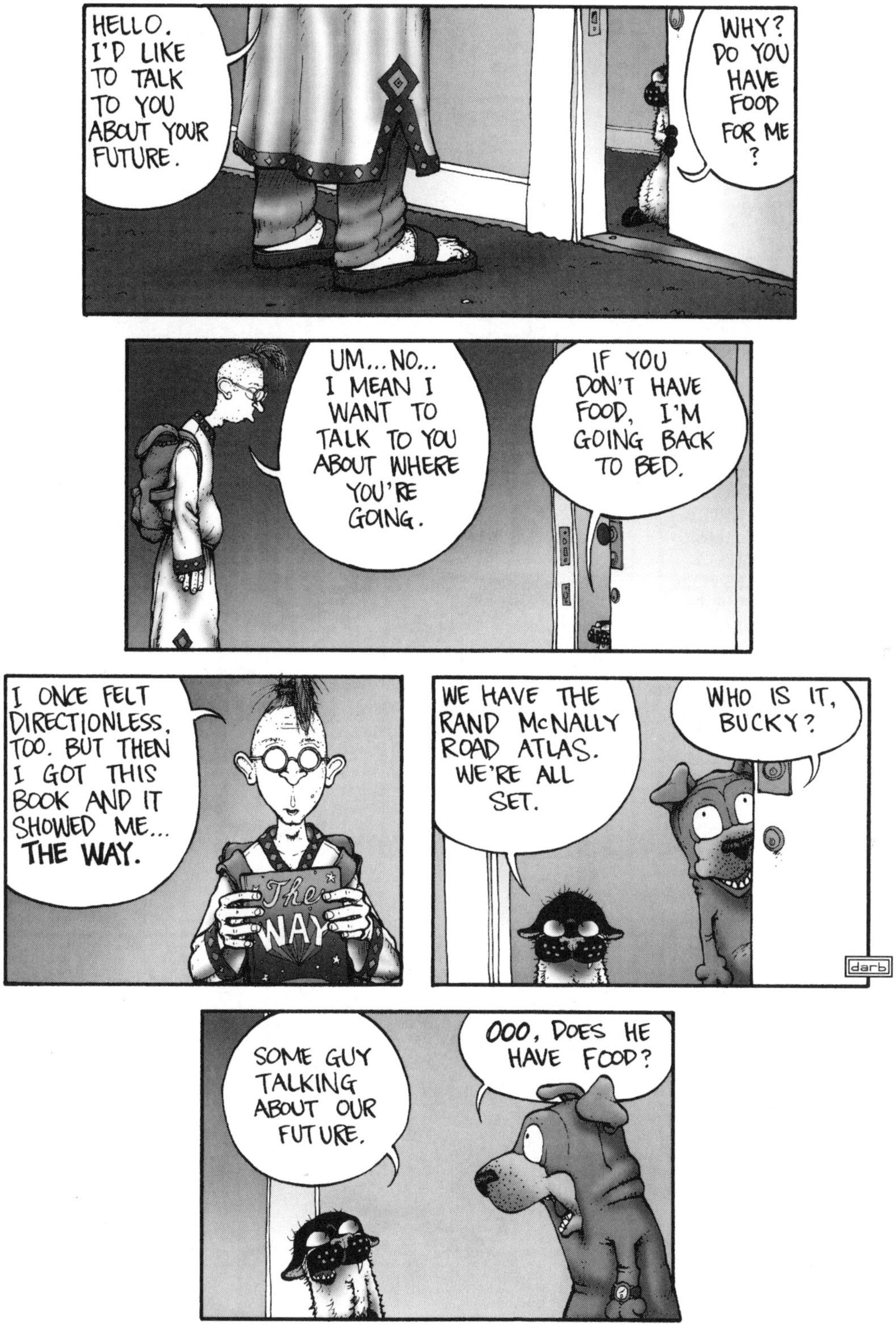
HELLO. I'D LIKE TO TALK TO YOU ABOUT YOUR FUTURE.
WHY? DO YOU HAVE FOOD FOR ME?
UM... NO... I MEAN I WANT TO TALK TO YOU ABOUT WHERE YOU'RE GOING.
IF YOU DON'T HAVE FOOD, I'M GOING BACK TO BED.
I ONCE FELT DIRECTIONLESS, TOO. BUT THEN I GOT THIS BOOK AND IT SHOWED ME... THE WAY.
The WAY
WE HAVE THE RAND McNALLY ROAD ATLAS. WE'RE ALL SET.
WHO IS IT, BUCKY?
darb
SOME GUY TALKING ABOUT OUR FUTURE.
OOO, DOES HE HAVE FOOD?

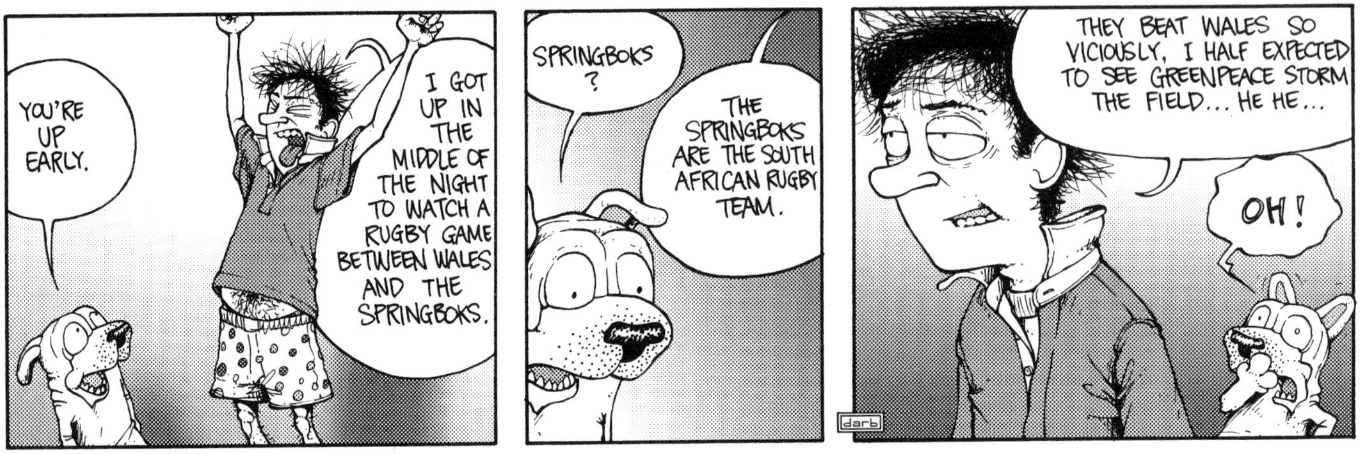
YOU'RE UP EARLY.
I GOT UP IN THE MIDDLE OF THE NIGHT TO WATCH A RUGBY GAME BETWEEN WALES AND THE SPRINGBOKS.
SPRINGBOKS ?
THE SPRINGBOKS ARE THE SOUTH AFRICAN RUGBY TEAM.
THEY BEAT WALES SO VICIOUSLY, I HALF EXPECTED TO SEE GREENPEACE STORM THE FIELD... HE HE...
OH!
darb

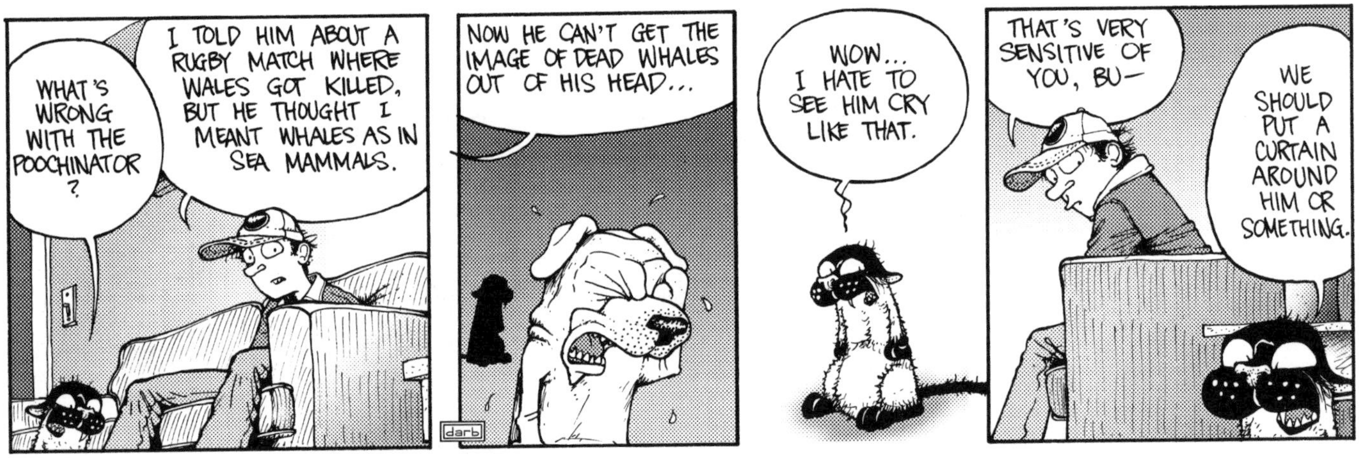
WHAT'S WRONG WITH THE POOCHINATOR ?
I TOLD HIM ABOUT A RUGBY MATCH WHERE WALES GOT KILLED, BUT HE THOUGHT I MEANT WHALES AS IN SEA MAMMALS.
darb
NOW HE CAN'T GET THE IMAGE OF DEAD WHALES OUT OF HIS HEAD...
WOW... I HATE TO SEE HIM CRY LIKE THAT.
THAT'S VERY SENSITIVE OF YOU, BU—
WE SHOULD PUT A CURTAIN AROUND HIM OR SOMETHING.

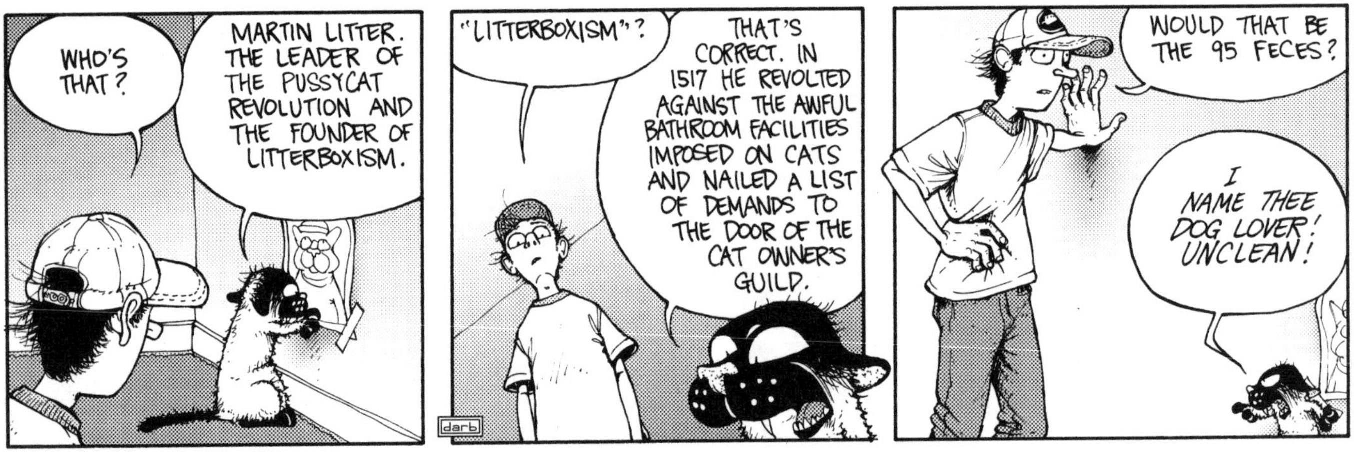
WHO'S THAT?
MARTIN LITTER. THE LEADER OF THE PUSSYCAT REVOLUTION AND THE FOUNDER OF LITTERBOXISM.
darb
"LITTERBOXISM"?
THAT'S CORRECT. IN 1517 HE REVOLTED AGAINST THE AWFUL BATHROOM FACILITIES IMPOSED ON CATS AND NAILED A LIST OF DEMANDS TO THE DOOR OF THE CAT OWNER'S GUILD.
WOULD THAT BE THE 95 FECES?
I NAME THEE DOG LOVER! UNCLEAN!

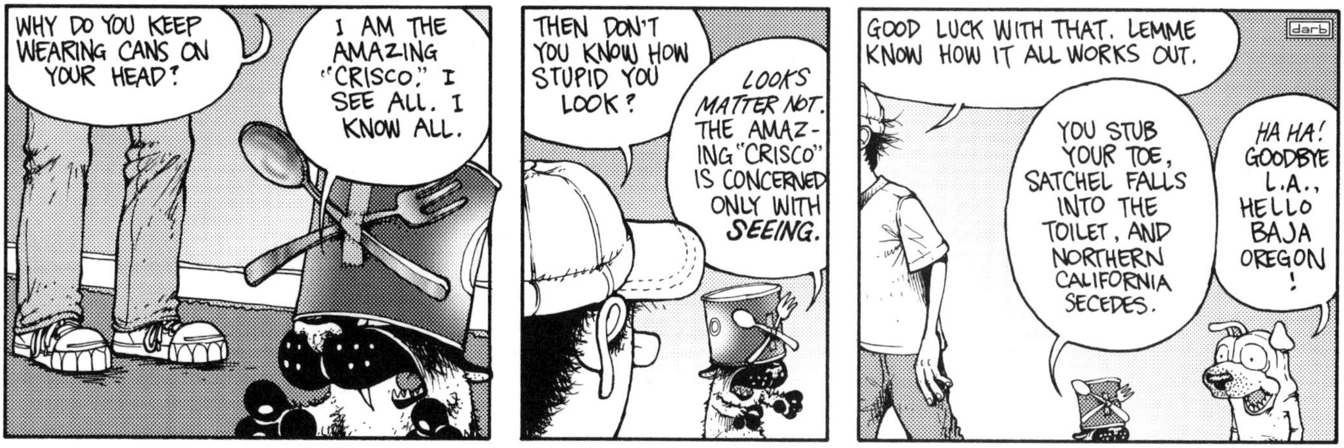
WHY DO YOU KEEP WEARING CANS ON YOUR HEAD?
I AM THE AMAZING "CRISCO." I SEE ALL. I KNOW ALL.
THEN DON'T YOU KNOW HOW STUPID YOU LOOK?
LOOKS MATTER NOT. THE AMAZING "CRISCO" IS CONCERNED ONLY WITH SEEING.
GOOD LUCK WITH THAT. LEMME KNOW HOW IT ALL WORKS OUT.
YOU STUB YOUR TOE, SATCHEL FALLS INTO THE TOILET, AND NORTHERN CALIFORNIA SECEDES.
HA HA! GOODBYE L.A., HELLO BAJA OREGON!
darb

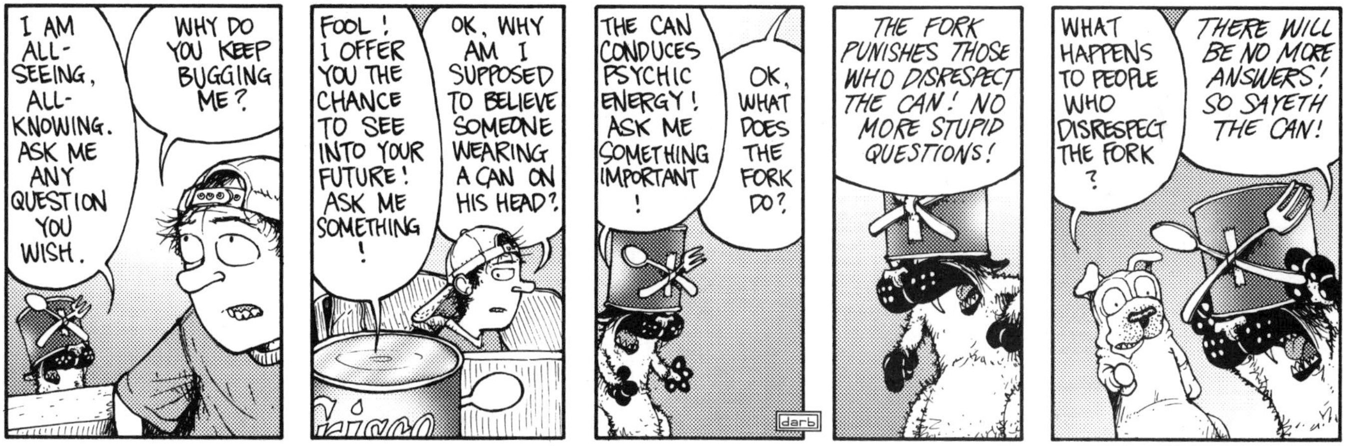
I AM ALL-SEEING, ALL-KNOWING. ASK ME ANY QUESTION YOU WISH.
WHY DO YOU KEEP BUGGING ME?
FOOL! I OFFER YOU THE CHANCE TO SEE INTO YOUR FUTURE! ASK ME SOMETHING!
OK, WHY AM I SUPPOSED TO BELIEVE SOMEONE WEARING A CAN ON HIS HEAD?
THE CAN CONDUCES PSYCHIC ENERGY! ASK ME SOMETHING IMPORTANT!
OK, WHAT DOES THE FORK DO?
darb
THE FORK PUNISHES THOSE WHO DISRESPECT THE CAN! NO MORE STUPID QUESTIONS!
WHAT HAPPENS TO PEOPLE WHO DISRESPECT THE FORK?
THERE WILL BE NO MORE ANSWERS! SO SAYETH THE CAN!

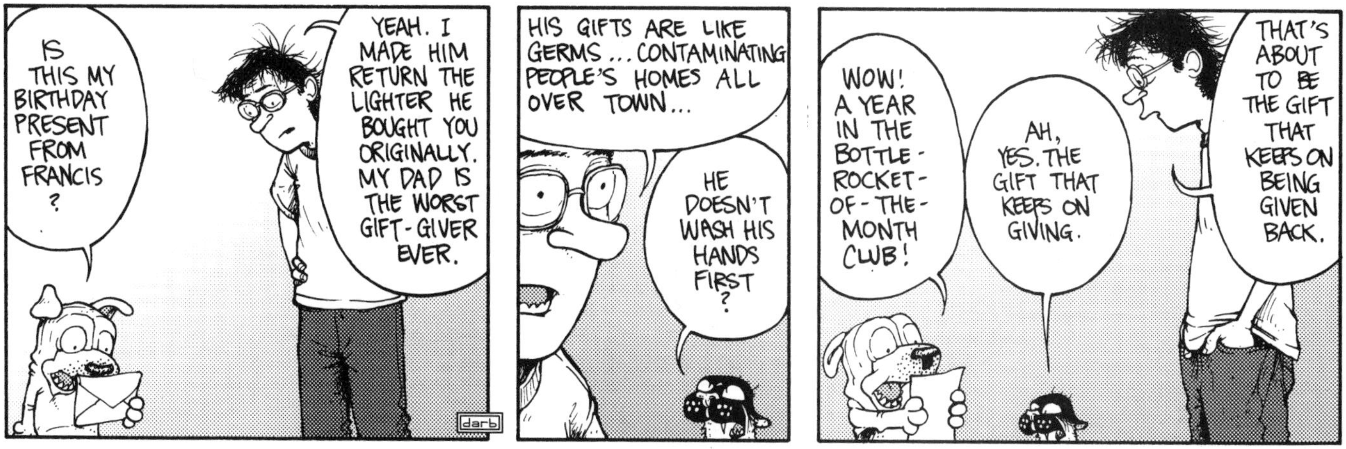
IS THIS MY BIRTHDAY PRESENT FROM FRANCIS?
YEAH. I MADE HIM RETURN THE LIGHTER HE BOUGHT YOU ORIGINALLY. MY DAD IS THE WORST GIFT-GIVER EVER.
darb
HIS GIFTS ARE LIKE GERMS... CONTAMINATING PEOPLE'S HOMES ALL OVER TOWN...
HE DOESN'T WASH HIS HANDS FIRST?
WOW! A YEAR IN THE BOTTLE-ROCKET-OF-THE-MONTH CLUB!
AH, YES. THE GIFT THAT KEEPS ON GIVING.
THAT'S ABOUT TO BE THE GIFT THAT KEEPS ON BEING GIVEN BACK.

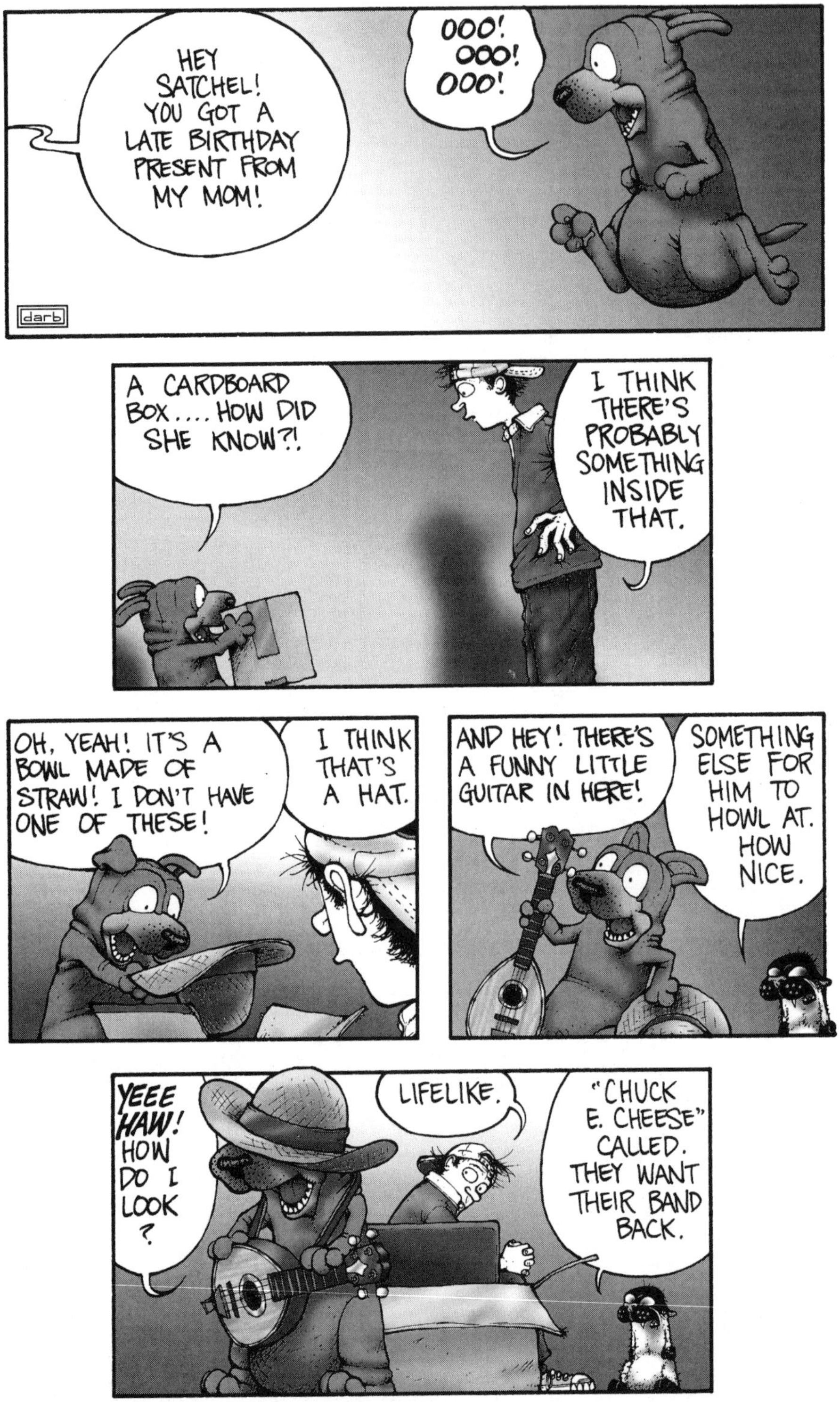
HEY SATCHEL! YOU GOT A LATE BIRTHDAY PRESENT FROM MY MOM!
OOO! OOO! OOO!
darb
A CARDBOARD BOX.... HOW DID SHE KNOW?!
I THINK THERE'S PROBABLY SOMETHING INSIDE THAT.
OH, YEAH! IT'S A BOWL MADE OF STRAW! I DON'T HAVE ONE OF THESE!
I THINK THAT'S A HAT.
AND HEY! THERE'S A FUNNY LITTLE GUITAR IN HERE!
SOMETHING ELSE FOR HIM TO HOWL AT. HOW NICE.
YEEE HAW! HOW DO I LOOK?
LIFELIKE.
"CHUCK E. CHEESE" CALLED. THEY WANT THEIR BAND BACK.

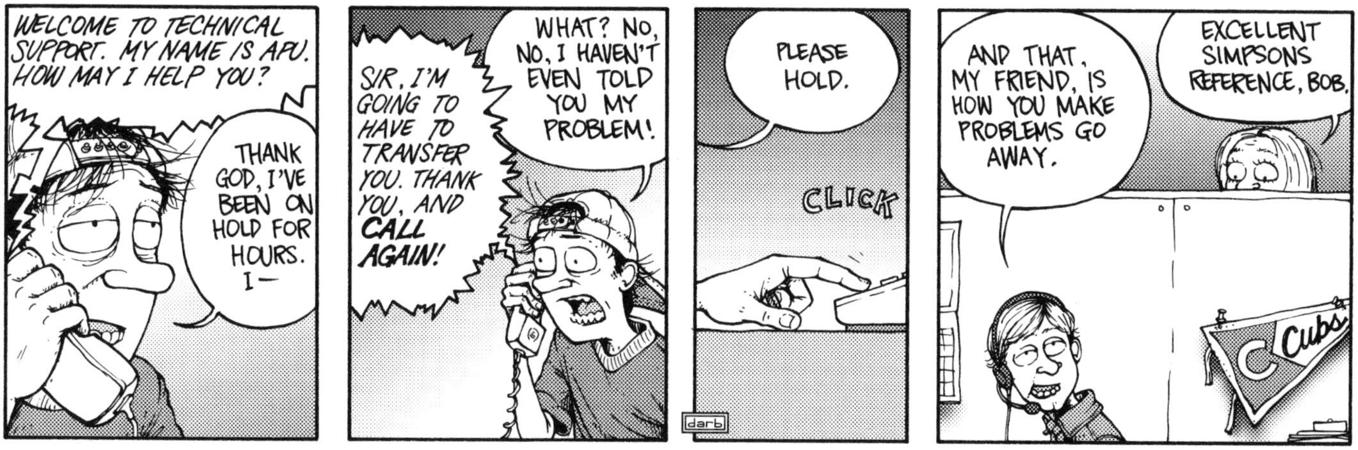

WELCOME TO TECHNICAL SUPPORT. MY NAME IS APU. HOW MAY I HELP YOU?
THANK GOD, I'VE BEEN ON HOLD FOR HOURS. I—
SIR, I'M GOING TO HAVE TO TRANSFER YOU. THANK YOU, AND CALL AGAIN!
WHAT? NO, NO, I HAVEN'T EVEN TOLD YOU MY PROBLEM!
PLEASE HOLD.
CLICK
darb
AND THAT, MY FRIEND, IS HOW YOU MAKE PROBLEMS GO AWAY.
EXCELLENT SIMPSONS REFERENCE, BOB.
Cubs

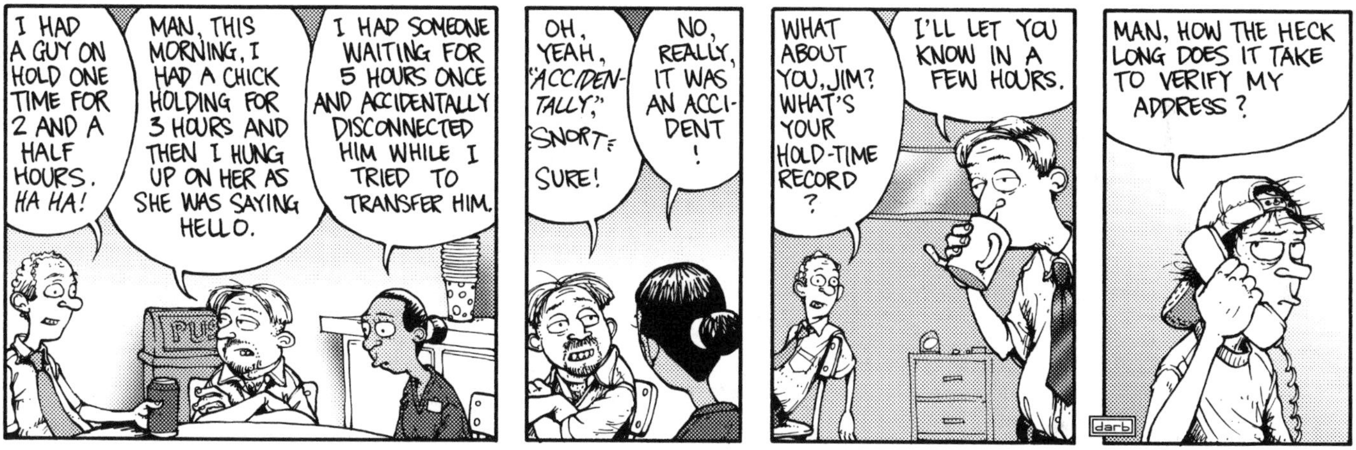

I HAD A GUY ON HOLD ONE TIME FOR 2 AND A HALF HOURS. HA HA!
MAN, THIS MORNING, I HAD A CHICK HOLDING FOR 3 HOURS AND THEN I HUNG UP ON HER AS SHE WAS SAYING HELLO.
I HAD SOMEONE WAITING FOR 5 HOURS ONCE AND ACCIDENTALLY DISCONNECTED HIM WHILE I TRIED TO TRANSFER HIM.
OH, YEAH, "ACCIDENTALLY," SNORT SURE!
NO, REALLY, IT WAS AN ACCIDENT!
WHAT ABOUT YOU, JIM? WHAT'S YOUR HOLD-TIME RECORD?
I'LL LET YOU KNOW IN A FEW HOURS.
darb
MAN, HOW THE HECK LONG DOES IT TAKE TO VERIFY MY ADDRESS?

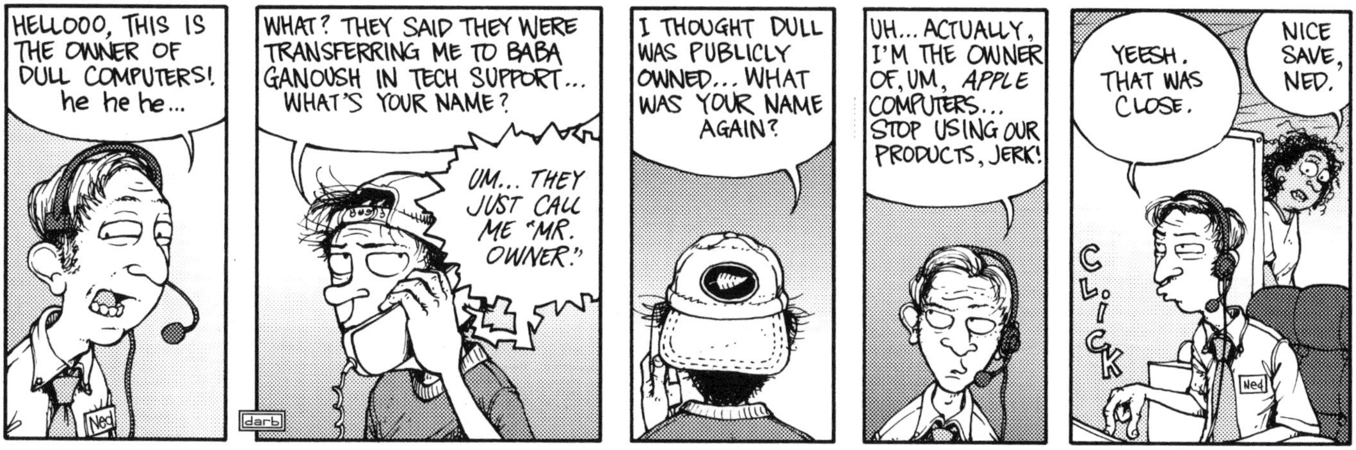

HELLOOO, THIS IS THE OWNER OF DULL COMPUTERS! he he he...
Ned
darb
WHAT? THEY SAID THEY WERE TRANSFERRING ME TO BABA GANOUSH IN TECH SUPPORT... WHAT'S YOUR NAME?
UM... THEY JUST CALL ME "MR. OWNER."
I THOUGHT DULL WAS PUBLICLY OWNED... WHAT WAS YOUR NAME AGAIN?
UH... ACTUALLY, I'M THE OWNER OF, UM, APPLE COMPUTERS... STOP USING OUR PRODUCTS, JERK!
YEESH. THAT WAS CLOSE.
NICE SAVE, NED.
CLICK
Ned

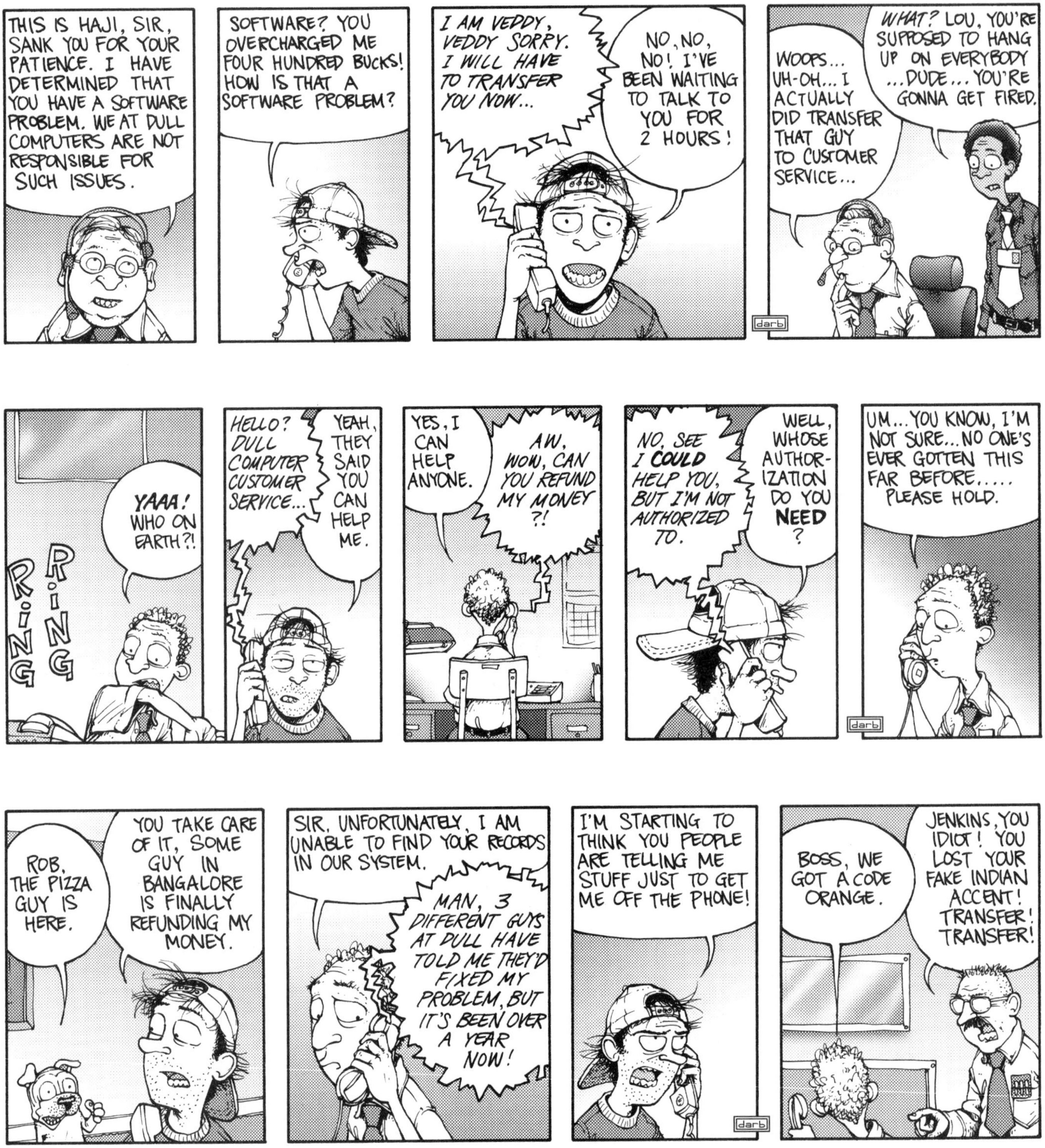
THIS IS HAJI, SIR, SANK YOU FOR YOUR PATIENCE. I HAVE DETERMINED THAT YOU HAVE A SOFTWARE PROBLEM. WE AT DULL COMPUTERS ARE NOT RESPONSIBLE FOR SUCH ISSUES.
SOFTWARE? YOU OVERCHARGED ME FOUR HUNDRED BUCKS! HOW IS THAT A SOFTWARE PROBLEM?
I AM VEDDY, VEDDY SORRY. I WILL HAVE TO TRANSFER YOU NOW...
NO, NO, NO! I'VE BEEN WAITING TO TALK TO YOU FOR 2 HOURS!
WOOPS... UH-OH... I ACTUALLY DID TRANSFER THAT GUY TO CUSTOMER SERVICE...
WHAT? LOU, YOU'RE SUPPOSED TO HANG UP ON EVERYBODY ...DUDE... YOU'RE GONNA GET FIRED.
darb
RING RING
YAAA! WHO ON EARTH?!
HELLO? DULL COMPUTER CUSTOMER SERVICE...
YEAH, THEY SAID YOU CAN HELP ME.
YES, I CAN HELP ANYONE.
AW, WOW, CAN YOU REFUND MY MONEY?!
NO, SEE I COULD HELP YOU, BUT I'M NOT AUTHORIZED TO.
WELL, WHOSE AUTHORIZATION DO YOU NEED?
UM... YOU KNOW, I'M NOT SURE... NO ONE'S EVER GOTTEN THIS FAR BEFORE..... PLEASE HOLD.
darb
ROB, THE PIZZA GUY IS HERE.
YOU TAKE CARE OF IT, SOME GUY IN BANGALORE IS FINALLY REFUNDING MY MONEY.
SIR, UNFORTUNATELY, I AM UNABLE TO FIND YOUR RECORDS IN OUR SYSTEM.
MAN, 3 DIFFERENT GUYS AT DULL HAVE TOLD ME THEY'D FIXED MY PROBLEM, BUT IT'S BEEN OVER A YEAR NOW!
I'M STARTING TO THINK YOU PEOPLE ARE TELLING ME STUFF JUST TO GET ME OFF THE PHONE!
darb
BOSS, WE GOT A CODE ORANGE.
JENKINS, YOU IDIOT! YOU LOST YOUR FAKE INDIAN ACCENT! TRANSFER! TRANSFER!

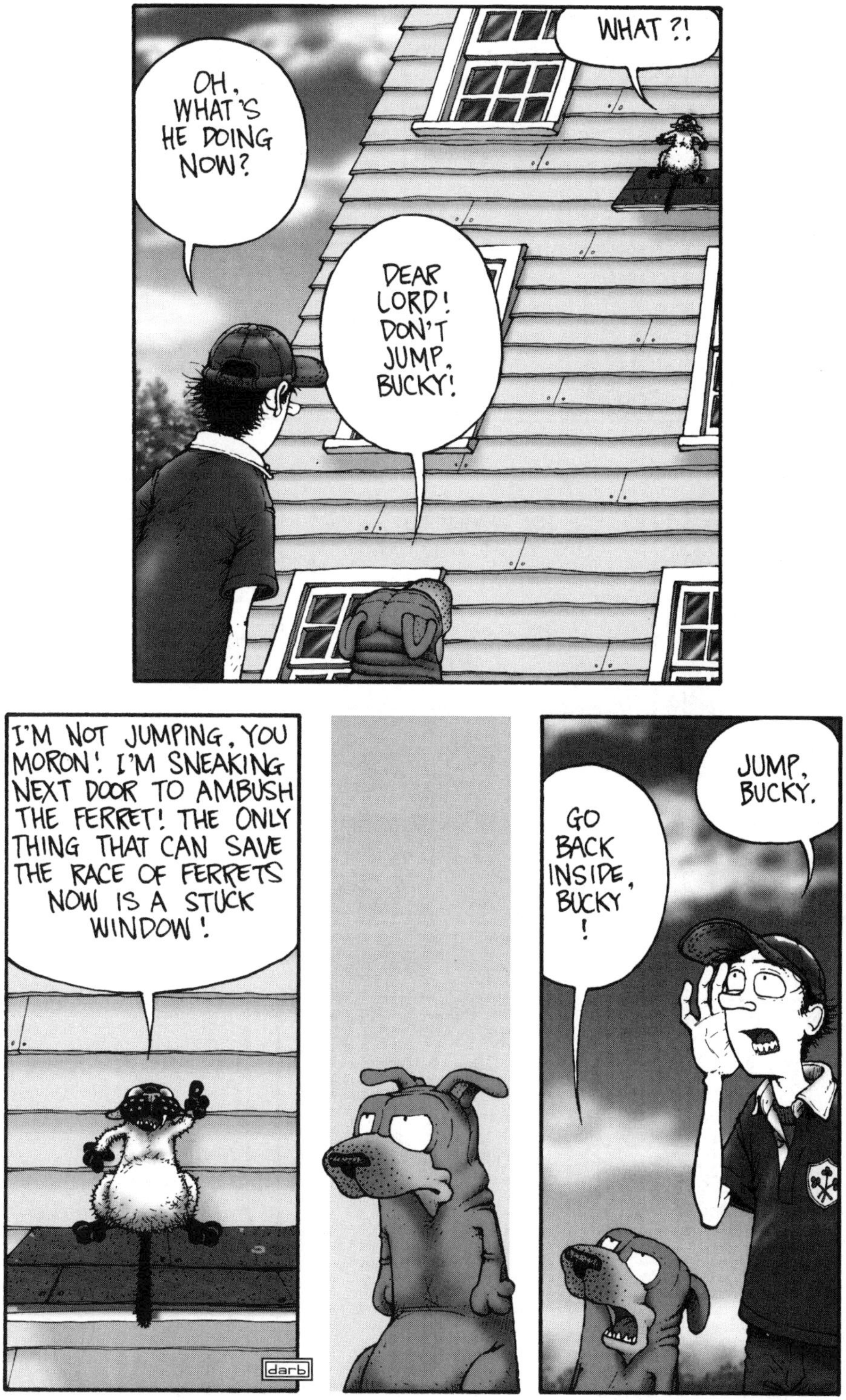
OH, WHAT'S HE DOING NOW?
WHAT?!
DEAR LORD! DON'T JUMP, BUCKY!
I'M NOT JUMPING, YOU MORON! I'M SNEAKING NEXT DOOR TO AMBUSH THE FERRET! THE ONLY THING THAT CAN SAVE THE RACE OF FERRETS NOW IS A STUCK WINDOW!
darb
JUMP, BUCKY.
GO BACK INSIDE, BUCKY!

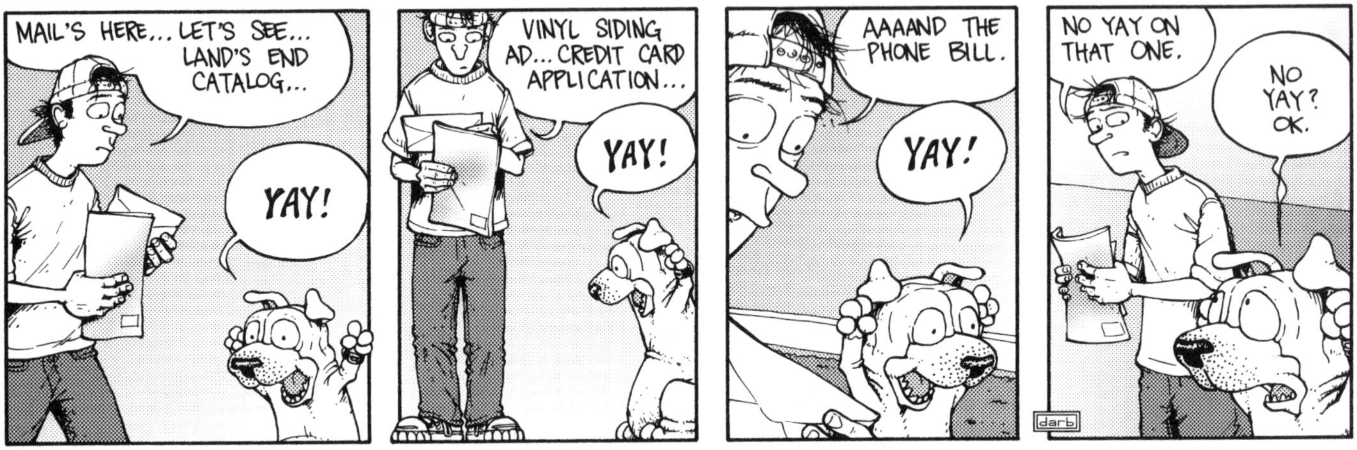
MAIL'S HERE... LET'S SEE... LAND'S END CATALOG...
YAY!
VINYL SIDING AD... CREDIT CARD APPLICATION...
YAY!
AAAAND THE PHONE BILL.
YAY!
NO YAY ON THAT ONE.
NO YAY? OK.
darb

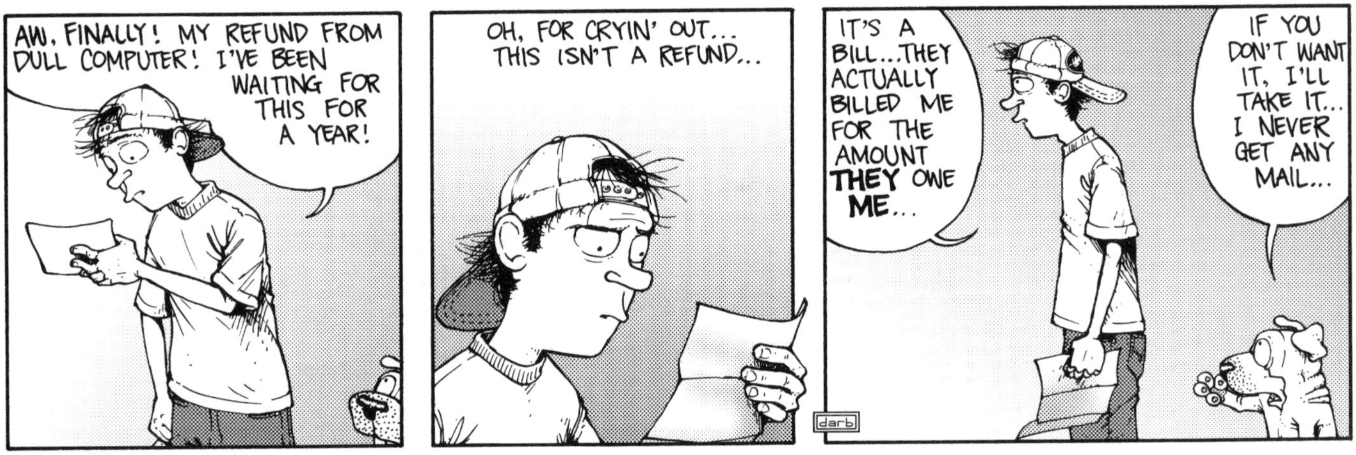
AW, FINALLY! MY REFUND FROM DULL COMPUTER! I'VE BEEN WAITING FOR THIS FOR A YEAR!
OH, FOR CRYIN' OUT... THIS ISN'T A REFUND...
darb
IT'S A BILL...THEY ACTUALLY BILLED ME FOR THE AMOUNT **THEY** OWE **ME**...
IF YOU DON'T WANT IT, I'LL TAKE IT... I NEVER GET ANY MAIL...

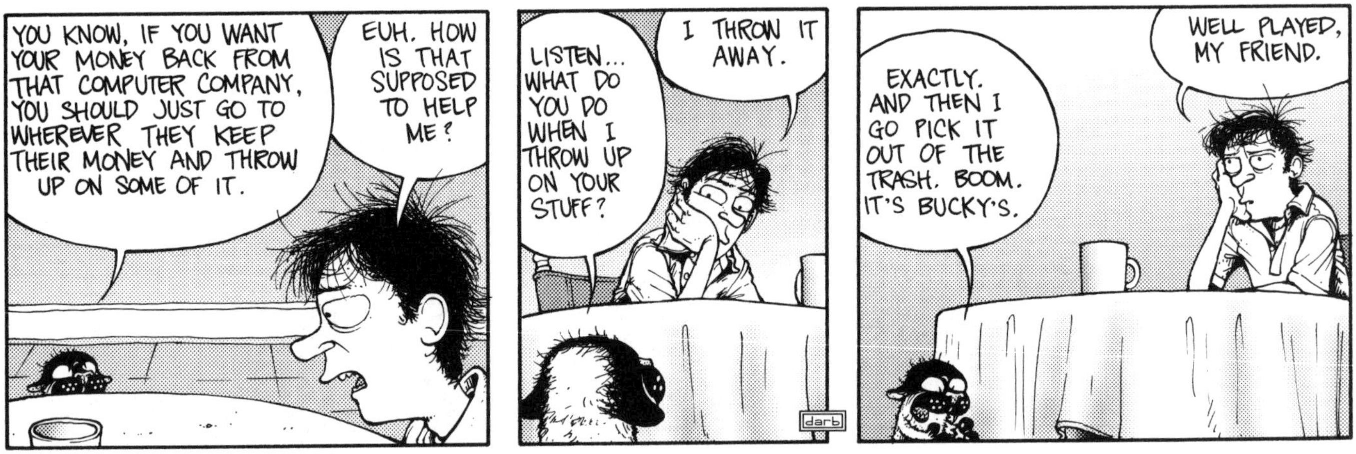
YOU KNOW, IF YOU WANT YOUR MONEY BACK FROM THAT COMPUTER COMPANY, YOU SHOULD JUST GO TO WHEREVER THEY KEEP THEIR MONEY AND THROW UP ON SOME OF IT.
EUH. HOW IS THAT SUPPOSED TO HELP ME?
LISTEN... WHAT DO YOU DO WHEN I THROW UP ON YOUR STUFF?
I THROW IT AWAY.
darb
EXACTLY. AND THEN I GO PICK IT OUT OF THE TRASH. BOOM. IT'S BUCKY'S.
WELL PLAYED, MY FRIEND.

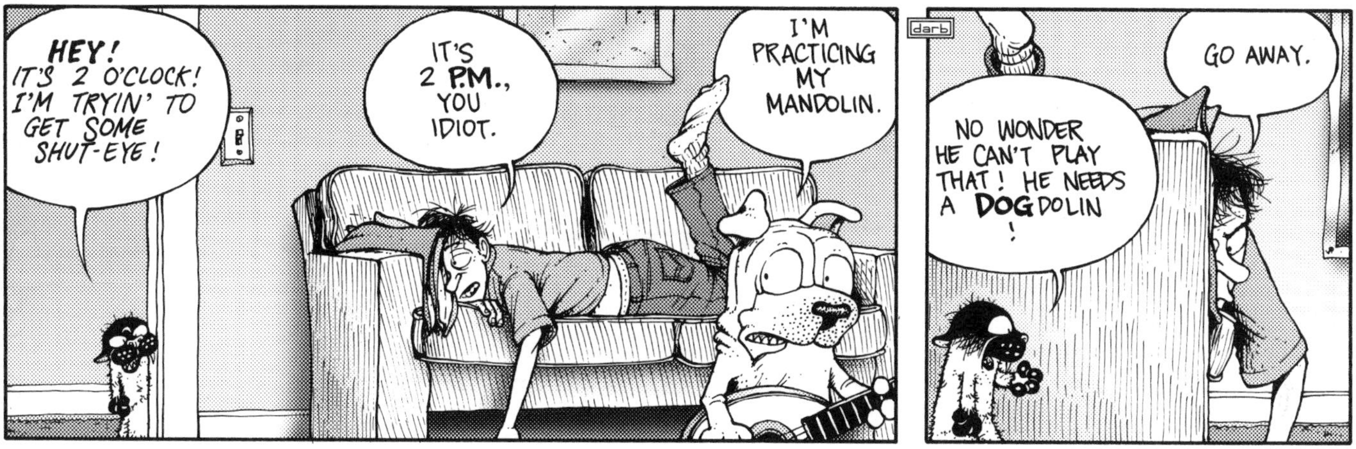
HEY! IT'S 2 O'CLOCK! I'M TRYIN' TO GET SOME SHUT-EYE!
IT'S 2 P.M., YOU IDIOT.
I'M PRACTICING MY MANDOLIN.
GO AWAY.
NO WONDER HE CAN'T PLAY THAT! HE NEEDS A DOGDOLIN!
darb

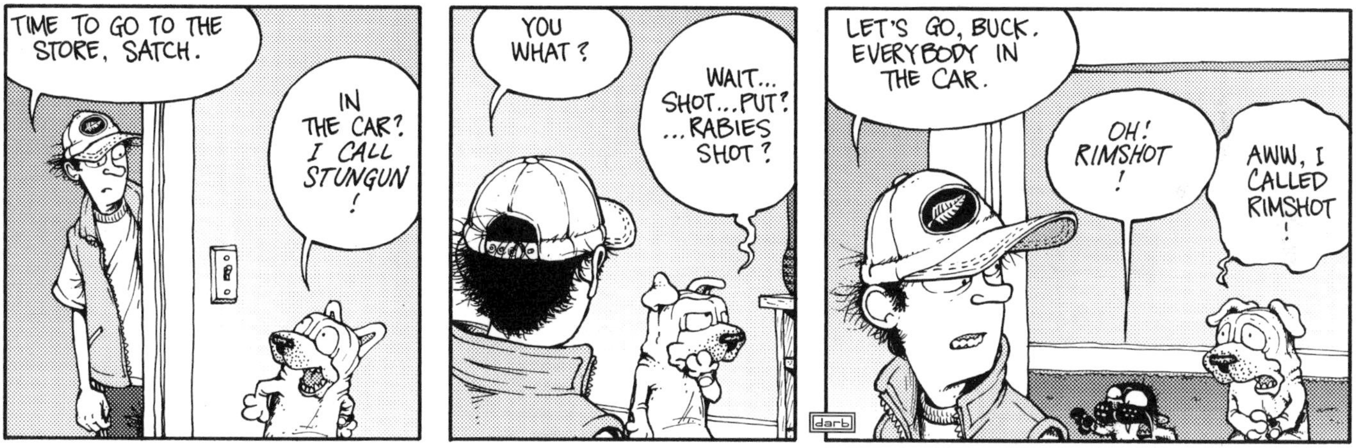
TIME TO GO TO THE STORE, SATCH.
IN THE CAR? I CALL STUNGUN!
YOU WHAT?
WAIT... SHOT...PUT? ...RABIES SHOT?
LET'S GO, BUCK. EVERYBODY IN THE CAR.
OH! RIMSHOT!
AWW, I CALLED RIMSHOT!
darb

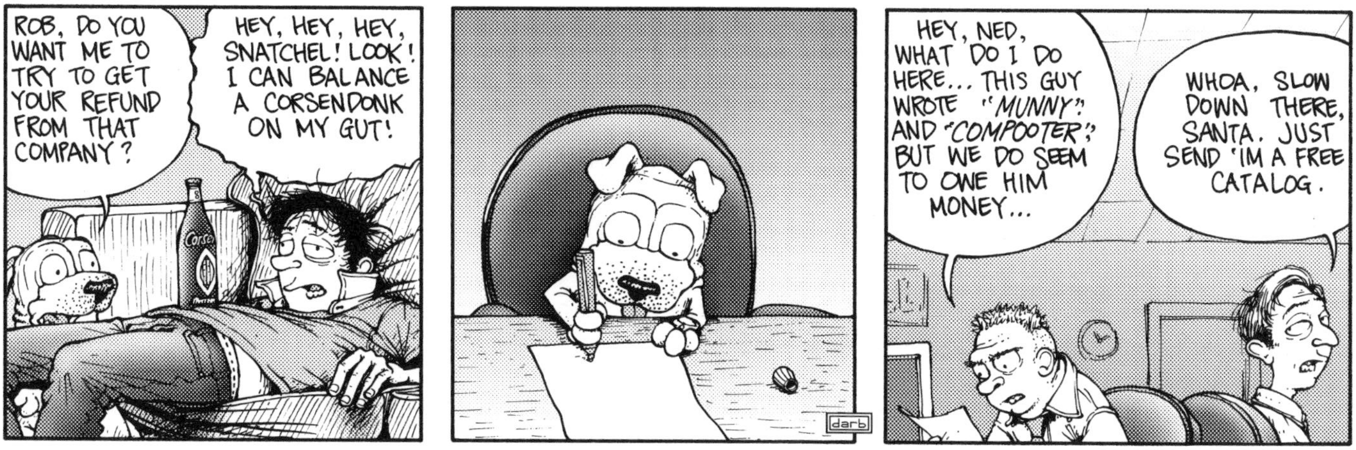
ROB, DO YOU WANT ME TO TRY TO GET YOUR REFUND FROM THAT COMPANY?
HEY, HEY, HEY, SNATCHEL! LOOK! I CAN BALANCE A CORSENDONK ON MY GUT!
HEY, NED, WHAT DO I DO HERE... THIS GUY WROTE "MUNNY" AND "COMPOOTER," BUT WE DO SEEM TO OWE HIM MONEY...
WHOA, SLOW DOWN THERE, SANTA. JUST SEND 'IM A FREE CATALOG.
darb

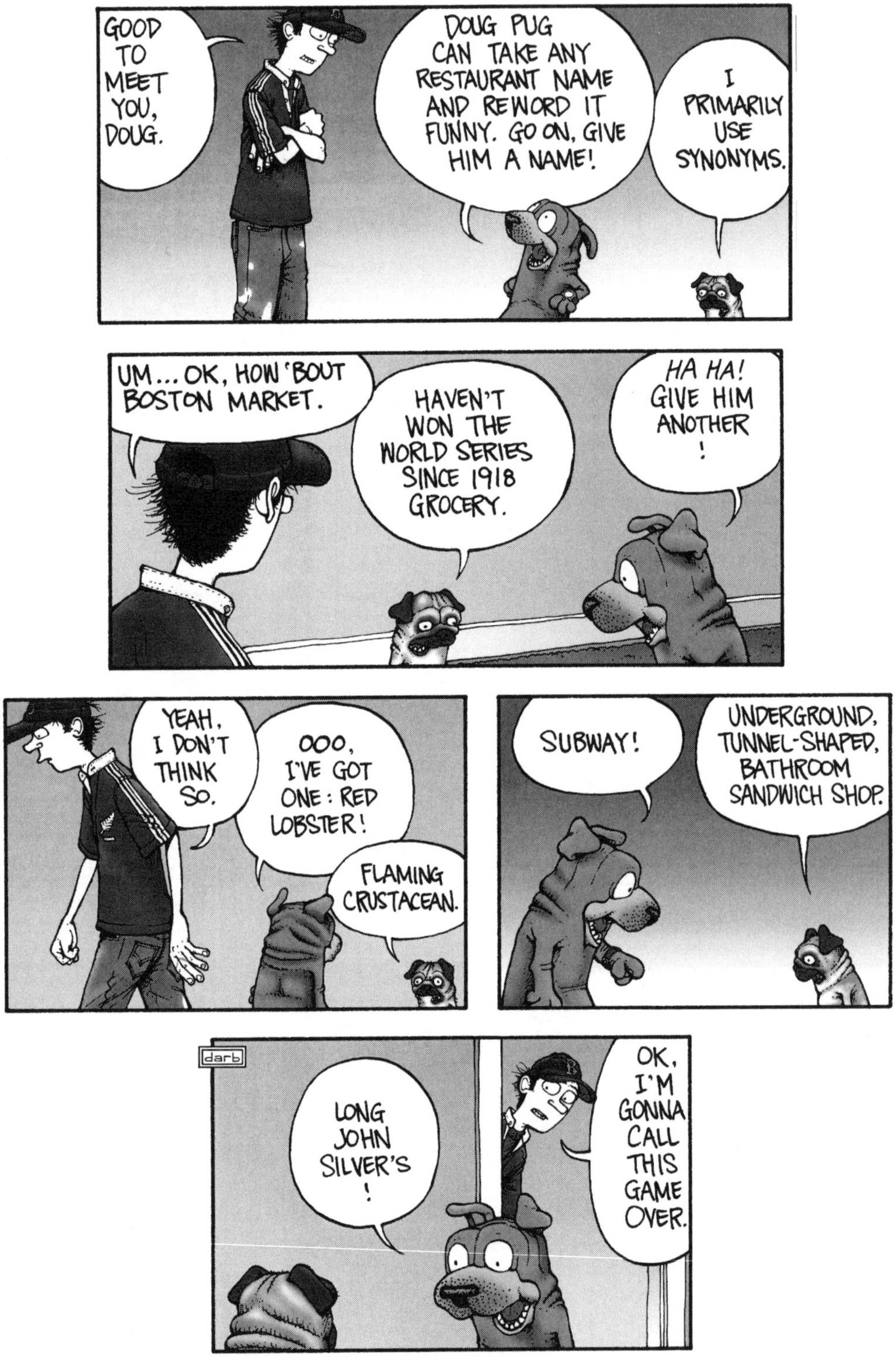
GOOD TO MEET YOU, DOUG.
DOUG PUG CAN TAKE ANY RESTAURANT NAME AND REWORD IT FUNNY. GO ON, GIVE HIM A NAME!
I PRIMARILY USE SYNONYMS.
UM... OK, HOW 'BOUT BOSTON MARKET.
HAVEN'T WON THE WORLD SERIES SINCE 1918 GROCERY.
HA HA! GIVE HIM ANOTHER!
YEAH, I DON'T THINK SO.
OOO, I'VE GOT ONE: RED LOBSTER!
FLAMING CRUSTACEAN.
SUBWAY!
UNDERGROUND, TUNNEL-SHAPED, BATHROOM SANDWICH SHOP.
darb
LONG JOHN SILVER'S!
OK, I'M GONNA CALL THIS GAME OVER.

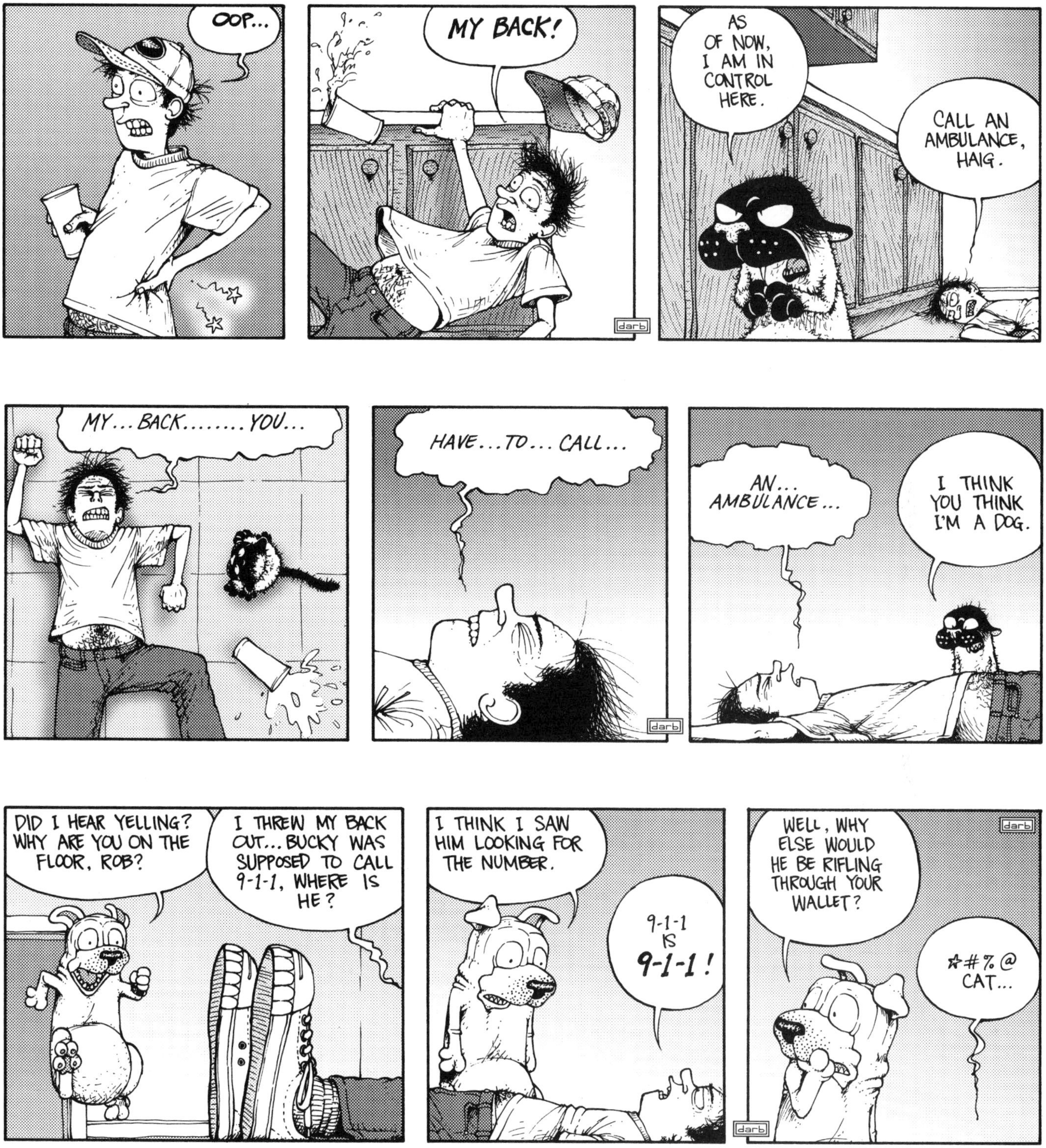
OOP...
MY BACK!
AS OF NOW, I AM IN CONTROL HERE.
CALL AN AMBULANCE, HAIG.
darb
MY... BACK........ YOU...
HAVE... TO... CALL...
AN... AMBULANCE...
I THINK YOU THINK I'M A DOG.
darb
DID I HEAR YELLING? WHY ARE YOU ON THE FLOOR, ROB?
I THREW MY BACK OUT... BUCKY WAS SUPPOSED TO CALL 9-1-1, WHERE IS HE?
I THINK I SAW HIM LOOKING FOR THE NUMBER.
9-1-1 IS 9-1-1!
WELL, WHY ELSE WOULD HE BE RIFLING THROUGH YOUR WALLET?
*#%@ CAT...
darb

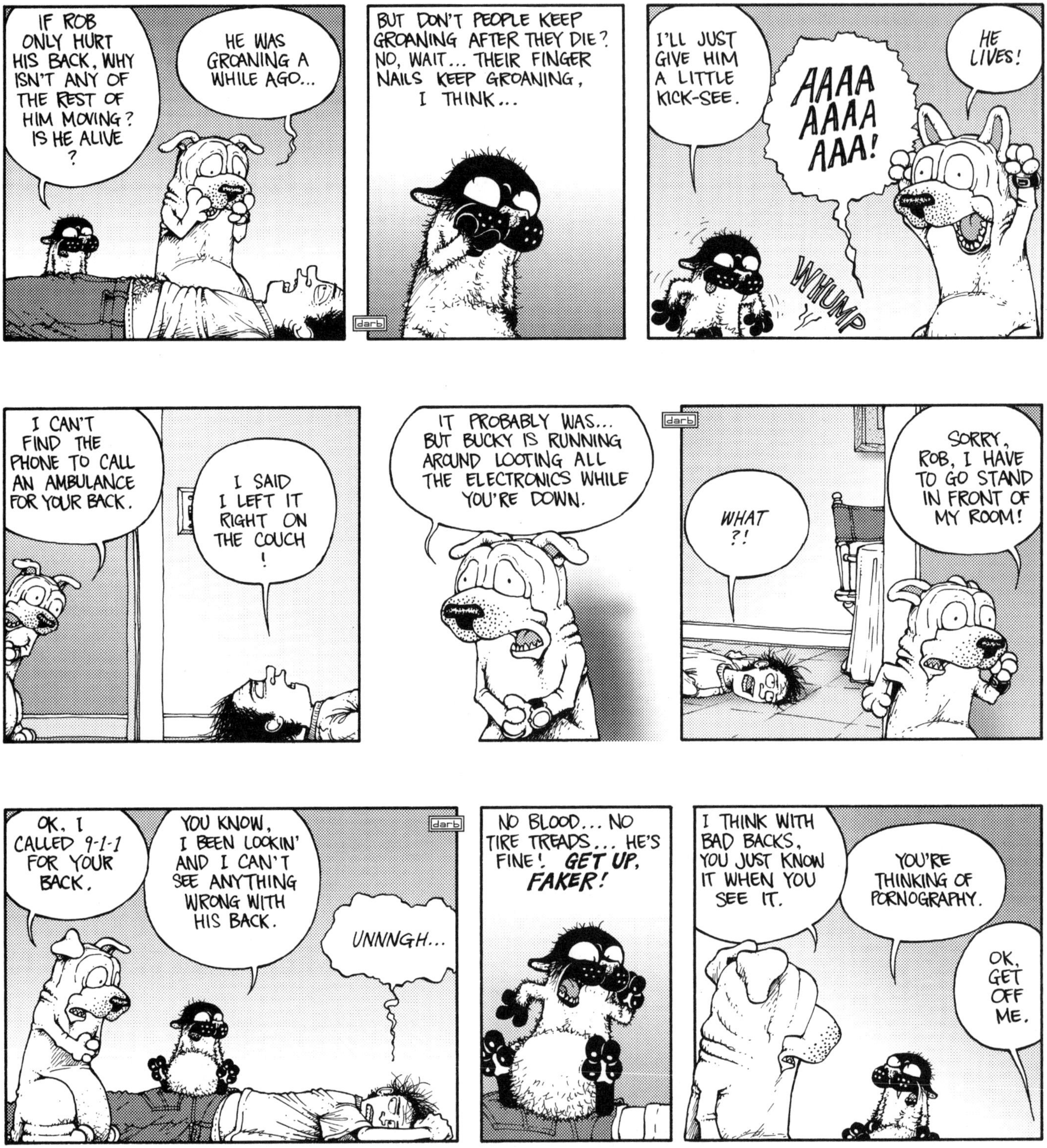
IF ROB ONLY HURT HIS BACK, WHY ISN'T ANY OF THE REST OF HIM MOVING? IS HE ALIVE ?
HE WAS GROANING A WHILE AGO...
darb
BUT DON'T PEOPLE KEEP GROANING AFTER THEY DIE? NO, WAIT... THEIR FINGER NAILS KEEP GROANING, I THINK...
I'LL JUST GIVE HIM A LITTLE KICK-SEE.
WHUMP
AAAA AAAA AAA!
HE LIVES!
I CAN'T FIND THE PHONE TO CALL AN AMBULANCE FOR YOUR BACK.
I SAID I LEFT IT RIGHT ON THE COUCH !
IT PROBABLY WAS... BUT BUCKY IS RUNNING AROUND LOOTING ALL THE ELECTRONICS WHILE YOU'RE DOWN.
darb
WHAT ?!
SORRY, ROB, I HAVE TO GO STAND IN FRONT OF MY ROOM!
OK, I CALLED 9-1-1 FOR YOUR BACK.
YOU KNOW, I BEEN LOOKIN' AND I CAN'T SEE ANYTHING WRONG WITH HIS BACK.
darb
UNNNGH...
NO BLOOD... NO TIRE TREADS... HE'S FINE! GET UP, FAKER!
I THINK WITH BAD BACKS, YOU JUST KNOW IT WHEN YOU SEE IT.
YOU'RE THINKING OF PORNOGRAPHY.
OK, GET OFF ME.

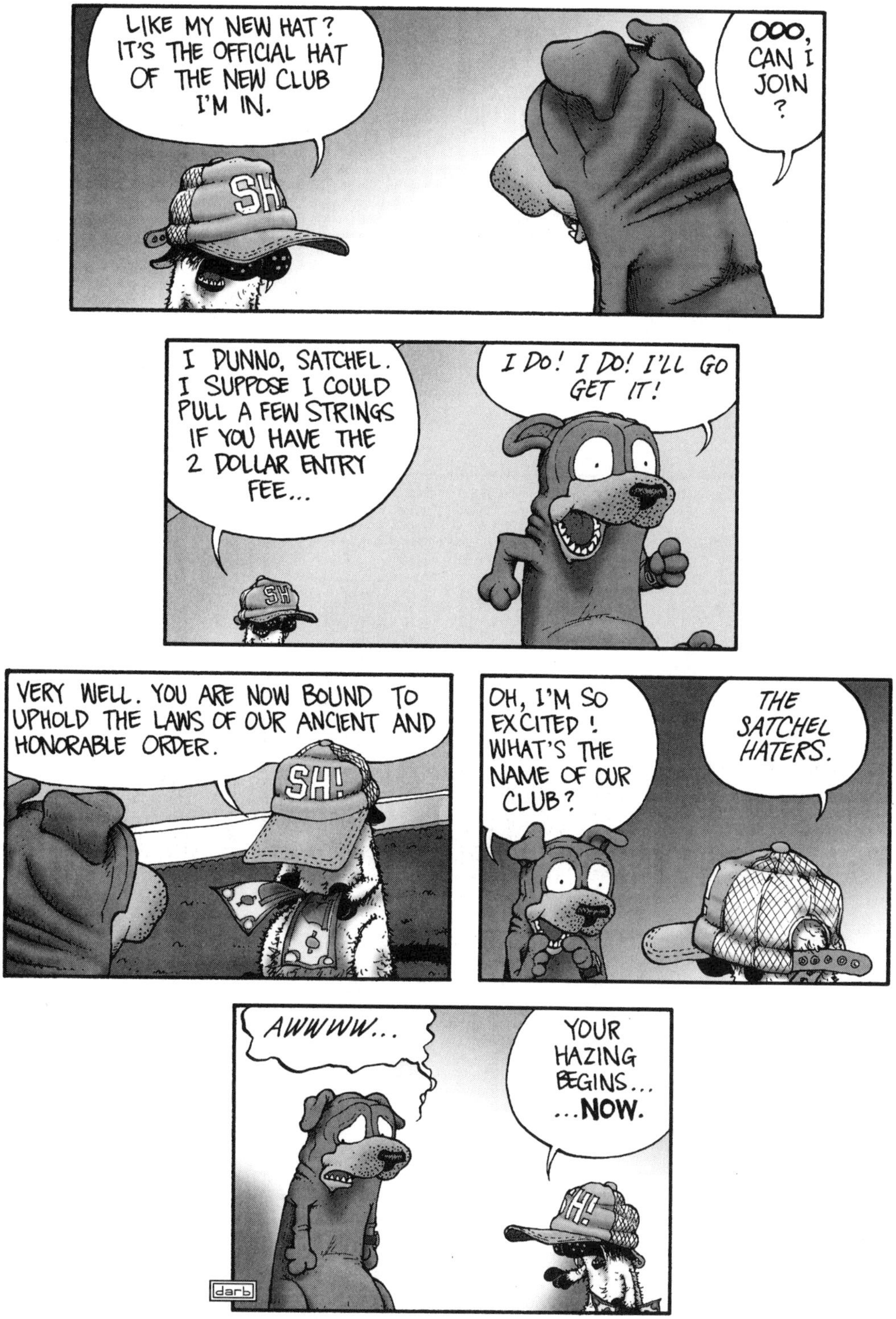
LIKE MY NEW HAT? IT'S THE OFFICIAL HAT OF THE NEW CLUB I'M IN.
SH
OOO, CAN I JOIN?
I DUNNO, SATCHEL. I SUPPOSE I COULD PULL A FEW STRINGS IF YOU HAVE THE 2 DOLLAR ENTRY FEE...
I DO! I DO! I'LL GO GET IT!
SH
VERY WELL. YOU ARE NOW BOUND TO UPHOLD THE LAWS OF OUR ANCIENT AND HONORABLE ORDER.
SH!
OH, I'M SO EXCITED! WHAT'S THE NAME OF OUR CLUB?
THE SATCHEL HATERS.
AWWWW...
YOUR HAZING BEGINS... ...**NOW**.
SH!
darb

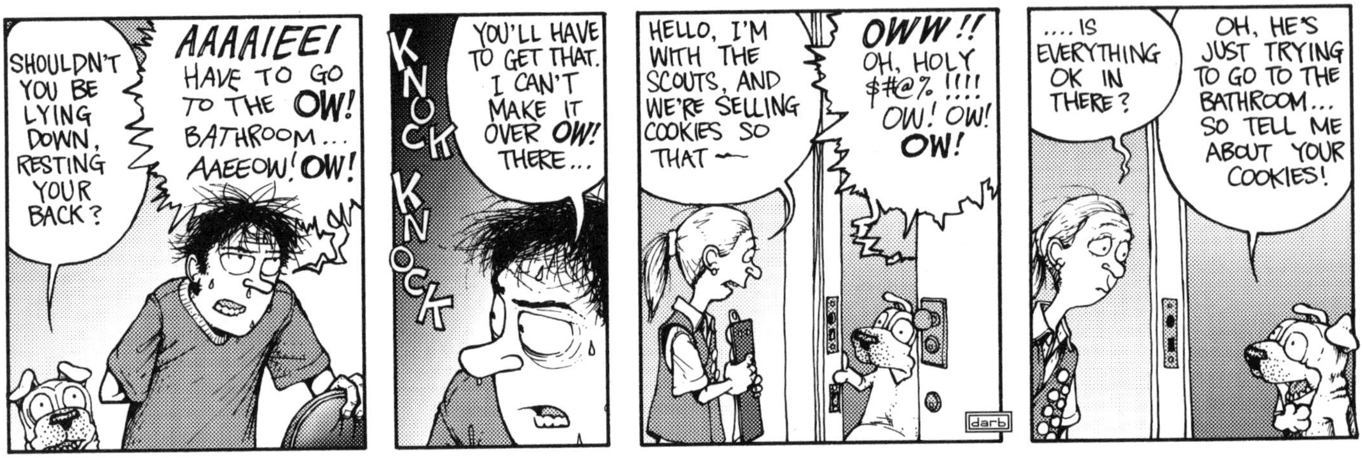
SHOULDN'T YOU BE LYING DOWN, RESTING YOUR BACK?
AAAAIEEE! HAVE TO GO TO THE OW! BATHROOM... AAEEOW! OW!
KNOCK KNOCK KNOCK
YOU'LL HAVE TO GET THAT. I CAN'T MAKE IT OVER OW! THERE...
HELLO, I'M WITH THE SCOUTS, AND WE'RE SELLING COOKIES SO THAT—
OWW!! OH, HOLY $#@%!!!!!!!! OW! OW! OW!
....IS EVERYTHING OK IN THERE?
OH, HE'S JUST TRYING TO GO TO THE BATHROOM... SO TELL ME ABOUT YOUR COOKIES!
darb

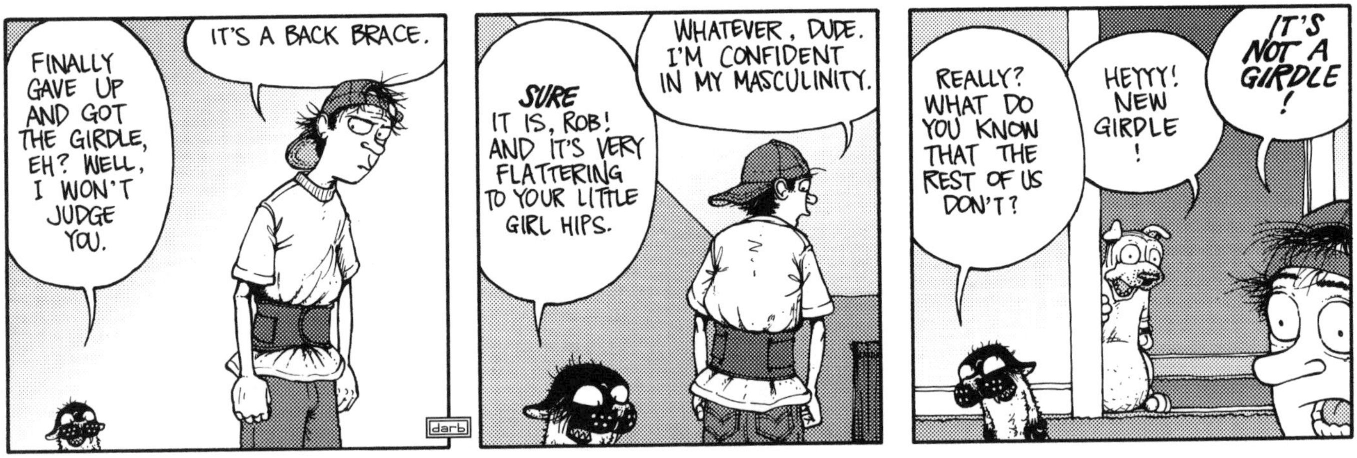
FINALLY GAVE UP AND GOT THE GIRDLE, EH? WELL, I WON'T JUDGE YOU.
IT'S A BACK BRACE.
darb
SURE IT IS, ROB! AND IT'S VERY FLATTERING TO YOUR LITTLE GIRL HIPS.
WHATEVER, DUDE. I'M CONFIDENT IN MY MASCULINITY.
REALLY? WHAT DO YOU KNOW THAT THE REST OF US DON'T?
HEYYY! NEW GIRDLE!
IT'S NOT A GIRDLE!

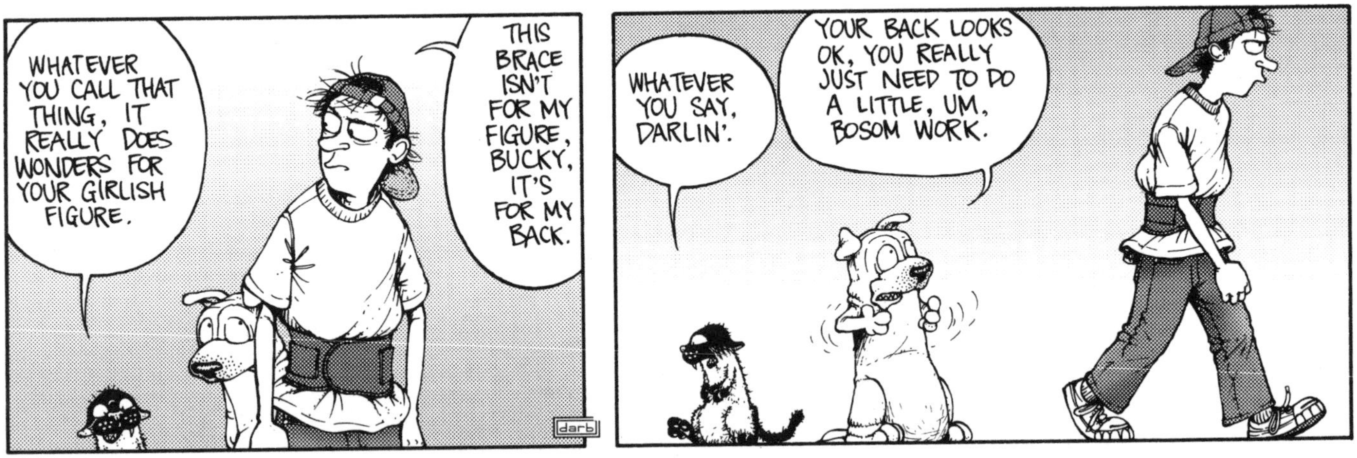
WHATEVER YOU CALL THAT THING, IT REALLY DOES WONDERS FOR YOUR GIRLISH FIGURE.
THIS BRACE ISN'T FOR MY FIGURE, BUCKY, IT'S FOR MY BACK.
darb
WHATEVER YOU SAY, DARLIN'.
YOUR BACK LOOKS OK, YOU REALLY JUST NEED TO DO A LITTLE, UM, BOSOM WORK.

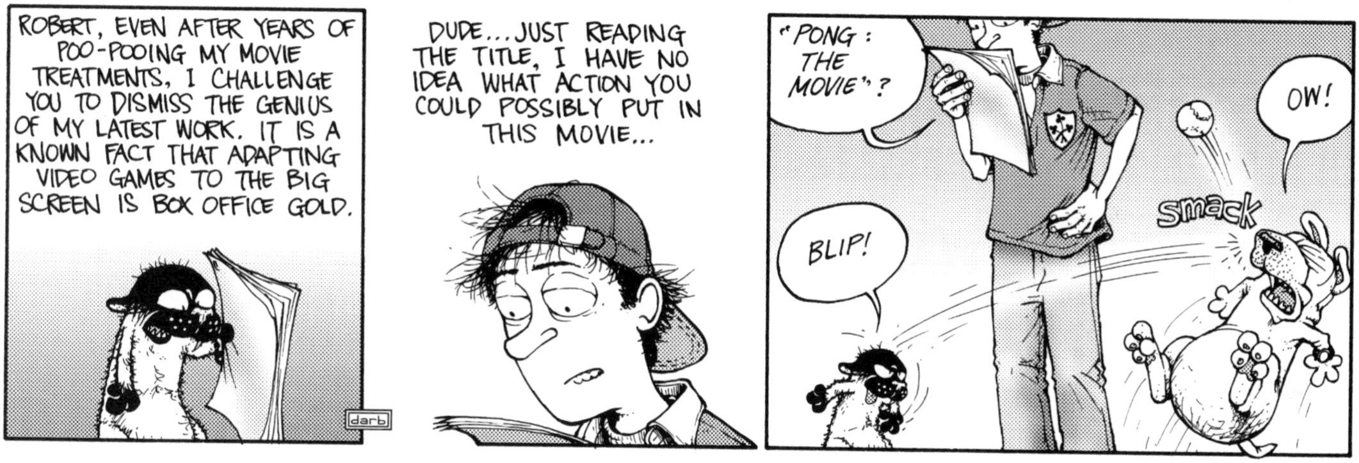
ROBERT, EVEN AFTER YEARS OF POO-POOING MY MOVIE TREATMENTS, I CHALLENGE YOU TO DISMISS THE GENIUS OF MY LATEST WORK. IT IS A KNOWN FACT THAT ADAPTING VIDEO GAMES TO THE BIG SCREEN IS BOX OFFICE GOLD.
darb
DUDE... JUST READING THE TITLE, I HAVE NO IDEA WHAT ACTION YOU COULD POSSIBLY PUT IN THIS MOVIE...
"PONG: THE MOVIE"?
BLIP!
SMACK
OW!

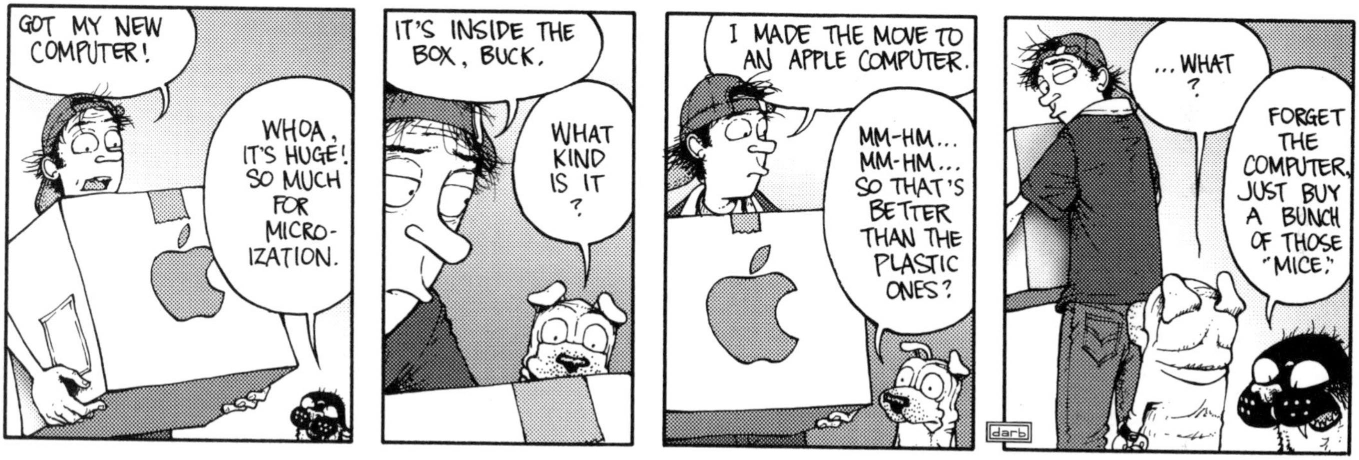
GOT MY NEW COMPUTER!
WHOA, IT'S HUGE! SO MUCH FOR MICRO-IZATION.
IT'S INSIDE THE BOX, BUCK.
WHAT KIND IS IT?
I MADE THE MOVE TO AN APPLE COMPUTER.
MM-HM... MM-HM... SO THAT'S BETTER THAN THE PLASTIC ONES?
darb
...WHAT?
FORGET THE COMPUTER. JUST BUY A BUNCH OF THOSE "MICE."

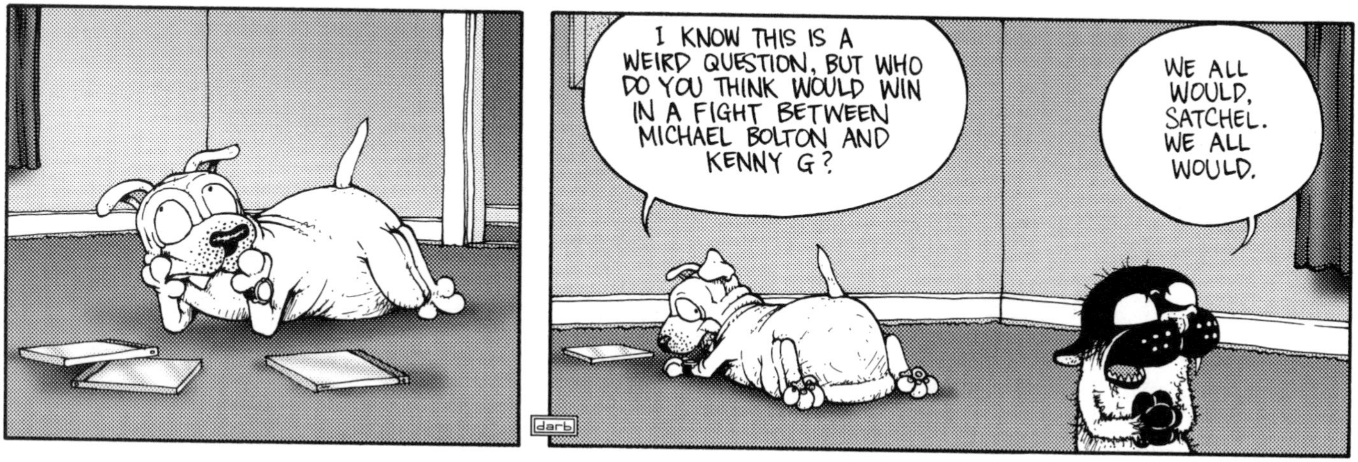
darb
I KNOW THIS IS A WEIRD QUESTION, BUT WHO DO YOU THINK WOULD WIN IN A FIGHT BETWEEN MICHAEL BOLTON AND KENNY G?
WE ALL WOULD, SATCHEL. WE ALL WOULD.

Today...
on a very
special
Get Fuzzy

darb
I LOVE YOU, SATCHEL.
OOP! HA HA!
HA HA HA! AHHHHH....
HEY, WHERE'S MY WATCH?
Kick Me!

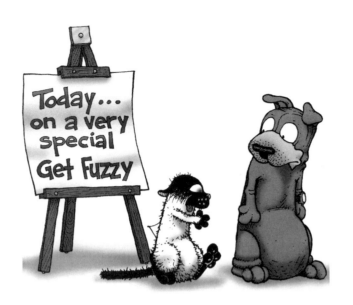

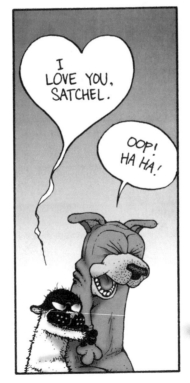

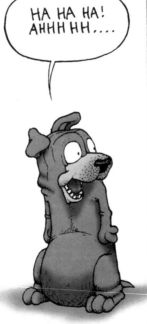

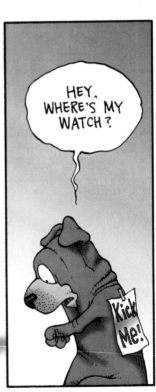

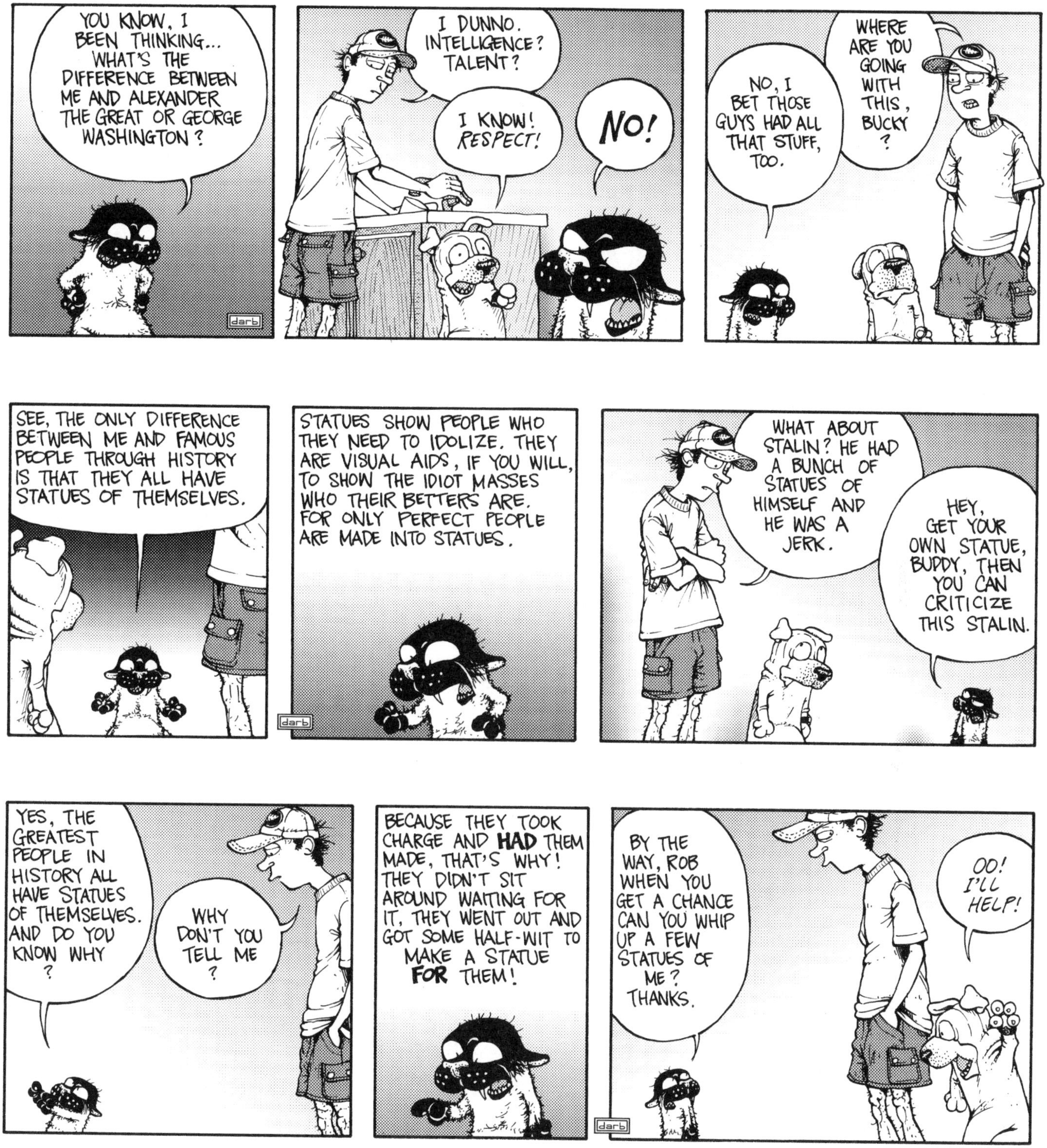
YOU KNOW, I BEEN THINKING... WHAT'S THE DIFFERENCE BETWEEN ME AND ALEXANDER THE GREAT OR GEORGE WASHINGTON?
I DUNNO. INTELLIGENCE? TALENT?
I KNOW! RESPECT!
NO!
WHERE ARE YOU GOING WITH THIS, BUCKY?
NO, I BET THOSE GUYS HAD ALL THAT STUFF, TOO.
SEE, THE ONLY DIFFERENCE BETWEEN ME AND FAMOUS PEOPLE THROUGH HISTORY IS THAT THEY ALL HAVE STATUES OF THEMSELVES.
STATUES SHOW PEOPLE WHO THEY NEED TO IDOLIZE. THEY ARE VISUAL AIDS, IF YOU WILL, TO SHOW THE IDIOT MASSES WHO THEIR BETTERS ARE. FOR ONLY PERFECT PEOPLE ARE MADE INTO STATUES.
WHAT ABOUT STALIN? HE HAD A BUNCH OF STATUES OF HIMSELF AND HE WAS A JERK.
HEY, GET YOUR OWN STATUE, BUDDY, THEN YOU CAN CRITICIZE THIS STALIN.
YES, THE GREATEST PEOPLE IN HISTORY ALL HAVE STATUES OF THEMSELVES. AND DO YOU KNOW WHY?
WHY DON'T YOU TELL ME?
BECAUSE THEY TOOK CHARGE AND HAD THEM MADE, THAT'S WHY! THEY DIDN'T SIT AROUND WAITING FOR IT, THEY WENT OUT AND GOT SOME HALF-WIT TO MAKE A STATUE FOR THEM!
BY THE WAY, ROB WHEN YOU GET A CHANCE CAN YOU WHIP UP A FEW STATUES OF ME? THANKS.
OO! I'LL HELP!
darb

REMEMBER HOW I SAID THAT THERE ARE STATUES OF ALL GREAT LEADERS? WELL, I GIVE YOU THE STATUE FOR THE MASSES: *BEHOLD!* THE BUCKY KATT ACTION FIGURE!

darb

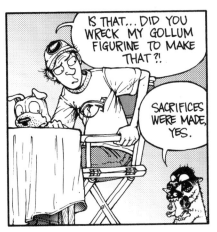

IS THAT... DID YOU WRECK MY GOLLUM FIGURINE TO MAKE THAT?!

SACRIFICES WERE MADE, YES.

BUCKY! I ORDERED THIS THING DIRECT FROM NEW ZEALAND! DO YOU KNOW HOW MUCH IT WAS WORTH?!

LEMME TELL YA SOMETHING... IT'S WORTH MORE NOW.

YOU TURNED MY BLUE SNAGGLETOOTH STAR WARS FIGURE INTO A BUCKY KATT ACTION FIGURE?

I CONVERTED ALL YOUR ACTION FIGURES INTO BUCKY KATTS.

ALL OF...? IS THAT FIGURE STICKING OUT OF THAT BOX MY LEGOLAS GREENLEAF STATUE?

YEAH, IT'S *WARRIOR BUCKY* NOW.

DUDE!!! THIS WAS A SPECIAL EDITION WETA WORKSHOP PIECE OF ART! THEY ONLY MADE A FEW HUNDRED OF THESE!

SEE? NOW HE'S TOTALLY UNIQUE.

darb

YOU EVEN MADE A BUCKY KATT ACTION FIGURE OUT OF MY HAN SOLO IN HOTH GEAR FIGURE?

THAT'S CORRECT.

STAR WARS & L.O.T.R FIGURE

DUDE... THAT ONE WAS STILL IN ITS ORIGINAL PACKAGING...

YEAH, YEAH, I GOT IT OUT. NO CHARGE.

darb

LEAVE ME...

ARE YOU CRYING, ROB?

STAR WARS L.O.T.R FIGURES

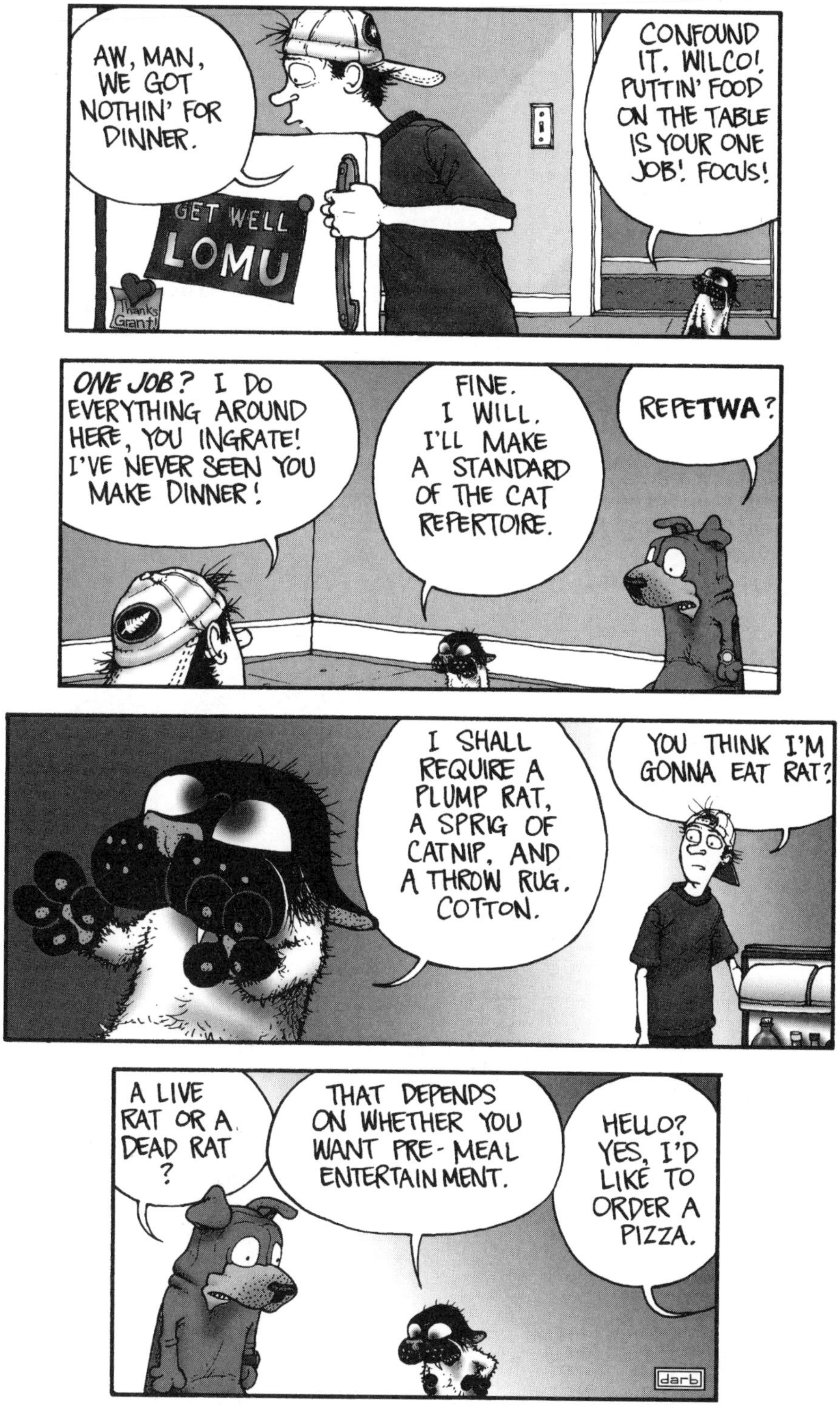
AW, MAN, WE GOT NOTHIN' FOR DINNER.
GET WELL LOMU
Thanks Grant!
CONFOUND IT, WILCO! PUTTIN' FOOD ON THE TABLE IS YOUR ONE JOB! FOCUS!
ONE JOB? I DO EVERYTHING AROUND HERE, YOU INGRATE! I'VE NEVER SEEN YOU MAKE DINNER!
FINE. I WILL. I'LL MAKE A STANDARD OF THE CAT REPERTOIRE.
REPETWA?
I SHALL REQUIRE A PLUMP RAT, A SPRIG OF CATNIP, AND A THROW RUG. COTTON.
YOU THINK I'M GONNA EAT RAT?
A LIVE RAT OR A DEAD RAT?
THAT DEPENDS ON WHETHER YOU WANT PRE-MEAL ENTERTAINMENT.
HELLO? YES, I'D LIKE TO ORDER A PIZZA.
darb

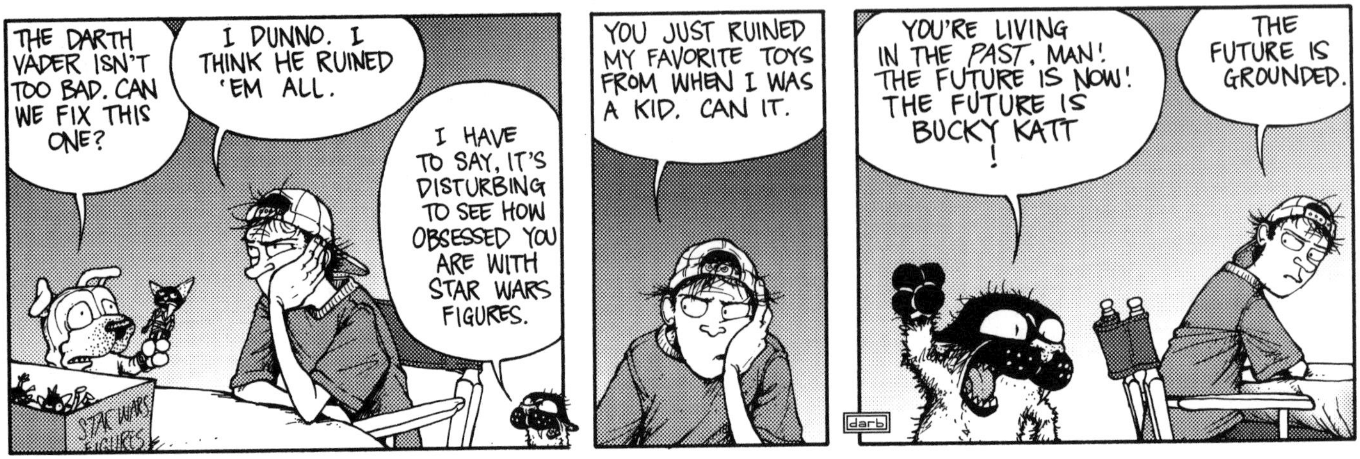
THE DARTH VADER ISN'T TOO BAD. CAN WE FIX THIS ONE?
I DUNNO. I THINK HE RUINED 'EM ALL.
I HAVE TO SAY, IT'S DISTURBING TO SEE HOW OBSESSED YOU ARE WITH STAR WARS FIGURES.
STAR WARS FIGURES
YOU JUST RUINED MY FAVORITE TOYS FROM WHEN I WAS A KID. CAN IT.
YOU'RE LIVING IN THE PAST, MAN! THE FUTURE IS NOW! THE FUTURE IS BUCKY KATT!
THE FUTURE IS GROUNDED.
darb

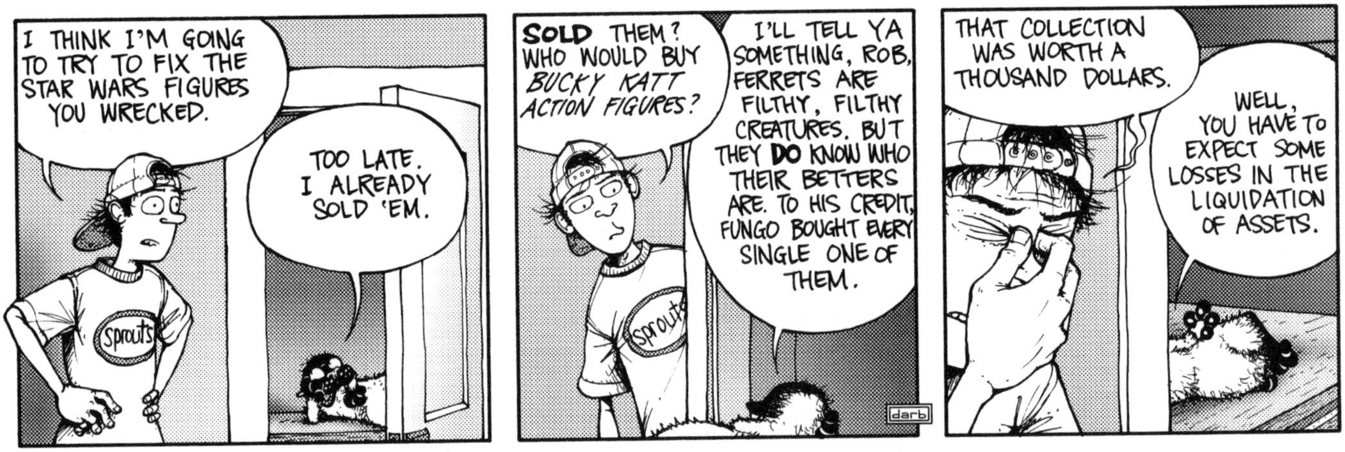
I THINK I'M GOING TO TRY TO FIX THE STAR WARS FIGURES YOU WRECKED.
TOO LATE. I ALREADY SOLD 'EM.
sprouts
SOLD THEM? WHO WOULD BUY BUCKY KATT ACTION FIGURES?
I'LL TELL YA SOMETHING, ROB, FERRETS ARE FILTHY, FILTHY CREATURES. BUT THEY DO KNOW WHO THEIR BETTERS ARE. TO HIS CREDIT, FUNGO BOUGHT EVERY SINGLE ONE OF THEM.
THAT COLLECTION WAS WORTH A THOUSAND DOLLARS.
WELL, YOU HAVE TO EXPECT SOME LOSSES IN THE LIQUIDATION OF ASSETS.
darb

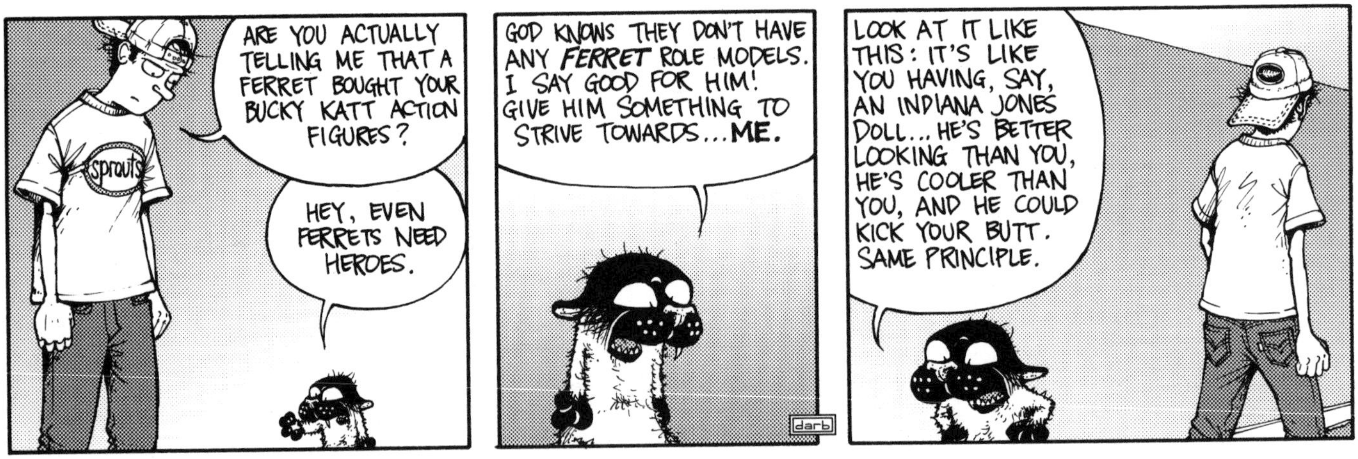
ARE YOU ACTUALLY TELLING ME THAT A FERRET BOUGHT YOUR BUCKY KATT ACTION FIGURES?
HEY, EVEN FERRETS NEED HEROES.
sprouts
GOD KNOWS THEY DON'T HAVE ANY FERRET ROLE MODELS. I SAY GOOD FOR HIM! GIVE HIM SOMETHING TO STRIVE TOWARDS...ME.
LOOK AT IT LIKE THIS: IT'S LIKE YOU HAVING, SAY, AN INDIANA JONES DOLL... HE'S BETTER LOOKING THAN YOU, HE'S COOLER THAN YOU, AND HE COULD KICK YOUR BUTT. SAME PRINCIPLE.
darb

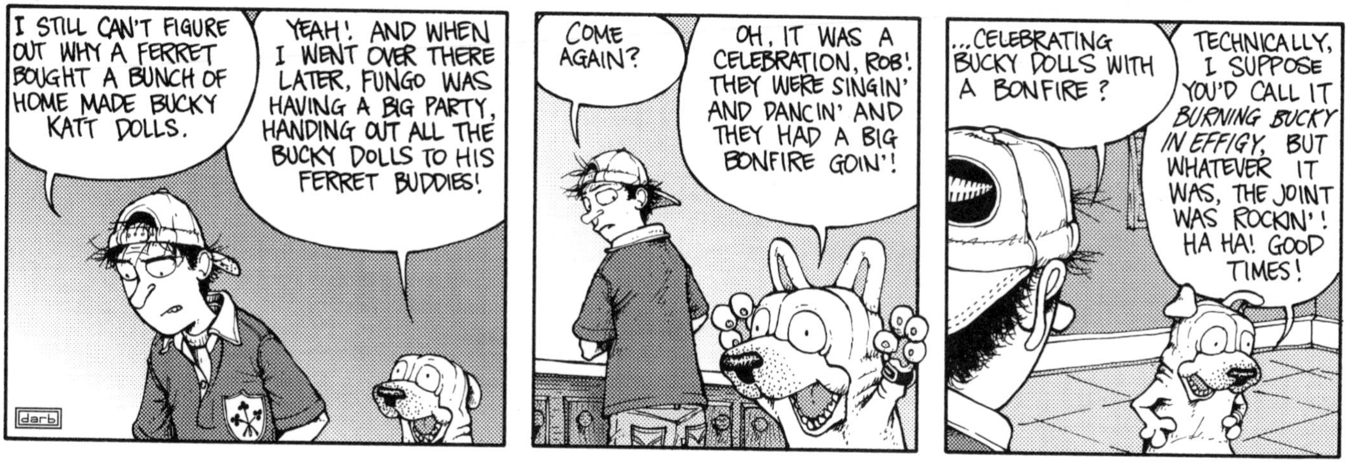
I STILL CAN'T FIGURE OUT WHY A FERRET BOUGHT A BUNCH OF HOME MADE BUCKY KATT DOLLS.
YEAH! AND WHEN I WENT OVER THERE LATER, FUNGO WAS HAVING A BIG PARTY, HANDING OUT ALL THE BUCKY DOLLS TO HIS FERRET BUDDIES!
COME AGAIN?
OH, IT WAS A CELEBRATION, ROB! THEY WERE SINGIN' AND DANCIN' AND THEY HAD A BIG BONFIRE GOIN'!
...CELEBRATING BUCKY DOLLS WITH A BONFIRE?
TECHNICALLY, I SUPPOSE YOU'D CALL IT *BURNING BUCKY IN EFFIGY*, BUT WHATEVER IT WAS, THE JOINT WAS ROCKIN'! HA HA! GOOD TIMES!
darb

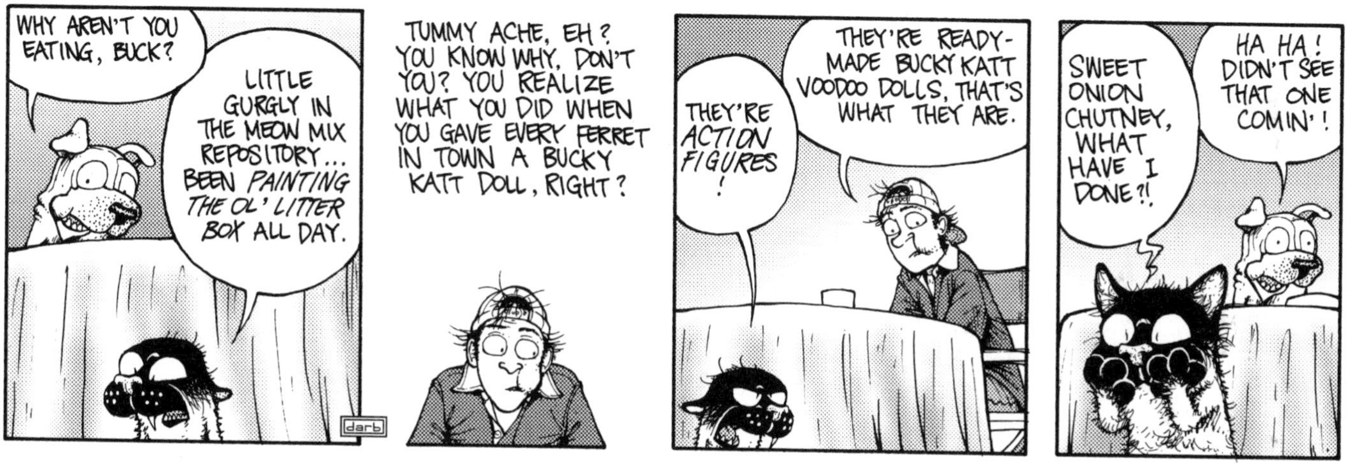
WHY AREN'T YOU EATING, BUCK?
LITTLE GURGLY IN THE MEOW MIX REPOSITORY... BEEN *PAINTING THE OL' LITTER BOX* ALL DAY.
darb
TUMMY ACHE, EH? YOU KNOW WHY, DON'T YOU? YOU REALIZE WHAT YOU DID WHEN YOU GAVE EVERY FERRET IN TOWN A BUCKY KATT DOLL, RIGHT?
THEY'RE *ACTION FIGURES*!
THEY'RE READY-MADE BUCKY KATT VOODOO DOLLS, THAT'S WHAT THEY ARE.
SWEET ONION CHUTNEY, WHAT HAVE I DONE?!
HA HA! DIDN'T SEE THAT ONE COMIN'!

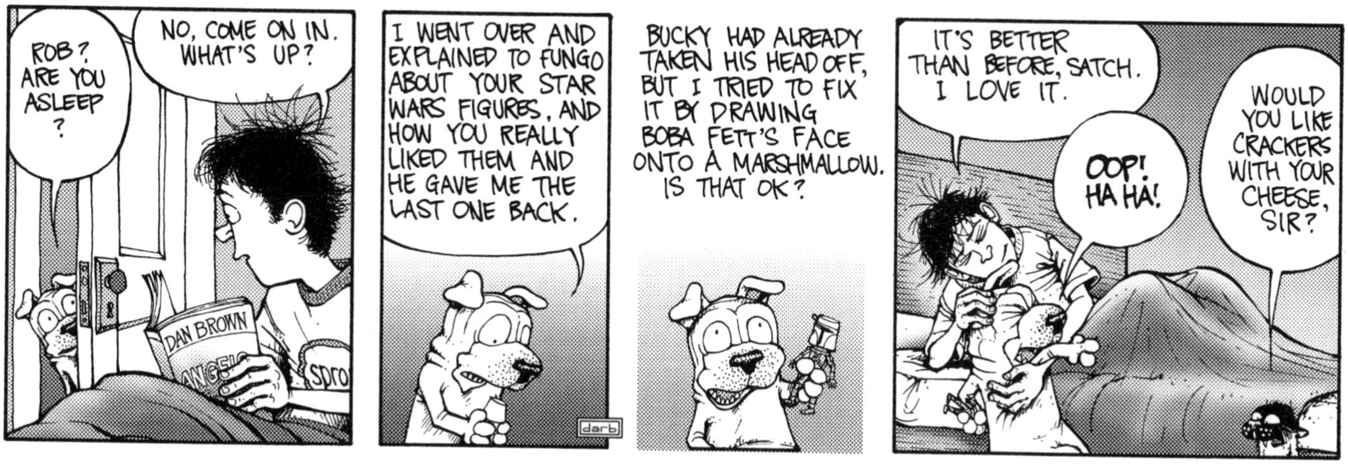
ROB? ARE YOU ASLEEP?
NO, COME ON IN. WHAT'S UP?
DAN BROWN
I WENT OVER AND EXPLAINED TO FUNGO ABOUT YOUR STAR WARS FIGURES, AND HOW YOU REALLY LIKED THEM AND HE GAVE ME THE LAST ONE BACK.
darb
BUCKY HAD ALREADY TAKEN HIS HEAD OFF, BUT I TRIED TO FIX IT BY DRAWING BOBA FETT'S FACE ONTO A MARSHMALLOW. IS THAT OK?
IT'S BETTER THAN BEFORE, SATCH. I LOVE IT.
OOP! HA HA!
WOULD YOU LIKE CRACKERS WITH YOUR CHEESE, SIR?

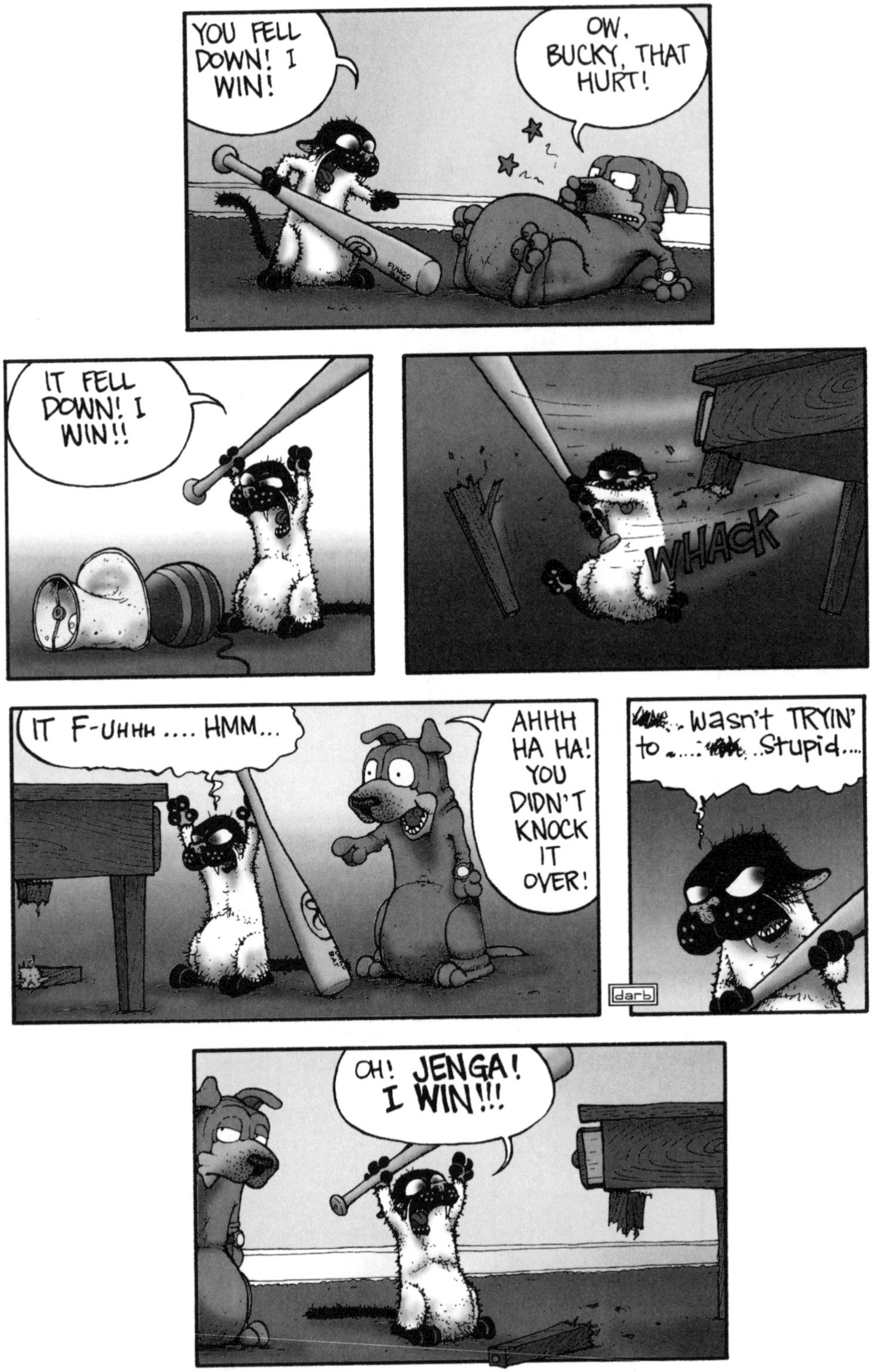
YOU FELL DOWN! I WIN!
OW, BUCKY, THAT HURT!
IT FELL DOWN! I WIN!!
WHACK
IT F-UHHH .... HMM...
AHHH HA HA! YOU DIDN'T KNOCK IT OVER!
wasn't TRYIN' to .... Stupid....
darb
OH! JENGA! I WIN!!!

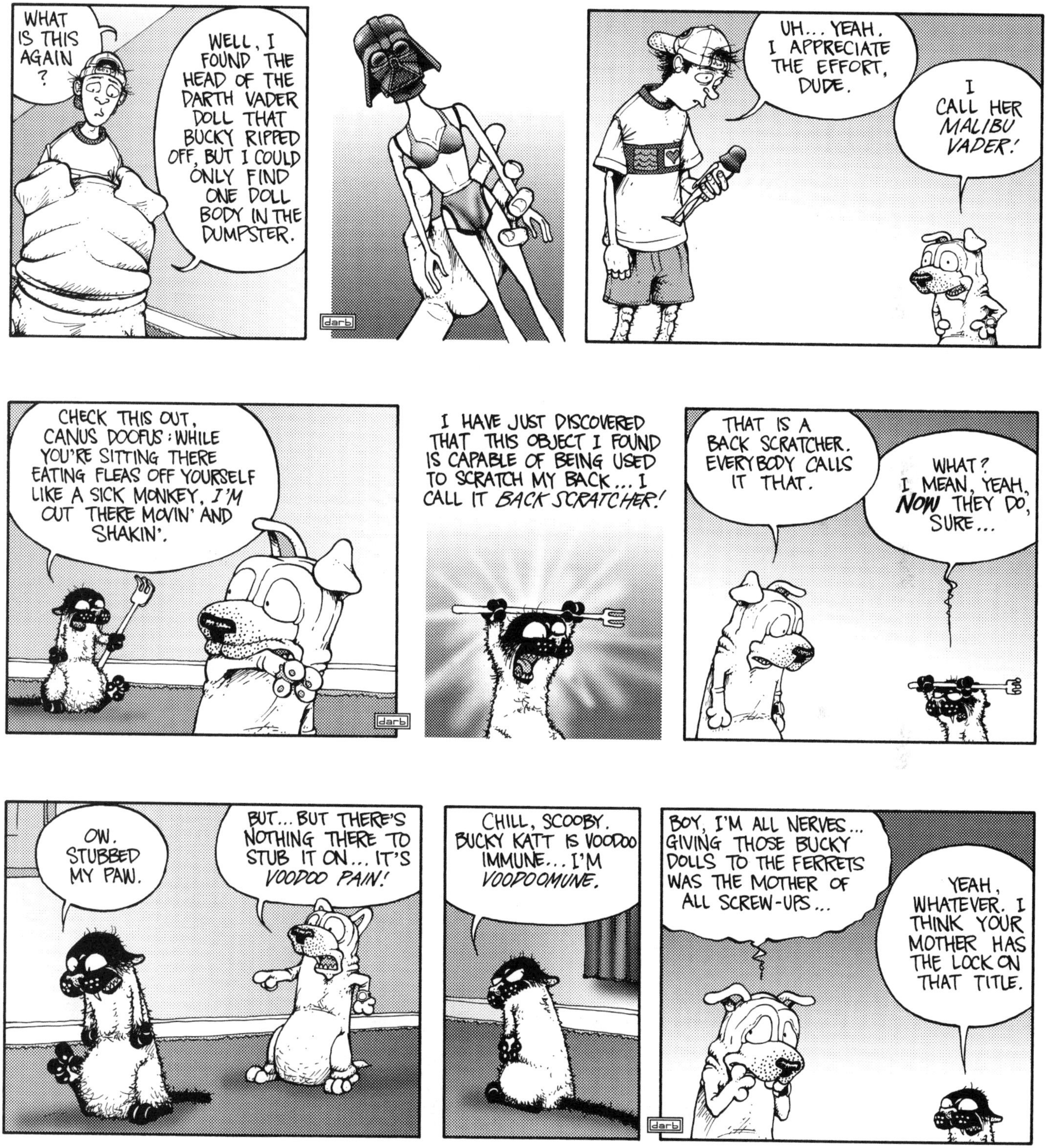
WHAT IS THIS AGAIN?
WELL, I FOUND THE HEAD OF THE DARTH VADER DOLL THAT BUCKY RIPPED OFF, BUT I COULD ONLY FIND ONE DOLL BODY IN THE DUMPSTER.
darb
UH... YEAH. I APPRECIATE THE EFFORT, DUDE.
I CALL HER *MALIBU VADER!*
CHECK THIS OUT, CANUS DOOFUS: WHILE YOU'RE SITTING THERE EATING FLEAS OFF YOURSELF LIKE A SICK MONKEY, *I'M* OUT THERE MOVIN' AND SHAKIN'.
darb
I HAVE JUST DISCOVERED THAT THIS OBJECT I FOUND IS CAPABLE OF BEING USED TO SCRATCH MY BACK... I CALL IT *BACK SCRATCHER!*
THAT IS A BACK SCRATCHER. EVERYBODY CALLS IT THAT.
WHAT? I MEAN, YEAH, ***NOW*** THEY DO, SURE...
OW. STUBBED MY PAW.
BUT... BUT THERE'S NOTHING THERE TO STUB IT ON... IT'S *VOODOO PAIN!*
CHILL, SCOOBY. BUCKY KATT IS VOODOO IMMUNE... I'M *VOODOOMUNE.*
darb
BOY, I'M ALL NERVES... GIVING THOSE BUCKY DOLLS TO THE FERRETS WAS THE MOTHER OF ALL SCREW-UPS...
YEAH, WHATEVER. I THINK YOUR MOTHER HAS THE LOCK ON THAT TITLE.

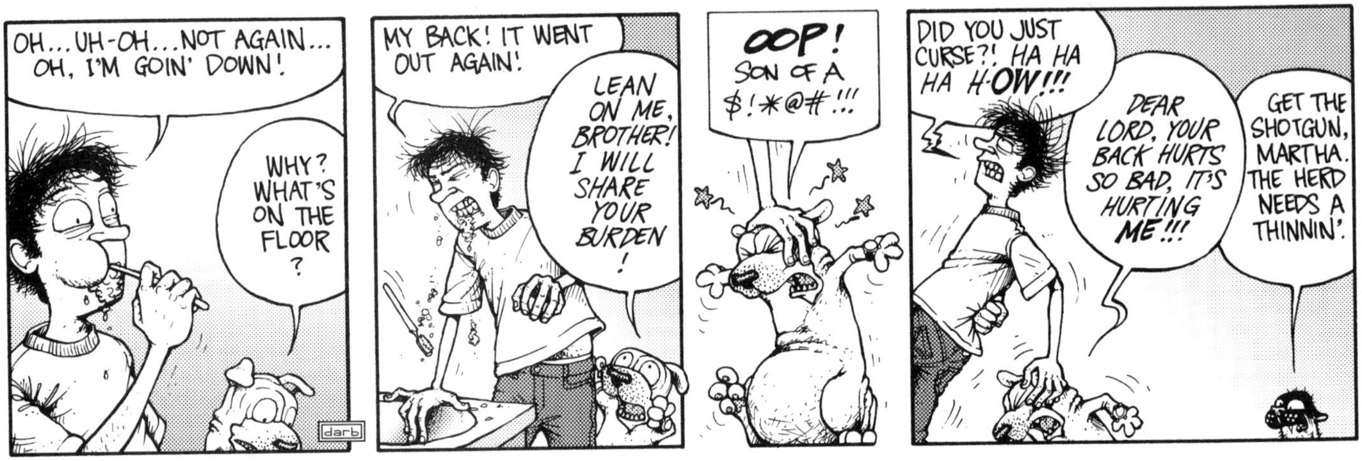
OH... UH-OH... NOT AGAIN... OH, I'M GOIN' DOWN!
WHY? WHAT'S ON THE FLOOR?
MY BACK! IT WENT OUT AGAIN!
LEAN ON ME, BROTHER! I WILL SHARE YOUR BURDEN!
OOP! SON OF A $!*@#!!!
DID YOU JUST CURSE?! HA HA HA H-OW!!!
DEAR LORD, YOUR BACK HURTS SO BAD, IT'S HURTING ME!!!
GET THE SHOTGUN, MARTHA. THE HERD NEEDS A THINNIN'.
darb

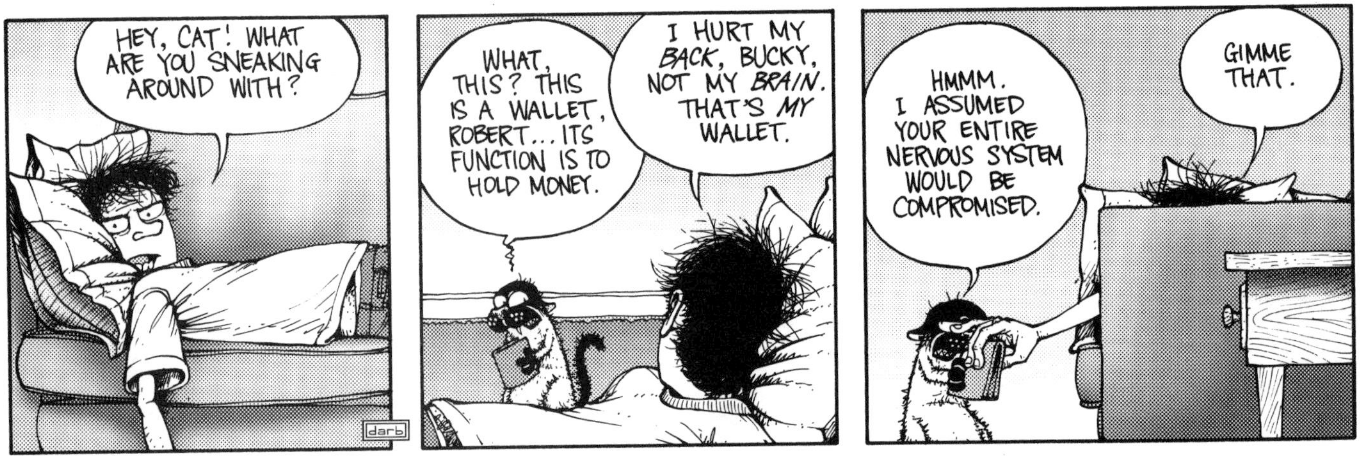
HEY, CAT! WHAT ARE YOU SNEAKING AROUND WITH?
WHAT, THIS? THIS IS A WALLET, ROBERT... ITS FUNCTION IS TO HOLD MONEY.
I HURT MY BACK, BUCKY, NOT MY BRAIN. THAT'S MY WALLET.
HMMM. I ASSUMED YOUR ENTIRE NERVOUS SYSTEM WOULD BE COMPROMISED.
GIMME THAT.
darb

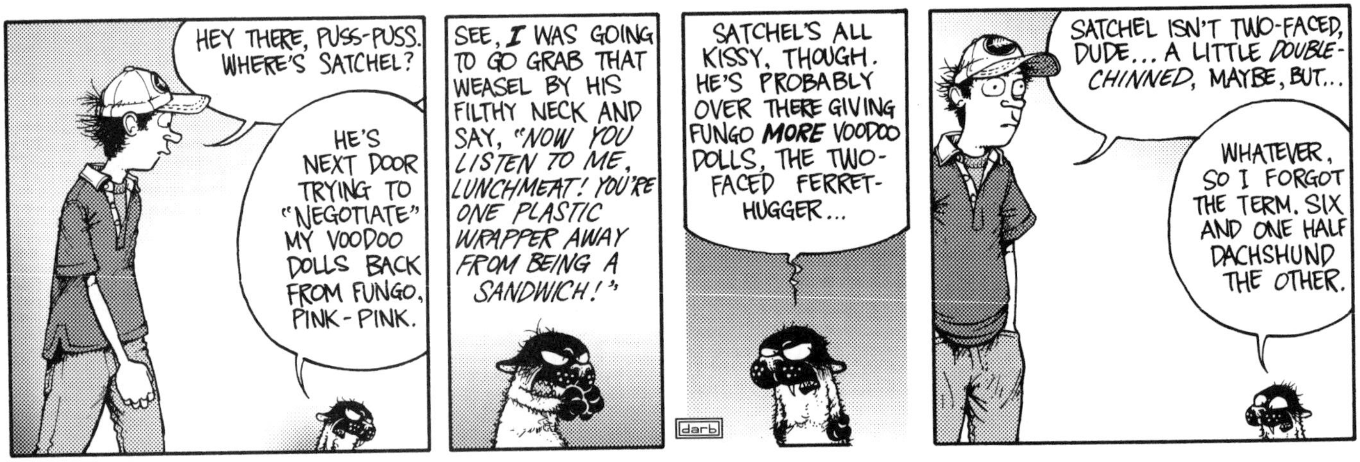
HEY THERE, PUSS-PUSS. WHERE'S SATCHEL?
HE'S NEXT DOOR TRYING TO "NEGOTIATE" MY VOODOO DOLLS BACK FROM FUNGO, PINK-PINK.
SEE, I WAS GOING TO GO GRAB THAT WEASEL BY HIS FILTHY NECK AND SAY, "NOW YOU LISTEN TO ME, LUNCHMEAT! YOU'RE ONE PLASTIC WRAPPER AWAY FROM BEING A SANDWICH!"
SATCHEL'S ALL KISSY, THOUGH. HE'S PROBABLY OVER THERE GIVING FUNGO MORE VOODOO DOLLS, THE TWO-FACED FERRET-HUGGER...
darb
SATCHEL ISN'T TWO-FACED, DUDE... A LITTLE DOUBLE-CHINNED, MAYBE, BUT...
WHATEVER, SO I FORGOT THE TERM. SIX AND ONE HALF DACHSHUND THE OTHER.

OH... IT'S YOU... WHAT ARE YOU DOING UP?
RUGBY CLUB ON T.V., BABY. GAMES FROM NEW ZEALAND START AT 3 A.M. yawn
darb
WELL, I DON'T KNOW IF I LIKE YOU BEING UP NOW... THIS IS BUCKY TIME.
TOO BAD YOU DON'T HAVE ANY SAY IN WHEN I'M UP, THEN, ISN'T IT?
...AND YET, I DO HAVE A SAY IN WHAT YOUR CARPET SMELLS LIKE...
BUCKY, I'M GONE, LIKE, TEN HOURS A DAY... HALF OF YOUR LIFE IS "BUCKY TIME," YOU... YOU, UH...
DUDE... WHAT IN THE WORLD ARE YOU DOING?
I WILL NOT STAND BY AND WATCH BUCKY TIME TREATED LIKE SOME FILTHY HAPPY HOUR!
HEY, YOU GUYS ARE UP, TOO? GUESS WHO MADE SMOOTHIES!

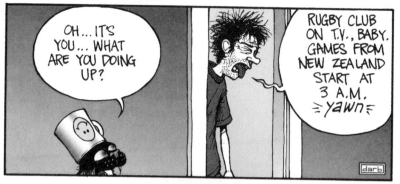

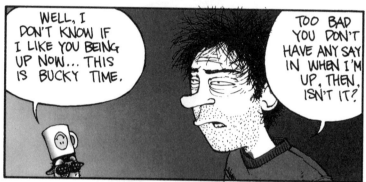

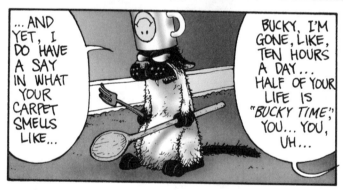

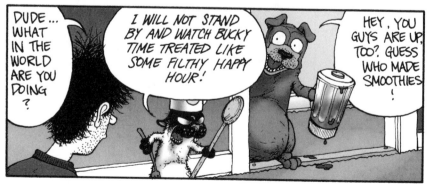

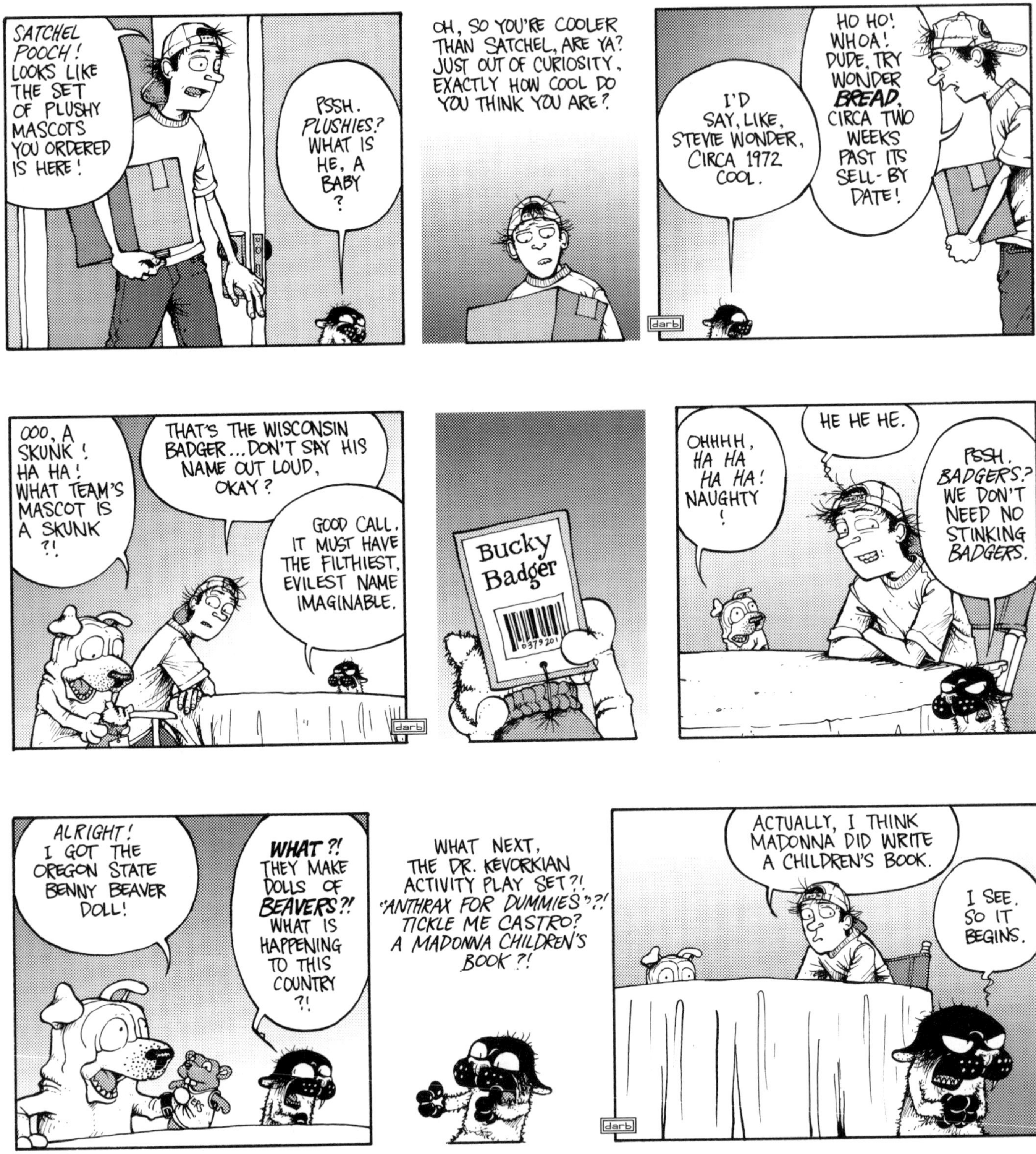
SATCHEL POOCH! LOOKS LIKE THE SET OF PLUSHY MASCOTS YOU ORDERED IS HERE!
PSSH. PLUSHIES? WHAT IS HE, A BABY?
OH, SO YOU'RE COOLER THAN SATCHEL, ARE YA? JUST OUT OF CURIOSITY, EXACTLY HOW COOL DO YOU THINK YOU ARE?
I'D SAY, LIKE, STEVIE WONDER, CIRCA 1972 COOL.
HO HO! WHOA! DUDE, TRY WONDER BREAD, CIRCA TWO WEEKS PAST ITS SELL-BY DATE!
darb
OOO, A SKUNK! HA HA! WHAT TEAM'S MASCOT IS A SKUNK?!
THAT'S THE WISCONSIN BADGER... DON'T SAY HIS NAME OUT LOUD, OKAY?
GOOD CALL. IT MUST HAVE THE FILTHIEST, EVILEST NAME IMAGINABLE.
darb
Bucky Badger
OHHHH, HA HA HA HA! NAUGHTY!
HE HE HE.
PSSH. BADGERS? WE DON'T NEED NO STINKING BADGERS.
ALRIGHT! I GOT THE OREGON STATE BENNY BEAVER DOLL!
WHAT?! THEY MAKE DOLLS OF BEAVERS?! WHAT IS HAPPENING TO THIS COUNTRY?!
WHAT NEXT, THE DR. KEVORKIAN ACTIVITY PLAY SET?! "ANTHRAX FOR DUMMIES"?! TICKLE ME CASTRO? A MADONNA CHILDREN'S BOOK?!
ACTUALLY, I THINK MADONNA DID WRITE A CHILDREN'S BOOK.
I SEE. SO IT BEGINS.
darb

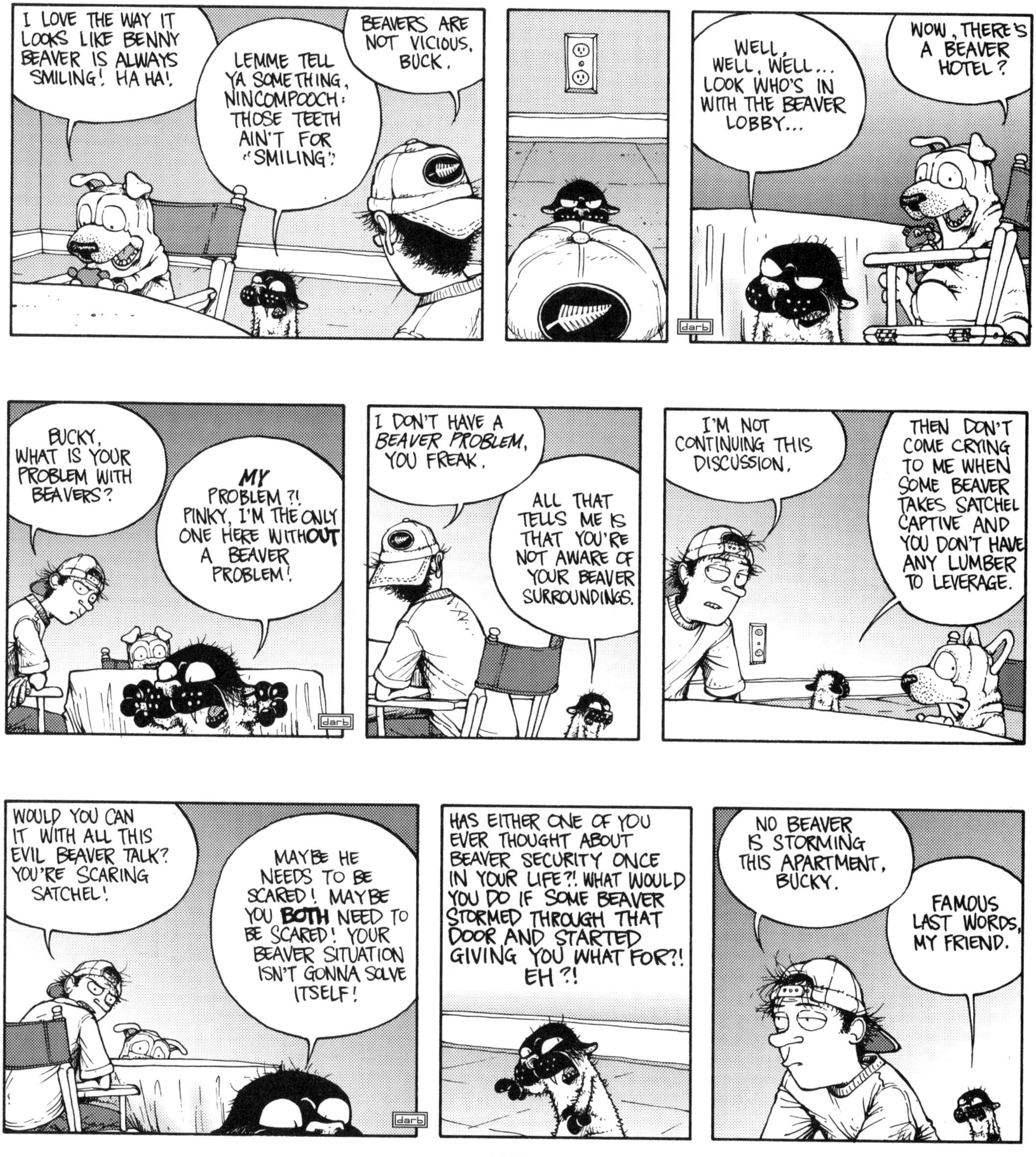
I LOVE THE WAY IT LOOKS LIKE BENNY BEAVER IS ALWAYS SMILING! HA HA!
LEMME TELL YA SOMETHING, NINCOMPOOCH: THOSE TEETH AIN'T FOR "SMILING."
BEAVERS ARE NOT VICIOUS, BUCK.
WELL, WELL, WELL... LOOK WHO'S IN WITH THE BEAVER LOBBY...
WOW, THERE'S A BEAVER HOTEL?
BUCKY, WHAT IS YOUR PROBLEM WITH BEAVERS?
MY PROBLEM?! PINKY, I'M THE ONLY ONE HERE WITHOUT A BEAVER PROBLEM!
I DON'T HAVE A BEAVER PROBLEM, YOU FREAK.
ALL THAT TELLS ME IS THAT YOU'RE NOT AWARE OF YOUR BEAVER SURROUNDINGS.
I'M NOT CONTINUING THIS DISCUSSION.
THEN DON'T COME CRYING TO ME WHEN SOME BEAVER TAKES SATCHEL CAPTIVE AND YOU DON'T HAVE ANY LUMBER TO LEVERAGE.
WOULD YOU CAN IT WITH ALL THIS EVIL BEAVER TALK? YOU'RE SCARING SATCHEL!
MAYBE HE NEEDS TO BE SCARED! MAYBE YOU BOTH NEED TO BE SCARED! YOUR BEAVER SITUATION ISN'T GONNA SOLVE ITSELF!
HAS EITHER ONE OF YOU EVER THOUGHT ABOUT BEAVER SECURITY ONCE IN YOUR LIFE?! WHAT WOULD YOU DO IF SOME BEAVER STORMED THROUGH THAT DOOR AND STARTED GIVING YOU WHAT FOR?! EH?!
NO BEAVER IS STORMING THIS APARTMENT, BUCKY.
FAMOUS LAST WORDS, MY FRIEND.

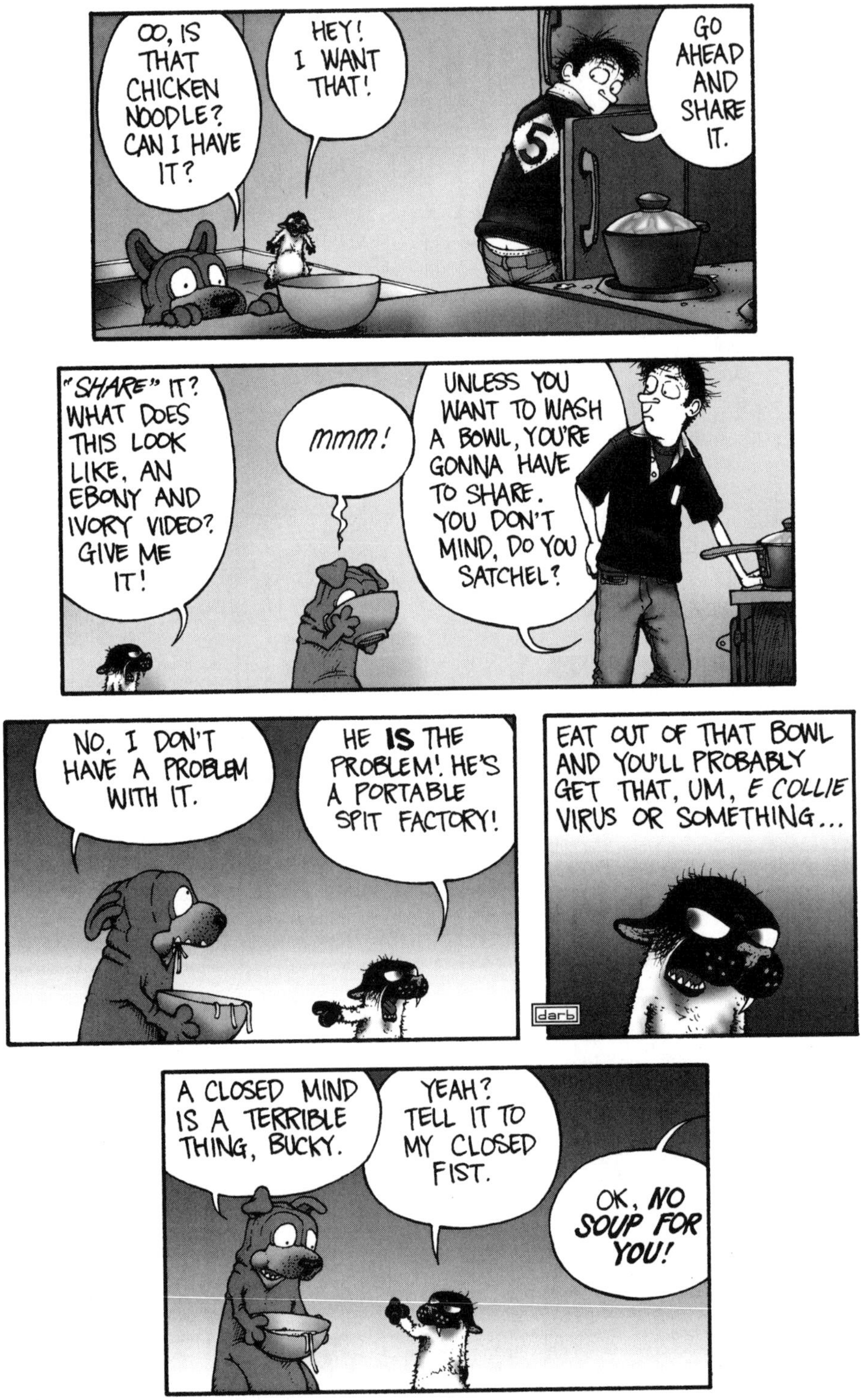
OO, IS THAT CHICKEN NOODLE? CAN I HAVE IT?
HEY! I WANT THAT!
GO AHEAD AND SHARE IT.
"SHARE" IT? WHAT DOES THIS LOOK LIKE, AN EBONY AND IVORY VIDEO? GIVE ME IT!
mmm!
UNLESS YOU WANT TO WASH A BOWL, YOU'RE GONNA HAVE TO SHARE. YOU DON'T MIND, DO YOU SATCHEL?
NO, I DON'T HAVE A PROBLEM WITH IT.
HE IS THE PROBLEM! HE'S A PORTABLE SPIT FACTORY!
EAT OUT OF THAT BOWL AND YOU'LL PROBABLY GET THAT, UM, E COLLIE VIRUS OR SOMETHING...
darb
A CLOSED MIND IS A TERRIBLE THING, BUCKY.
YEAH? TELL IT TO MY CLOSED FIST.
OK, NO SOUP FOR YOU!

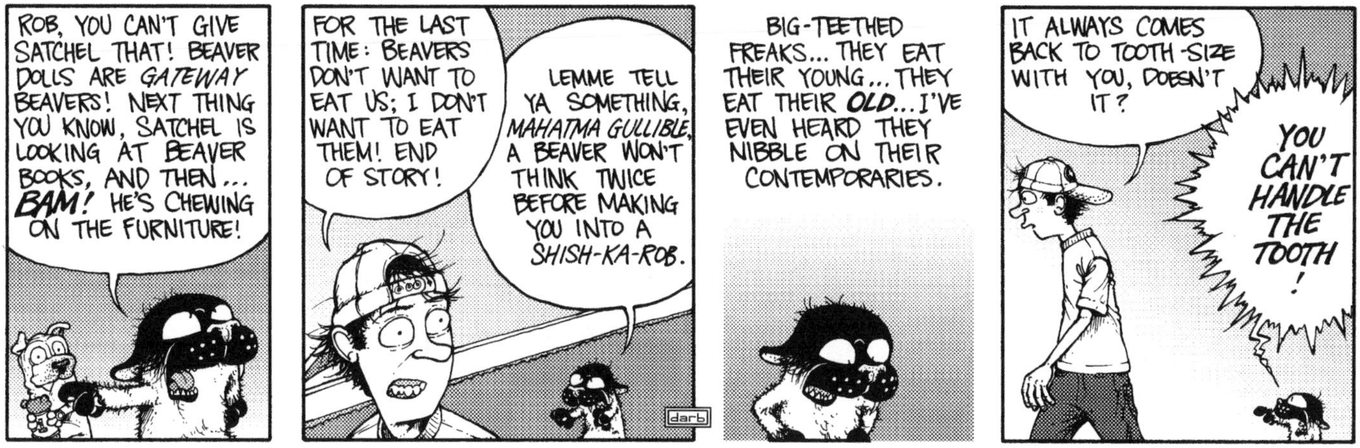
ROB, YOU CAN'T GIVE SATCHEL THAT! BEAVER DOLLS ARE *GATEWAY* BEAVERS! NEXT THING YOU KNOW, SATCHEL IS LOOKING AT BEAVER BOOKS, AND THEN... **BAM!** HE'S CHEWING ON THE FURNITURE!
FOR THE LAST TIME: BEAVERS DON'T WANT TO EAT US; I DON'T WANT TO EAT THEM! END OF STORY!
LEMME TELL YA SOMETHING, *MAHATMA GULLIBLE*, A BEAVER WON'T THINK TWICE BEFORE MAKING YOU INTO A *SHISH-KA-ROB*.
BIG-TEETHED FREAKS... THEY EAT THEIR YOUNG... THEY EAT THEIR **OLD**... I'VE EVEN HEARD THEY NIBBLE ON THEIR CONTEMPORARIES.
IT ALWAYS COMES BACK TO TOOTH-SIZE WITH YOU, DOESN'T IT?
YOU CAN'T HANDLE THE TOOTH!

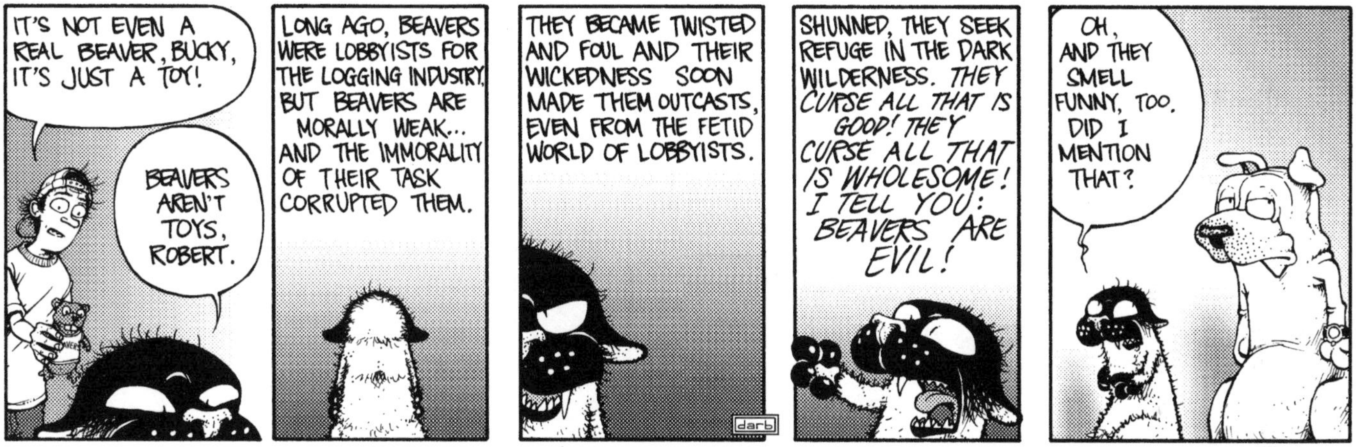
IT'S NOT EVEN A REAL BEAVER, BUCKY, IT'S JUST A TOY!
BEAVERS AREN'T TOYS, ROBERT.
LONG AGO, BEAVERS WERE LOBBYISTS FOR THE LOGGING INDUSTRY, BUT BEAVERS ARE MORALLY WEAK... AND THE IMMORALITY OF THEIR TASK CORRUPTED THEM.
THEY BECAME TWISTED AND FOUL AND THEIR WICKEDNESS SOON MADE THEM OUTCASTS, EVEN FROM THE FETID WORLD OF LOBBYISTS.
SHUNNED, THEY SEEK REFUGE IN THE DARK WILDERNESS. *THEY CURSE ALL THAT IS GOOD! THEY CURSE ALL THAT IS WHOLESOME! I TELL YOU: BEAVERS ARE EVIL!*
OH, AND THEY SMELL FUNNY, TOO. DID I MENTION THAT?

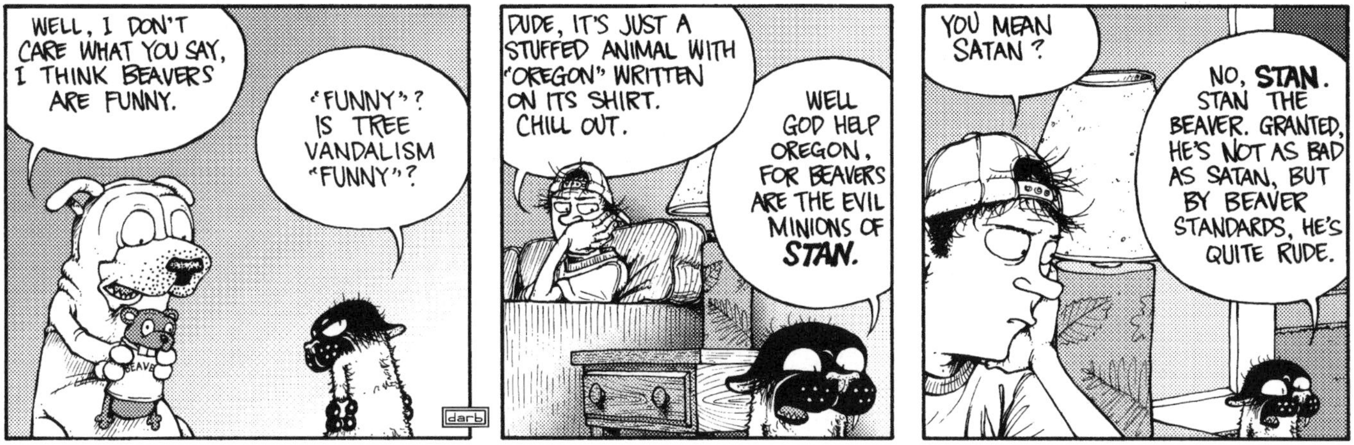
WELL, I DON'T CARE WHAT YOU SAY, I THINK BEAVERS ARE FUNNY.
"FUNNY"? IS TREE VANDALISM "FUNNY"?
DUDE, IT'S JUST A STUFFED ANIMAL WITH "OREGON" WRITTEN ON ITS SHIRT. CHILL OUT.
WELL GOD HELP OREGON, FOR BEAVERS ARE THE EVIL MINIONS OF **STAN.**
YOU MEAN SATAN?
NO, **STAN**. STAN THE BEAVER. GRANTED, HE'S NOT AS BAD AS SATAN, BUT BY BEAVER STANDARDS, HE'S QUITE RUDE.

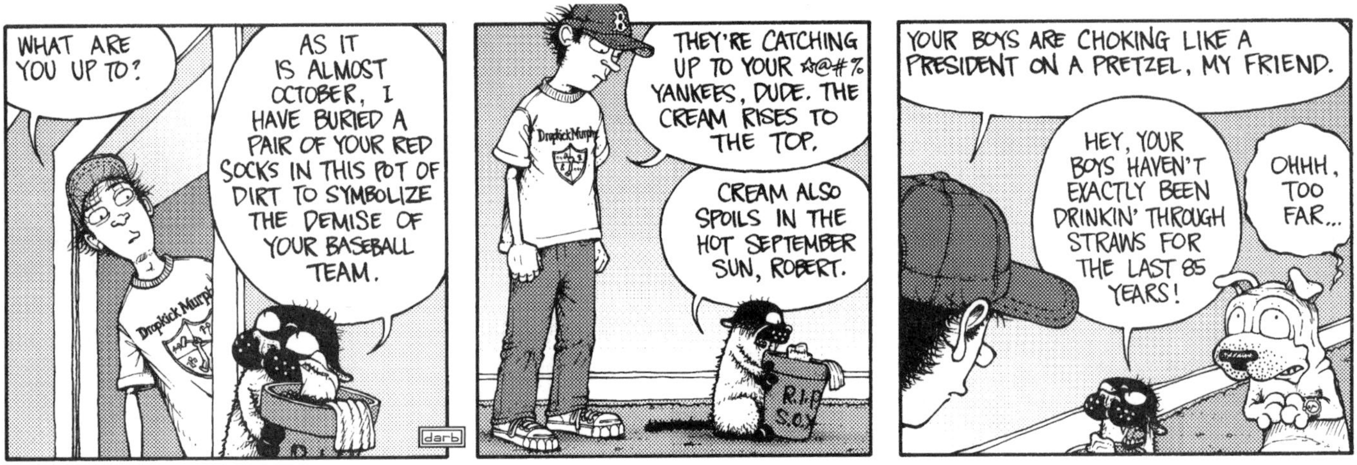
WHAT ARE YOU UP TO?
AS IT IS ALMOST OCTOBER, I HAVE BURIED A PAIR OF YOUR RED SOCKS IN THIS POT OF DIRT TO SYMBOLIZE THE DEMISE OF YOUR BASEBALL TEAM.
darb
THEY'RE CATCHING UP TO YOUR ☆@#% YANKEES, DUDE. THE CREAM RISES TO THE TOP.
CREAM ALSO SPOILS IN THE HOT SEPTEMBER SUN, ROBERT.
R.I.P. S.O.X.
YOUR BOYS ARE CHOKING LIKE A PRESIDENT ON A PRETZEL, MY FRIEND.
HEY, YOUR BOYS HAVEN'T EXACTLY BEEN DRINKIN' THROUGH STRAWS FOR THE LAST 85 YEARS!
OHHH, TOO FAR...

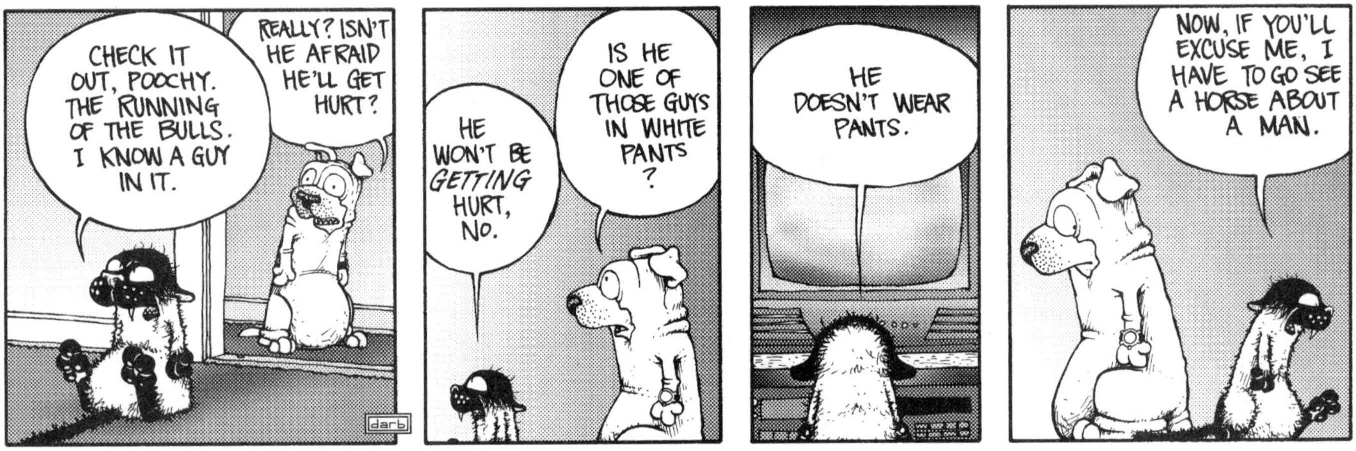
CHECK IT OUT, POOCHY. THE RUNNING OF THE BULLS. I KNOW A GUY IN IT.
REALLY? ISN'T HE AFRAID HE'LL GET HURT?
darb
HE WON'T BE *GETTING* HURT, NO.
IS HE ONE OF THOSE GUYS IN WHITE PANTS?
HE DOESN'T WEAR PANTS.
NOW, IF YOU'LL EXCUSE ME, I HAVE TO GO SEE A HORSE ABOUT A MAN.

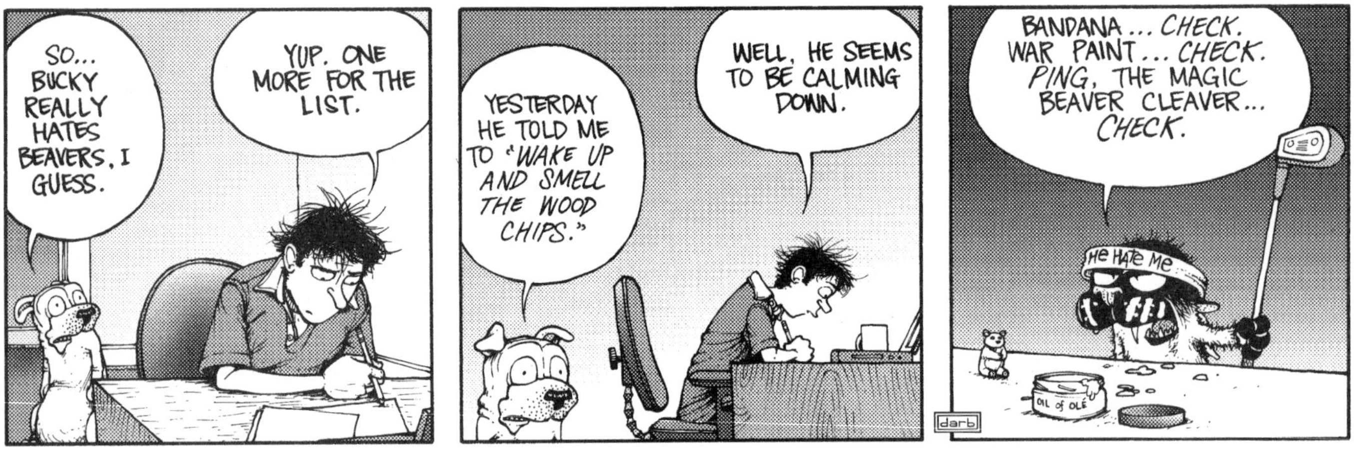
SO... BUCKY REALLY HATES BEAVERS, I GUESS.
YUP. ONE MORE FOR THE LIST.
WELL, HE SEEMS TO BE CALMING DOWN.
YESTERDAY HE TOLD ME TO "*WAKE UP AND SMELL THE WOOD CHIPS.*"
BANDANA... *CHECK*. WAR PAINT... *CHECK*. *PING*, THE MAGIC BEAVER CLEAVER... *CHECK*.
HE HATE ME
OIL of OLÉ
darb

15 MINUTES? GREAT, THANKS.

YOU ORDERED A PIZZA? DID YOU GET MONKEY ON IT?

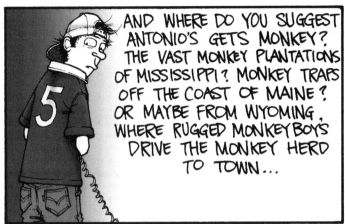

AND WHERE DO YOU SUGGEST ANTONIO'S GETS MONKEY? THE VAST MONKEY PLANTATIONS OF MISSISSIPPI? MONKEY TRAPS OFF THE COAST OF MAINE? OR MAYBE FROM WYOMING, WHERE RUGGED MONKEY BOYS DRIVE THE MONKEY HERD TO TOWN...

ROBERT, THIS COUNTRY IS INFESTED WITH MONKEYS! WILD MONKEYS, STRAY MONKEYS, FERAL MONKEYS EMERGING NIGHTLY FROM SEWERS AND TERRORIZING THE CHILDREN...

darb

THERE ARE NO "SEWER MONKEYS," BUCKY.

I HATE TO BURST THE BUBBLE OF YOUR MONKEY-FREE UTOPIA, ROB, BUT IT'S A KNOWN FACT THAT WHEN PET MONKEYS GET TOO VIOLENT, PEOPLE FLUSH 'EM.

DUDE, YOU CAN'T EAT MONKEYS. YOU CAN'T FLUSH MONKEYS.

WHAT ARE YOU, THE S.P.C. MONKEY ALL OF A SUDDEN?

NO, I'M S-A-N-E.

WHAT, STUPID AND AGAINST NORMAL EATING?

COULD WE GET HALF ONION, HALF MONKEY?

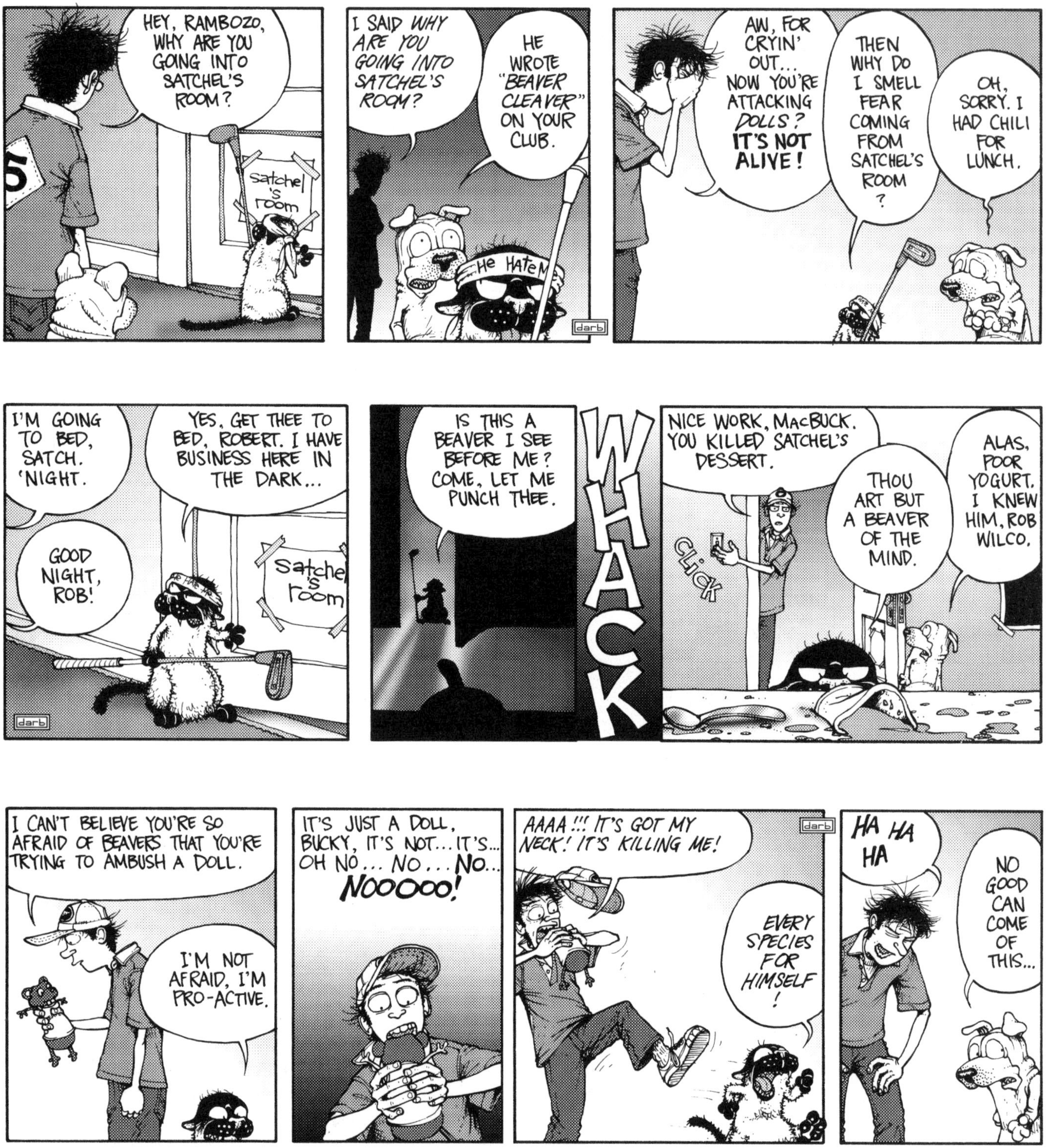
HEY, RAMBOZO, WHY ARE YOU GOING INTO SATCHEL'S ROOM?
Satchel 's room
I SAID *WHY ARE YOU GOING INTO SATCHEL'S ROOM?*
HE WROTE "*BEAVER CLEAVER*" ON YOUR CLUB.
He HateM
darb
AW, FOR CRYIN' OUT... NOW YOU'RE ATTACKING *DOLLS?* **IT'S NOT ALIVE!**
THEN WHY DO I SMELL FEAR COMING FROM SATCHEL'S ROOM?
OH, SORRY. I HAD CHILI FOR LUNCH.
I'M GOING TO BED, SATCH. 'NIGHT.
YES, GET THEE TO BED, ROBERT. I HAVE BUSINESS HERE IN THE DARK...
GOOD NIGHT, ROB!
Satchel 's room
darb
IS THIS A BEAVER I SEE BEFORE ME? COME, LET ME PUNCH THEE.
WHACK
NICE WORK, MACBUCK. YOU KILLED SATCHEL'S DESSERT.
CLICK
THOU ART BUT A BEAVER OF THE MIND.
ALAS, POOR YOGURT. I KNEW HIM, ROB WILCO.
I CAN'T BELIEVE YOU'RE SO AFRAID OF BEAVERS THAT YOU'RE TRYING TO AMBUSH A DOLL.
I'M NOT AFRAID, I'M PRO-ACTIVE.
IT'S JUST A DOLL, BUCKY, IT'S NOT... IT'S... OH NO... NO... **NO...**
NOOOOO!
darb
AAAA!!! IT'S GOT MY NECK! IT'S KILLING ME!
EVERY SPECIES FOR HIMSELF!
HA HA HA
NO GOOD CAN COME OF THIS...

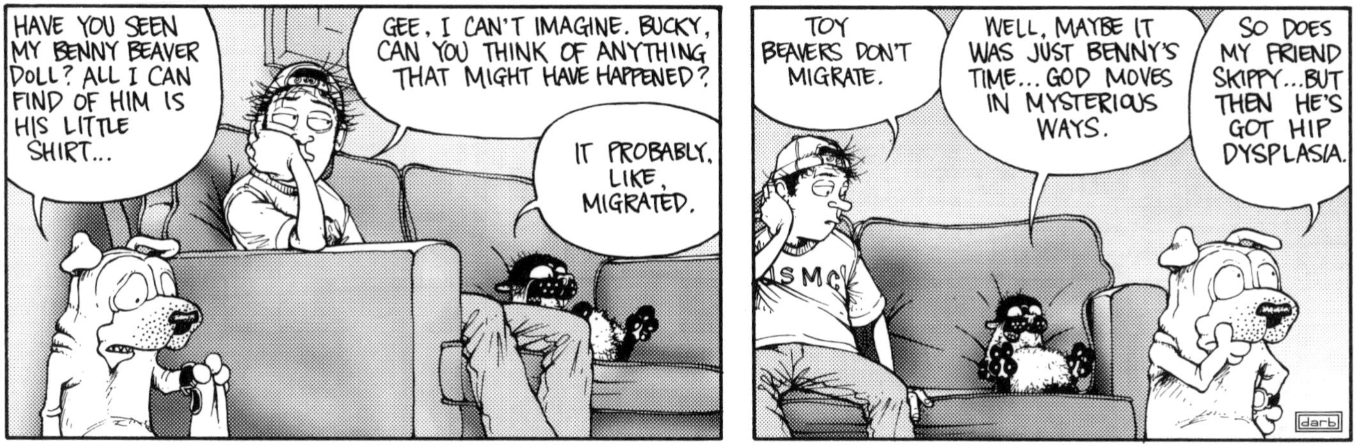
HAVE YOU SEEN MY BENNY BEAVER DOLL? ALL I CAN FIND OF HIM IS HIS LITTLE SHIRT...
GEE, I CAN'T IMAGINE. BUCKY, CAN YOU THINK OF ANYTHING THAT MIGHT HAVE HAPPENED?
IT PROBABLY, LIKE, MIGRATED.
TOY BEAVERS DON'T MIGRATE.
WELL, MAYBE IT WAS JUST BENNY'S TIME... GOD MOVES IN MYSTERIOUS WAYS.
SO DOES MY FRIEND SKIPPY...BUT THEN HE'S GOT HIP DYSPLASIA.
USMC
darb

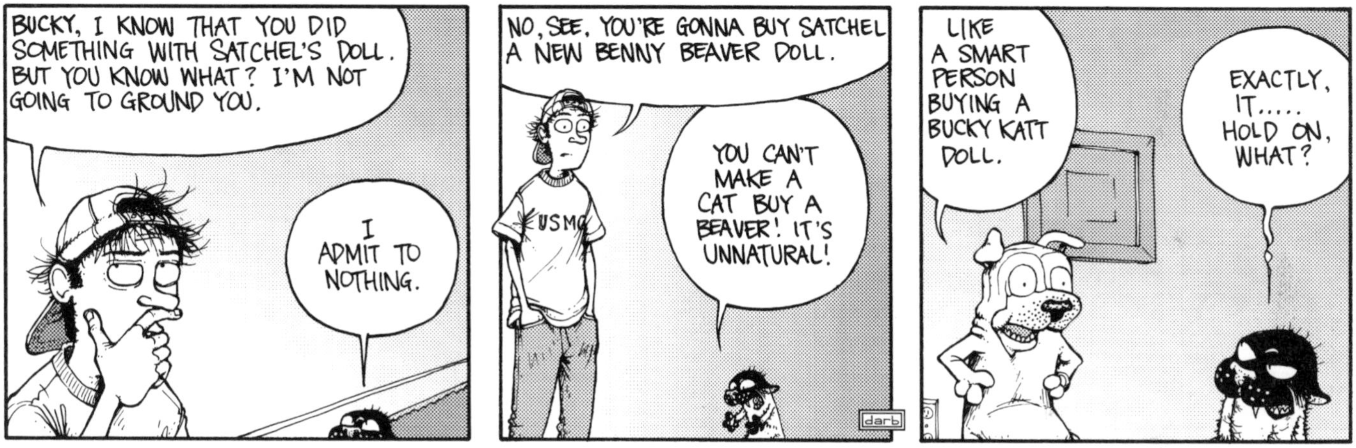
BUCKY, I KNOW THAT YOU DID SOMETHING WITH SATCHEL'S DOLL. BUT YOU KNOW WHAT? I'M NOT GOING TO GROUND YOU.
I ADMIT TO NOTHING.
NO, SEE, YOU'RE GONNA BUY SATCHEL A NEW BENNY BEAVER DOLL.
YOU CAN'T MAKE A CAT BUY A BEAVER! IT'S UNNATURAL!
USMC
darb
LIKE A SMART PERSON BUYING A BUCKY KATT DOLL.
EXACTLY, IT..... HOLD ON, WHAT?

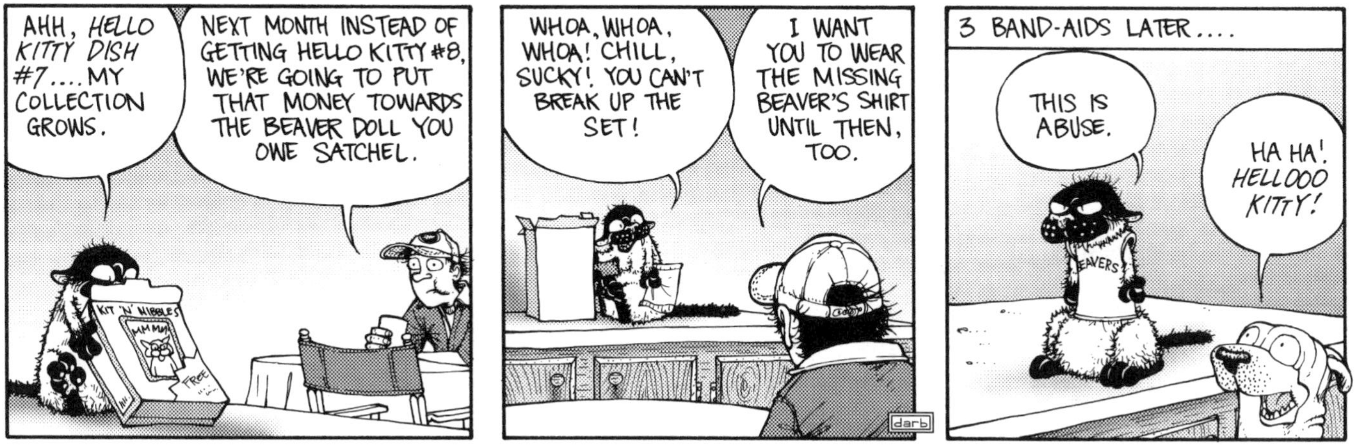
AHH, *HELLO KITTY DISH* #7.... MY COLLECTION GROWS.
NEXT MONTH INSTEAD OF GETTING HELLO KITTY #8, WE'RE GOING TO PUT THAT MONEY TOWARDS THE BEAVER DOLL YOU OWE SATCHEL.
KIT 'N' NIBBLES
MMMM
FREE
WHOA, WHOA, WHOA! CHILL, SUCKY! YOU CAN'T BREAK UP THE SET!
I WANT YOU TO WEAR THE MISSING BEAVER'S SHIRT UNTIL THEN, TOO.
darb
3 BAND-AIDS LATER....
THIS IS ABUSE.
HA HA! *HELLOOO KITTY!*
BEAVERS

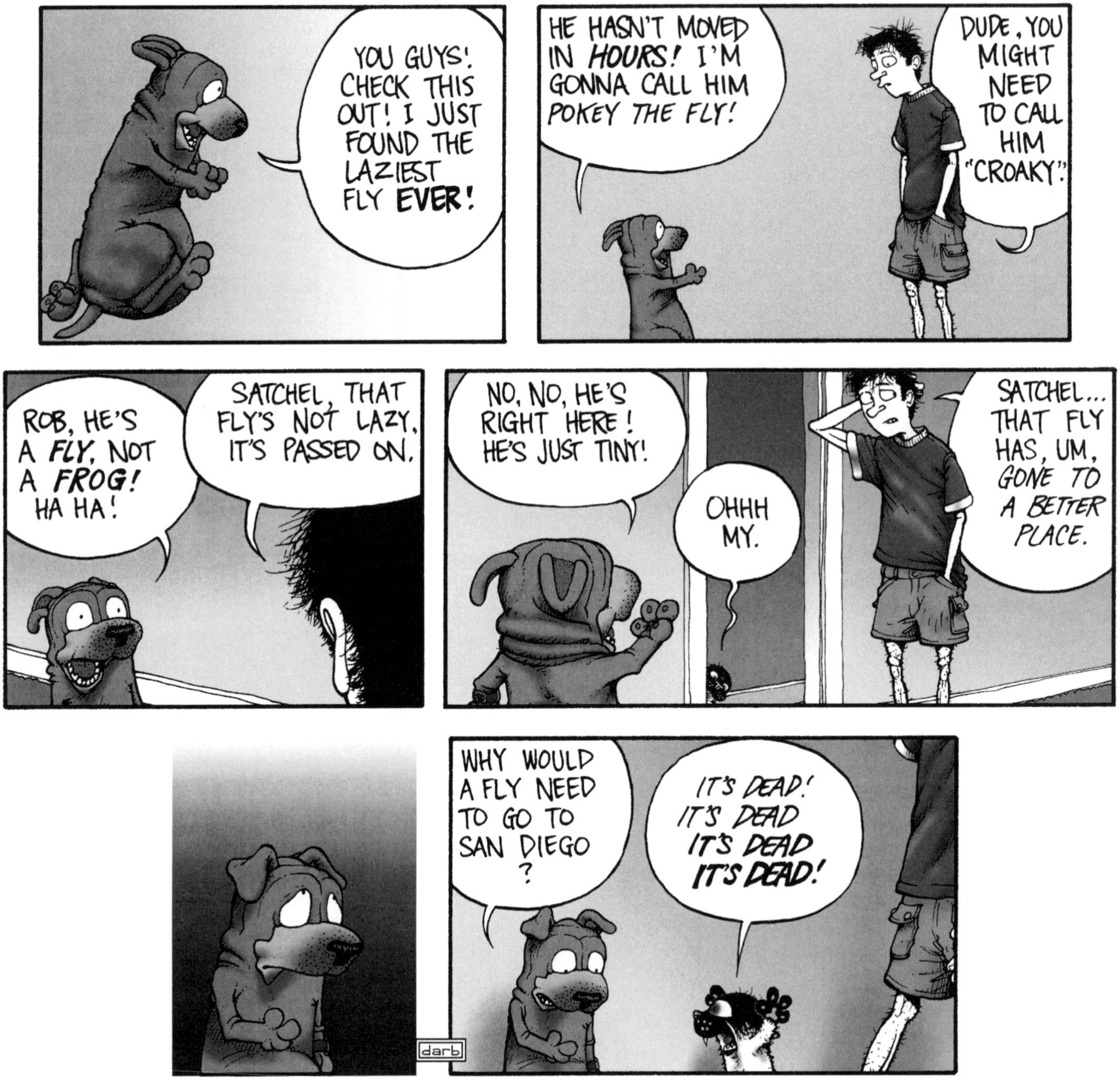
YOU GUYS! CHECK THIS OUT! I JUST FOUND THE LAZIEST FLY **EVER**!
HE HASN'T MOVED IN ***HOURS!*** I'M GONNA CALL HIM *POKEY THE FLY!*
DUDE, YOU MIGHT NEED TO CALL HIM "CROAKY".
SATCHEL, THAT FLY'S NOT LAZY, IT'S PASSED ON.
ROB, HE'S A ***FLY,*** NOT A ***FROG!*** HA HA!
NO, NO, HE'S RIGHT HERE! HE'S JUST TINY!
OHHH MY.
SATCHEL... THAT FLY HAS, UM, *GONE TO A BETTER PLACE.*
WHY WOULD A FLY NEED TO GO TO SAN DIEGO ?
IT'S DEAD! IT'S DEAD ***IT'S DEAD IT'S DEAD!***
darb

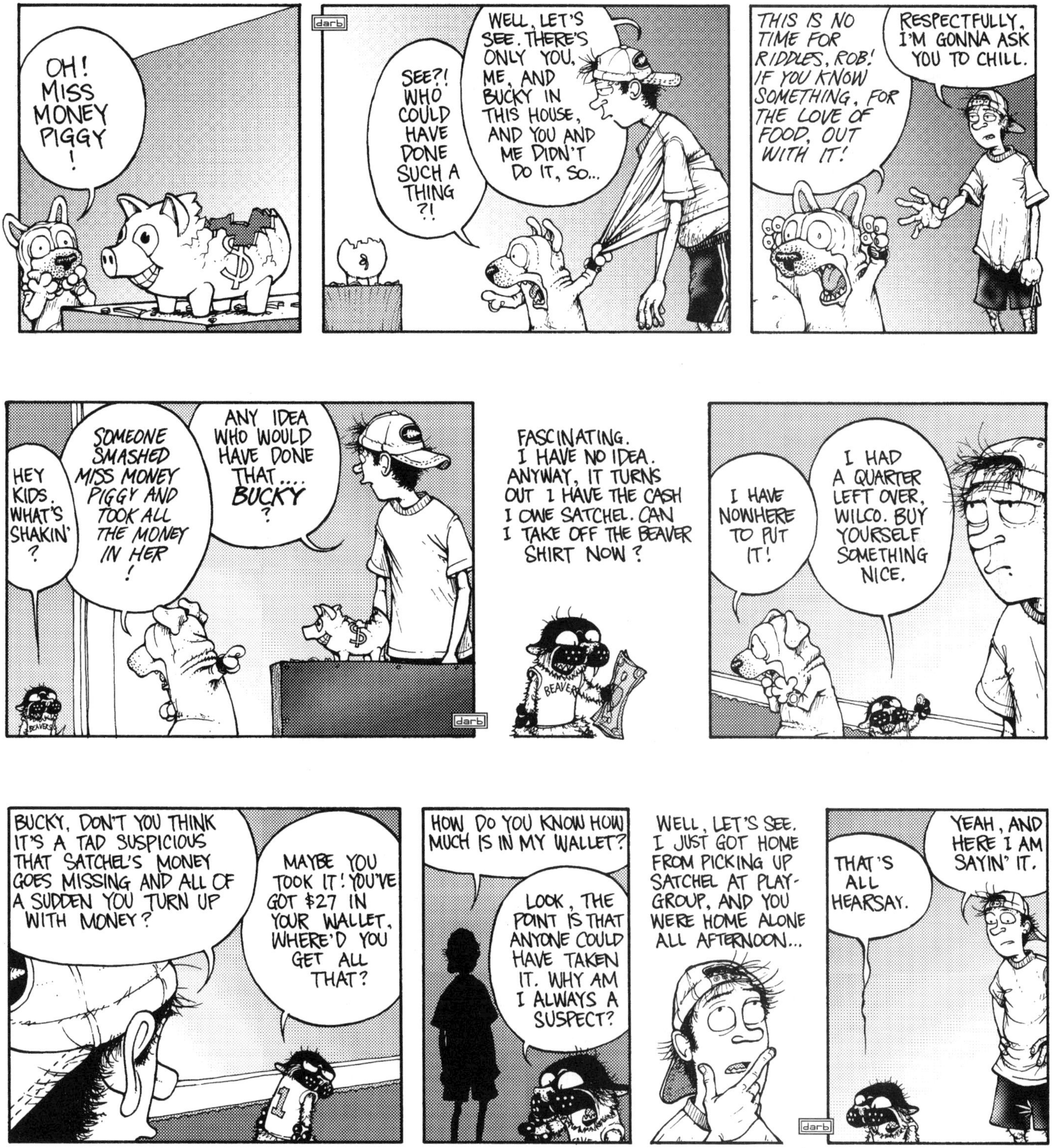
OH! MISS MONEY PIGGY!
darb
SEE?! WHO COULD HAVE DONE SUCH A THING?!
WELL, LET'S SEE. THERE'S ONLY YOU, ME, AND BUCKY IN THIS HOUSE, AND YOU AND ME DIDN'T DO IT, SO...
THIS IS NO TIME FOR RIDDLES, ROB! IF YOU KNOW SOMETHING, FOR THE LOVE OF FOOD, OUT WITH IT!
RESPECTFULLY, I'M GONNA ASK YOU TO CHILL.
HEY KIDS. WHAT'S SHAKIN'?
SOMEONE SMASHED MISS MONEY PIGGY AND TOOK ALL THE MONEY IN HER!
ANY IDEA WHO WOULD HAVE DONE THAT.... BUCKY?
BEAVERS
darb
FASCINATING. I HAVE NO IDEA. ANYWAY, IT TURNS OUT I HAVE THE CASH I OWE SATCHEL. CAN I TAKE OFF THE BEAVER SHIRT NOW?
BEAVER
I HAVE NOWHERE TO PUT IT!
I HAD A QUARTER LEFT OVER, WILCO. BUY YOURSELF SOMETHING NICE.
BUCKY, DON'T YOU THINK IT'S A TAD SUSPICIOUS THAT SATCHEL'S MONEY GOES MISSING AND ALL OF A SUDDEN YOU TURN UP WITH MONEY?
MAYBE YOU TOOK IT! YOU'VE GOT $27 IN YOUR WALLET. WHERE'D YOU GET ALL THAT?
HOW DO YOU KNOW HOW MUCH IS IN MY WALLET?
LOOK, THE POINT IS THAT ANYONE COULD HAVE TAKEN IT. WHY AM I ALWAYS A SUSPECT?
WELL, LET'S SEE. I JUST GOT HOME FROM PICKING UP SATCHEL AT PLAY-GROUP, AND YOU WERE HOME ALONE ALL AFTERNOON...
darb
THAT'S ALL HEARSAY.
YEAH, AND HERE I AM SAYIN' IT.

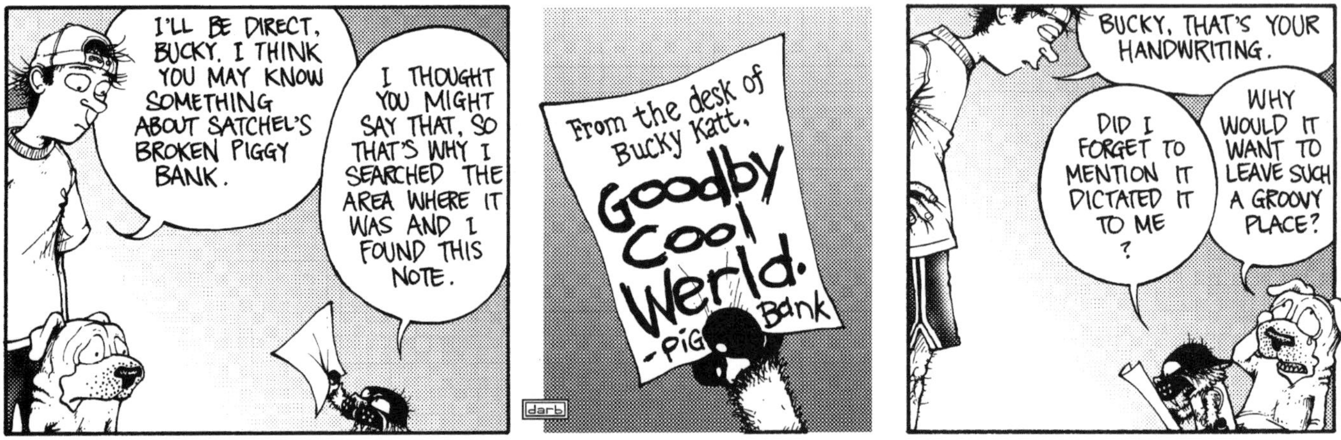
I'LL BE DIRECT, BUCKY. I THINK YOU MAY KNOW SOMETHING ABOUT SATCHEL'S BROKEN PIGGY BANK.
I THOUGHT YOU MIGHT SAY THAT, SO THAT'S WHY I SEARCHED THE AREA WHERE IT WAS AND I FOUND THIS NOTE.
From the desk of Bucky Katt.
Goodby Cool Werld. -Pig Bank
BUCKY, THAT'S YOUR HANDWRITING.
DID I FORGET TO MENTION IT DICTATED IT TO ME ?
WHY WOULD IT WANT TO LEAVE SUCH A GROOVY PLACE?

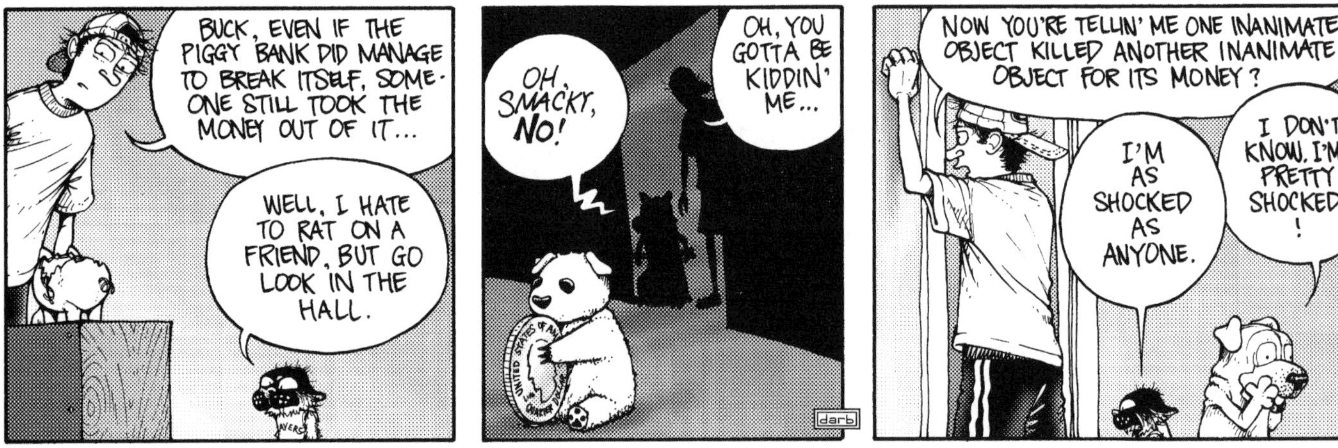
BUCK, EVEN IF THE PIGGY BANK DID MANAGE TO BREAK ITSELF, SOME-ONE STILL TOOK THE MONEY OUT OF IT...
WELL, I HATE TO RAT ON A FRIEND, BUT GO LOOK IN THE HALL.
OH, SMACKY, NO!
OH, YOU GOTTA BE KIDDIN' ME...
NOW YOU'RE TELLIN' ME ONE INANIMATE OBJECT KILLED ANOTHER INANIMATE OBJECT FOR ITS MONEY ?
I'M AS SHOCKED AS ANYONE.
I DON'T KNOW. I'M PRETTY SHOCKED !

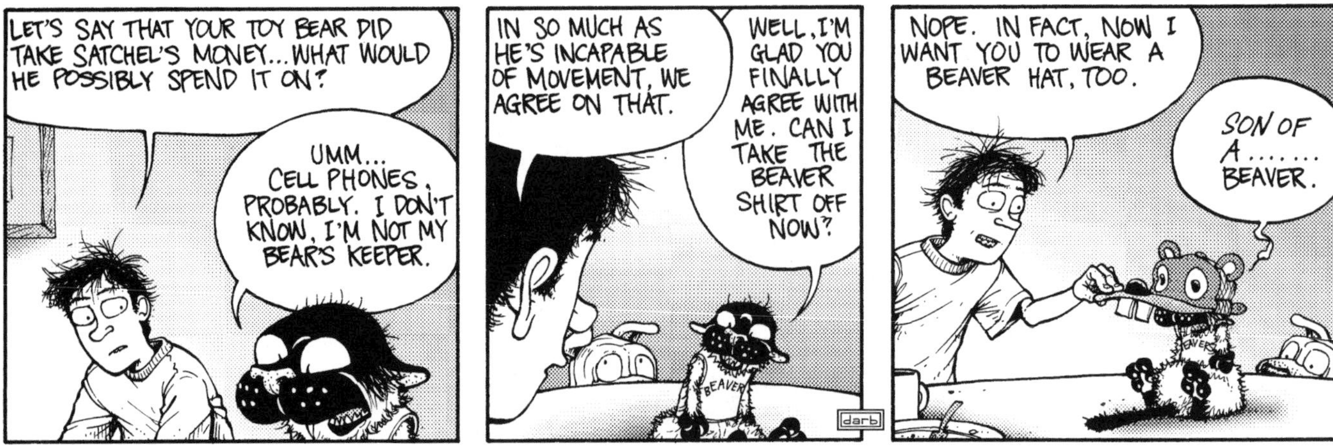
LET'S SAY THAT YOUR TOY BEAR DID TAKE SATCHEL'S MONEY... WHAT WOULD HE POSSIBLY SPEND IT ON?
UMM... CELL PHONES, PROBABLY. I DON'T KNOW, I'M NOT MY BEAR'S KEEPER.
IN SO MUCH AS HE'S INCAPABLE OF MOVEMENT, WE AGREE ON THAT.
WELL, I'M GLAD YOU FINALLY AGREE WITH ME. CAN I TAKE THE BEAVER SHIRT OFF NOW?
NOPE. IN FACT, NOW I WANT YOU TO WEAR A BEAVER HAT, TOO.
SON OF A....... BEAVER.

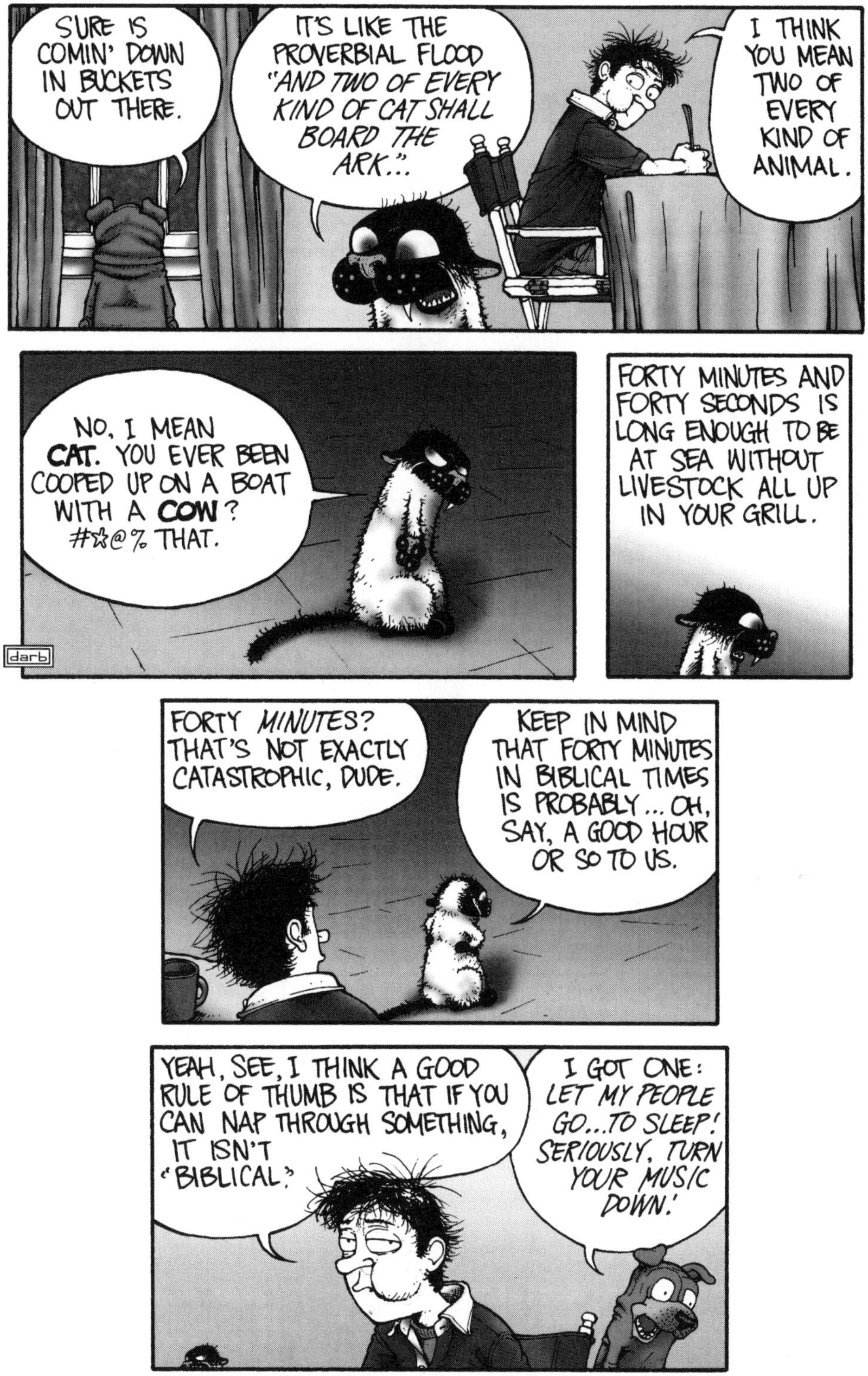
SURE IS COMIN' DOWN IN BUCKETS OUT THERE.
IT'S LIKE THE PROVERBIAL FLOOD "AND TWO OF EVERY KIND OF CAT SHALL BOARD THE ARK."...
I THINK YOU MEAN TWO OF EVERY KIND OF ANIMAL.
NO, I MEAN CAT. YOU EVER BEEN COOPED UP ON A BOAT WITH A COW? #☆@% THAT.
darb
FORTY MINUTES AND FORTY SECONDS IS LONG ENOUGH TO BE AT SEA WITHOUT LIVESTOCK ALL UP IN YOUR GRILL.
FORTY MINUTES? THAT'S NOT EXACTLY CATASTROPHIC, DUDE.
KEEP IN MIND THAT FORTY MINUTES IN BIBLICAL TIMES IS PROBABLY... OH, SAY, A GOOD HOUR OR SO TO US.
YEAH, SEE, I THINK A GOOD RULE OF THUMB IS THAT IF YOU CAN NAP THROUGH SOMETHING, IT ISN'T "BIBLICAL."
I GOT ONE: LET MY PEOPLE GO...TO SLEEP! SERIOUSLY, TURN YOUR MUSIC DOWN.'

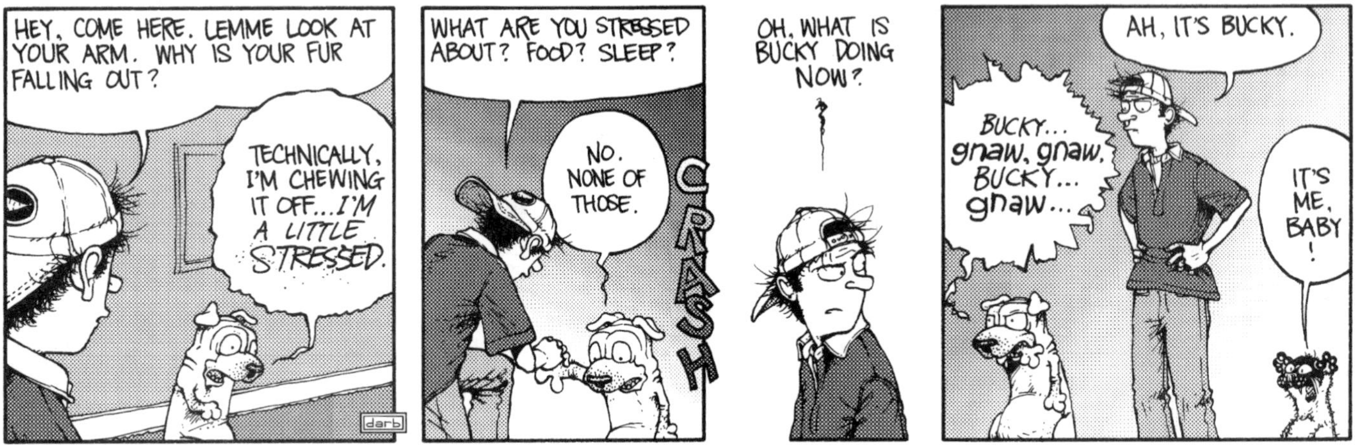
HEY, COME HERE. LEMME LOOK AT YOUR ARM. WHY IS YOUR FUR FALLING OUT?
TECHNICALLY, I'M CHEWING IT OFF...I'M A LITTLE STRESSED.
darb
WHAT ARE YOU STRESSED ABOUT? FOOD? SLEEP?
NO. NONE OF THOSE.
CRASH
OH, WHAT IS BUCKY DOING NOW?
AH, IT'S BUCKY.
BUCKY... gnaw, gnaw, BUCKY... gnaw...
IT'S ME, BABY!

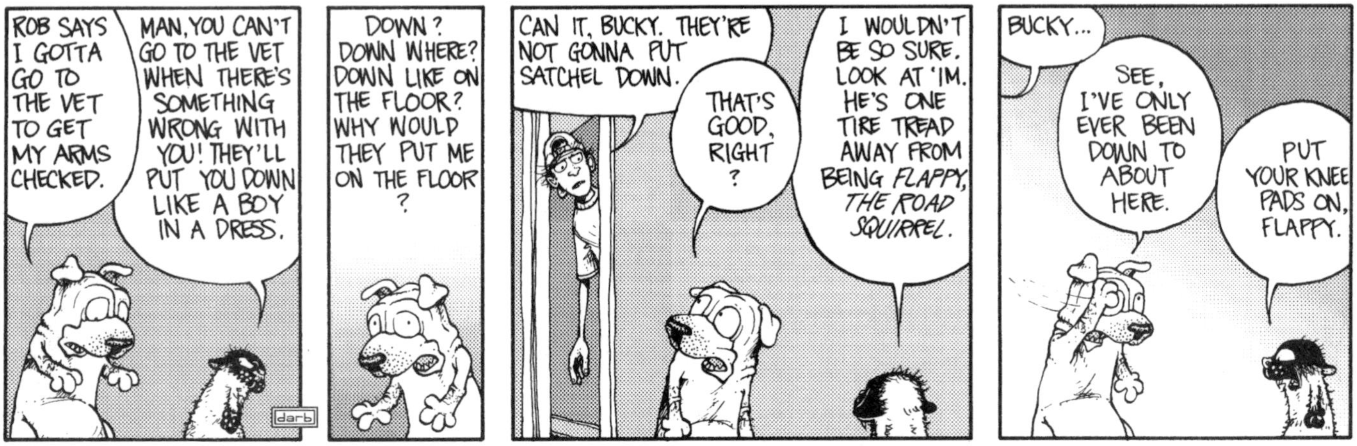
ROB SAYS I GOTTA GO TO THE VET TO GET MY ARMS CHECKED.
MAN, YOU CAN'T GO TO THE VET WHEN THERE'S SOMETHING WRONG WITH YOU! THEY'LL PUT YOU DOWN LIKE A BOY IN A DRESS.
darb
DOWN? DOWN WHERE? DOWN LIKE ON THE FLOOR? WHY WOULD THEY PUT ME ON THE FLOOR?
CAN IT, BUCKY. THEY'RE NOT GONNA PUT SATCHEL DOWN.
THAT'S GOOD, RIGHT?
I WOULDN'T BE SO SURE. LOOK AT 'IM. HE'S ONE TIRE TREAD AWAY FROM BEING FLAPPY, THE ROAD SQUIRREL.
BUCKY...
SEE, I'VE ONLY EVER BEEN DOWN TO ABOUT HERE.
PUT YOUR KNEE PADS ON, FLAPPY.

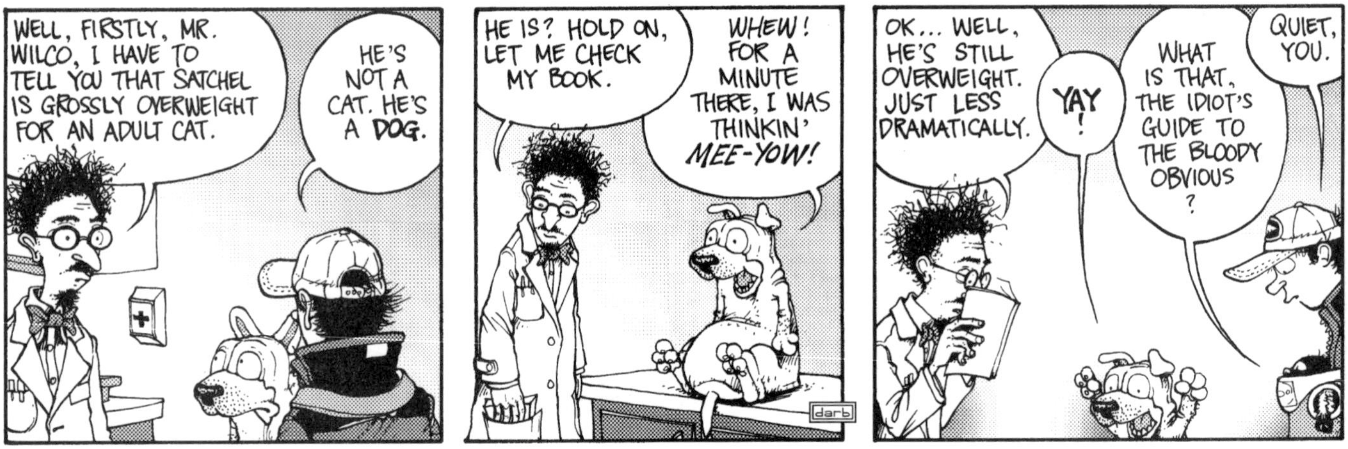
WELL, FIRSTLY, MR. WILCO, I HAVE TO TELL YOU THAT SATCHEL IS GROSSLY OVERWEIGHT FOR AN ADULT CAT.
HE'S NOT A CAT. HE'S A DOG.
HE IS? HOLD ON, LET ME CHECK MY BOOK.
WHEW! FOR A MINUTE THERE, I WAS THINKIN' MEE-YOW!
darb
OK... WELL, HE'S STILL OVERWEIGHT. JUST LESS DRAMATICALLY.
YAY!
WHAT IS THAT, THE IDIOT'S GUIDE TO THE BLOODY OBVIOUS?
QUIET, YOU.

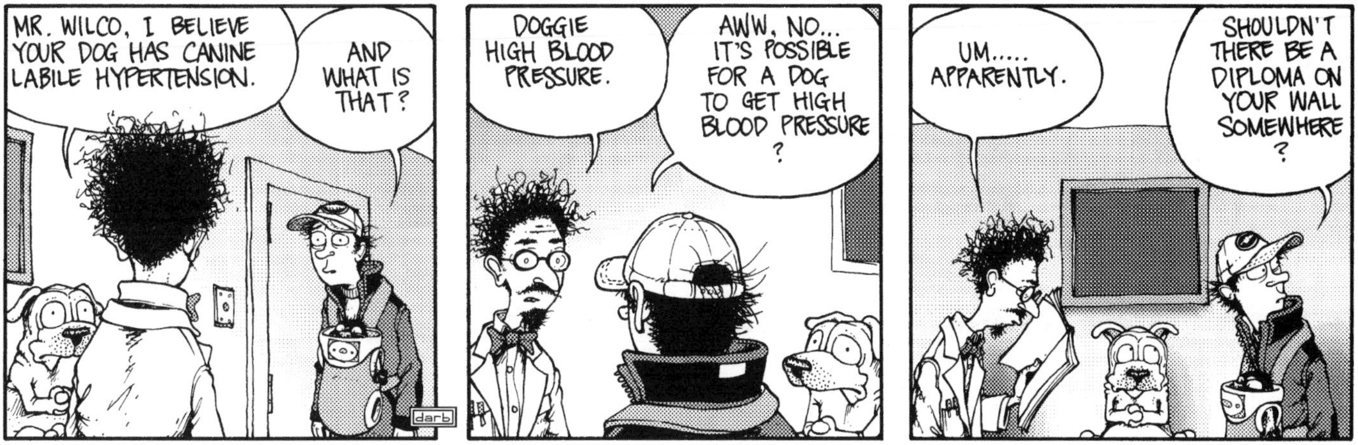
MR. WILCO, I BELIEVE YOUR DOG HAS CANINE LABILE HYPERTENSION.
AND WHAT IS THAT?
DOGGIE HIGH BLOOD PRESSURE.
AWW, NO... IT'S POSSIBLE FOR A DOG TO GET HIGH BLOOD PRESSURE?
UM..... APPARENTLY.
SHOULDN'T THERE BE A DIPLOMA ON YOUR WALL SOMEWHERE?
darb

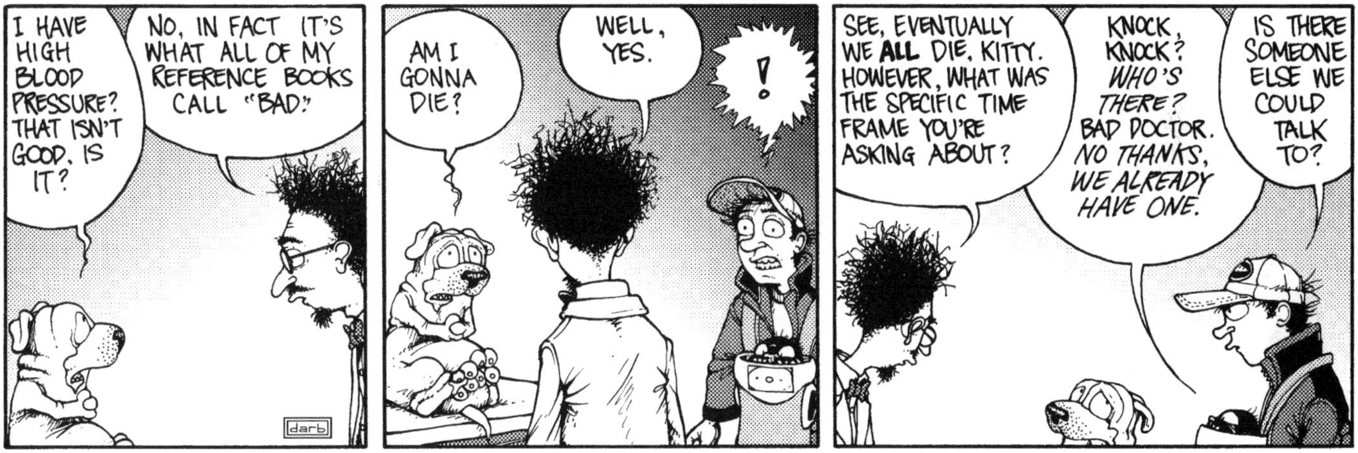
I HAVE HIGH BLOOD PRESSURE? THAT ISN'T GOOD, IS IT?
NO, IN FACT IT'S WHAT ALL OF MY REFERENCE BOOKS CALL "BAD."
AM I GONNA DIE?
WELL, YES.
!
SEE, EVENTUALLY WE **ALL** DIE, KITTY. HOWEVER, WHAT WAS THE SPECIFIC TIME FRAME YOU'RE ASKING ABOUT?
KNOCK, KNOCK? *WHO'S THERE?* BAD DOCTOR. *NO THANKS, WE ALREADY HAVE ONE.*
IS THERE SOMEONE ELSE WE COULD TALK TO?
darb

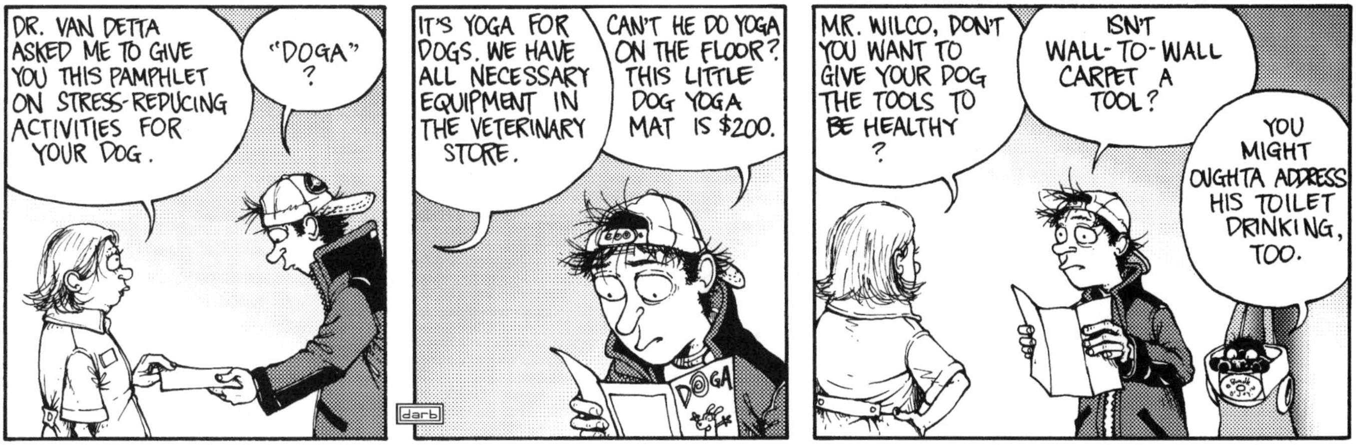
DR. VAN DETTA ASKED ME TO GIVE YOU THIS PAMPHLET ON STRESS-REDUCING ACTIVITIES FOR YOUR DOG.
"DOGA"?
IT'S YOGA FOR DOGS. WE HAVE ALL NECESSARY EQUIPMENT IN THE VETERINARY STORE.
CAN'T HE DO YOGA ON THE FLOOR? THIS LITTLE DOG YOGA MAT IS $200.
DOGA
MR. WILCO, DON'T YOU WANT TO GIVE YOUR DOG THE TOOLS TO BE HEALTHY?
ISN'T WALL-TO-WALL CARPET A TOOL?
YOU MIGHT OUGHTA ADDRESS HIS TOILET DRINKING, TOO.
darb

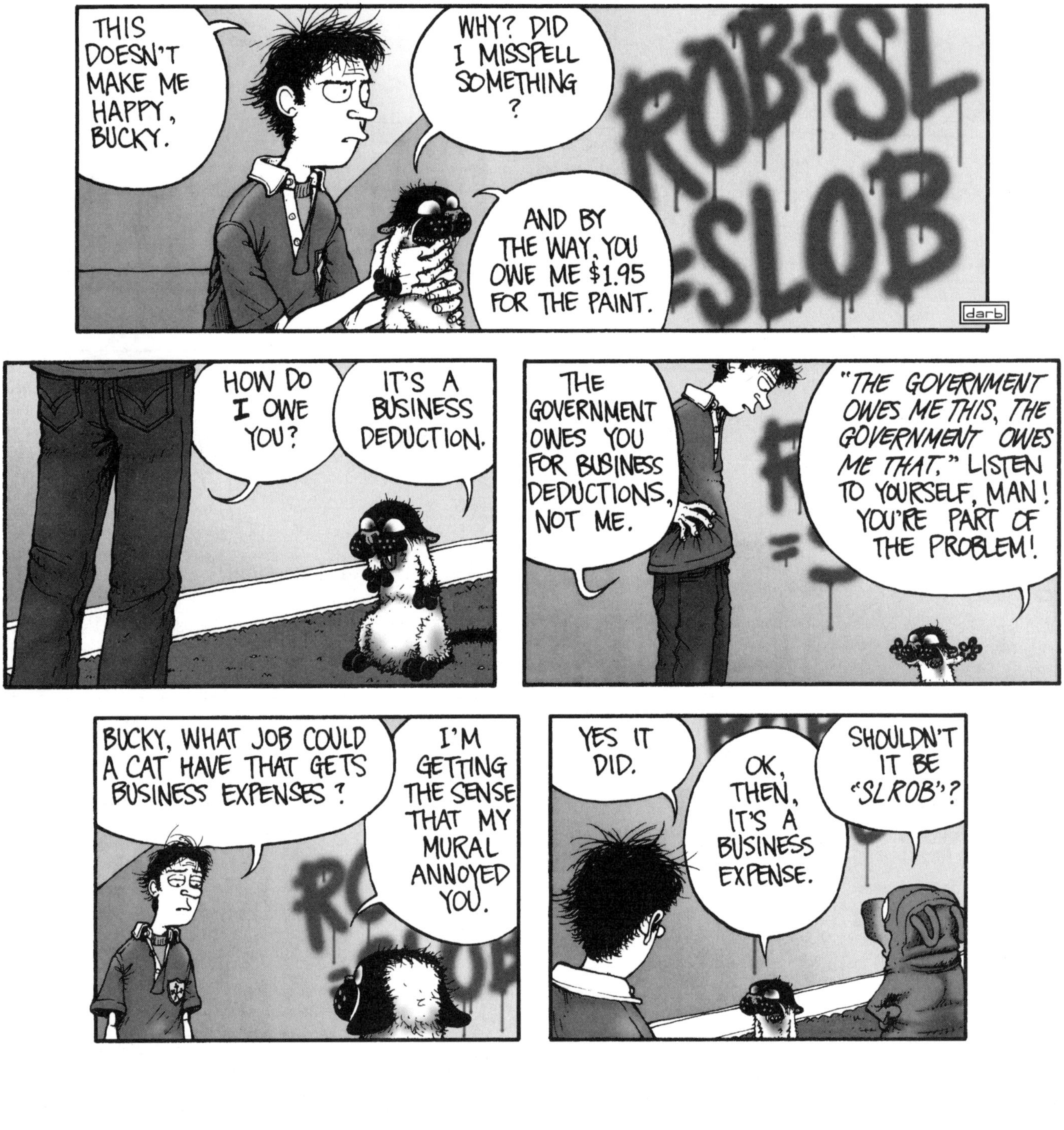
THIS DOESN'T MAKE ME HAPPY, BUCKY.
WHY? DID I MISSPELL SOMETHING?
ROB+SL =SLOB
AND BY THE WAY, YOU OWE ME $1.95 FOR THE PAINT.
darb
HOW DO I OWE YOU?
IT'S A BUSINESS DEDUCTION.
THE GOVERNMENT OWES YOU FOR BUSINESS DEDUCTIONS, NOT ME.
"THE GOVERNMENT OWES ME THIS, THE GOVERNMENT OWES ME THAT." LISTEN TO YOURSELF, MAN! YOU'RE PART OF THE PROBLEM!
BUCKY, WHAT JOB COULD A CAT HAVE THAT GETS BUSINESS EXPENSES?
I'M GETTING THE SENSE THAT MY MURAL ANNOYED YOU.
YES IT DID.
OK, THEN, IT'S A BUSINESS EXPENSE.
SHOULDN'T IT BE "SLROB"?

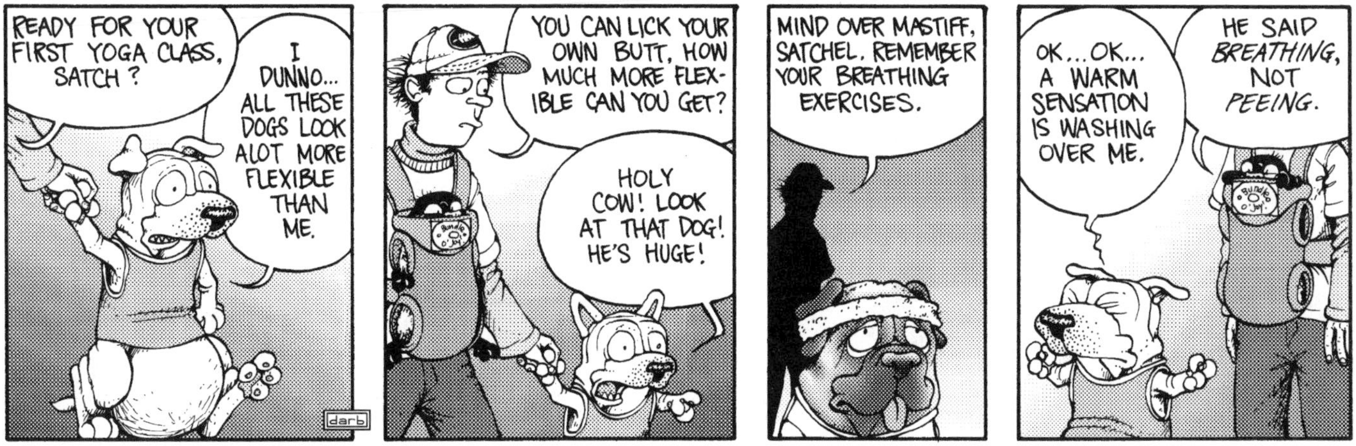
READY FOR YOUR FIRST YOGA CLASS, SATCH?
I DUNNO... ALL THESE DOGS LOOK ALOT MORE FLEXIBLE THAN ME.
YOU CAN LICK YOUR OWN BUTT. HOW MUCH MORE FLEX-IBLE CAN YOU GET?
HOLY COW! LOOK AT THAT DOG! HE'S HUGE!
MIND OVER MASTIFF, SATCHEL. REMEMBER YOUR BREATHING EXERCISES.
OK...OK... A WARM SENSATION IS WASHING OVER ME.
HE SAID *BREATHING*, NOT *PEEING*.

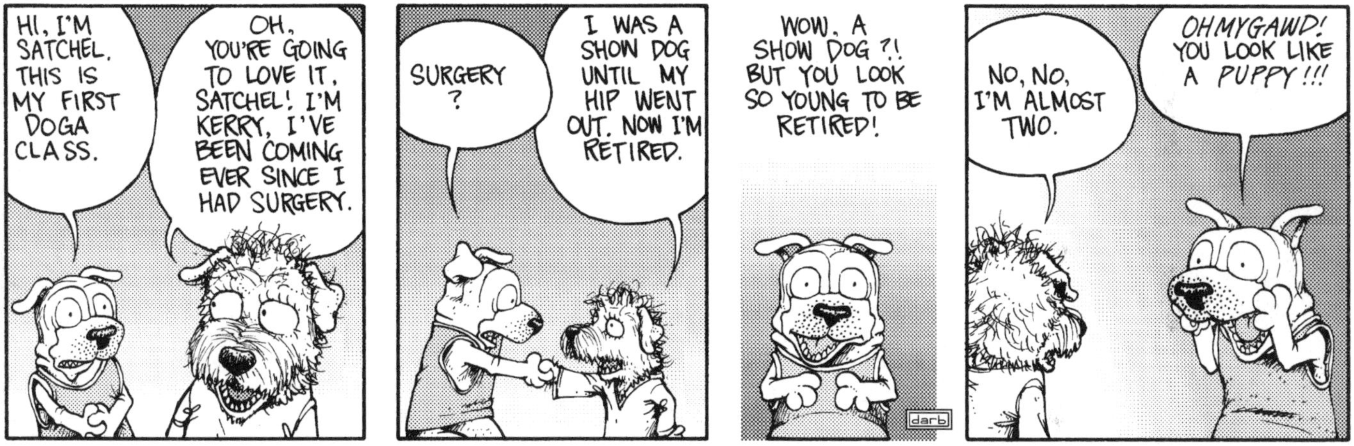
HI, I'M SATCHEL. THIS IS MY FIRST DOGA CLASS.
OH, YOU'RE GOING TO LOVE IT, SATCHEL! I'M KERRY, I'VE BEEN COMING EVER SINCE I HAD SURGERY.
SURGERY?
I WAS A SHOW DOG UNTIL MY HIP WENT OUT. NOW I'M RETIRED.
WOW. A SHOW DOG?! BUT YOU LOOK SO YOUNG TO BE RETIRED!
NO, NO, I'M ALMOST TWO.
OHMYGAWD! YOU LOOK LIKE A *PUPPY!!!*

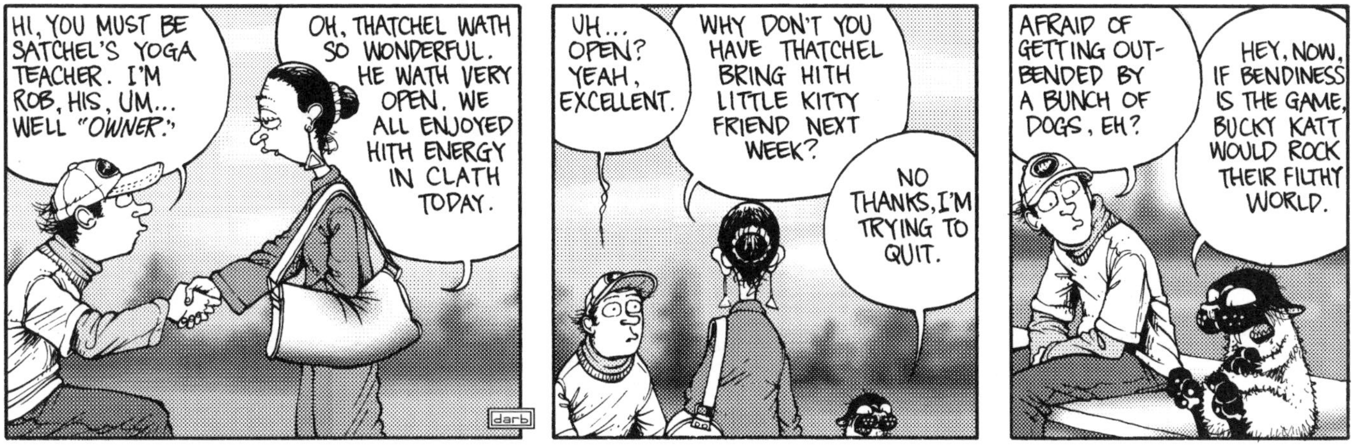
HI, YOU MUST BE SATCHEL'S YOGA TEACHER. I'M ROB, HIS, UM... WELL "*OWNER*."
OH, THATCHEL WATH SO WONDERFUL. HE WATH VERY OPEN. WE ALL ENJOYED HITH ENERGY IN CLATH TODAY.
UH... OPEN? YEAH, EXCELLENT.
WHY DON'T YOU HAVE THATCHEL BRING HITH LITTLE KITTY FRIEND NEXT WEEK?
NO THANKS, I'M TRYING TO QUIT.
AFRAID OF GETTING OUT-BENDED BY A BUNCH OF DOGS, EH?
HEY, NOW, IF BENDINESS IS THE GAME, BUCKY KATT WOULD ROCK THEIR FILTHY WORLD.

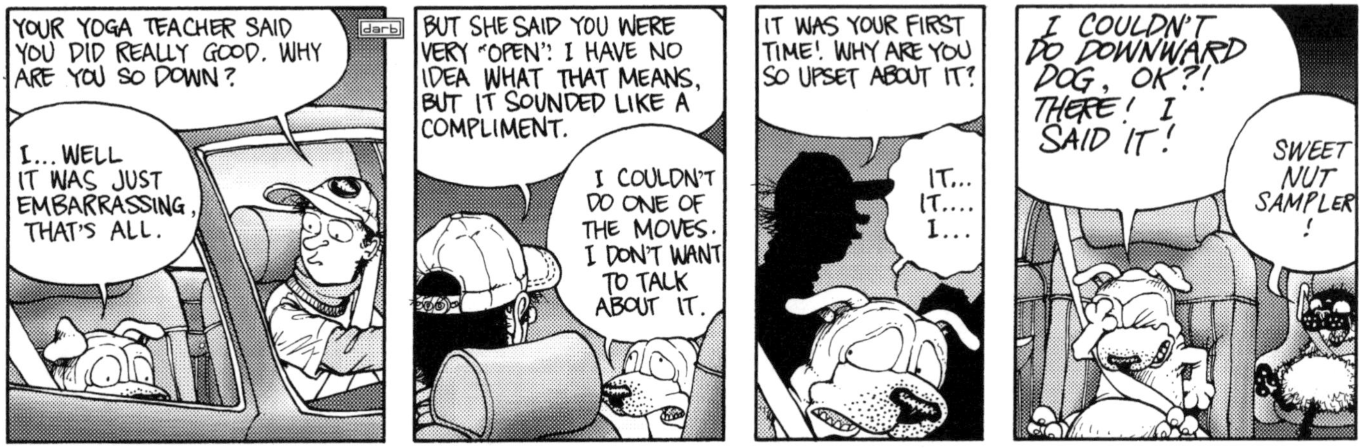
YOUR YOGA TEACHER SAID YOU DID REALLY GOOD. WHY ARE YOU SO DOWN?
I... WELL IT WAS JUST EMBARRASSING, THAT'S ALL.
BUT SHE SAID YOU WERE VERY "OPEN". I HAVE NO IDEA WHAT THAT MEANS, BUT IT SOUNDED LIKE A COMPLIMENT.
I COULDN'T DO ONE OF THE MOVES. I DON'T WANT TO TALK ABOUT IT.
IT WAS YOUR FIRST TIME! WHY ARE YOU SO UPSET ABOUT IT?
IT... IT.... I...
I COULDN'T DO DOWNWARD DOG, OK?! THERE! I SAID IT!
SWEET NUT SAMPLER!

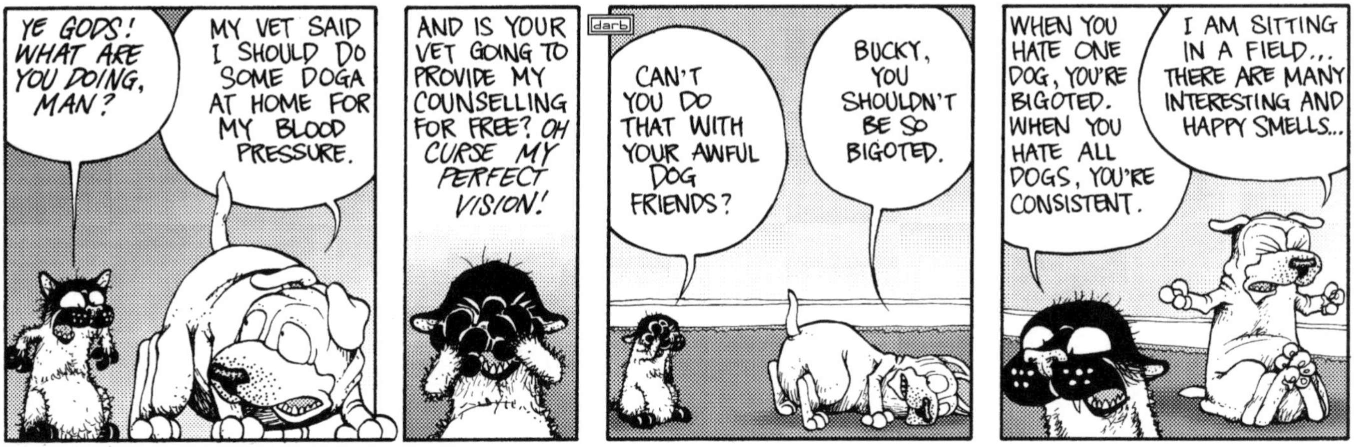
YE GODS! WHAT ARE YOU DOING, MAN?
MY VET SAID I SHOULD DO SOME DOGA AT HOME FOR MY BLOOD PRESSURE.
AND IS YOUR VET GOING TO PROVIDE MY COUNSELLING FOR FREE? OH CURSE MY PERFECT VISION!
CAN'T YOU DO THAT WITH YOUR AWFUL DOG FRIENDS?
BUCKY, YOU SHOULDN'T BE SO BIGOTED.
WHEN YOU HATE ONE DOG, YOU'RE BIGOTED. WHEN YOU HATE ALL DOGS, YOU'RE CONSISTENT.
I AM SITTING IN A FIELD... THERE ARE MANY INTERESTING AND HAPPY SMELLS...

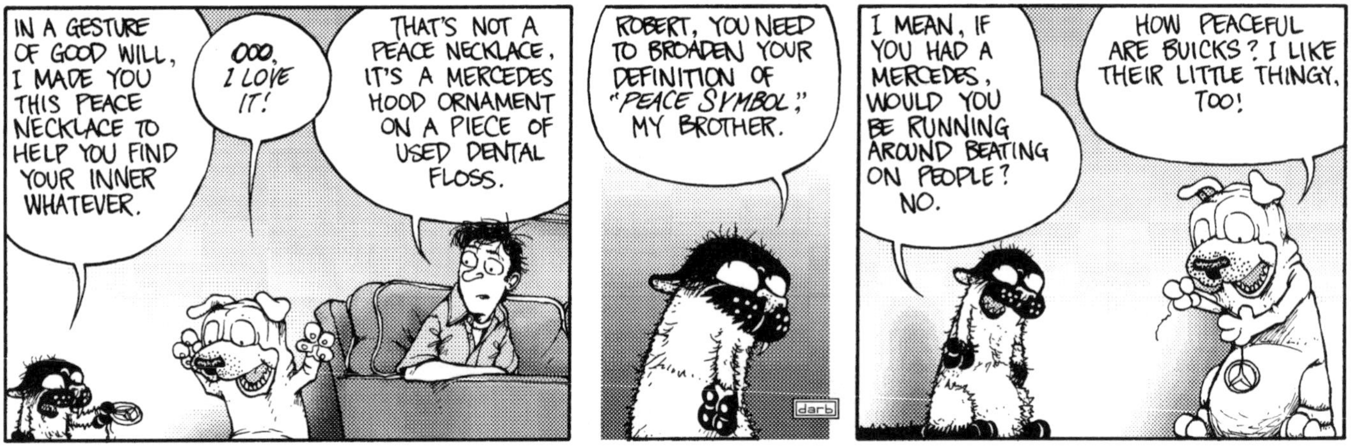
IN A GESTURE OF GOOD WILL, I MADE YOU THIS PEACE NECKLACE TO HELP YOU FIND YOUR INNER WHATEVER.
OOO, I LOVE IT!
THAT'S NOT A PEACE NECKLACE, IT'S A MERCEDES HOOD ORNAMENT ON A PIECE OF USED DENTAL FLOSS.
ROBERT, YOU NEED TO BROADEN YOUR DEFINITION OF "PEACE SYMBOL," MY BROTHER.
I MEAN, IF YOU HAD A MERCEDES, WOULD YOU BE RUNNING AROUND BEATING ON PEOPLE? NO.
HOW PEACEFUL ARE BUICKS? I LIKE THEIR LITTLE THINGY, TOO!

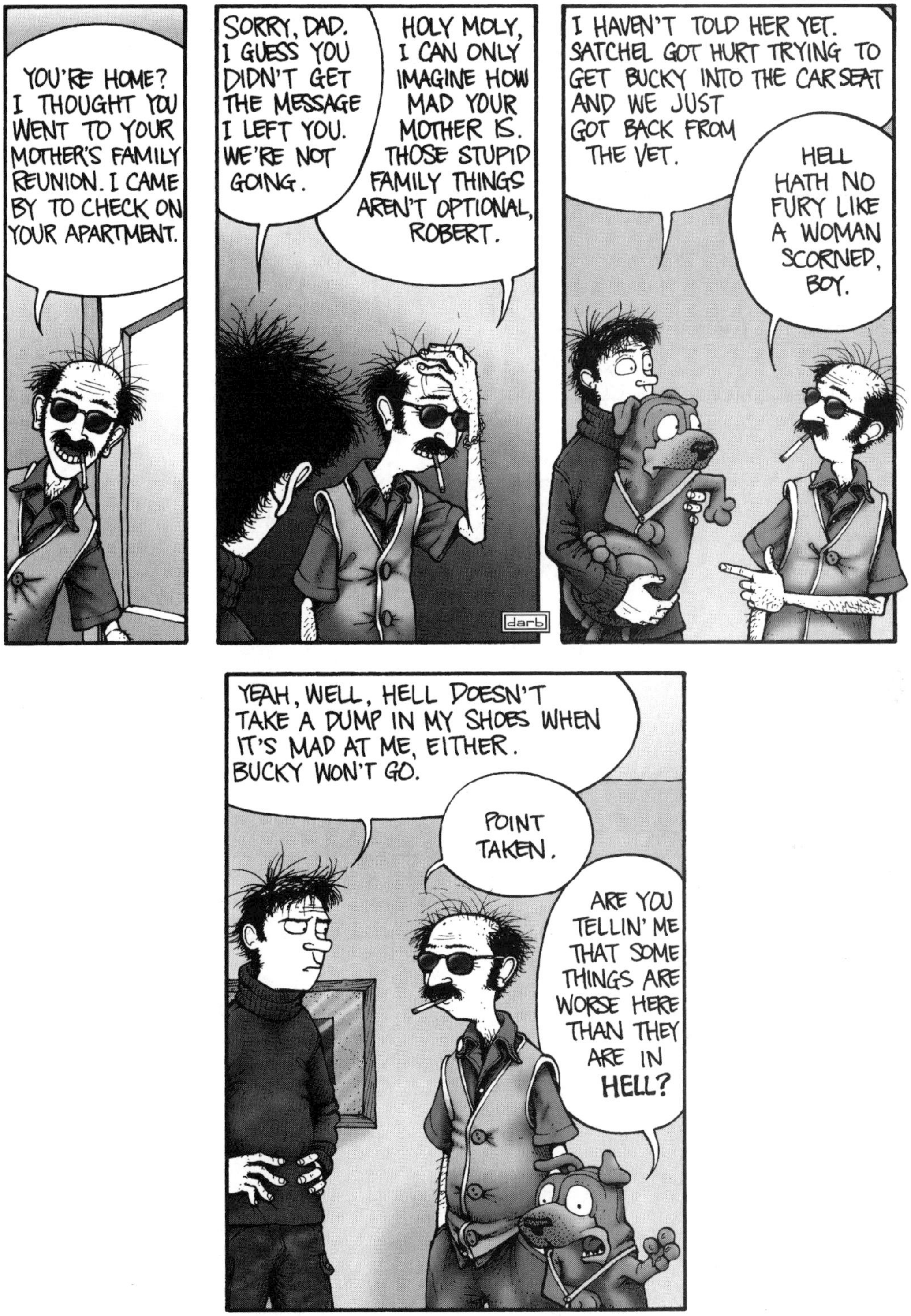
YOU'RE HOME? I THOUGHT YOU WENT TO YOUR MOTHER'S FAMILY REUNION. I CAME BY TO CHECK ON YOUR APARTMENT.
SORRY, DAD. I GUESS YOU DIDN'T GET THE MESSAGE I LEFT YOU. WE'RE NOT GOING.
HOLY MOLY, I CAN ONLY IMAGINE HOW MAD YOUR MOTHER IS. THOSE STUPID FAMILY THINGS AREN'T OPTIONAL, ROBERT.
darb
I HAVEN'T TOLD HER YET. SATCHEL GOT HURT TRYING TO GET BUCKY INTO THE CAR SEAT AND WE JUST GOT BACK FROM THE VET.
HELL HATH NO FURY LIKE A WOMAN SCORNED, BOY.
YEAH, WELL, HELL DOESN'T TAKE A DUMP IN MY SHOES WHEN IT'S MAD AT ME, EITHER. BUCKY WON'T GO.
POINT TAKEN.
ARE YOU TELLIN' ME THAT SOME THINGS ARE WORSE HERE THAN THEY ARE IN HELL?

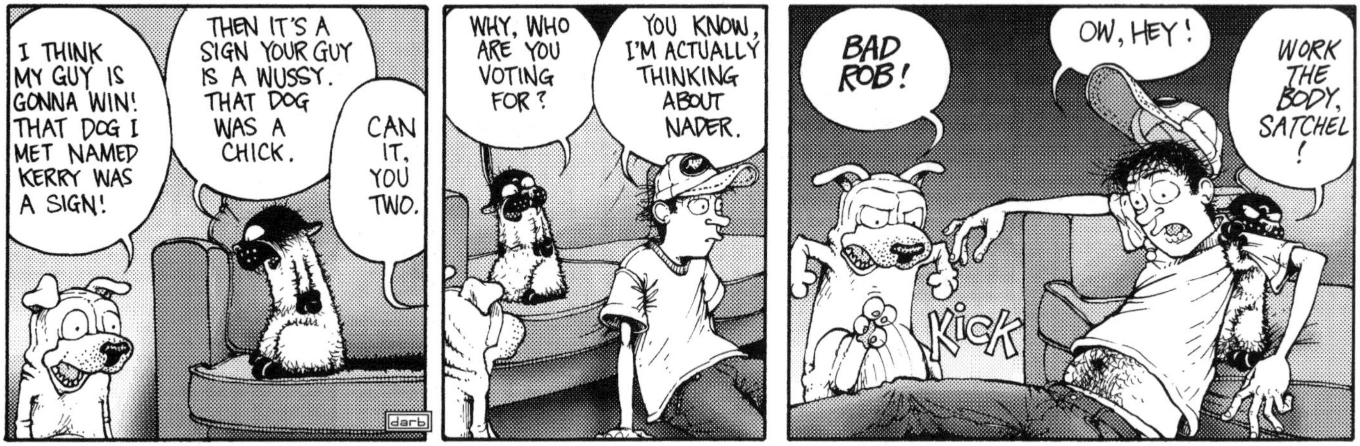
I THINK MY GUY IS GONNA WIN! THAT DOG I MET NAMED KERRY WAS A SIGN!
THEN IT'S A SIGN YOUR GUY IS A WUSSY. THAT DOG WAS A CHICK.
CAN IT, YOU TWO.
darb
WHY, WHO ARE YOU VOTING FOR?
YOU KNOW, I'M ACTUALLY THINKING ABOUT NADER.
BAD ROB!
OW, HEY!
WORK THE BODY, SATCHEL!
KICK

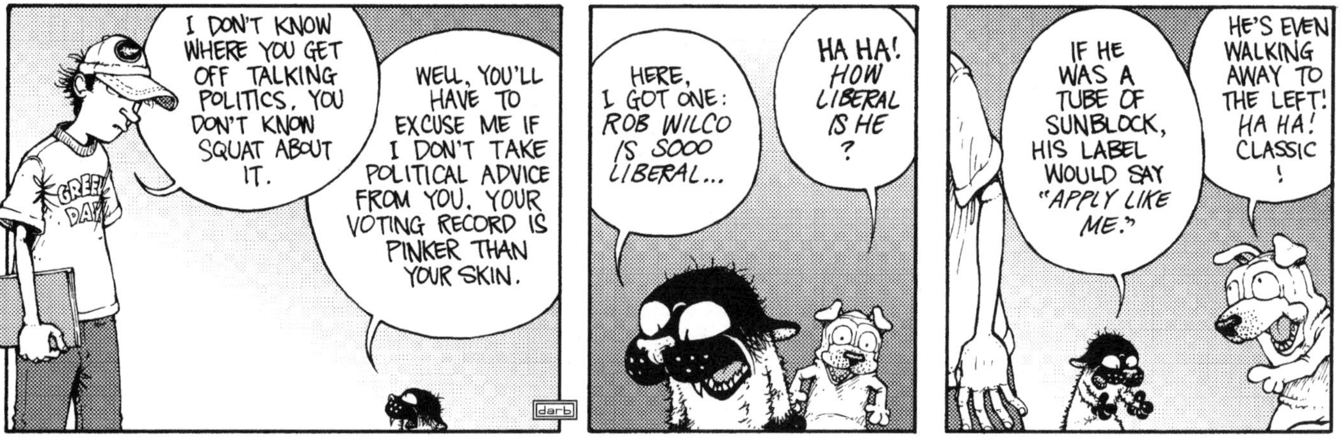
I DON'T KNOW WHERE YOU GET OFF TALKING POLITICS. YOU DON'T KNOW SQUAT ABOUT IT.
WELL, YOU'LL HAVE TO EXCUSE ME IF I DON'T TAKE POLITICAL ADVICE FROM YOU. YOUR VOTING RECORD IS PINKER THAN YOUR SKIN.
GREEN DAY
darb
HERE, I GOT ONE: ROB WILCO IS SOOO LIBERAL...
HA HA! HOW LIBERAL IS HE?
IF HE WAS A TUBE OF SUNBLOCK, HIS LABEL WOULD SAY "APPLY LIKE ME."
HE'S EVEN WALKING AWAY TO THE LEFT! HA HA! CLASSIC!

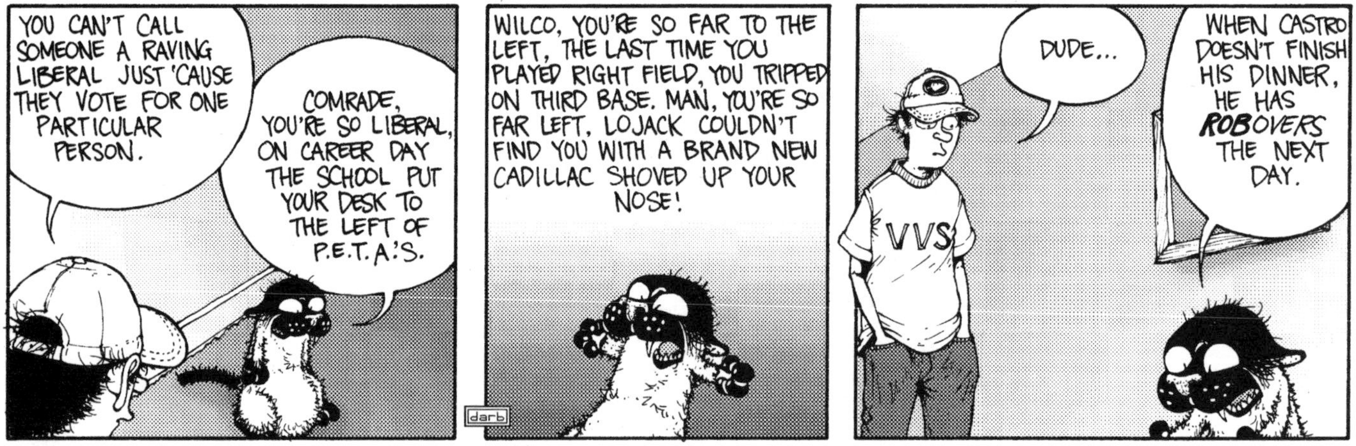
YOU CAN'T CALL SOMEONE A RAVING LIBERAL JUST 'CAUSE THEY VOTE FOR ONE PARTICULAR PERSON.
COMRADE, YOU'RE SO LIBERAL, ON CAREER DAY THE SCHOOL PUT YOUR DESK TO THE LEFT OF P.E.T.A.'S.
darb
WILCO, YOU'RE SO FAR TO THE LEFT, THE LAST TIME YOU PLAYED RIGHT FIELD, YOU TRIPPED ON THIRD BASE. MAN, YOU'RE SO FAR LEFT, LOJACK COULDN'T FIND YOU WITH A BRAND NEW CADILLAC SHOVED UP YOUR NOSE!
DUDE...
WHEN CASTRO DOESN'T FINISH HIS DINNER, HE HAS ROBOVERS THE NEXT DAY.
VVS

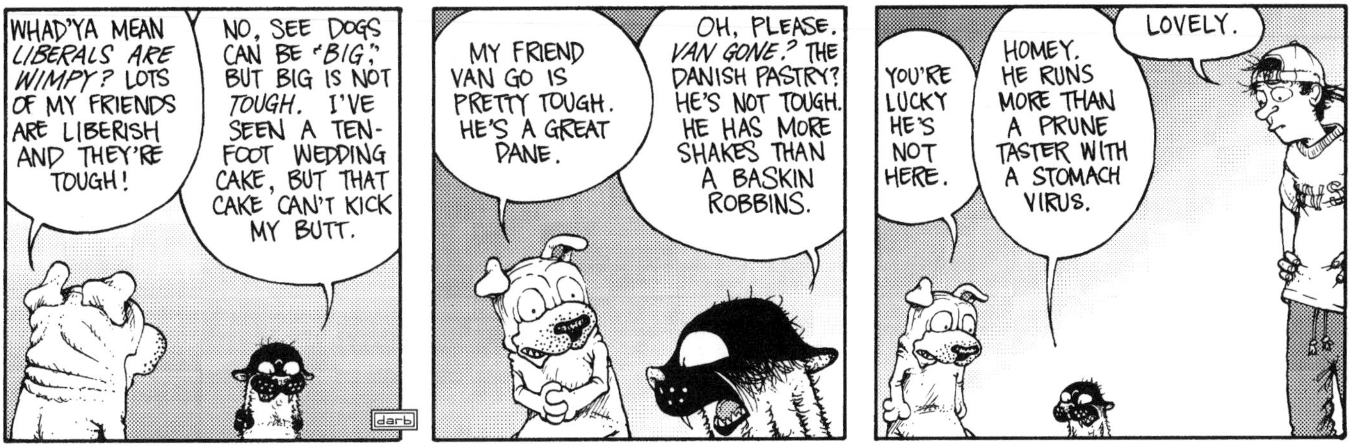
WHAD'YA MEAN *LIBERALS ARE WIMPY?* LOTS OF MY FRIENDS ARE LIBERISH AND THEY'RE TOUGH!
NO, SEE DOGS CAN BE "*BIG*," BUT BIG IS NOT *TOUGH*. I'VE SEEN A TEN-FOOT WEDDING CAKE, BUT THAT CAKE CAN'T KICK MY BUTT.
darb
MY FRIEND VAN GO IS PRETTY TOUGH. HE'S A GREAT DANE.
OH, PLEASE. *VAN GONE?* THE DANISH PASTRY? HE'S NOT TOUGH. HE HAS MORE SHAKES THAN A BASKIN ROBBINS.
YOU'RE LUCKY HE'S NOT HERE.
HOMEY. HE RUNS MORE THAN A PRUNE TASTER WITH A STOMACH VIRUS.
LOVELY.

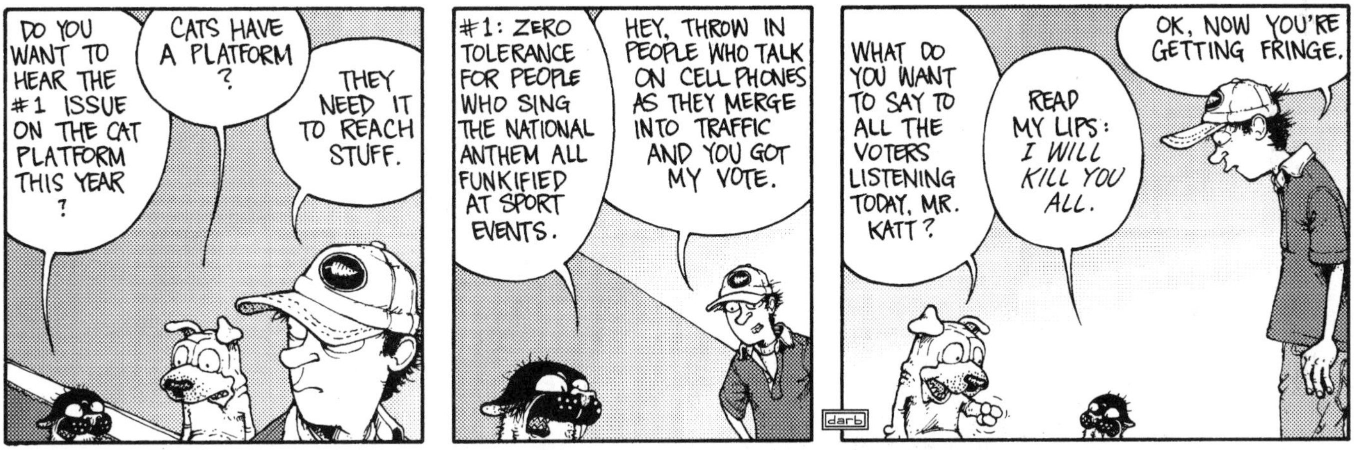
DO YOU WANT TO HEAR THE #1 ISSUE ON THE CAT PLATFORM THIS YEAR ?
CATS HAVE A PLATFORM ?
THEY NEED IT TO REACH STUFF.
#1: ZERO TOLERANCE FOR PEOPLE WHO SING THE NATIONAL ANTHEM ALL FUNKIFIED AT SPORT EVENTS.
HEY, THROW IN PEOPLE WHO TALK ON CELL PHONES AS THEY MERGE INTO TRAFFIC AND YOU GOT MY VOTE.
darb
WHAT DO YOU WANT TO SAY TO ALL THE VOTERS LISTENING TODAY, MR. KATT ?
READ MY LIPS: *I WILL KILL YOU ALL.*
OK, NOW YOU'RE GETTING FRINGE.

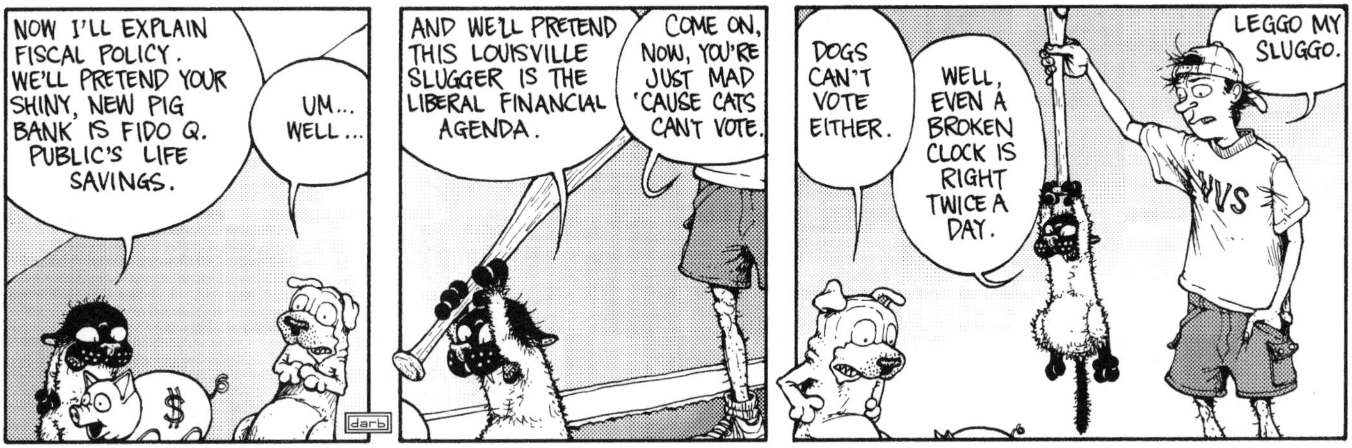
NOW I'LL EXPLAIN FISCAL POLICY. WE'LL PRETEND YOUR SHINY, NEW PIG BANK IS FIDO Q. PUBLIC'S LIFE SAVINGS.
UM... WELL...
darb
AND WE'LL PRETEND THIS LOUISVILLE SLUGGER IS THE LIBERAL FINANCIAL AGENDA.
COME ON, NOW, YOU'RE JUST MAD 'CAUSE CATS CAN'T VOTE.
DOGS CAN'T VOTE EITHER.
WELL, EVEN A BROKEN CLOCK IS RIGHT TWICE A DAY.
LEGGO MY SLUGGO.

AHHH! I LOVE LAZY SUNDAYS! A GOOD NIGHT'S SLEEP, THE SUN IS SHINING, I'M UP FOR ANYTHING!
REALLY? I HAVE A FUN IDEA.
PUT THIS SHIRT ON AND STAND OVER THERE.
WHAT IS THIS?
I'LL BE RIGHT BACK. I HAVE TO GO GET SOMETHING.
100
75
50
5 MINUTES LATER...
YOU'RE GETTING ME IN THE FACE!
I'M CALIBRATING THE SIGHT! HOLD STILL!
La Super Doucher!
... AND 5 MINUTES AFTER THAT...
I QUIT! THIS ISN'T FUN AT ALL!
DID YOU THINK I MEANT FUN FOR **YOU**? WOOPS.
darb

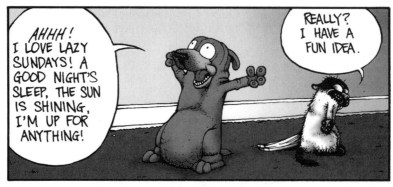

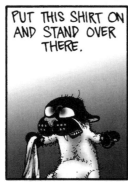

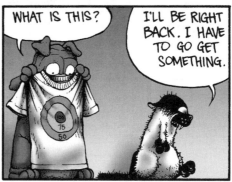

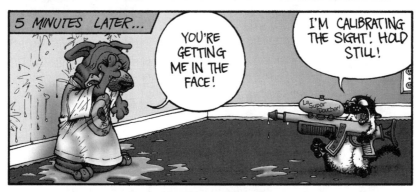

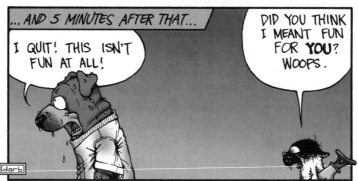

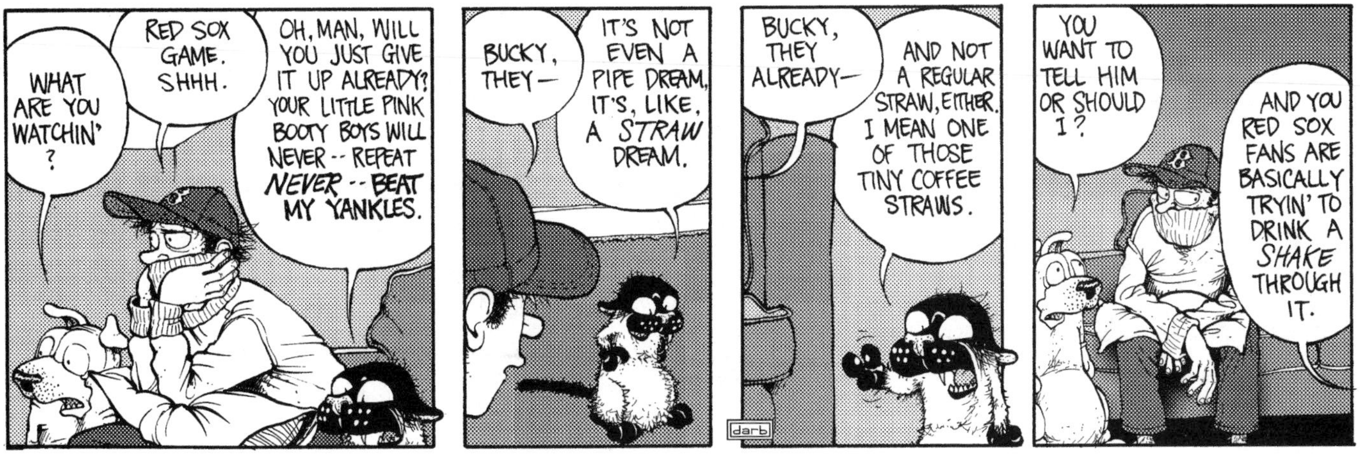
WHAT ARE YOU WATCHIN' ?
RED SOX GAME. SHHH.
OH, MAN, WILL YOU JUST GIVE IT UP ALREADY? YOUR LITTLE PINK BOOTY BOYS WILL NEVER -- REPEAT *NEVER* -- BEAT MY YANKLES.
BUCKY, THEY—
IT'S NOT EVEN A PIPE DREAM, IT'S, LIKE, A *STRAW* DREAM.
BUCKY, THEY ALREADY—
AND NOT A REGULAR STRAW, EITHER. I MEAN ONE OF THOSE TINY COFFEE STRAWS.
YOU WANT TO TELL HIM OR SHOULD I ?
AND YOU RED SOX FANS ARE BASICALLY TRYIN' TO DRINK A *SHAKE* THROUGH IT.
darb

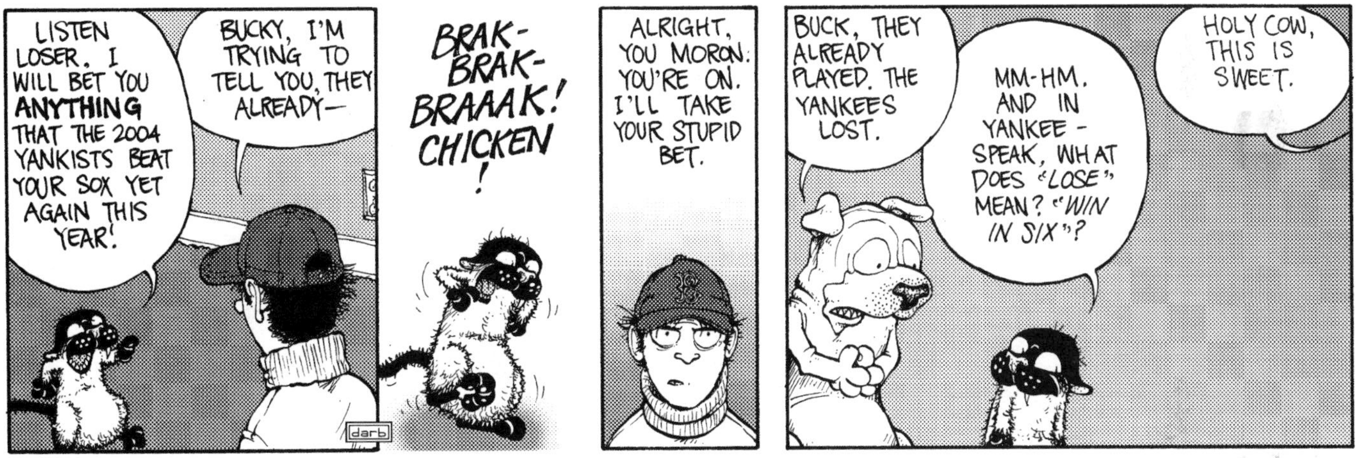
LISTEN LOSER. I WILL BET YOU **ANYTHING** THAT THE 2004 YANKISTS BEAT YOUR SOX YET AGAIN THIS YEAR!
BUCKY, I'M TRYING TO TELL YOU, THEY ALREADY—
darb
BRAK-BRAK-BRAAAK! CHICKEN!
ALRIGHT, YOU MORON: YOU'RE ON. I'LL TAKE YOUR STUPID BET.
BUCK, THEY ALREADY PLAYED. THE YANKEES LOST.
MM-HM. AND IN YANKEE-SPEAK, WHAT DOES "*LOSE*" MEAN? "*WIN IN SIX*"?
HOLY COW, THIS IS SWEET.

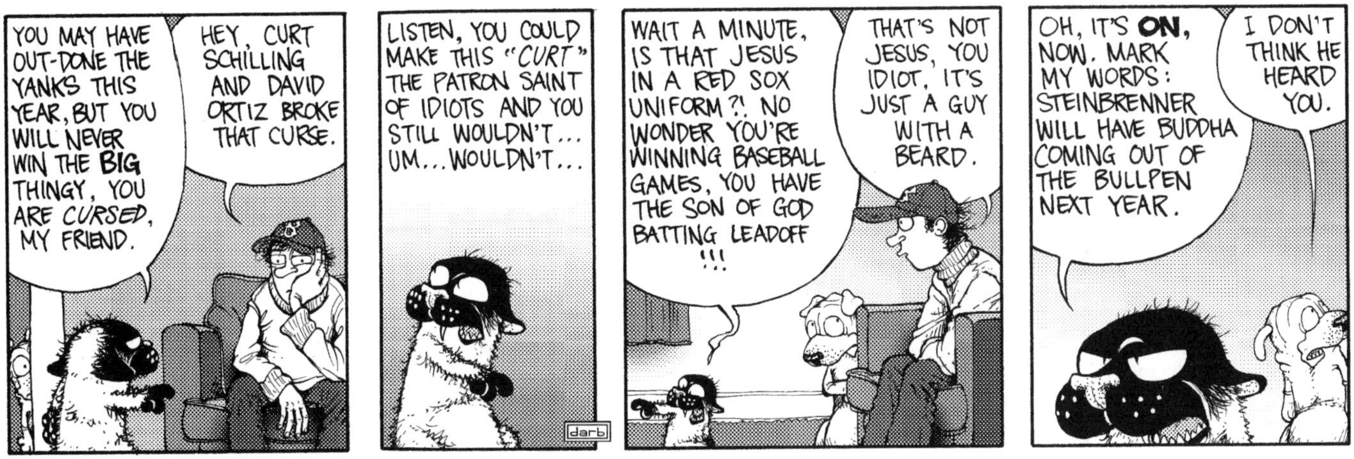
YOU MAY HAVE OUT-DONE THE YANKS THIS YEAR, BUT YOU WILL NEVER WIN THE **BIG** THINGY. YOU ARE *CURSED*, MY FRIEND.
HEY, CURT SCHILLING AND DAVID ORTIZ BROKE THAT CURSE.
LISTEN, YOU COULD MAKE THIS "*CURT*" THE PATRON SAINT OF IDIOTS AND YOU STILL WOULDN'T... UM... WOULDN'T...
darb
WAIT A MINUTE, IS THAT JESUS IN A RED SOX UNIFORM?! NO WONDER YOU'RE WINNING BASEBALL GAMES, YOU HAVE THE SON OF GOD BATTING LEADOFF !!!
THAT'S NOT JESUS, YOU IDIOT, IT'S JUST A GUY WITH A BEARD.
OH, IT'S **ON**, NOW. MARK MY WORDS: STEINBRENNER WILL HAVE BUDDHA COMING OUT OF THE BULLPEN NEXT YEAR.
I DON'T THINK HE HEARD YOU.

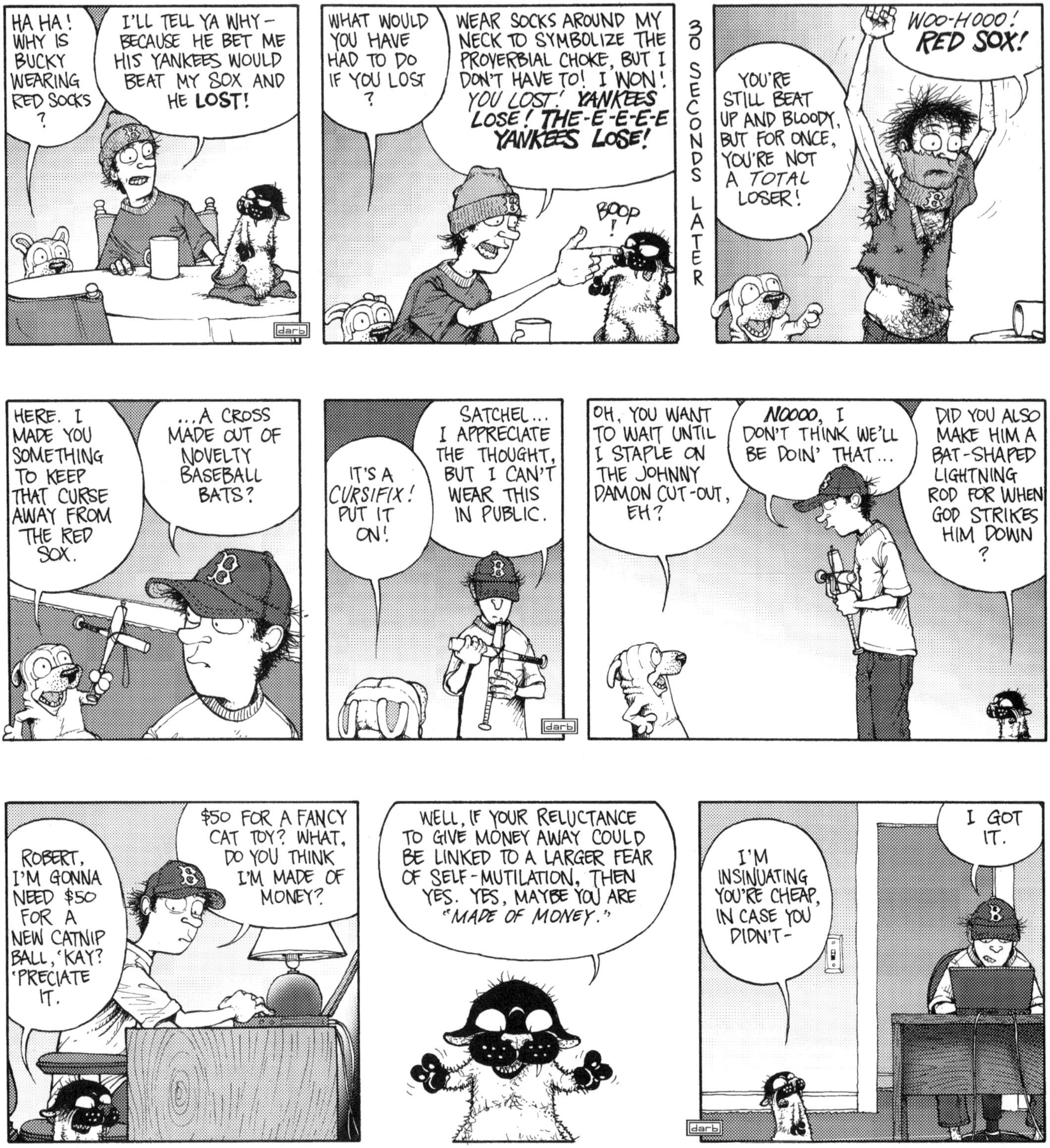
HA HA! WHY IS BUCKY WEARING RED SOCKS?
I'LL TELL YA WHY - BECAUSE HE BET ME HIS YANKEES WOULD BEAT MY SOX AND HE LOST!
WHAT WOULD YOU HAVE HAD TO DO IF YOU LOST?
WEAR SOCKS AROUND MY NECK TO SYMBOLIZE THE PROVERBIAL CHOKE, BUT I DON'T HAVE TO! I WON! YOU LOST! YANKEES LOSE! THE-E-E-E-E YANKEES LOSE!
BOOP!
30 SECONDS LATER
WOO-HOOO! RED SOX!
YOU'RE STILL BEAT UP AND BLOODY, BUT FOR ONCE, YOU'RE NOT A TOTAL LOSER!
darb
HERE. I MADE YOU SOMETHING TO KEEP THAT CURSE AWAY FROM THE RED SOX.
...A CROSS MADE OUT OF NOVELTY BASEBALL BATS?
IT'S A CURSIFIX! PUT IT ON!
SATCHEL... I APPRECIATE THE THOUGHT, BUT I CAN'T WEAR THIS IN PUBLIC.
OH, YOU WANT TO WAIT UNTIL I STAPLE ON THE JOHNNY DAMON CUT-OUT, EH?
NOOOO, I DON'T THINK WE'LL BE DOIN' THAT...
DID YOU ALSO MAKE HIM A BAT-SHAPED LIGHTNING ROD FOR WHEN GOD STRIKES HIM DOWN?
darb
ROBERT, I'M GONNA NEED $50 FOR A NEW CATNIP BALL, 'KAY? 'PRECIATE IT.
$50 FOR A FANCY CAT TOY? WHAT, DO YOU THINK I'M MADE OF MONEY?
WELL, IF YOUR RELUCTANCE TO GIVE MONEY AWAY COULD BE LINKED TO A LARGER FEAR OF SELF-MUTILATION, THEN YES. YES, MAYBE YOU ARE "MADE OF MONEY."
I'M INSINUATING YOU'RE CHEAP, IN CASE YOU DIDN'T-
I GOT IT.
darb

SITTING HERE WATCHING THE BIRDS SOAR THROUGH THE SKY SO MAJESTICALLY, I CAN'T HELP BUT BE INSPIRED...
SURELY A MACHINE COULD BE DEVISED THAT MIGHT HELP US ATTAIN EQUALITY WITH THE BIRDS.
WE ALREADY HAVE AIRPLANES, BUCKY.
NO, NO, I'M TALKIN' **SMALLER.** SOMETHING THAT COULD PROPEL LITTLE THINGS INTO THE SKY!
darb
SOMETHING THAT WOULD CATAPULT YOU INTO THE AIR?
NO! SMALLER STUFF!
MM-HM. I THINK YOU MIGHT BE DESCRIBING A GUN.
YES, EXACTLY! A **GUN** WOULD BRING THOSE ARROGANT BIRDS DOWN TO THE GROUND WITH US!

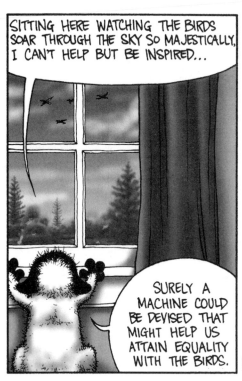

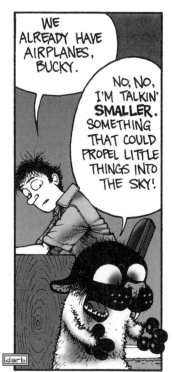

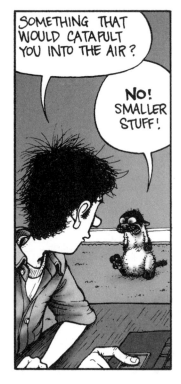

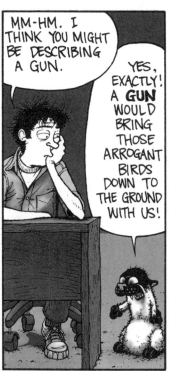

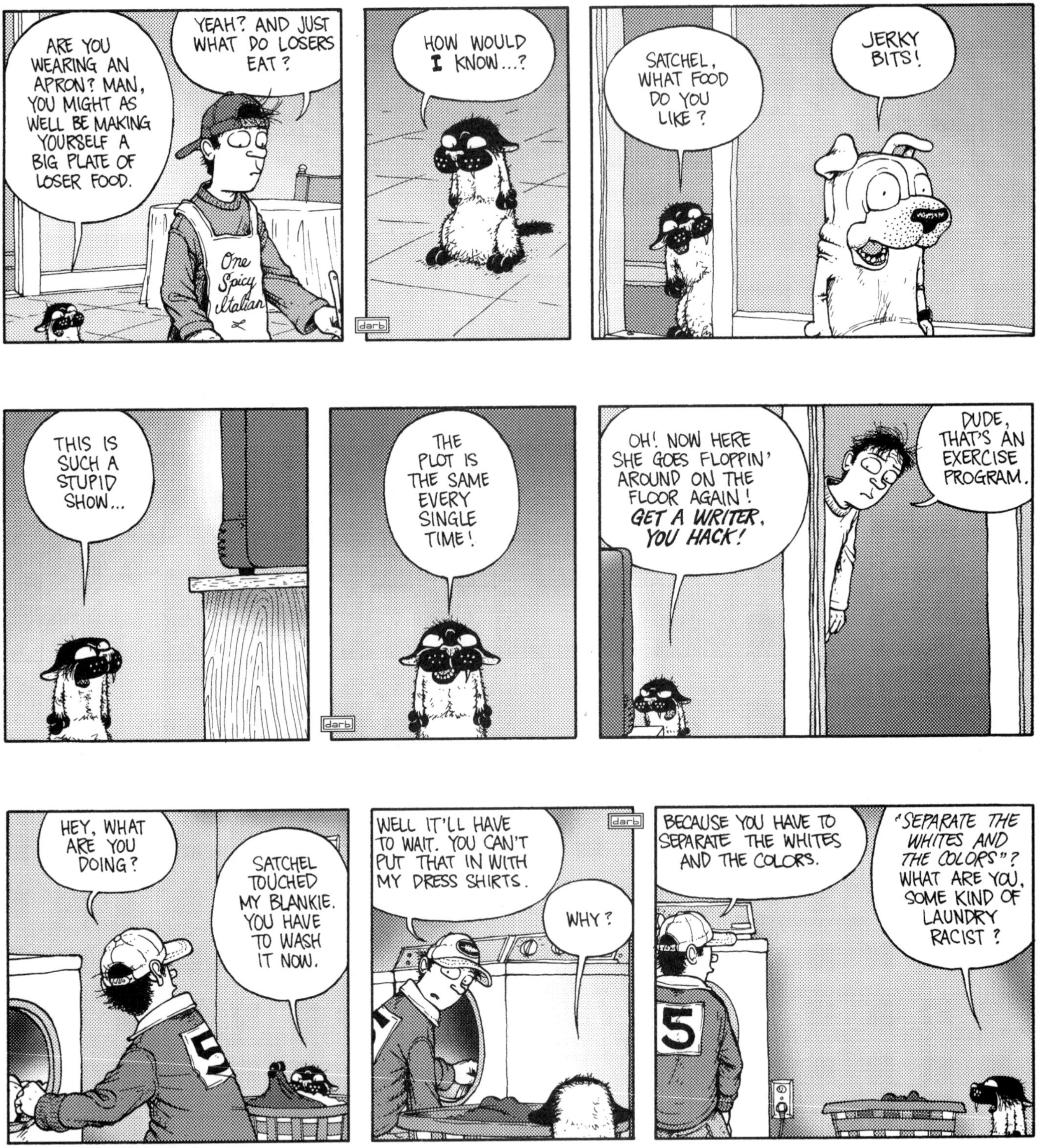
ARE YOU WEARING AN APRON? MAN, YOU MIGHT AS WELL BE MAKING YOURSELF A BIG PLATE OF LOSER FOOD.
YEAH? AND JUST WHAT DO LOSERS EAT?
One Spicy Italian
HOW WOULD I KNOW...?
darb
SATCHEL, WHAT FOOD DO YOU LIKE?
JERKY BITS!
THIS IS SUCH A STUPID SHOW...
THE PLOT IS THE SAME EVERY SINGLE TIME!
darb
OH! NOW HERE SHE GOES FLOPPIN' AROUND ON THE FLOOR AGAIN! GET A WRITER, YOU HACK!
DUDE, THAT'S AN EXERCISE PROGRAM.
HEY, WHAT ARE YOU DOING?
SATCHEL TOUCHED MY BLANKIE. YOU HAVE TO WASH IT NOW.
WELL IT'LL HAVE TO WAIT. YOU CAN'T PUT THAT IN WITH MY DRESS SHIRTS.
darb
WHY?
BECAUSE YOU HAVE TO SEPARATE THE WHITES AND THE COLORS.
"SEPARATE THE WHITES AND THE COLORS"? WHAT ARE YOU, SOME KIND OF LAUNDRY RACIST?

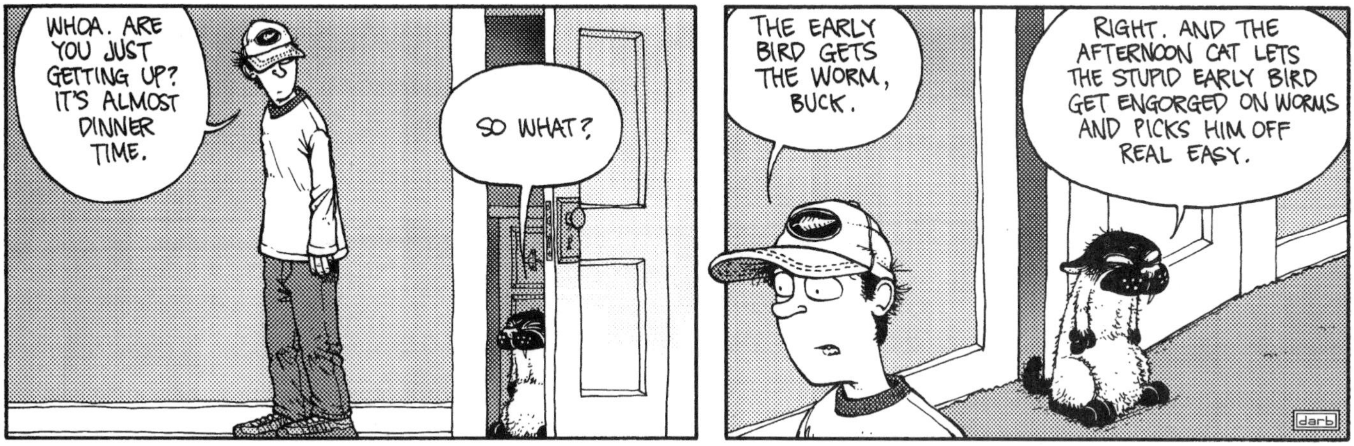
WHOA. ARE YOU JUST GETTING UP? IT'S ALMOST DINNER TIME.
SO WHAT?
THE EARLY BIRD GETS THE WORM, BUCK.
RIGHT. AND THE AFTERNOON CAT LETS THE STUPID EARLY BIRD GET ENGORGED ON WORMS AND PICKS HIM OFF REAL EASY.
darb

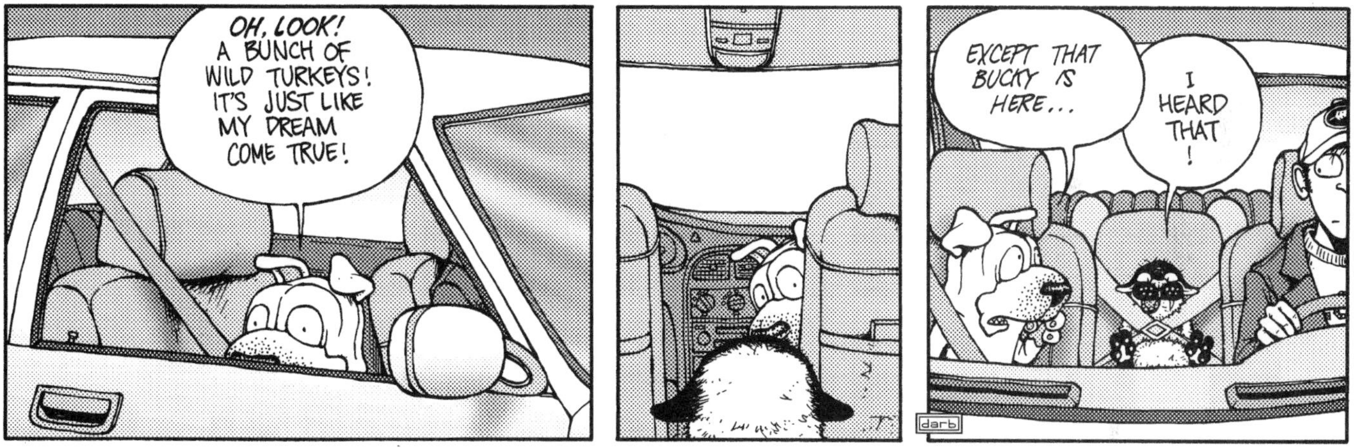
OH, LOOK! A BUNCH OF WILD TURKEYS! IT'S JUST LIKE MY DREAM COME TRUE!
EXCEPT THAT BUCKY IS HERE...
I HEARD THAT!
darb

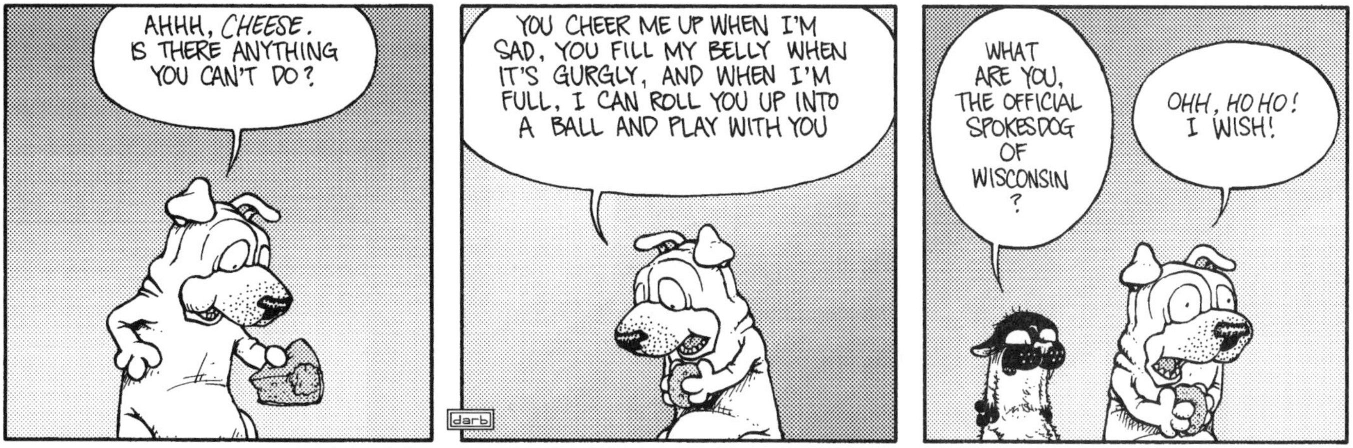
AHHH, CHEESE. IS THERE ANYTHING YOU CAN'T DO?
YOU CHEER ME UP WHEN I'M SAD, YOU FILL MY BELLY WHEN IT'S GURGLY, AND WHEN I'M FULL, I CAN ROLL YOU UP INTO A BALL AND PLAY WITH YOU
WHAT ARE YOU, THE OFFICIAL SPOKESDOG OF WISCONSIN?
OHH, HO HO! I WISH!
darb

WHY? WHY WOULD BUCKY JUST BITE ME LIKE THAT ?
OH, LET'S SEE... BECAUSE CATS ARE EVIL?
CATS ARE NOT EVIL, ROBERT.
WELL NOT AS A GROUP, NO. CATS DON'T WORK WELL ENOUGH WITH EACH OTHER TO COORDINATE IT.
THE NOTION THAT CATS ARE EVIL IS A MYTH PROPAGATED BY THE MEDIA, MANY OF WHOM HAVE AN AGENDA.
THAT WOULD BE THE LESSER KNOWN LITERAL MEDIA.
SO WHY DID YOU BITE ME?
I'M GLAD YOU ASKED ME THAT, SATCHEL...
...THING IS THAT IN THE DIM LIGHT, IT LOOKED LIKE YOU WERE ATTACKING ME...
DUDE, IT'S NOON.
AND YOU CAN SEE IN THE DARK! YOU'RE ALWAYS BRAGGING ABOUT IT!
SCHILLING
38
darb
HAVE YOU NO SHAME, BUCKY?
I PICK UP A LOT OF STUFF ON THE STREET, MAYBE I DO. DESCRIBE IT.

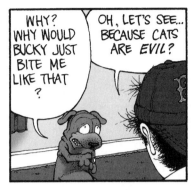

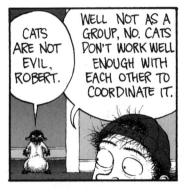

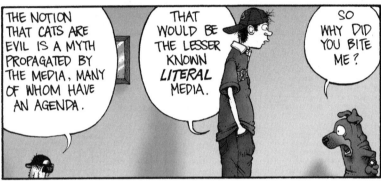

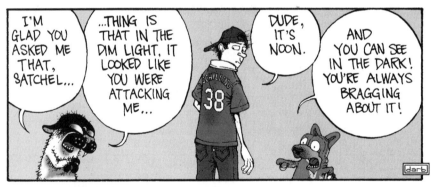

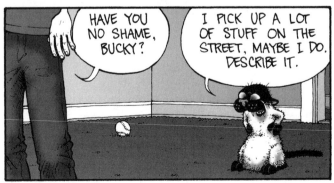

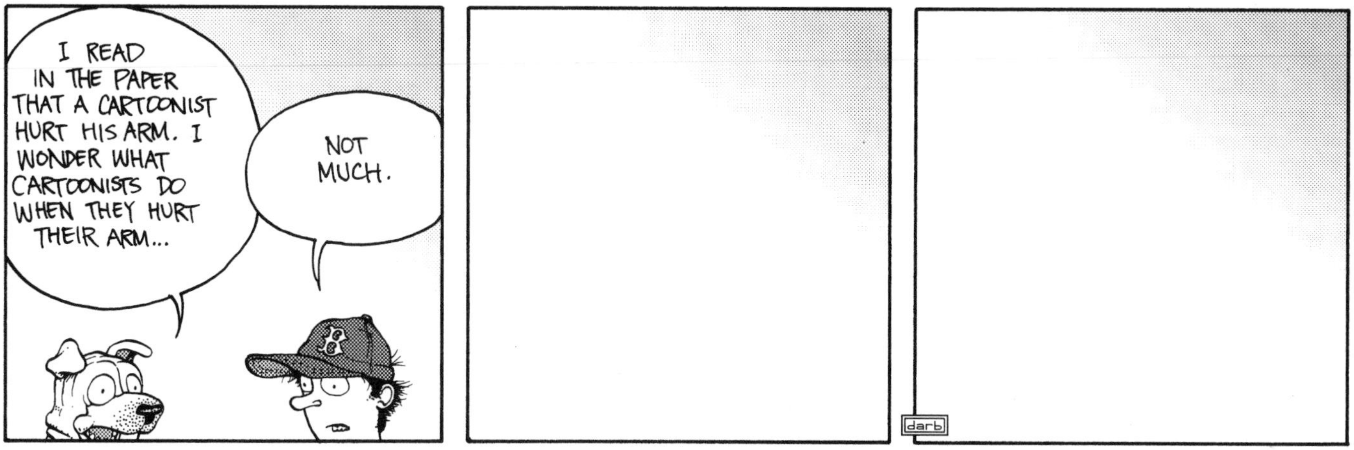
I READ IN THE PAPER THAT A CARTOONIST HURT HIS ARM. I WONDER WHAT CARTOONISTS DO WHEN THEY HURT THEIR ARM...
NOT MUCH.
darb

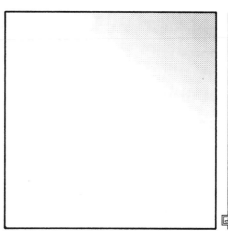

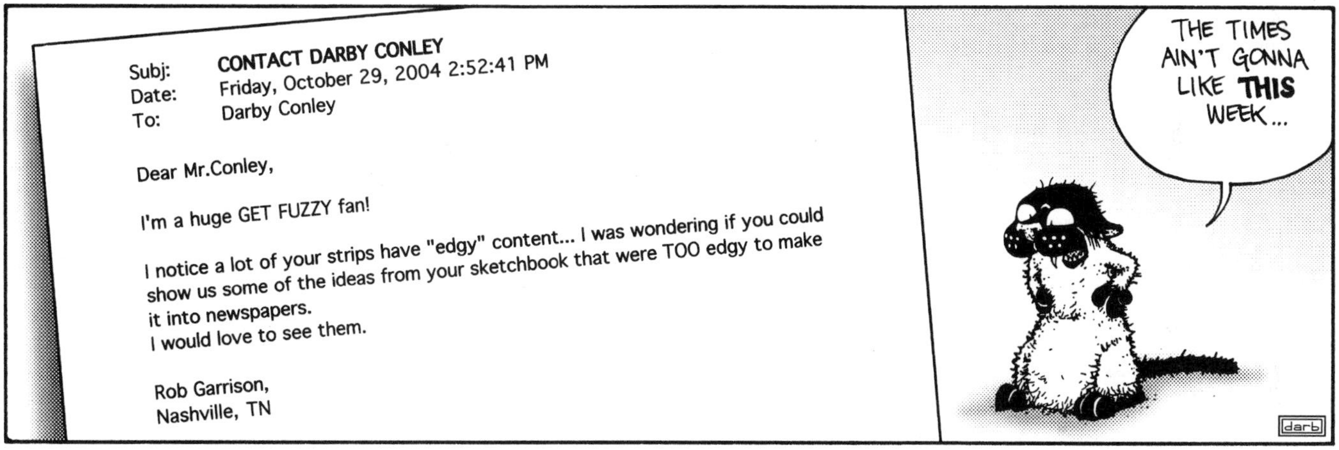
Subj: CONTACT DARBY CONLEY
Date: Friday, October 29, 2004 2:52:41 PM
To: Darby Conley
Dear Mr.Conley,
I'm a huge GET FUZZY fan!
I notice a lot of your strips have "edgy" content... I was wondering if you could show us some of the ideas from your sketchbook that were TOO edgy to make it into newspapers.
I would love to see them.
Rob Garrison,
Nashville, TN
THE TIMES AIN'T GONNA LIKE **THIS** WEEK...
darb

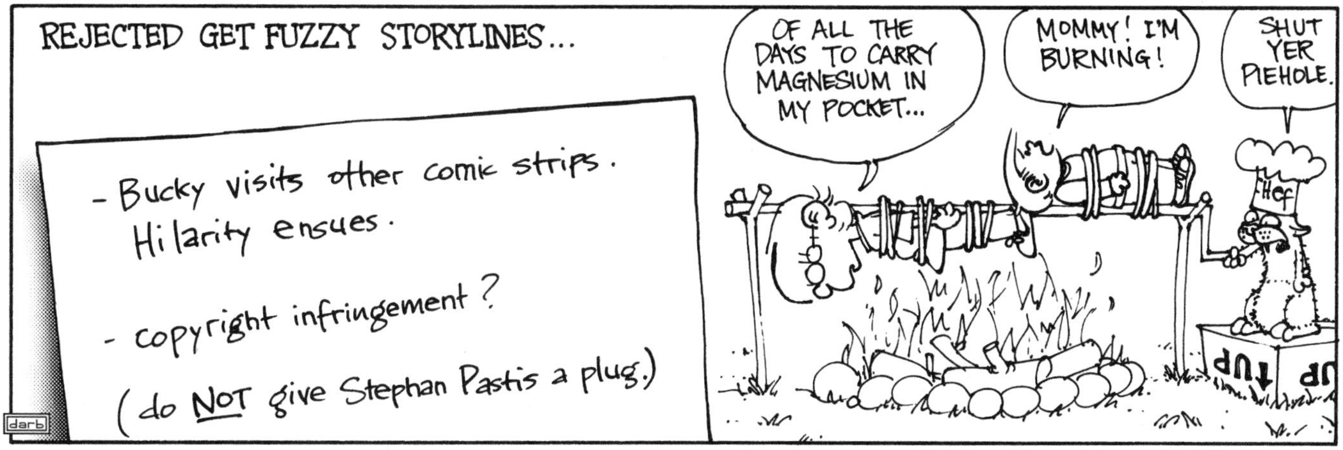
REJECTED GET FUZZY STORYLINES...
- Bucky visits other comic strips. Hilarity ensues.
- copyright infringement?
(do NOT give Stephan Pastis a plug.)
OF ALL THE DAYS TO CARRY MAGNESIUM IN MY POCKET...
MOMMY! I'M BURNING!
SHUT YER PIEHOLE.
Chef
UP
UP
darb

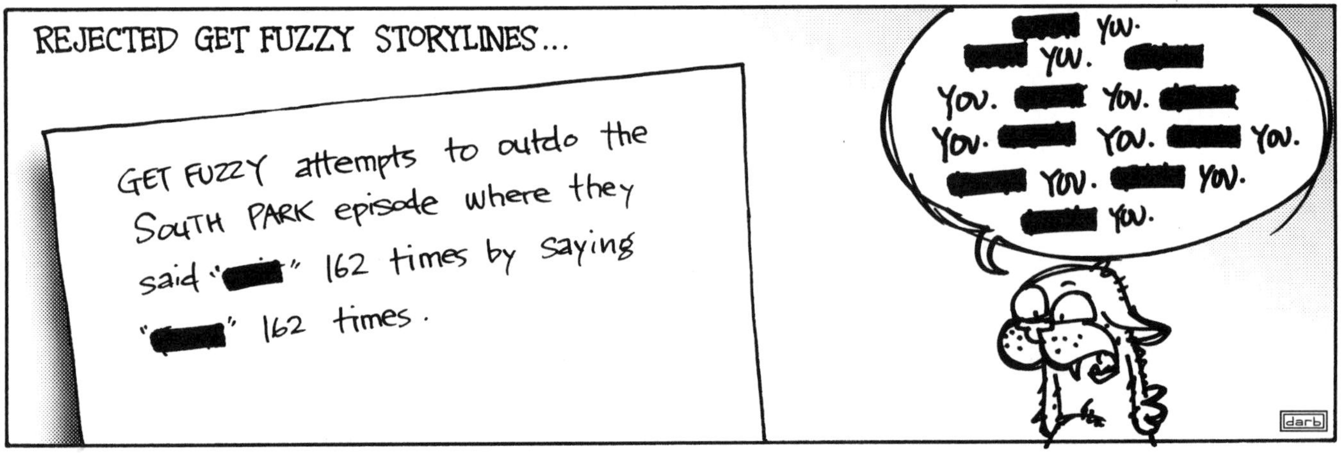
REJECTED GET FUZZY STORYLINES...
GET FUZZY attempts to outdo the SOUTH PARK episode where they said "[redacted]" 162 times by saying "[redacted]" 162 times.
[redacted] YOU.
[redacted] YOU. [redacted]
YOU. [redacted] YOU. [redacted]
YOU. [redacted] YOU. [redacted] YOU.
[redacted] YOU. [redacted] YOU.
[redacted] YOU.
darb

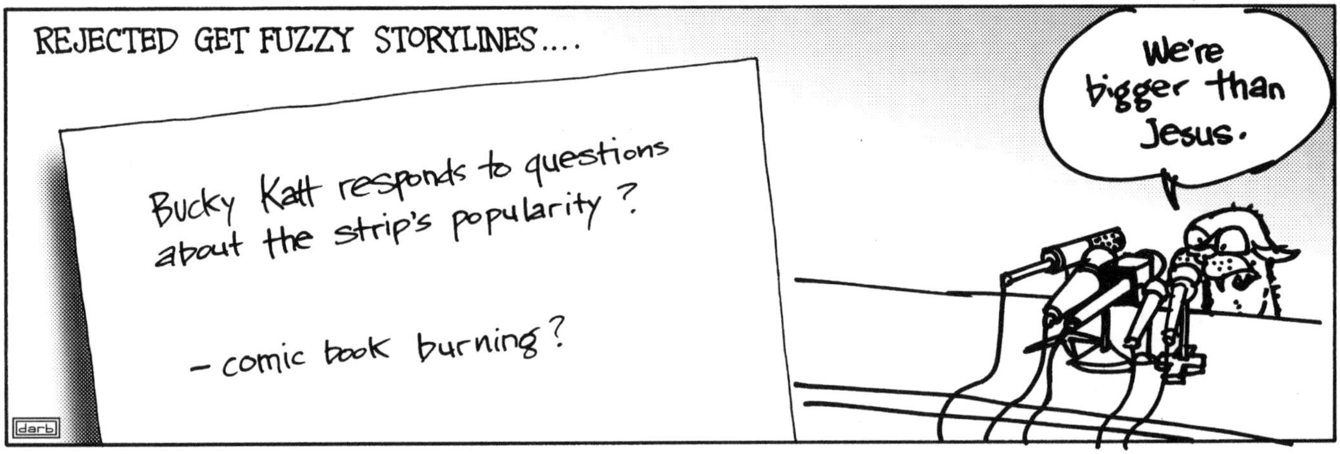
REJECTED GET FUZZY STORYLINES....
Bucky Katt responds to questions about the strip's popularity?
- comic book burning?
We're bigger than Jesus.
darb

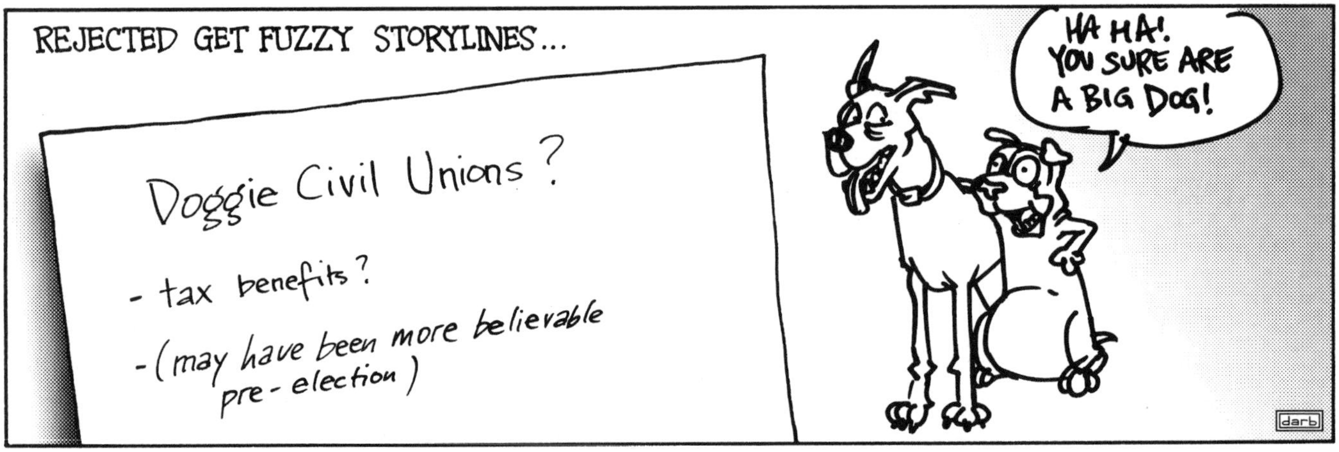
REJECTED GET FUZZY STORYLINES...
Doggie Civil Unions?
- tax benefits?
- (may have been more believable pre-election)
HA HA! YOU SURE ARE A BIG DOG!
darb

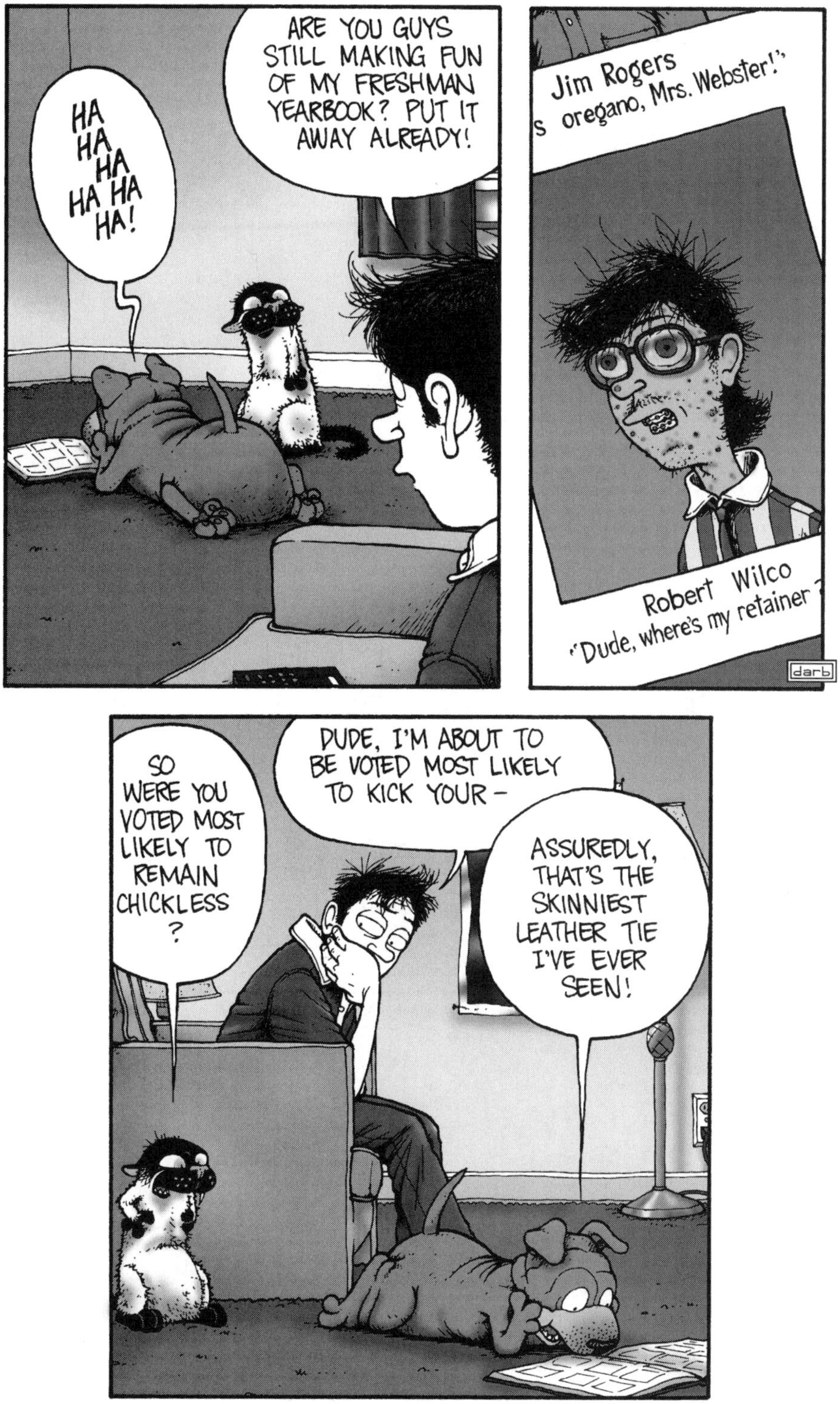
HA HA HA HA HA HA!
ARE YOU GUYS STILL MAKING FUN OF MY FRESHMAN YEARBOOK? PUT IT AWAY ALREADY!
Jim Rogers
s oregano, Mrs. Webster!"
Robert Wilco
"Dude, where's my retainer?
darb
SO WERE YOU VOTED MOST LIKELY TO REMAIN CHICKLESS?
DUDE, I'M ABOUT TO BE VOTED MOST LIKELY TO KICK YOUR–
ASSUREDLY, THAT'S THE SKINNIEST LEATHER TIE I'VE EVER SEEN!

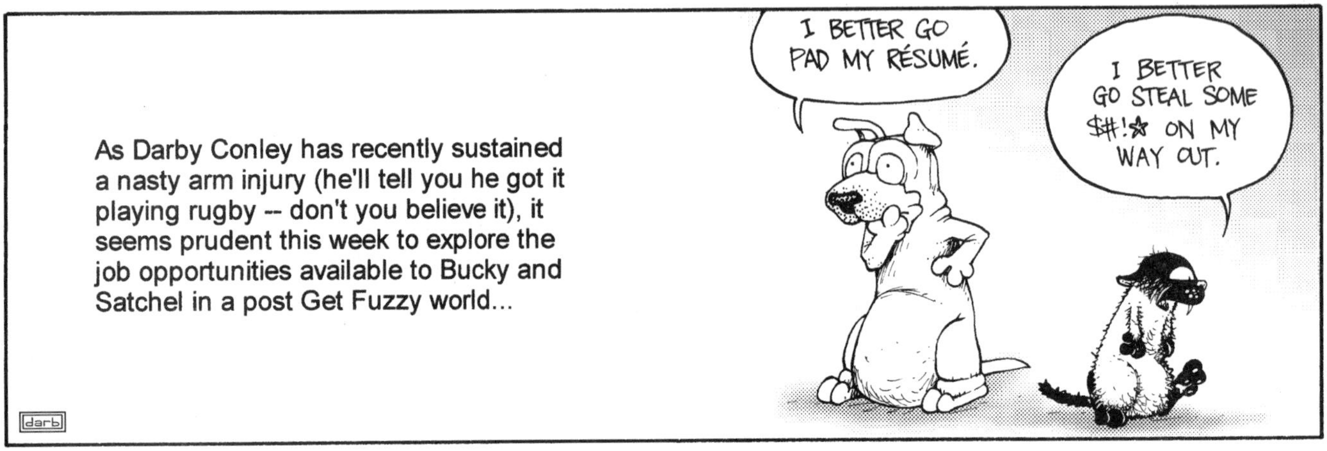
As Darby Conley has recently sustained a nasty arm injury (he'll tell you he got it playing rugby -- don't you believe it), it seems prudent this week to explore the job opportunities available to Bucky and Satchel in a post Get Fuzzy world...
I BETTER GO PAD MY RÉSUMÉ.
I BETTER GO STEAL SOME $#!☆ ON MY WAY OUT.
darb

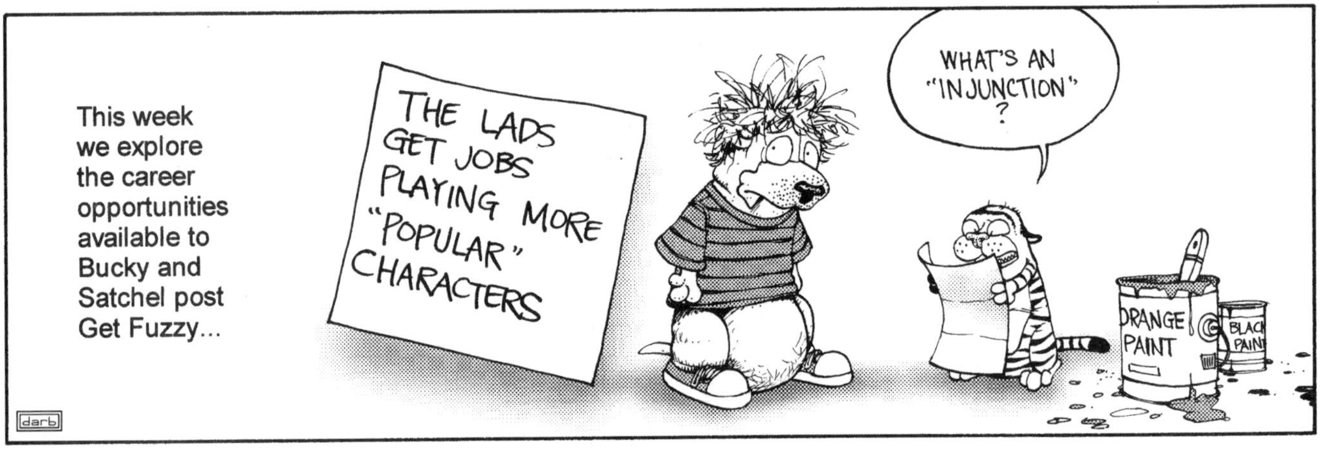
This week we explore the career opportunities available to Bucky and Satchel post Get Fuzzy...
THE LADS GET JOBS PLAYING MORE "POPULAR" CHARACTERS
WHAT'S AN "INJUNCTION"?
ORANGE PAINT
darb

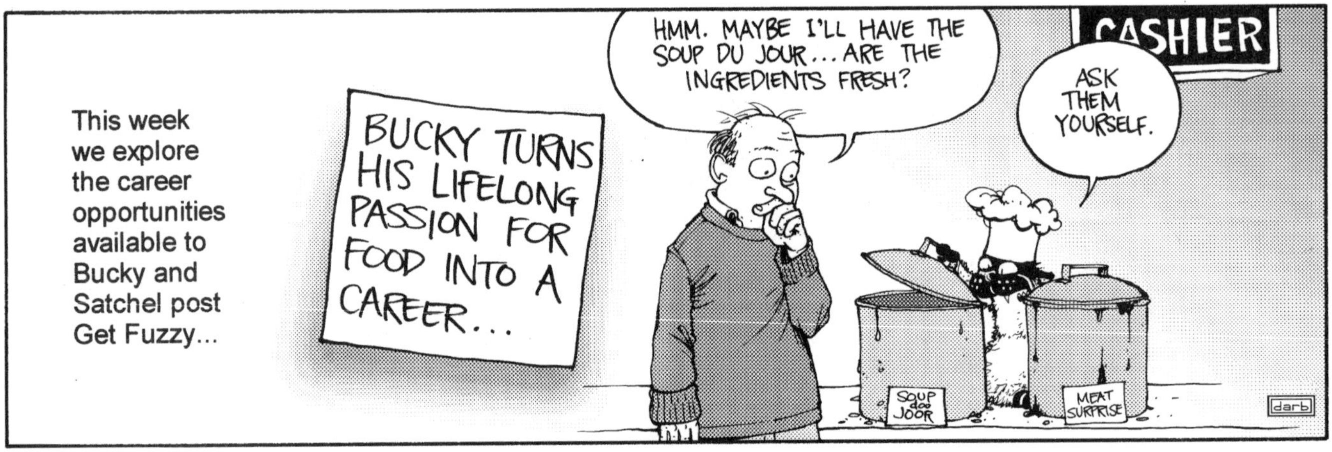
This week we explore the career opportunities available to Bucky and Satchel post Get Fuzzy...
BUCKY TURNS HIS LIFELONG PASSION FOR FOOD INTO A CAREER...
CASHIER
HMM. MAYBE I'LL HAVE THE SOUP DU JOUR... ARE THE INGREDIENTS FRESH?
ASK THEM YOURSELF.
SOUP doo JOOR
MEAT SURPRISE
darb

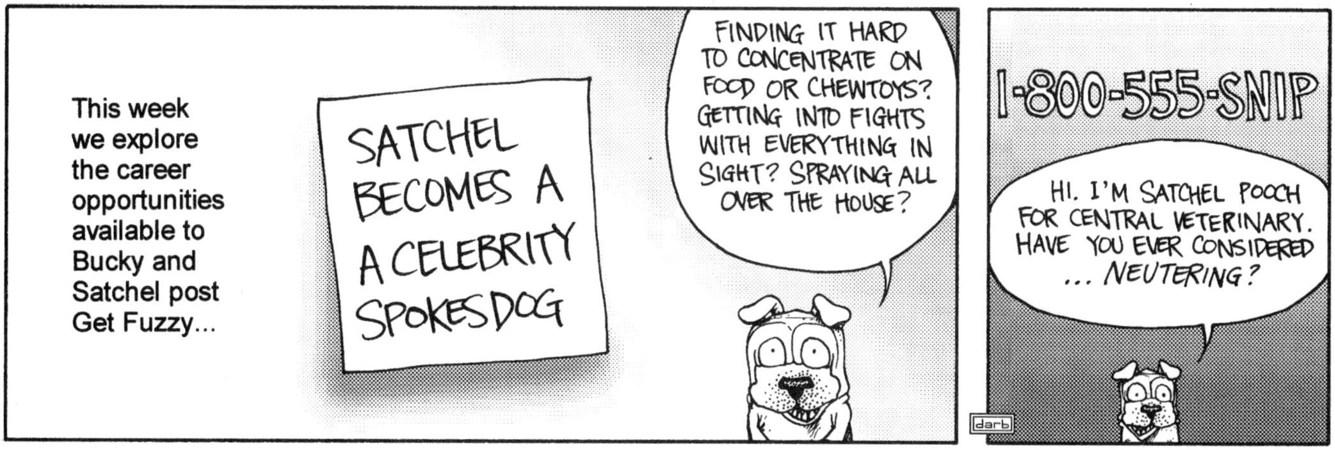
This week we explore the career opportunities available to Bucky and Satchel post Get Fuzzy...
SATCHEL BECOMES A A CELEBRITY SPOKESDOG
FINDING IT HARD TO CONCENTRATE ON FOOD OR CHEWTOYS? GETTING INTO FIGHTS WITH EVERYTHING IN SIGHT? SPRAYING ALL OVER THE HOUSE?
1-800-555-SNIP
HI. I'M SATCHEL POOCH FOR CENTRAL VETERINARY. HAVE YOU EVER CONSIDERED ... NEUTERING?
darb

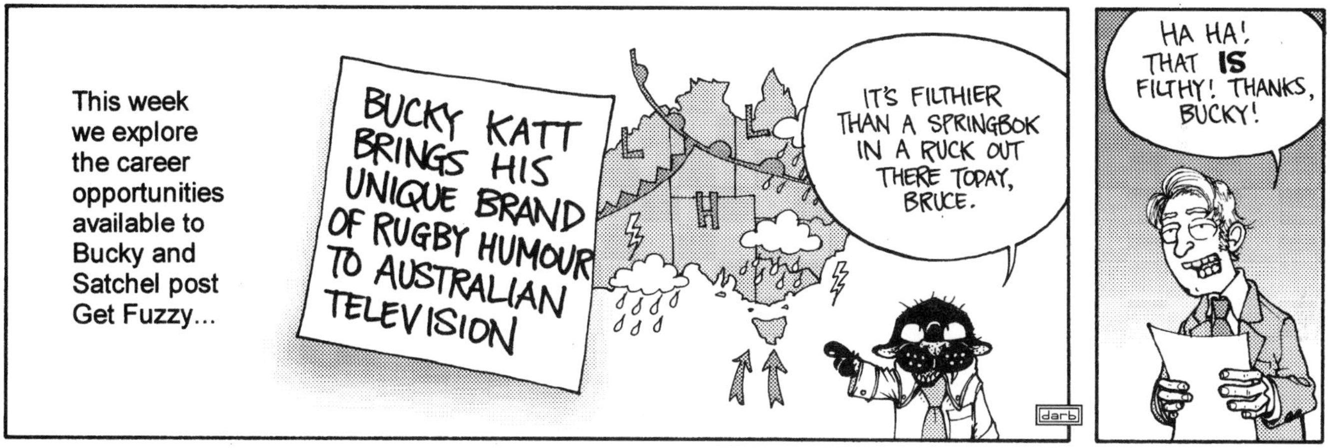
This week we explore the career opportunities available to Bucky and Satchel post Get Fuzzy...
BUCKY KATT BRINGS HIS UNIQUE BRAND OF RUGBY HUMOUR TO AUSTRALIAN TELEVISION
IT'S FILTHIER THAN A SPRINGBOK IN A RUCK OUT THERE TODAY, BRUCE.
HA HA! THAT IS FILTHY! THANKS, BUCKY!
darb

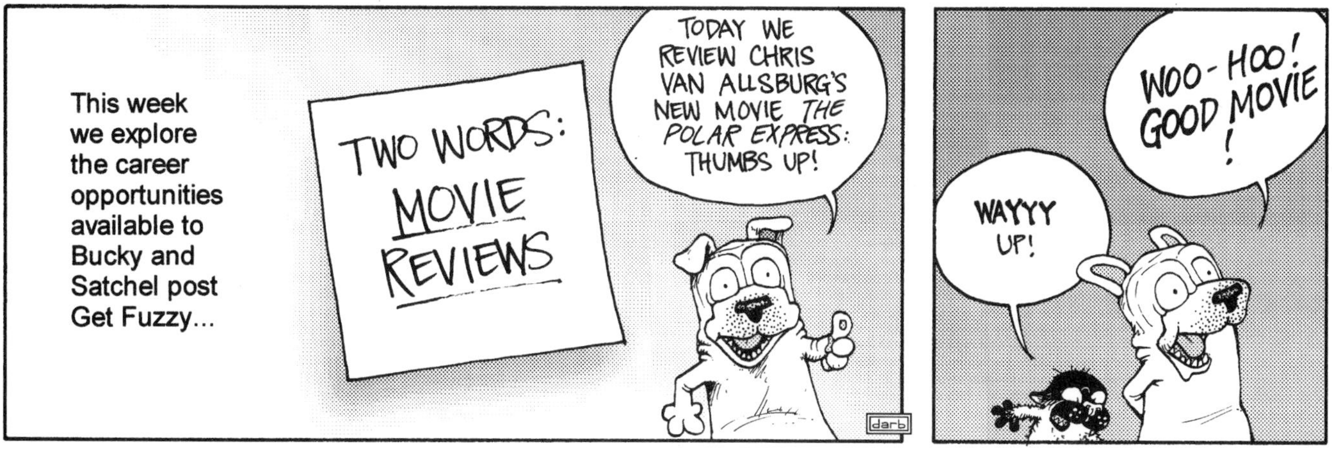
This week we explore the career opportunities available to Bucky and Satchel post Get Fuzzy...
TWO WORDS: MOVIE REVIEWS
TODAY WE REVIEW CHRIS VAN ALLSBURG'S NEW MOVIE THE POLAR EXPRESS: THUMBS UP!
WAYYY UP!
WOO-HOO! GOOD MOVIE!
darb

WHAT ARE WE DOING WITH OURSELVES, SATCHEL?
WE'RE EATING TOAST!
NO, NO, I MEAN IN LIFE. WE'RE NOT CONTRIBUTING ANYTHING! WE'RE JUST TAKING UP SPACE!
YOU HAVE TO FIGHT FOR SOMETHING... FORESTS... STEEL TRAP HUNTING... ALTERNATIVE ENERGY...
darb
I LIKE TOAST... I COULD DO SOMETHING FOR TOAST...
SATCHEL...
OF COURSE, I ALSO RIP IT TO SHREDS WITH MY TEETH. SO...
HEY, I JUST FOUND A BIRD NEST! WANNA KNOCK IT OUT OF THE TREE AND EAT THE EGGS?

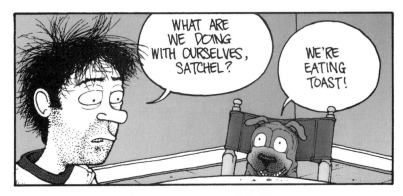

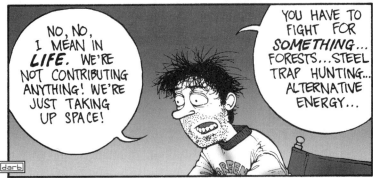

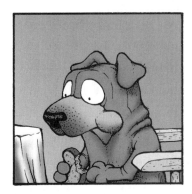

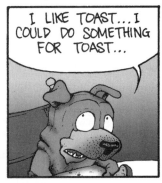

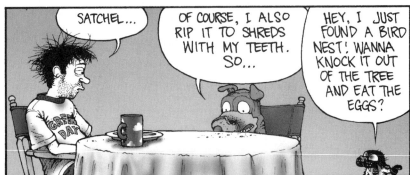

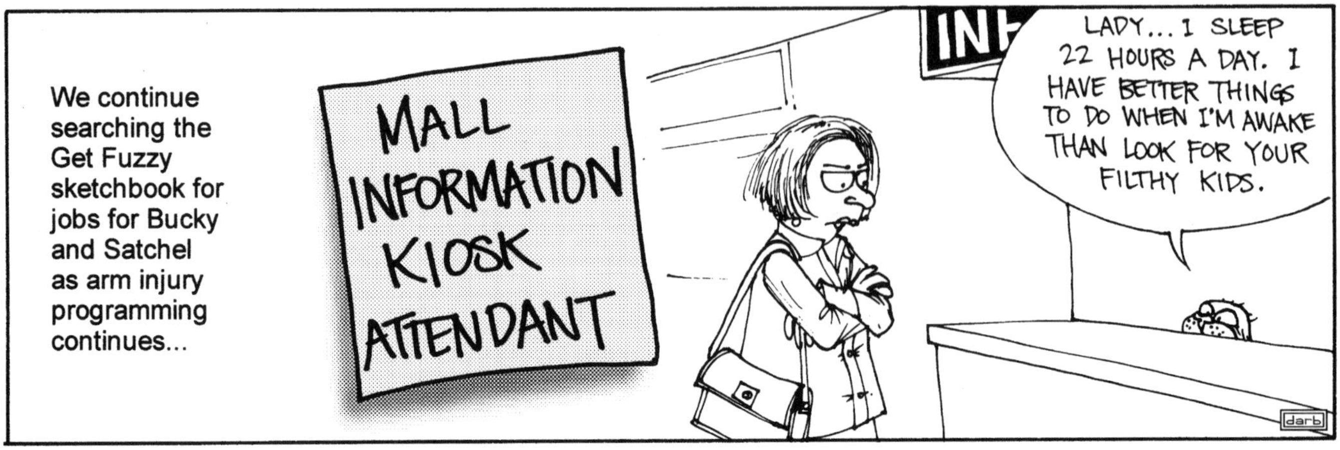
We continue searching the Get Fuzzy sketchbook for jobs for Bucky and Satchel as arm injury programming continues...
MALL INFORMATION KIOSK ATTENDANT
LADY... I SLEEP 22 HOURS A DAY. I HAVE BETTER THINGS TO DO WHEN I'M AWAKE THAN LOOK FOR YOUR FILTHY KIDS.

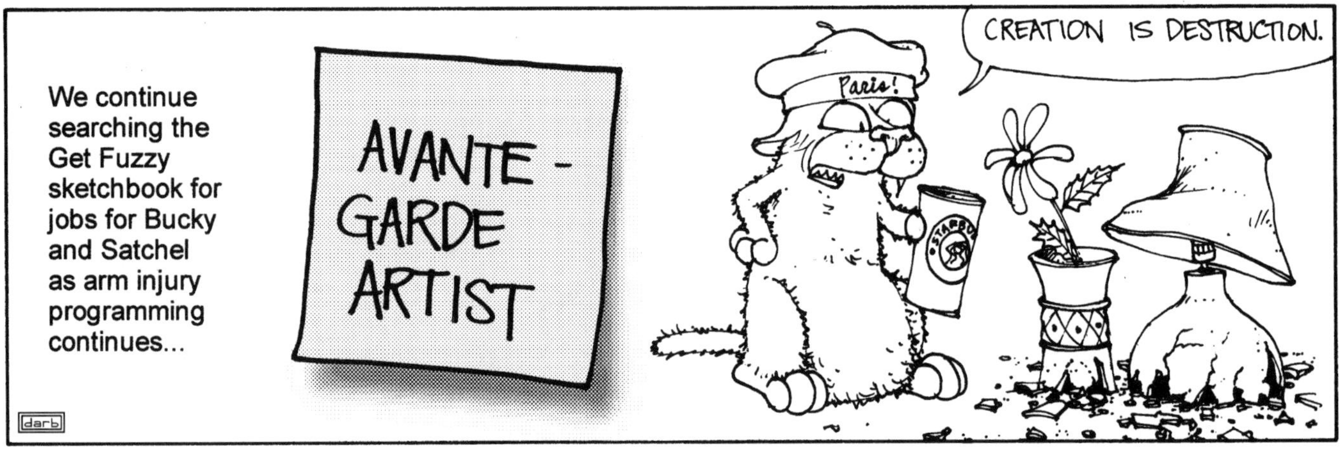
We continue searching the Get Fuzzy sketchbook for jobs for Bucky and Satchel as arm injury programming continues...
AVANTE-GARDE ARTIST
CREATION IS DESTRUCTION.
Paris!

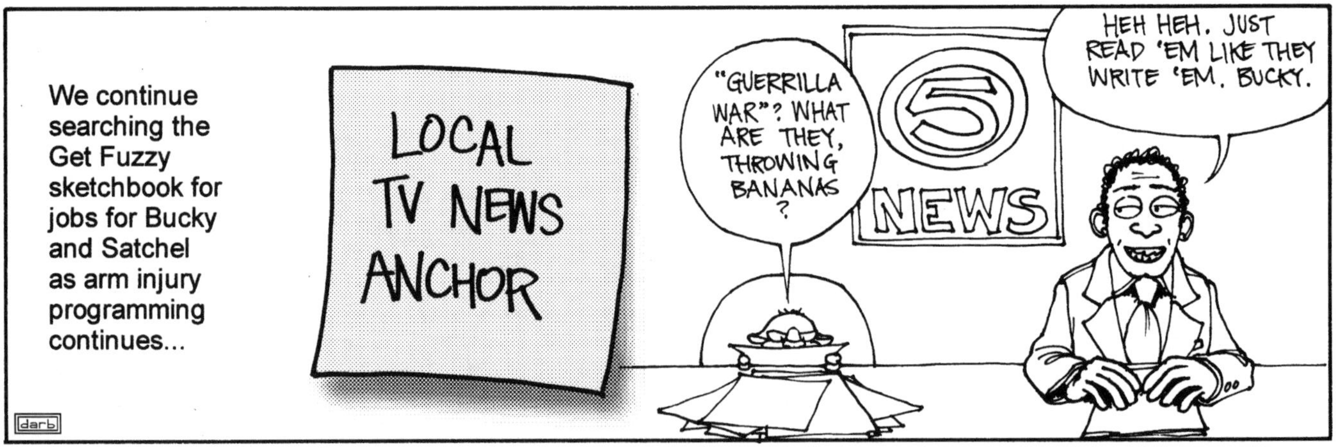
We continue searching the Get Fuzzy sketchbook for jobs for Bucky and Satchel as arm injury programming continues...
LOCAL TV NEWS ANCHOR
"GUERRILLA WAR"? WHAT ARE THEY, THROWING BANANAS?
HEH HEH. JUST READ 'EM LIKE THEY WRITE 'EM, BUCKY.
5
NEWS

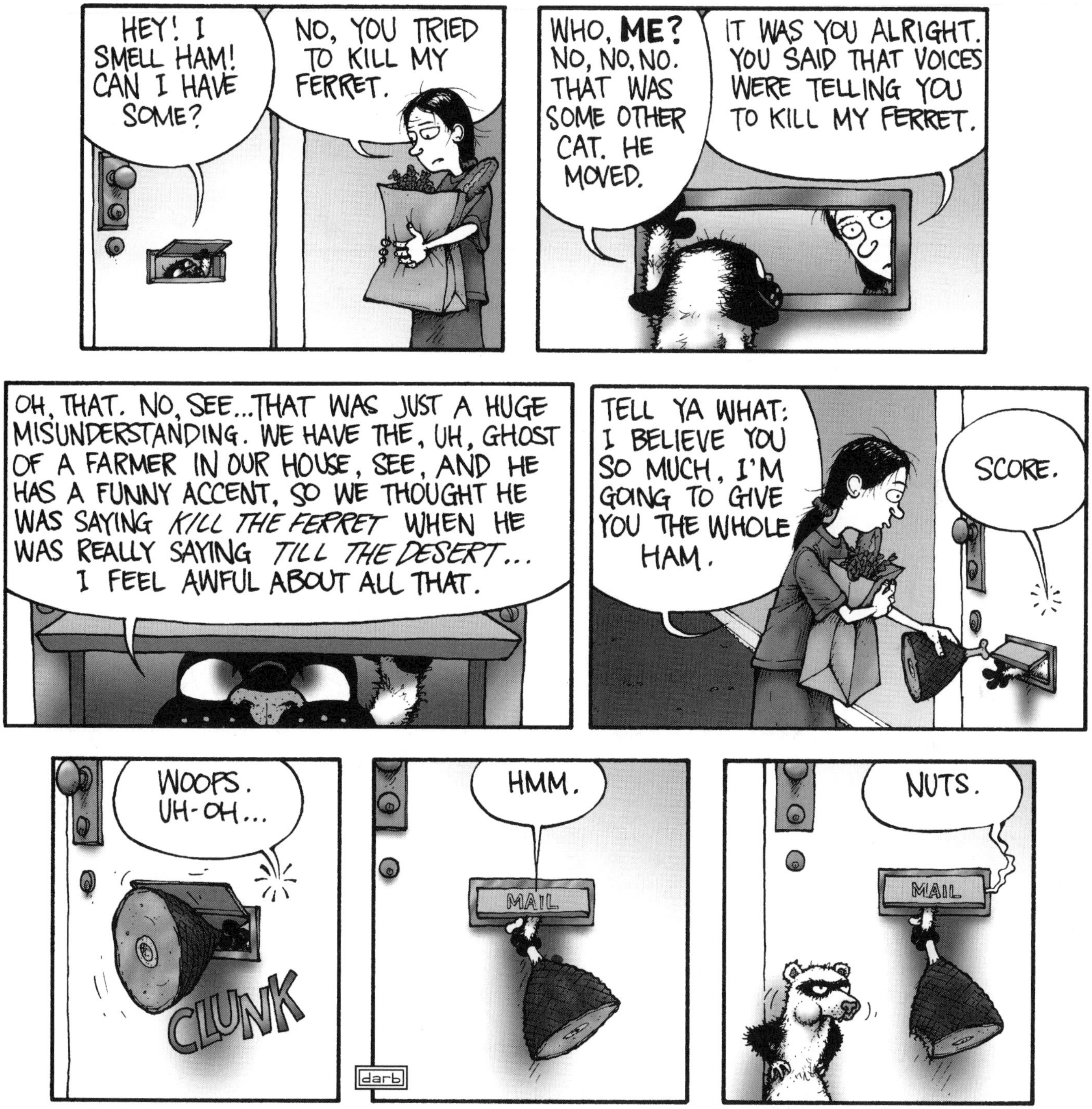
HEY! I SMELL HAM! CAN I HAVE SOME?
NO, YOU TRIED TO KILL MY FERRET.
WHO, **ME?** NO, NO, NO. THAT WAS SOME OTHER CAT. HE MOVED.
IT WAS YOU ALRIGHT. YOU SAID THAT VOICES WERE TELLING YOU TO KILL MY FERRET.
OH, THAT. NO, SEE...THAT WAS JUST A HUGE MISUNDERSTANDING. WE HAVE THE, UH, GHOST OF A FARMER IN OUR HOUSE, SEE, AND HE HAS A FUNNY ACCENT, SO WE THOUGHT HE WAS SAYING *KILL THE FERRET* WHEN HE WAS REALLY SAYING *TILL THE DESERT*... I FEEL AWFUL ABOUT ALL THAT.
TELL YA WHAT: I BELIEVE YOU SO MUCH, I'M GOING TO GIVE YOU THE WHOLE HAM.
SCORE.
WOOPS. UH-OH...
CLUNK
HMM.
MAIL
darb
NUTS.
MAIL

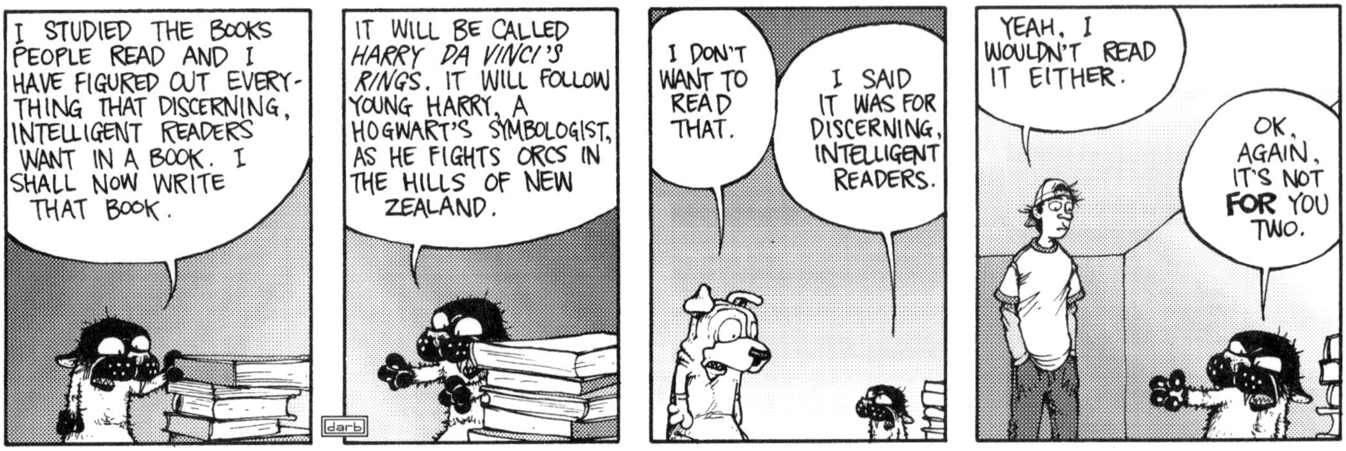
I STUDIED THE BOOKS PEOPLE READ AND I HAVE FIGURED OUT EVERYTHING THAT DISCERNING, INTELLIGENT READERS WANT IN A BOOK. I SHALL NOW WRITE THAT BOOK.
darb
IT WILL BE CALLED *HARRY DA VINCI'S RINGS*. IT WILL FOLLOW YOUNG HARRY, A HOGWART'S SYMBOLOGIST, AS HE FIGHTS ORCS IN THE HILLS OF NEW ZEALAND.
I DON'T WANT TO READ THAT.
I SAID IT WAS FOR DISCERNING, INTELLIGENT READERS.
YEAH, I WOULDN'T READ IT EITHER.
OK, AGAIN, IT'S NOT **FOR** YOU TWO.

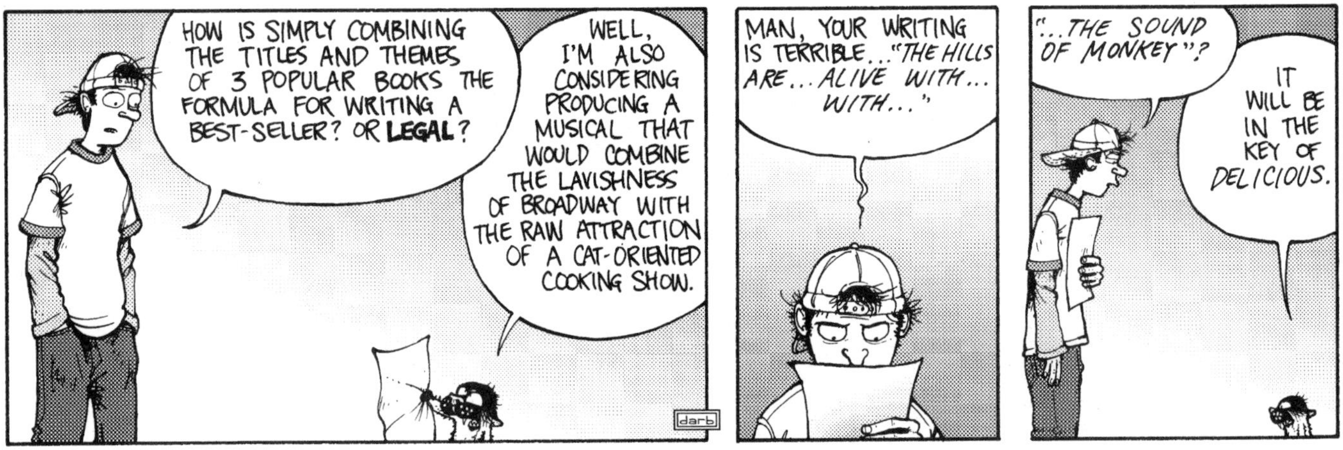
HOW IS SIMPLY COMBINING THE TITLES AND THEMES OF 3 POPULAR BOOKS THE FORMULA FOR WRITING A BEST-SELLER? OR **LEGAL**?
WELL, I'M ALSO CONSIDERING PRODUCING A MUSICAL THAT WOULD COMBINE THE LAVISHNESS OF BROADWAY WITH THE RAW ATTRACTION OF A CAT-ORIENTED COOKING SHOW.
darb
MAN, YOUR WRITING IS TERRIBLE..."*THE HILLS ARE... ALIVE WITH... WITH...*"
"*...THE SOUND OF MONKEY*"?
IT WILL BE IN THE KEY OF *DELICIOUS*.

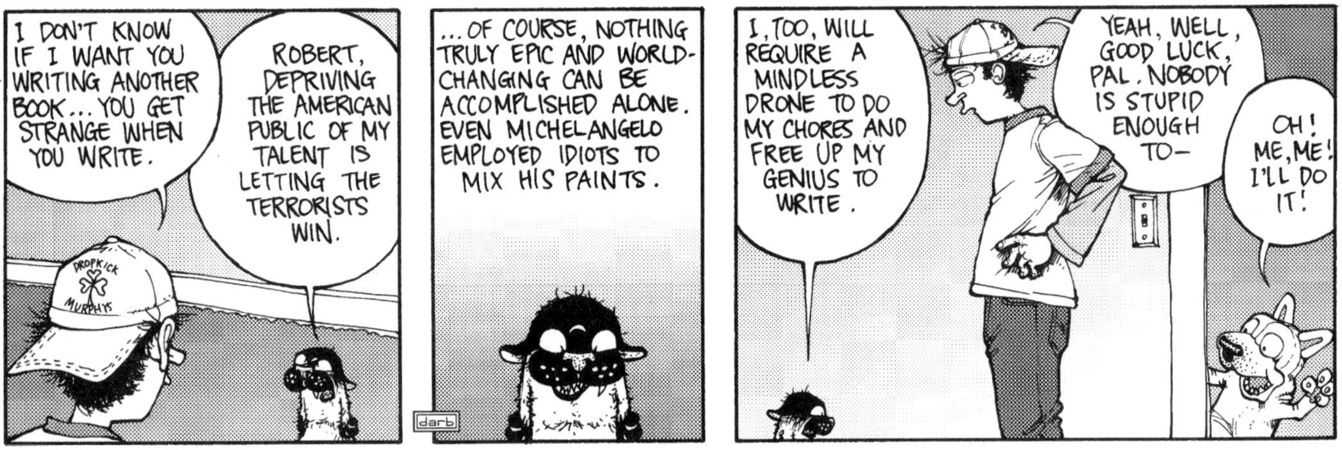
I DON'T KNOW IF I WANT YOU WRITING ANOTHER BOOK... YOU GET STRANGE WHEN YOU WRITE.
ROBERT, DEPRIVING THE AMERICAN PUBLIC OF MY TALENT IS LETTING THE TERRORISTS WIN.
DROPKICK MURPHYS
darb
...OF COURSE, NOTHING TRULY EPIC AND WORLD-CHANGING CAN BE ACCOMPLISHED ALONE. EVEN MICHELANGELO EMPLOYED IDIOTS TO MIX HIS PAINTS.
I, TOO, WILL REQUIRE A MINDLESS DRONE TO DO MY CHORES AND FREE UP MY GENIUS TO WRITE.
YEAH, WELL, GOOD LUCK, PAL. NOBODY IS STUPID ENOUGH TO—
OH! ME, ME! I'LL DO IT!

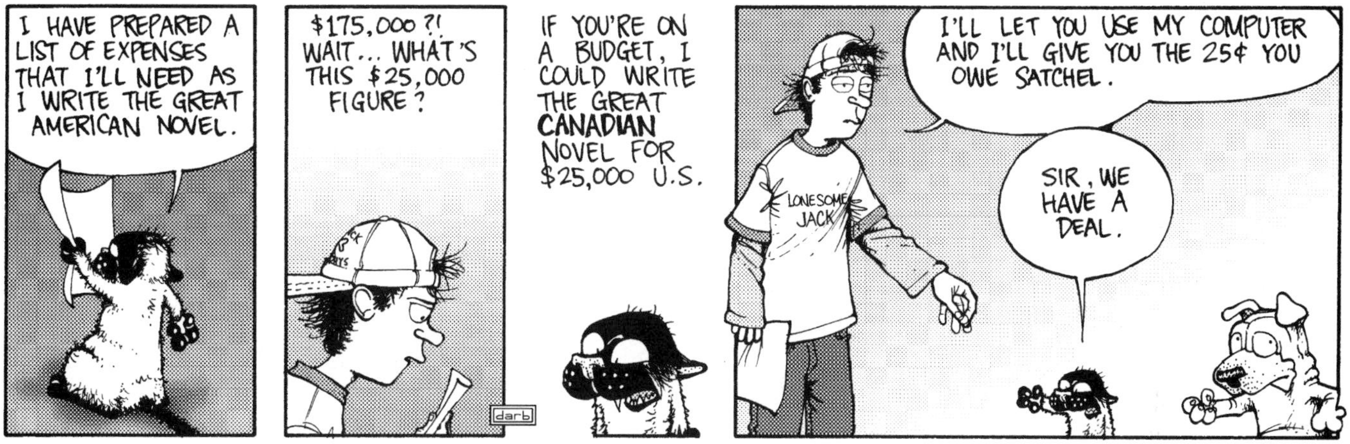
I HAVE PREPARED A LIST OF EXPENSES THAT I'LL NEED AS I WRITE THE GREAT AMERICAN NOVEL.
$175,000 ?! WAIT... WHAT'S THIS $25,000 FIGURE?
IF YOU'RE ON A BUDGET, I COULD WRITE THE GREAT **CANADIAN** NOVEL FOR $25,000 U.S.
I'LL LET YOU USE MY COMPUTER AND I'LL GIVE YOU THE 25¢ YOU OWE SATCHEL.
LONESOME JACK
SIR, WE HAVE A DEAL.

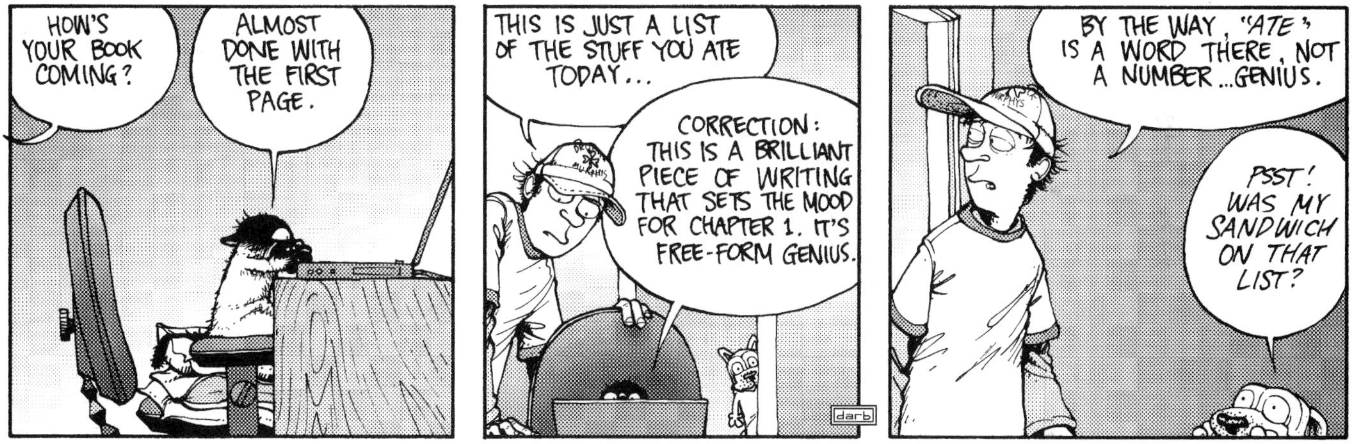
HOW'S YOUR BOOK COMING?
ALMOST DONE WITH THE FIRST PAGE.
THIS IS JUST A LIST OF THE STUFF YOU ATE TODAY...
CORRECTION: THIS IS A BRILLIANT PIECE OF WRITING THAT SETS THE MOOD FOR CHAPTER 1. IT'S FREE-FORM GENIUS.
BY THE WAY, "ATE" IS A WORD THERE, NOT A NUMBER...GENIUS.
PSST! WAS MY SANDWICH ON THAT LIST?

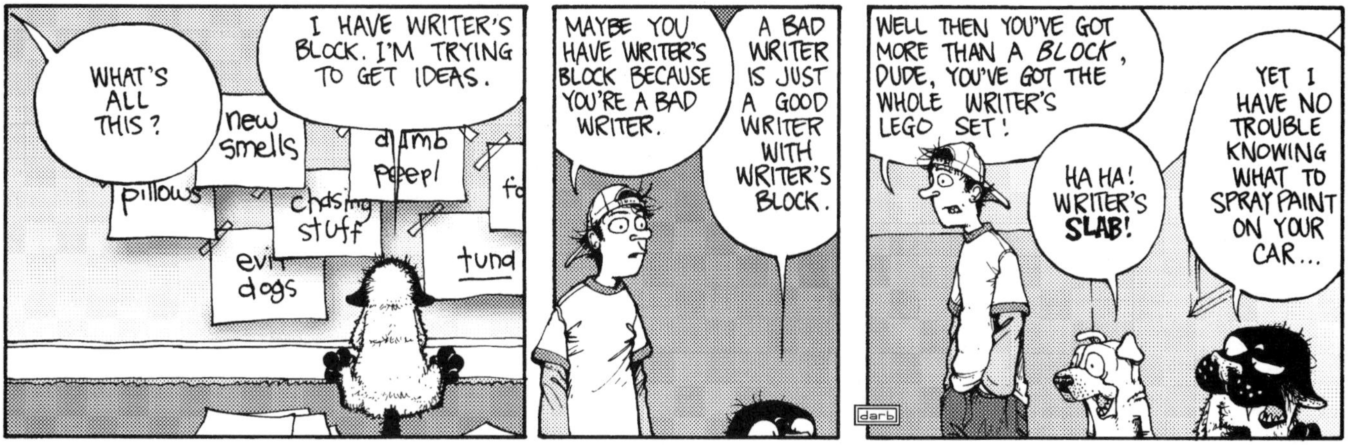
WHAT'S ALL THIS?
I HAVE WRITER'S BLOCK. I'M TRYING TO GET IDEAS.
new smells
dumb peepl
pillows
chasing stuff
MAYBE YOU HAVE WRITER'S BLOCK BECAUSE YOU'RE A BAD WRITER.
A BAD WRITER IS JUST A GOOD WRITER WITH WRITER'S BLOCK.
WELL THEN YOU'VE GOT MORE THAN A *BLOCK*, DUDE, YOU'VE GOT THE WHOLE WRITER'S LEGO SET!
HA HA! WRITER'S **SLAB**!
YET I HAVE NO TROUBLE KNOWING WHAT TO SPRAY PAINT ON YOUR CAR...

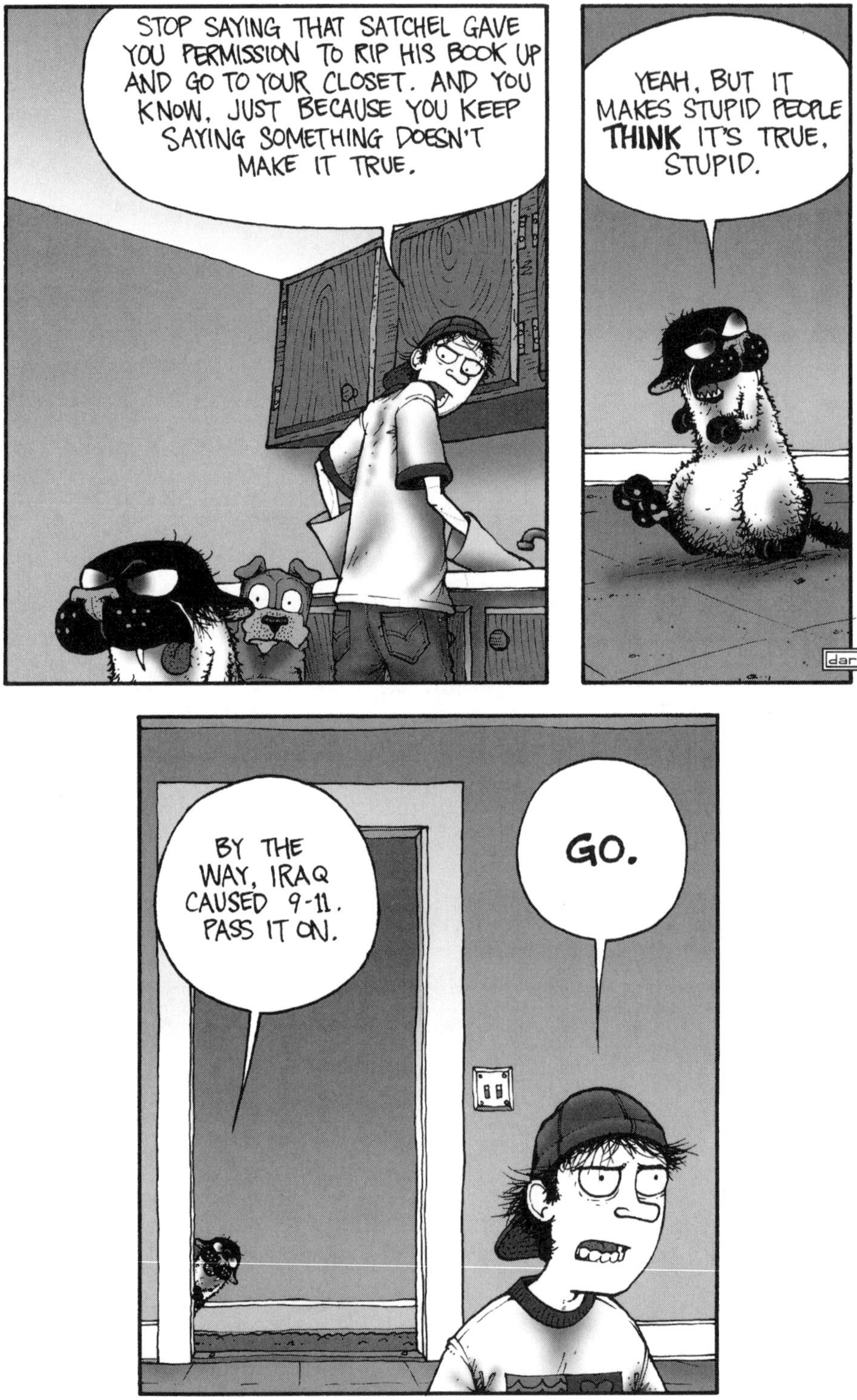
STOP SAYING THAT SATCHEL GAVE YOU PERMISSION TO RIP HIS BOOK UP AND GO TO YOUR CLOSET. AND YOU KNOW, JUST BECAUSE YOU KEEP SAYING SOMETHING DOESN'T MAKE IT TRUE.
YEAH, BUT IT MAKES STUPID PEOPLE THINK IT'S TRUE, STUPID.
darb
BY THE WAY, IRAQ CAUSED 9-11. PASS IT ON.
GO.

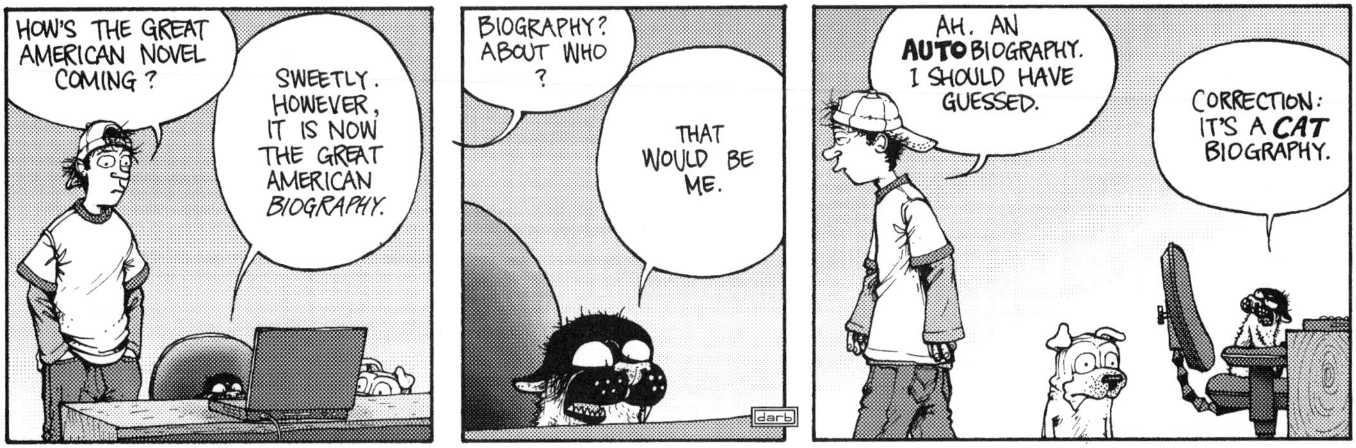
HOW'S THE GREAT AMERICAN NOVEL COMING?
SWEETLY. HOWEVER, IT IS NOW THE GREAT AMERICAN *BIOGRAPHY.*
BIOGRAPHY? ABOUT WHO?
THAT WOULD BE ME.
darb
AH. AN **AUTO**BIOGRAPHY. I SHOULD HAVE GUESSED.
CORRECTION: IT'S A ***CAT*** BIOGRAPHY.

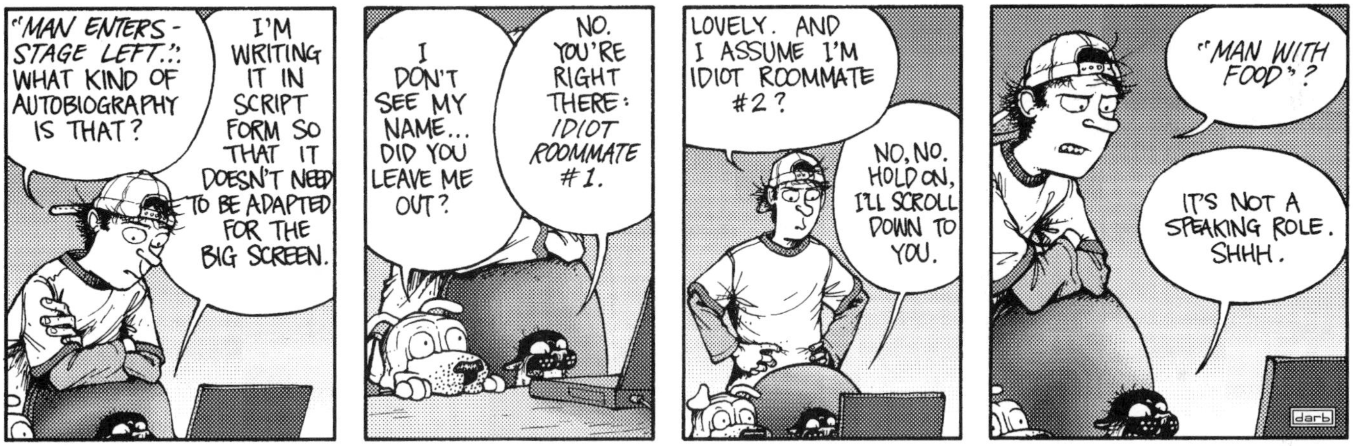
"*MAN ENTERS - STAGE LEFT.*": WHAT KIND OF AUTOBIOGRAPHY IS THAT?
I'M WRITING IT IN SCRIPT FORM SO THAT IT DOESN'T NEED TO BE ADAPTED FOR THE BIG SCREEN.
I DON'T SEE MY NAME... DID YOU LEAVE ME OUT?
NO. YOU'RE RIGHT THERE: *IDIOT ROOMMATE #1.*
LOVELY. AND I ASSUME I'M IDIOT ROOMMATE #2?
NO, NO. HOLD ON, I'LL SCROLL DOWN TO YOU.
"*MAN WITH FOOD*"?
IT'S NOT A SPEAKING ROLE. SHHH.
darb

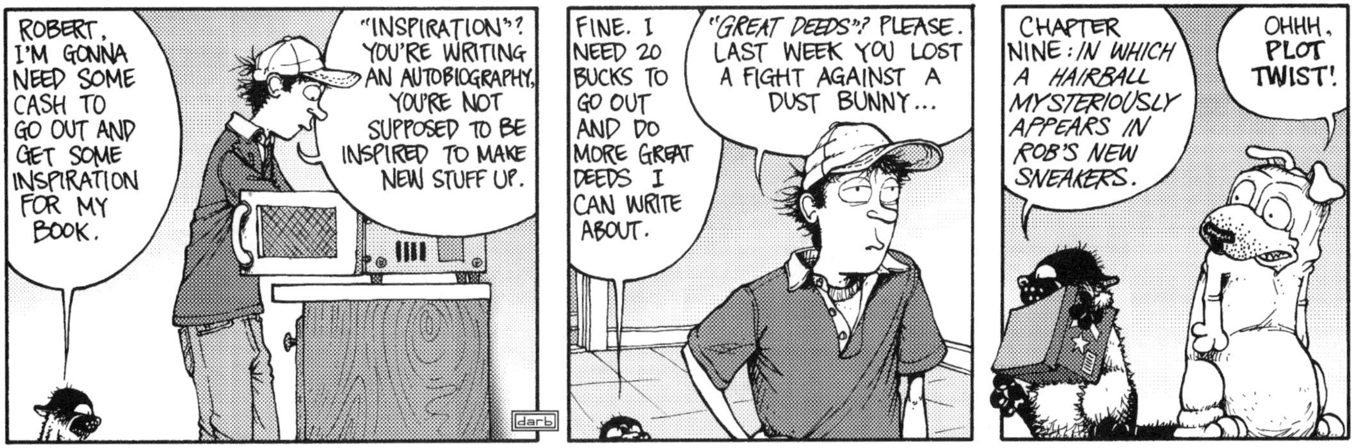
ROBERT, I'M GONNA NEED SOME CASH TO GO OUT AND GET SOME INSPIRATION FOR MY BOOK.
"INSPIRATION"? YOU'RE WRITING AN AUTOBIOGRAPHY, YOU'RE NOT SUPPOSED TO BE INSPIRED TO MAKE NEW STUFF UP.
darb
FINE. I NEED 20 BUCKS TO GO OUT AND DO MORE GREAT DEEDS I CAN WRITE ABOUT.
"*GREAT DEEDS*"? PLEASE. LAST WEEK YOU LOST A FIGHT AGAINST A DUST BUNNY...
CHAPTER NINE: *IN WHICH A HAIRBALL MYSTERIOUSLY APPEARS IN ROB'S NEW SNEAKERS.*
OHHH, **PLOT TWIST**!

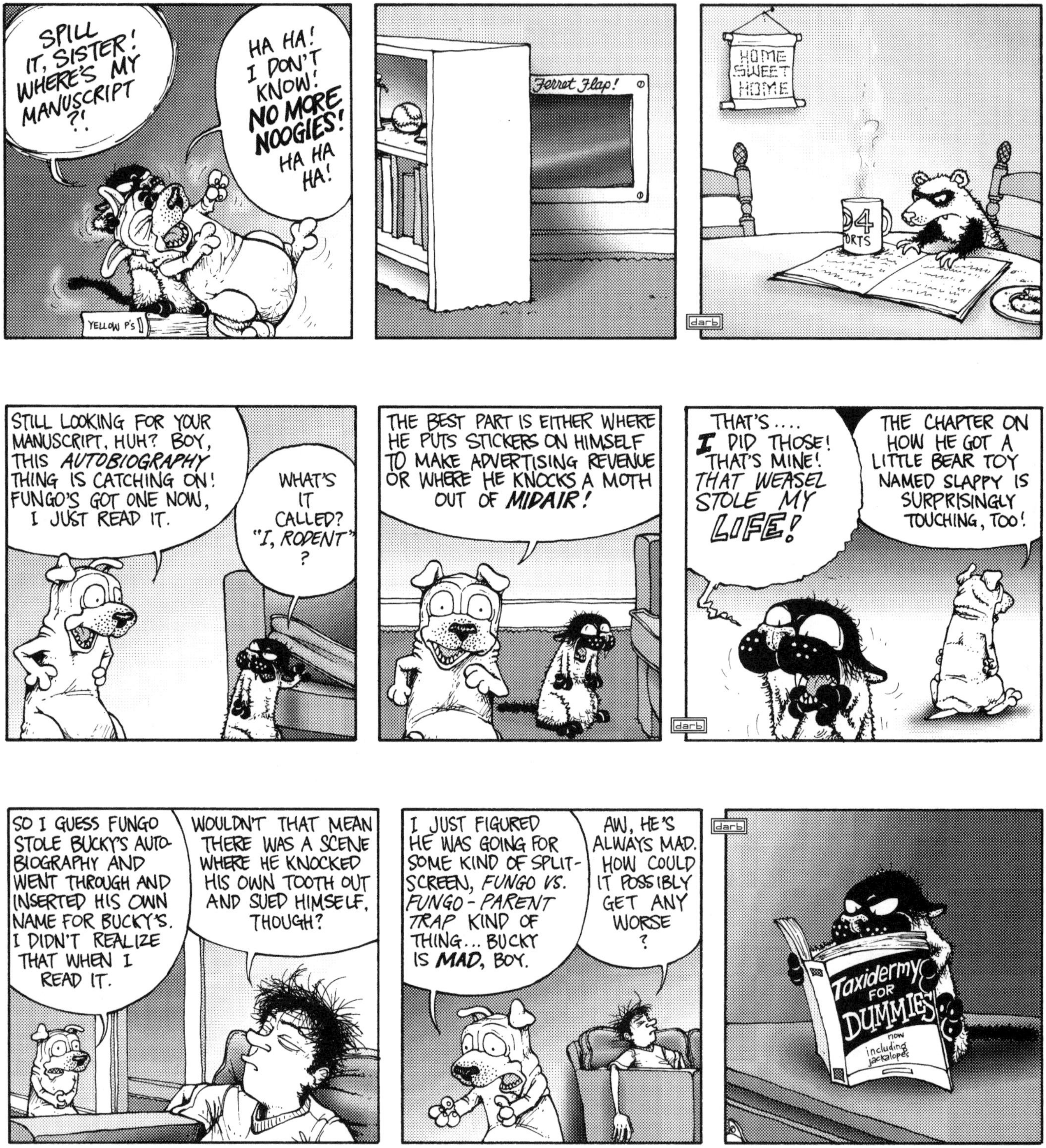
SPILL IT, SISTER! WHERE'S MY MANUSCRIPT ?!
HA HA! I DON'T KNOW! NO MORE NOOGIES! HA HA HA!
YELLOW P's
Ferret Flap!
HOME SWEET HOME
darb
STILL LOOKING FOR YOUR MANUSCRIPT, HUH? BOY, THIS AUTOBIOGRAPHY THING IS CATCHING ON! FUNGO'S GOT ONE NOW, I JUST READ IT.
WHAT'S IT CALLED? "I, RODENT"?
THE BEST PART IS EITHER WHERE HE PUTS STICKERS ON HIMSELF TO MAKE ADVERTISING REVENUE OR WHERE HE KNOCKS A MOTH OUT OF MIDAIR!
THAT'S.... I DID THOSE! THAT'S MINE! THAT WEASEL STOLE MY LIFE!
THE CHAPTER ON HOW HE GOT A LITTLE BEAR TOY NAMED SLAPPY IS SURPRISINGLY TOUCHING, TOO!
darb
SO I GUESS FUNGO STOLE BUCKY'S AUTOBIOGRAPHY AND WENT THROUGH AND INSERTED HIS OWN NAME FOR BUCKY'S. I DIDN'T REALIZE THAT WHEN I READ IT.
WOULDN'T THAT MEAN THERE WAS A SCENE WHERE HE KNOCKED HIS OWN TOOTH OUT AND SUED HIMSELF, THOUGH?
I JUST FIGURED HE WAS GOING FOR SOME KIND OF SPLIT-SCREEN, FUNGO VS. FUNGO - PARENT TRAP KIND OF THING... BUCKY IS MAD, BOY.
AW, HE'S ALWAYS MAD. HOW COULD IT POSSIBLY GET ANY WORSE?
darb
Taxidermy FOR DUMMIES now including jackalopes

A Kitty Litter-ary
Moment With
Bucky B. Katt

WHOSE TOADS THESE ARE I THINK I KNEW.
HIS FROGS ARE IN THE VISCOUS STEW;
HE WILL NOT SEE ME STOOPING HERE
TO LAUNCH HIS TOADS TO FROG FONDUE.

THE LITTLE PUSS WOULD THINK IT QUEER
TO STOP WITH NO FROGS TO TOSS NEAR
BETWEEN THE TOADS AND FROGGY FLING
THE FARTHEST FROG TOSSED O'ER THE PIER.

HE GIVES THE SLIMY NEWTS A SWING
AS IF THEY ARE SOME GREEN PLAYTHING...

THE ONLY OTHER SOUND'S THE CHEEP
OF PEEPERS PINNED AND SENT FLYING.
THE TOADS ARE BEST FOUND SOUND ASLEEP,
BUT I HAVE PRODIGIOUS FROGS TO REAP,
REPTILES TO THROW BEFORE I SLEEP,
REPTILES TO THROW BEFORE I SLEEP.

darb

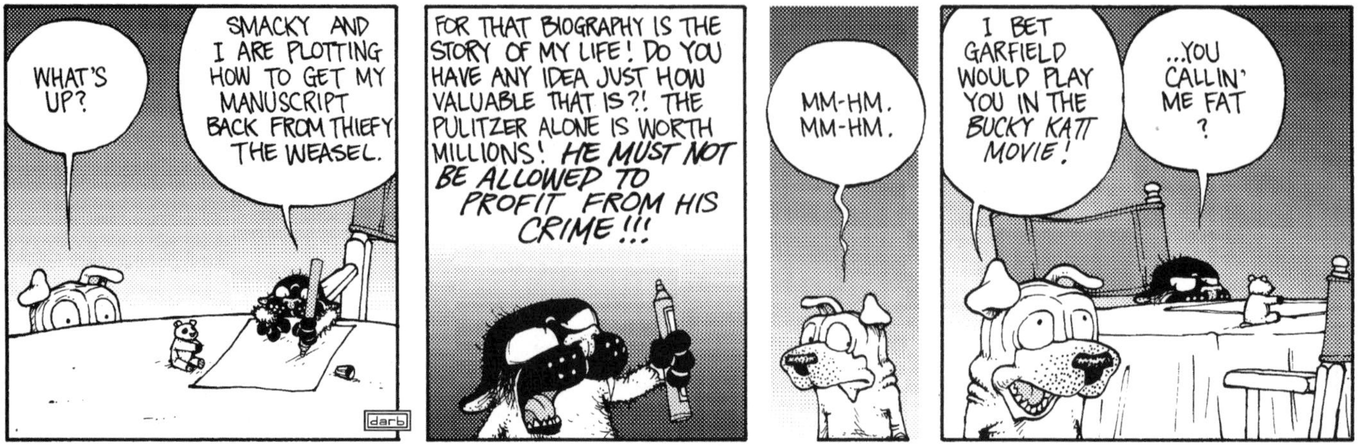
WHAT'S UP?
SMACKY AND I ARE PLOTTING HOW TO GET MY MANUSCRIPT BACK FROM THIEFY THE WEASEL.
FOR THAT BIOGRAPHY IS THE STORY OF MY LIFE! DO YOU HAVE ANY IDEA JUST HOW VALUABLE THAT IS?! THE PULITZER ALONE IS WORTH MILLIONS! HE MUST NOT BE ALLOWED TO PROFIT FROM HIS CRIME!!!
MM-HM. MM-HM.
I BET GARFIELD WOULD PLAY YOU IN THE BUCKY KATT MOVIE!
...YOU CALLIN' ME FAT ?
darb

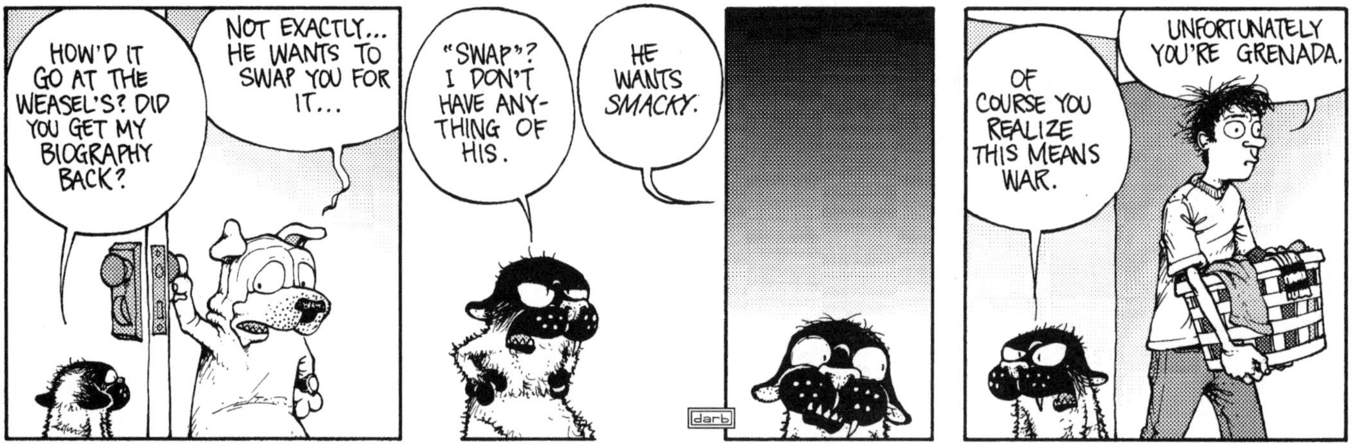
HOW'D IT GO AT THE WEASEL'S? DID YOU GET MY BIOGRAPHY BACK?
NOT EXACTLY... HE WANTS TO SWAP YOU FOR IT...
"SWAP"? I DON'T HAVE ANY-THING OF HIS.
HE WANTS SMACKY.
OF COURSE YOU REALIZE THIS MEANS WAR.
UNFORTUNATELY YOU'RE GRENADA.
darb

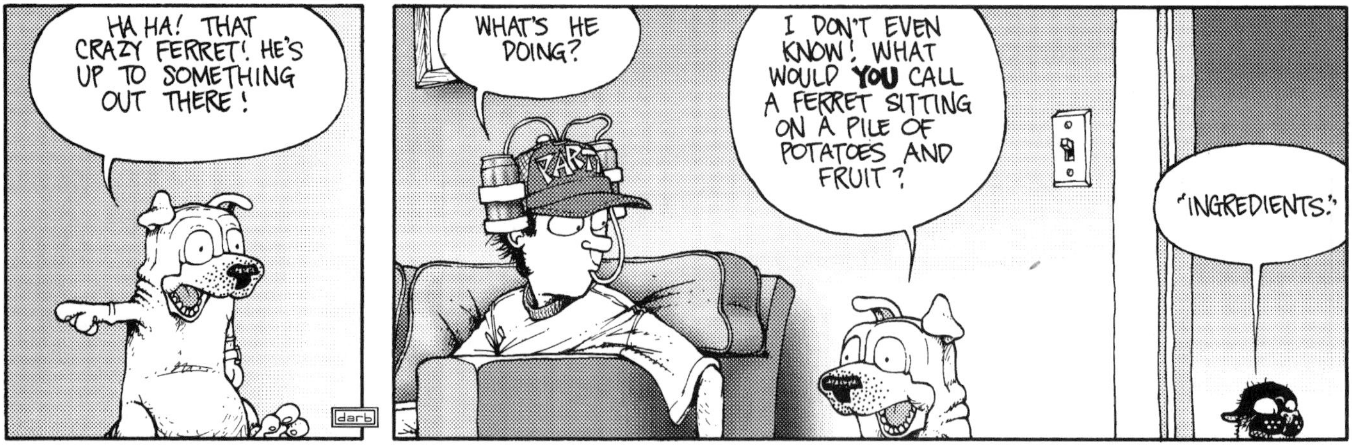
HA HA! THAT CRAZY FERRET! HE'S UP TO SOMETHING OUT THERE!
WHAT'S HE DOING?
I DON'T EVEN KNOW! WHAT WOULD YOU CALL A FERRET SITTING ON A PILE OF POTATOES AND FRUIT?
"INGREDIENTS."
darb

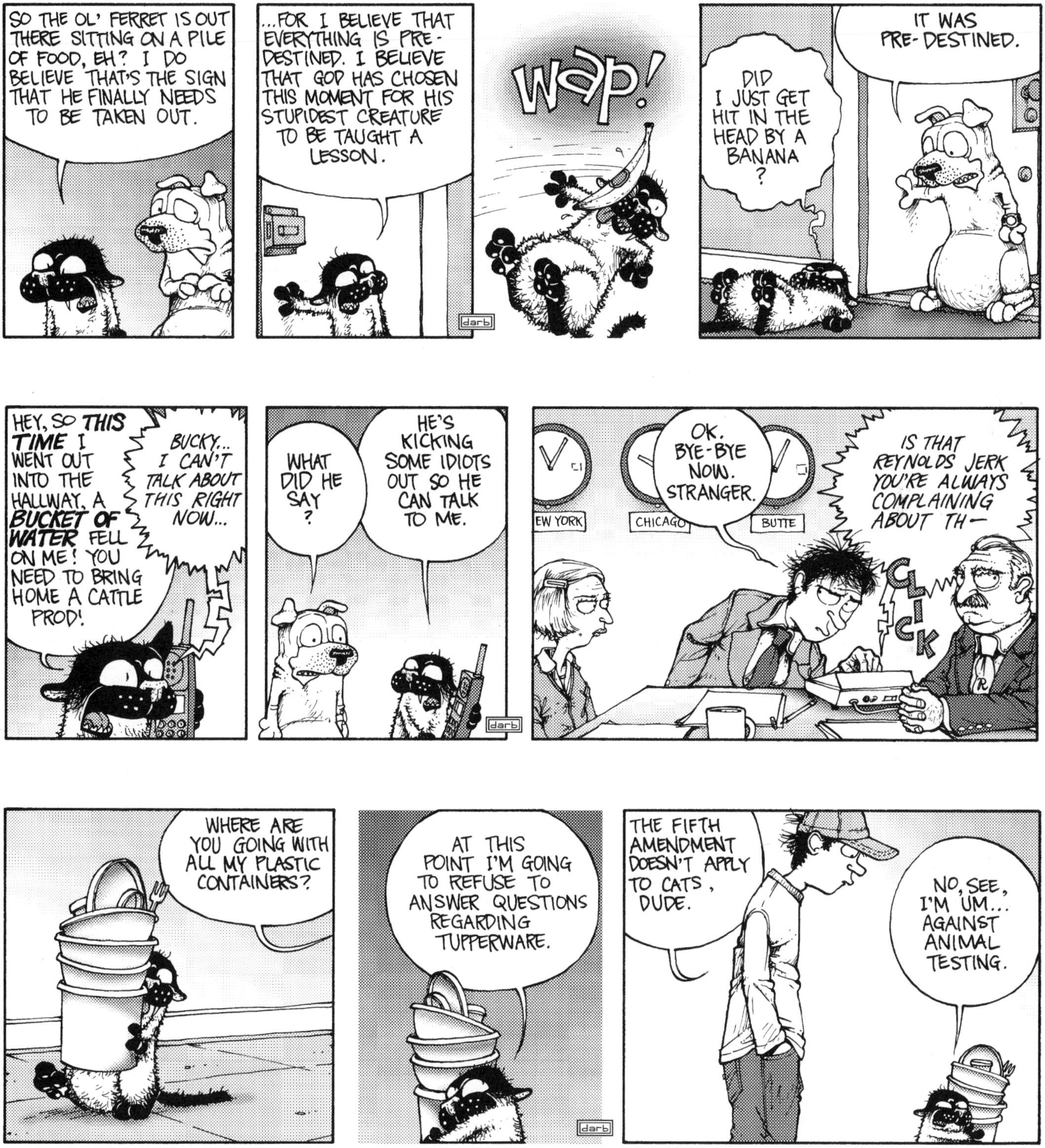
SO THE OL' FERRET IS OUT THERE SITTING ON A PILE OF FOOD, EH? I DO BELIEVE THAT'S THE SIGN THAT HE FINALLY NEEDS TO BE TAKEN OUT.
...FOR I BELIEVE THAT EVERYTHING IS PRE-DESTINED. I BELIEVE THAT GOD HAS CHOSEN THIS MOMENT FOR HIS STUPIDEST CREATURE TO BE TAUGHT A LESSON.
darb
WAP!
DID I JUST GET HIT IN THE HEAD BY A BANANA?
IT WAS PRE-DESTINED.
HEY, SO THIS TIME I WENT OUT INTO THE HALLWAY, A BUCKET OF WATER FELL ON ME! YOU NEED TO BRING HOME A CATTLE PROD!
BUCKY... I CAN'T TALK ABOUT THIS RIGHT NOW...
WHAT DID HE SAY?
HE'S KICKING SOME IDIOTS OUT SO HE CAN TALK TO ME.
darb
EW YORK
CHICAGO
BUTTE
OK. BYE-BYE NOW. STRANGER.
IS THAT REYNOLDS JERK YOU'RE ALWAYS COMPLAINING ABOUT TH—
CLICK
WHERE ARE YOU GOING WITH ALL MY PLASTIC CONTAINERS?
AT THIS POINT I'M GOING TO REFUSE TO ANSWER QUESTIONS REGARDING TUPPERWARE.
darb
THE FIFTH AMENDMENT DOESN'T APPLY TO CATS, DUDE.
NO, SEE, I'M UM... AGAINST ANIMAL TESTING.

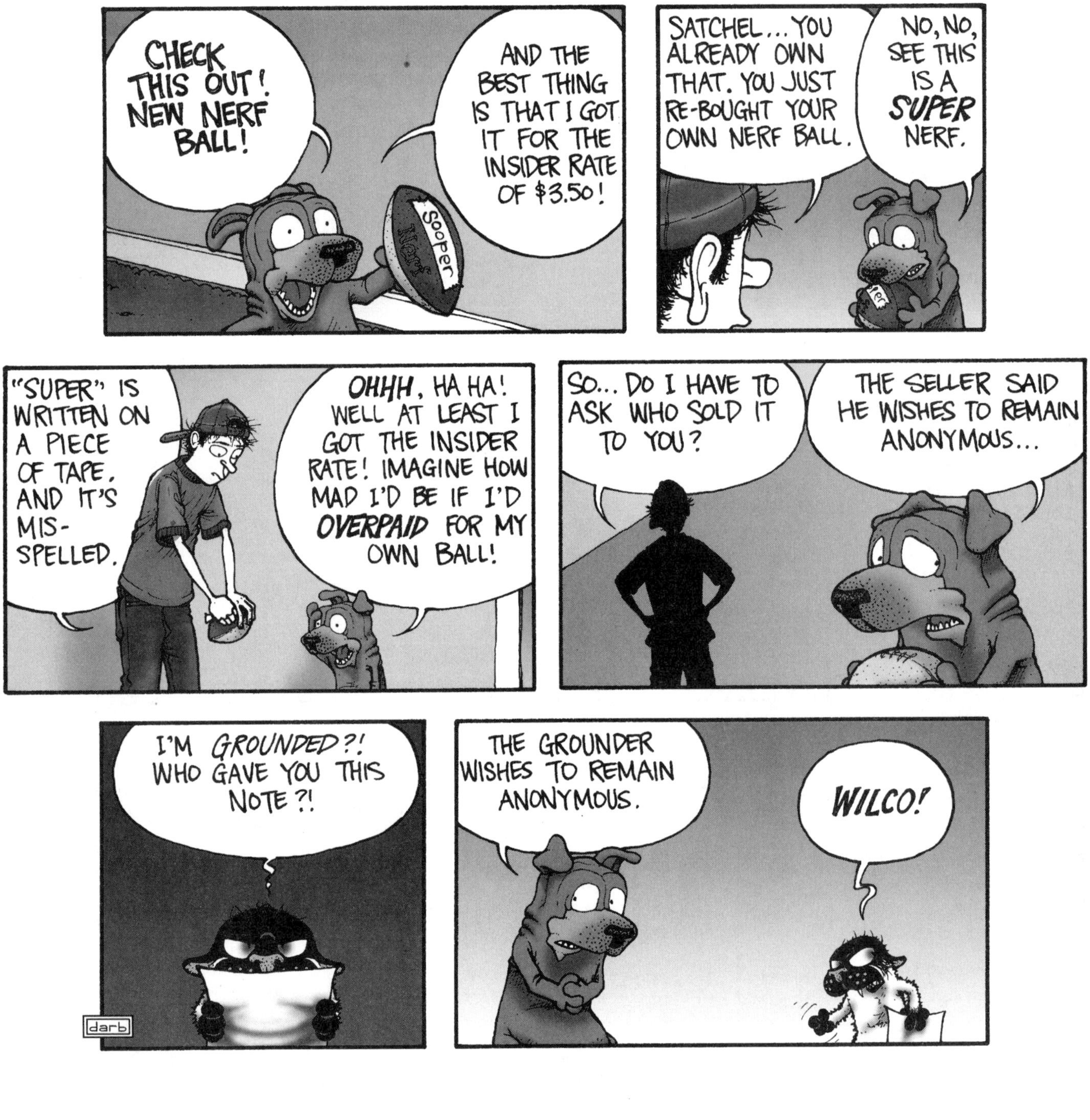
CHECK THIS OUT! NEW NERF BALL!
AND THE BEST THING IS THAT I GOT IT FOR THE INSIDER RATE OF $3.50!
Sooper Nerf
SATCHEL... YOU ALREADY OWN THAT. YOU JUST RE-BOUGHT YOUR OWN NERF BALL.
NO, NO, SEE THIS IS A SUPER NERF.
"SUPER" IS WRITTEN ON A PIECE OF TAPE, AND IT'S MIS-SPELLED.
OHHH, HA HA! WELL AT LEAST I GOT THE INSIDER RATE! IMAGINE HOW MAD I'D BE IF I'D OVERPAID FOR MY OWN BALL!
SO... DO I HAVE TO ASK WHO SOLD IT TO YOU?
THE SELLER SAID HE WISHES TO REMAIN ANONYMOUS...
I'M GROUNDED?! WHO GAVE YOU THIS NOTE?!
darb
THE GROUNDER WISHES TO REMAIN ANONYMOUS.
WILCO!

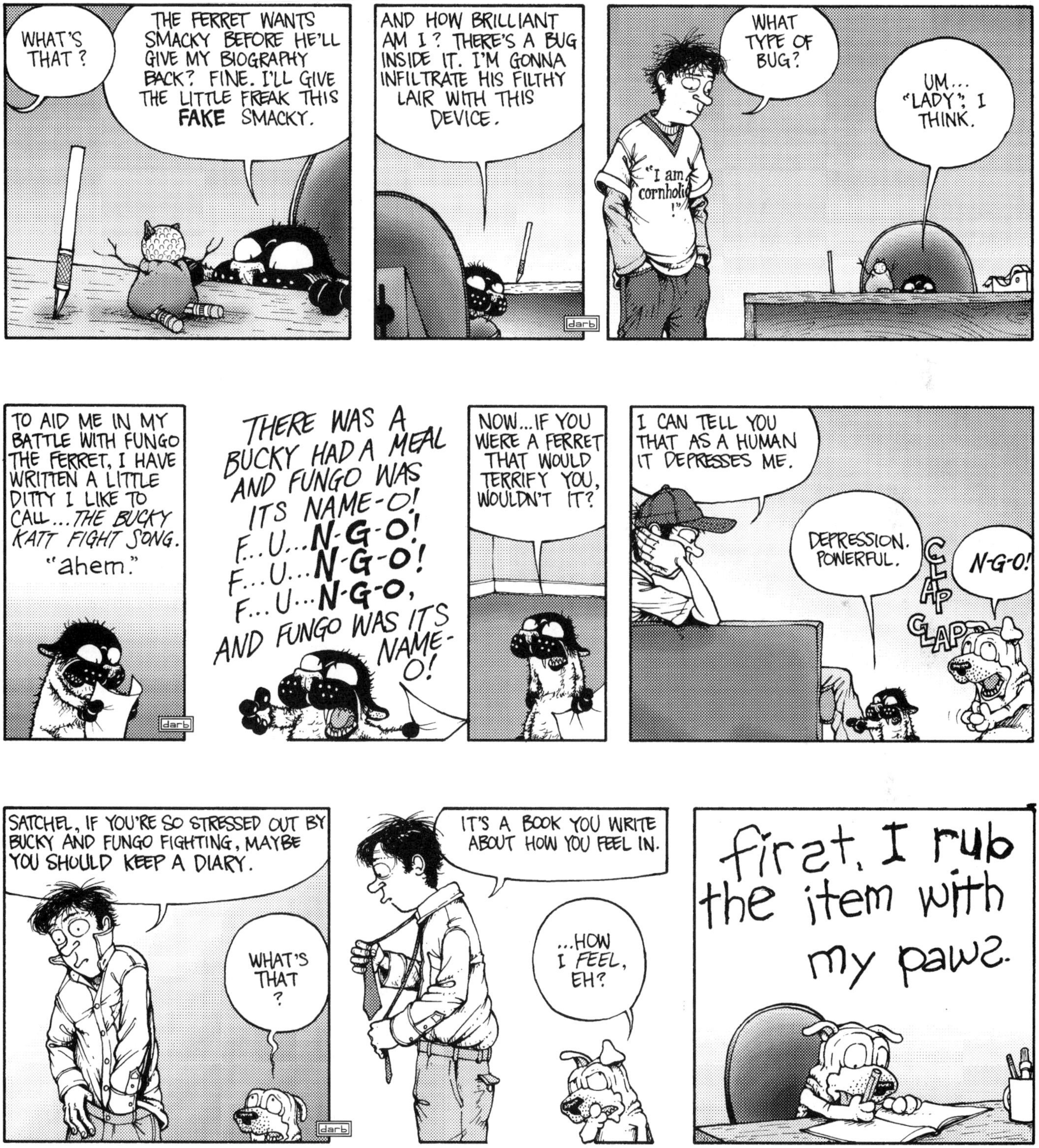
WHAT'S THAT?
THE FERRET WANTS SMACKY BEFORE HE'LL GIVE MY BIOGRAPHY BACK? FINE. I'LL GIVE THE LITTLE FREAK THIS FAKE SMACKY.
AND HOW BRILLIANT AM I? THERE'S A BUG INSIDE IT. I'M GONNA INFILTRATE HIS FILTHY LAIR WITH THIS DEVICE.
darb
WHAT TYPE OF BUG?
"I am cornholio!"
UM... "LADY", I THINK.
TO AID ME IN MY BATTLE WITH FUNGO THE FERRET, I HAVE WRITTEN A LITTLE DITTY I LIKE TO CALL... THE BUCKY KATT FIGHT SONG. "ahem."
darb
THERE WAS A BUCKY HAD A MEAL AND FUNGO WAS ITS NAME-O! F...U...N-G-O! F...U...N-G-O! F...U...N-G-O, AND FUNGO WAS ITS NAME-O!
NOW...IF YOU WERE A FERRET THAT WOULD TERRIFY YOU, WOULDN'T IT?
I CAN TELL YOU THAT AS A HUMAN IT DEPRESSES ME.
DEPRESSION. POWERFUL.
CLAP CLAP
N-G-O!
SATCHEL, IF YOU'RE SO STRESSED OUT BY BUCKY AND FUNGO FIGHTING, MAYBE YOU SHOULD KEEP A DIARY.
WHAT'S THAT?
darb
IT'S A BOOK YOU WRITE ABOUT HOW YOU FEEL IN.
...HOW I FEEL, EH?
first, I rub the item with my paws.

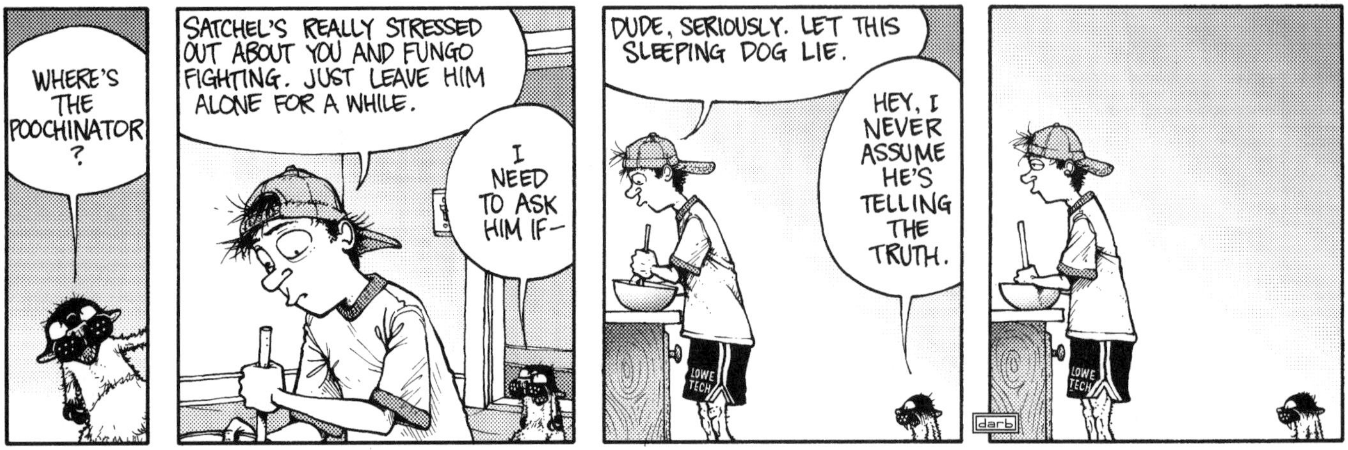
WHERE'S THE POOCHINATOR?
SATCHEL'S REALLY STRESSED OUT ABOUT YOU AND FUNGO FIGHTING. JUST LEAVE HIM ALONE FOR A WHILE.
I NEED TO ASK HIM IF–
DUDE, SERIOUSLY. LET THIS SLEEPING DOG LIE.
HEY, I NEVER ASSUME HE'S TELLING THE TRUTH.
LOWE TECH
LOWE TECH
darb

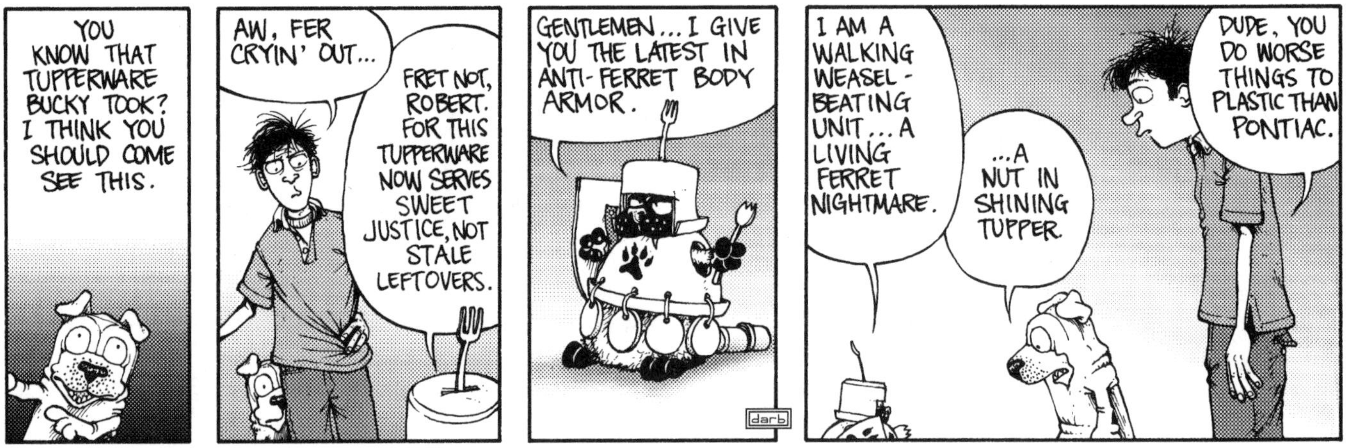
YOU KNOW THAT TUPPERWARE BUCKY TOOK? I THINK YOU SHOULD COME SEE THIS.
AW, FER CRYIN' OUT...
FRET NOT, ROBERT. FOR THIS TUPPERWARE NOW SERVES SWEET JUSTICE, NOT STALE LEFTOVERS.
GENTLEMEN... I GIVE YOU THE LATEST IN ANTI-FERRET BODY ARMOR.
darb
I AM A WALKING WEASEL-BEATING UNIT... A LIVING FERRET NIGHTMARE.
...A NUT IN SHINING TUPPER.
DUDE, YOU DO WORSE THINGS TO PLASTIC THAN PONTIAC.

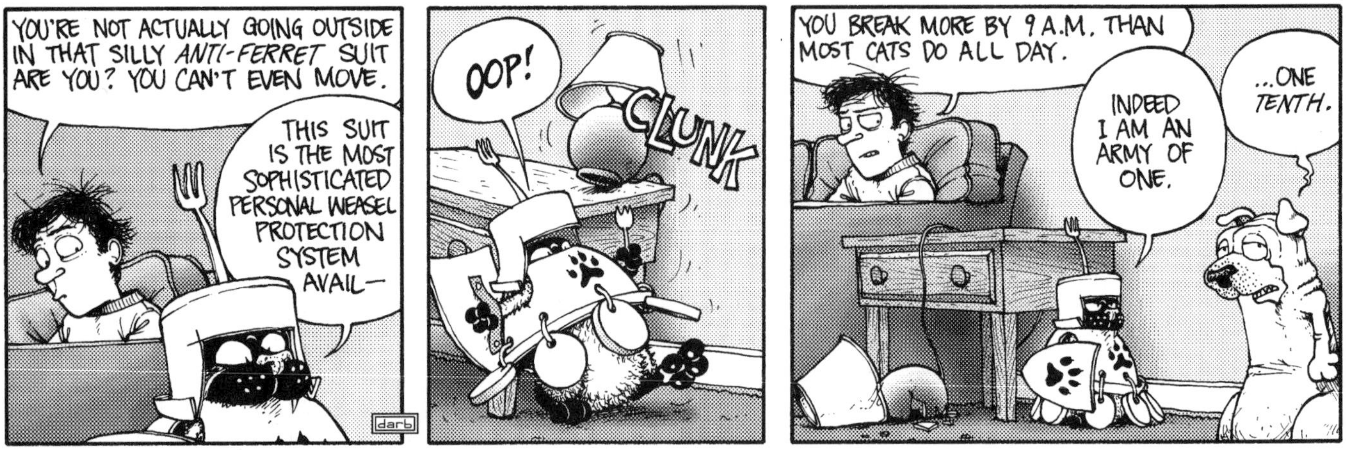
YOU'RE NOT ACTUALLY GOING OUTSIDE IN THAT SILLY *ANTI-FERRET* SUIT ARE YOU? YOU CAN'T EVEN MOVE.
THIS SUIT IS THE MOST SOPHISTICATED PERSONAL WEASEL PROTECTION SYSTEM AVAIL–
darb
OOP!
CLUNK
YOU BREAK MORE BY 9 A.M. THAN MOST CATS DO ALL DAY.
INDEED I AM AN ARMY OF ONE.
...ONE *TENTH*.

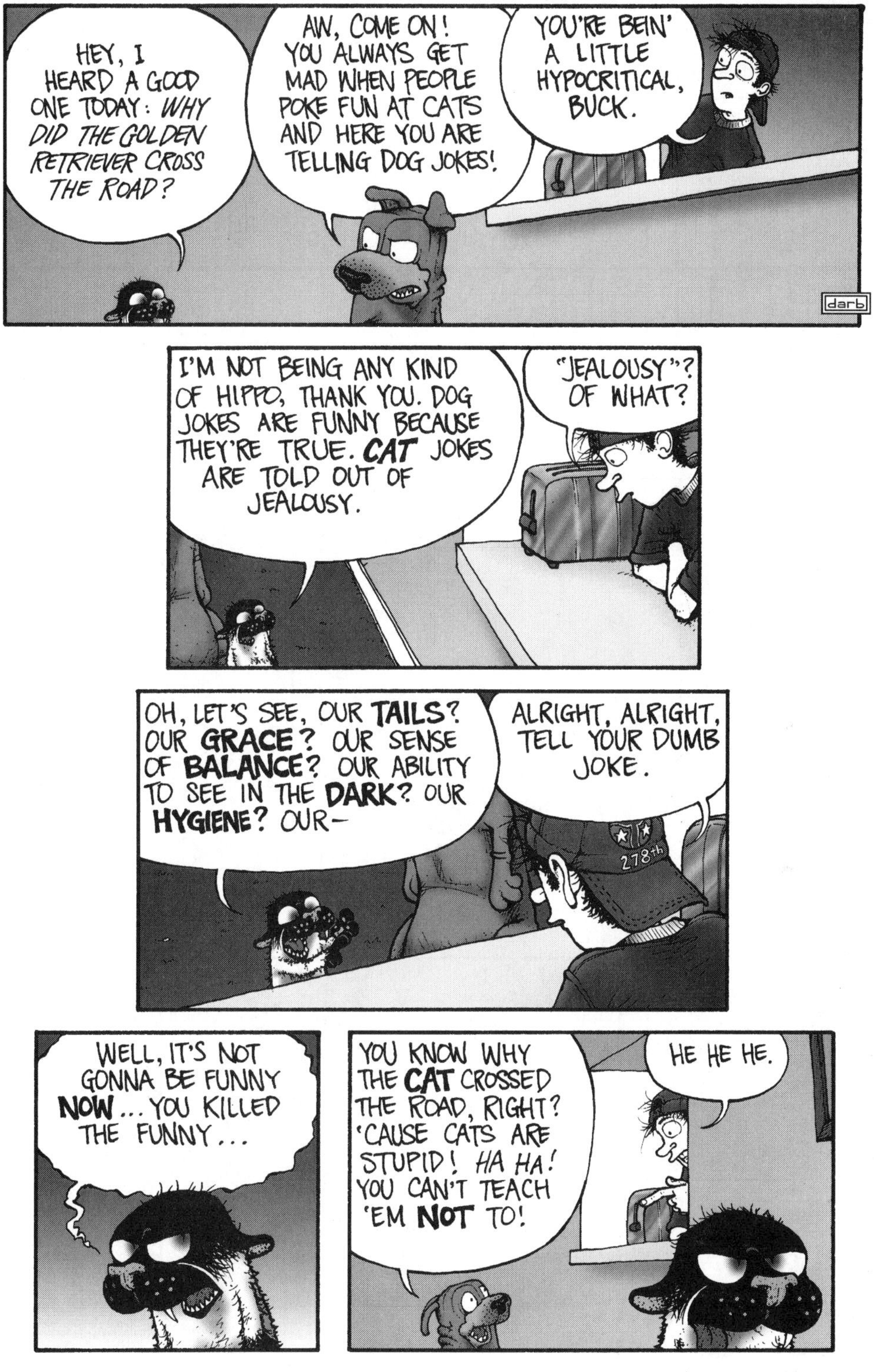
HEY, I HEARD A GOOD ONE TODAY: WHY DID THE GOLDEN RETRIEVER CROSS THE ROAD?
AW, COME ON! YOU ALWAYS GET MAD WHEN PEOPLE POKE FUN AT CATS AND HERE YOU ARE TELLING DOG JOKES!
YOU'RE BEIN' A LITTLE HYPOCRITICAL, BUCK.
darb
I'M NOT BEING ANY KIND OF HIPPO, THANK YOU. DOG JOKES ARE FUNNY BECAUSE THEY'RE TRUE. CAT JOKES ARE TOLD OUT OF JEALOUSY.
"JEALOUSY"? OF WHAT?
OH, LET'S SEE, OUR TAILS? OUR GRACE? OUR SENSE OF BALANCE? OUR ABILITY TO SEE IN THE DARK? OUR HYGIENE? OUR–
ALRIGHT, ALRIGHT, TELL YOUR DUMB JOKE.
278th
WELL, IT'S NOT GONNA BE FUNNY NOW... YOU KILLED THE FUNNY...
YOU KNOW WHY THE CAT CROSSED THE ROAD, RIGHT? 'CAUSE CATS ARE STUPID! HA HA! YOU CAN'T TEACH 'EM NOT TO!
HE HE HE.

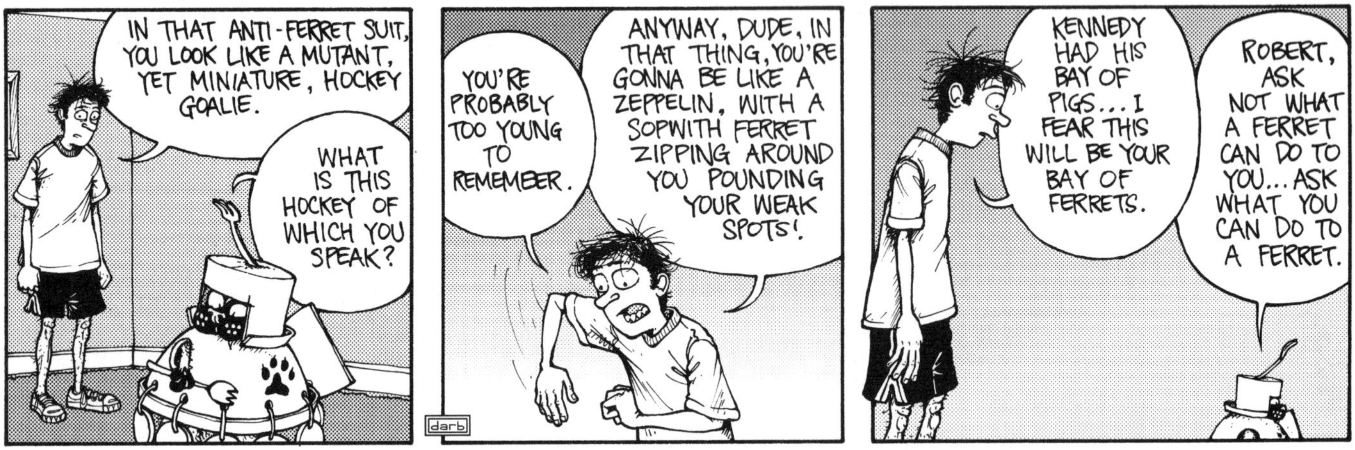
IN THAT ANTI-FERRET SUIT, YOU LOOK LIKE A MUTANT, YET MINIATURE, HOCKEY GOALIE.
WHAT IS THIS HOCKEY OF WHICH YOU SPEAK?
YOU'RE PROBABLY TOO YOUNG TO REMEMBER.
ANYWAY, DUDE, IN THAT THING, YOU'RE GONNA BE LIKE A ZEPPELIN, WITH A SOPWITH FERRET ZIPPING AROUND YOU POUNDING YOUR WEAK SPOTS!
KENNEDY HAD HIS BAY OF PIGS... I FEAR THIS WILL BE YOUR BAY OF FERRETS.
ROBERT, ASK NOT WHAT A FERRET CAN DO TO YOU... ASK WHAT YOU CAN DO TO A FERRET.

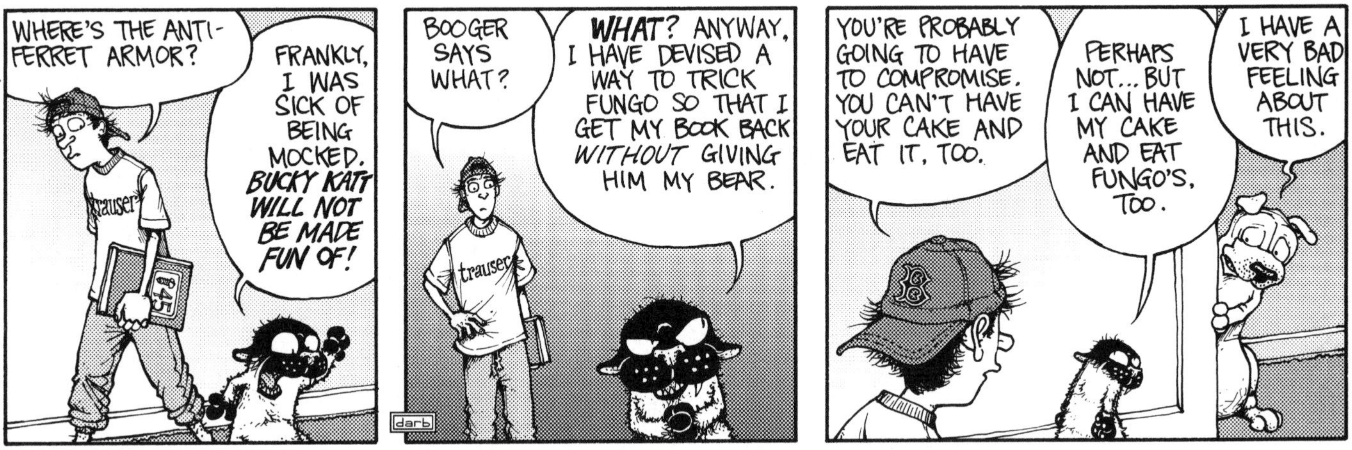
WHERE'S THE ANTI-FERRET ARMOR?
FRANKLY, I WAS SICK OF BEING MOCKED. BUCKY KATT WILL NOT BE MADE FUN OF!
BOOGER SAYS WHAT?
WHAT? ANYWAY, I HAVE DEVISED A WAY TO TRICK FUNGO SO THAT I GET MY BOOK BACK WITHOUT GIVING HIM MY BEAR.
YOU'RE PROBABLY GOING TO HAVE TO COMPROMISE. YOU CAN'T HAVE YOUR CAKE AND EAT IT, TOO.
PERHAPS NOT... BUT I CAN HAVE MY CAKE AND EAT FUNGO'S, TOO.
I HAVE A VERY BAD FEELING ABOUT THIS.

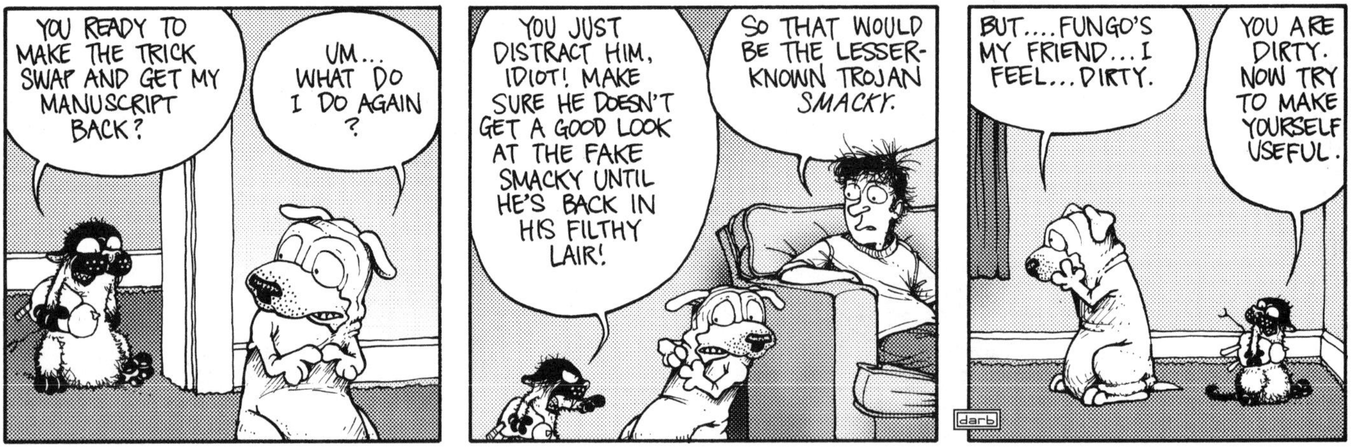
YOU READY TO MAKE THE TRICK SWAP AND GET MY MANUSCRIPT BACK?
UM... WHAT DO I DO AGAIN ?
YOU JUST DISTRACT HIM, IDIOT! MAKE SURE HE DOESN'T GET A GOOD LOOK AT THE FAKE SMACKY UNTIL HE'S BACK IN HIS FILTHY LAIR!
SO THAT WOULD BE THE LESSER-KNOWN TROJAN SMACKY.
BUT.... FUNGO'S MY FRIEND... I FEEL... DIRTY.
YOU ARE DIRTY. NOW TRY TO MAKE YOURSELF USEFUL.

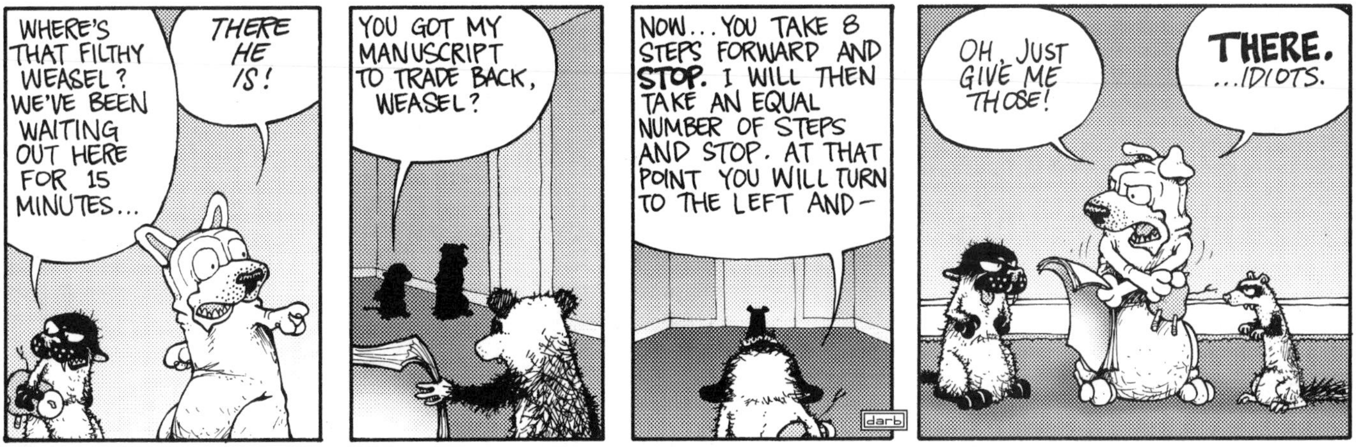
WHERE'S THAT FILTHY WEASEL? WE'VE BEEN WAITING OUT HERE FOR 15 MINUTES...
THERE HE IS!
YOU GOT MY MANUSCRIPT TO TRADE BACK, WEASEL?
NOW... YOU TAKE 8 STEPS FORWARD AND STOP. I WILL THEN TAKE AN EQUAL NUMBER OF STEPS AND STOP. AT THAT POINT YOU WILL TURN TO THE LEFT AND—
darb
OH, JUST GIVE ME THOSE!
THERE. ...IDIOTS.

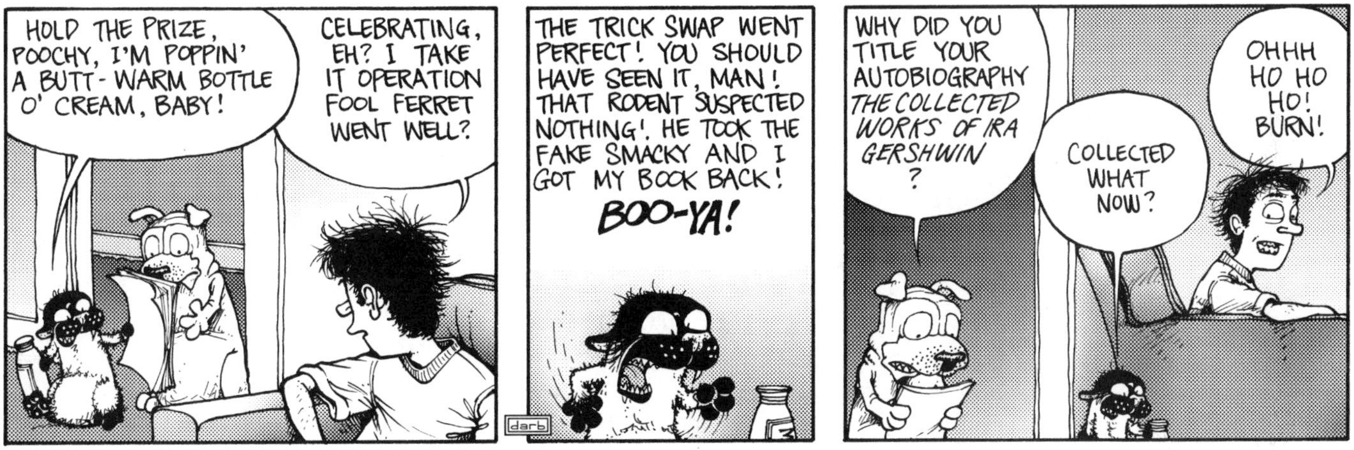
HOLD THE PRIZE, POOCHY, I'M POPPIN' A BUTT-WARM BOTTLE O' CREAM, BABY!
CELEBRATING, EH? I TAKE IT OPERATION FOOL FERRET WENT WELL?
darb
THE TRICK SWAP WENT PERFECT! YOU SHOULD HAVE SEEN IT, MAN! THAT RODENT SUSPECTED NOTHING! HE TOOK THE FAKE SMACKY AND I GOT MY BOOK BACK!
BOO-YA!
WHY DID YOU TITLE YOUR AUTOBIOGRAPHY THE COLLECTED WORKS OF IRA GERSHWIN?
COLLECTED WHAT NOW?
OHHH HO HO HO! BURN!

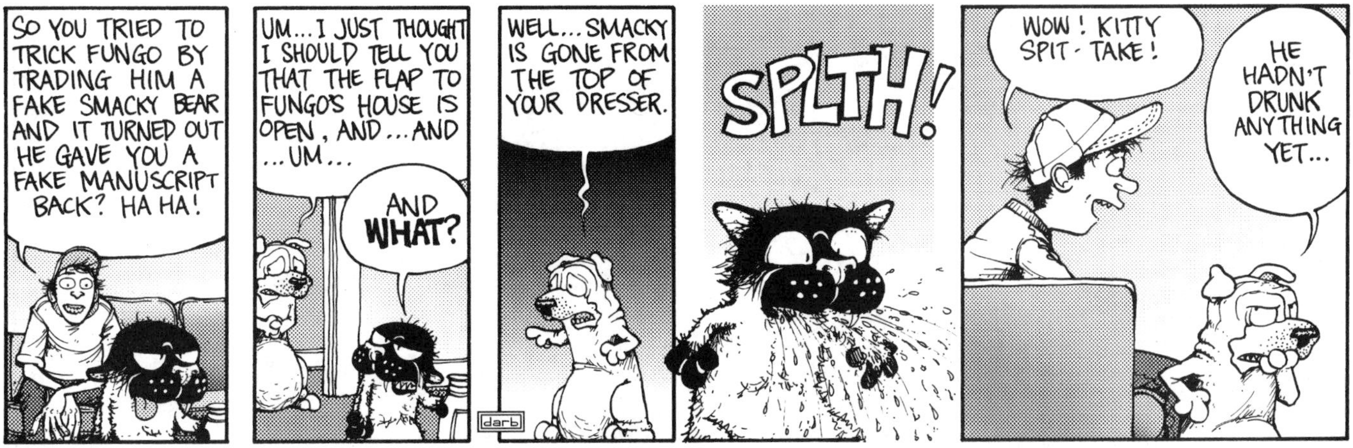
SO YOU TRIED TO TRICK FUNGO BY TRADING HIM A FAKE SMACKY BEAR AND IT TURNED OUT HE GAVE YOU A FAKE MANUSCRIPT BACK? HA HA!
UM... I JUST THOUGHT I SHOULD TELL YOU THAT THE FLAP TO FUNGO'S HOUSE IS OPEN, AND... AND ...UM...
AND WHAT?
darb
WELL... SMACKY IS GONE FROM THE TOP OF YOUR DRESSER.
SPLTH!
WOW! KITTY SPIT-TAKE!
HE HADN'T DRUNK ANYTHING YET...

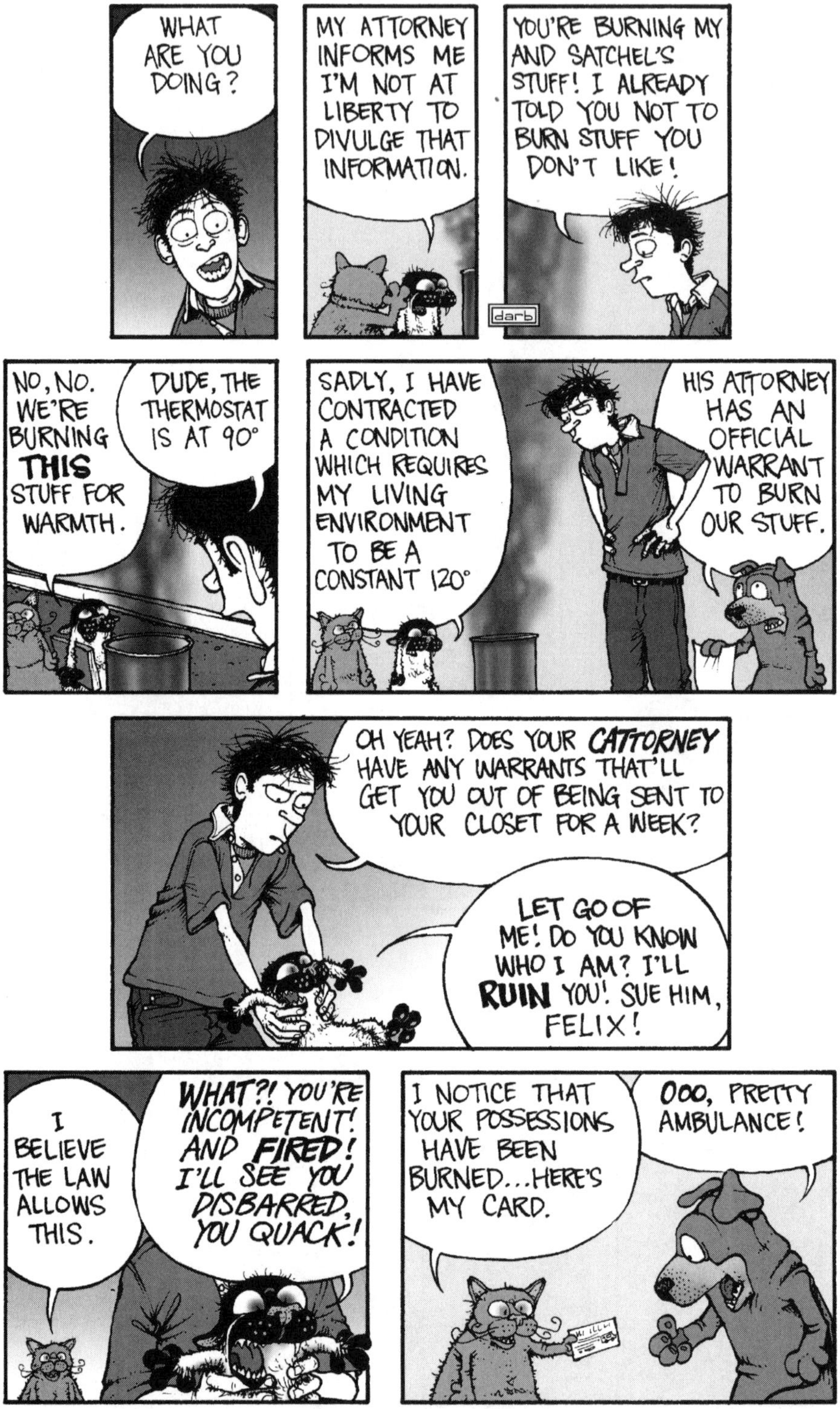
WHAT ARE YOU DOING?
MY ATTORNEY INFORMS ME I'M NOT AT LIBERTY TO DIVULGE THAT INFORMATION.
darb
YOU'RE BURNING MY AND SATCHEL'S STUFF! I ALREADY TOLD YOU NOT TO BURN STUFF YOU DON'T LIKE!
NO, NO. WE'RE BURNING **THIS** STUFF FOR WARMTH.
DUDE, THE THERMOSTAT IS AT 90°
SADLY, I HAVE CONTRACTED A CONDITION WHICH REQUIRES MY LIVING ENVIRONMENT TO BE A CONSTANT 120°
HIS ATTORNEY HAS AN OFFICIAL WARRANT TO BURN OUR STUFF.
OH YEAH? DOES YOUR ***CATTORNEY*** HAVE ANY WARRANTS THAT'LL GET YOU OUT OF BEING SENT TO YOUR CLOSET FOR A WEEK?
LET GO OF ME! DO YOU KNOW WHO I AM? I'LL **RUIN** YOU! SUE HIM, FELIX!
I BELIEVE THE LAW ALLOWS THIS.
WHAT?! YOU'RE INCOMPETENT! AND ***FIRED****! I'LL SEE YOU DISBARRED, YOU QUACK!*
I NOTICE THAT YOUR POSSESSIONS HAVE BEEN BURNED... HERE'S MY CARD.
OOO, PRETTY AMBULANCE!

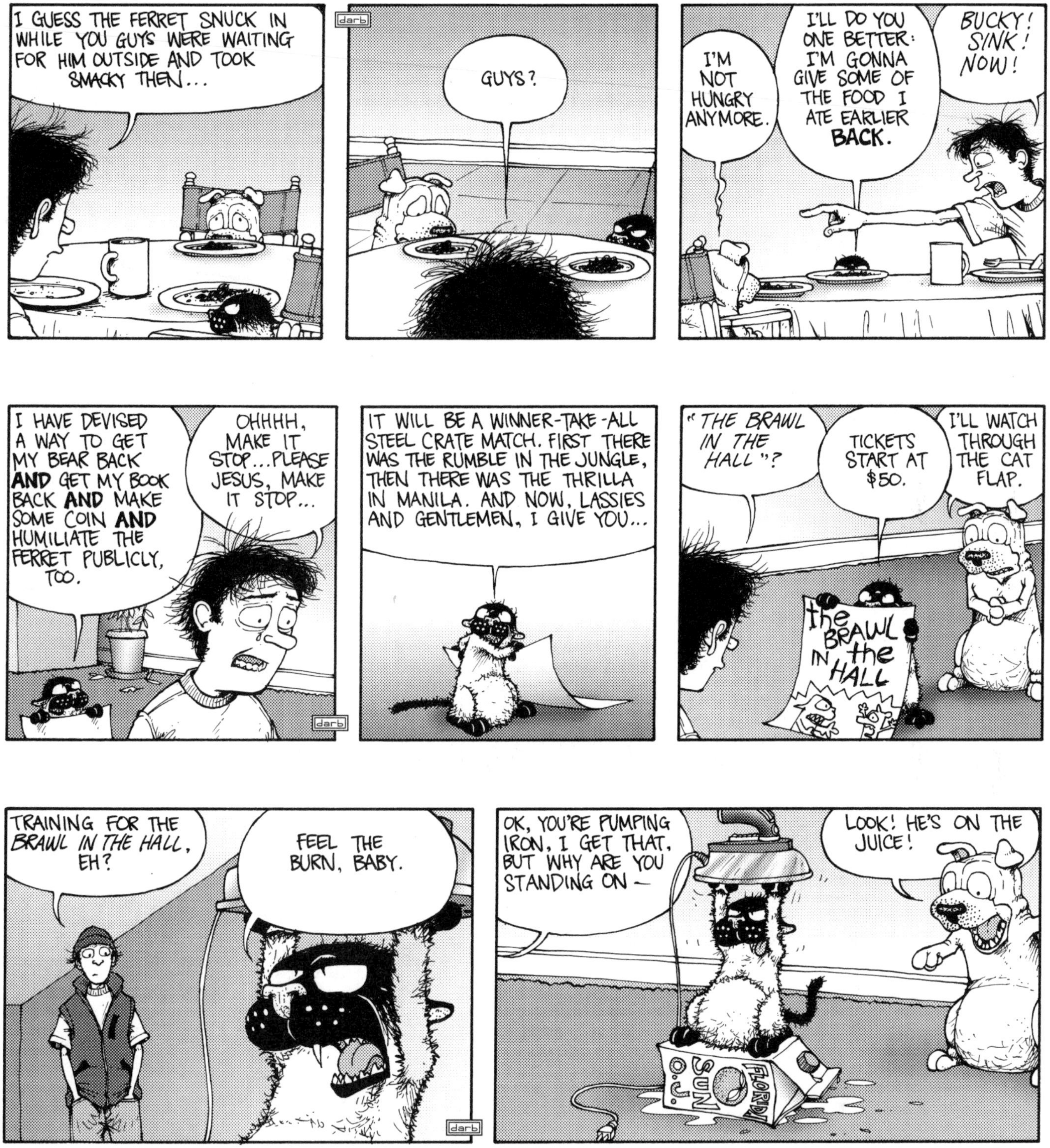
I GUESS THE FERRET SNUCK IN WHILE YOU GUYS WERE WAITING FOR HIM OUTSIDE AND TOOK SMACKY THEN...
darb
GUYS?
I'M NOT HUNGRY ANYMORE.
I'LL DO YOU ONE BETTER: I'M GONNA GIVE SOME OF THE FOOD I ATE EARLIER BACK.
BUCKY! SINK! NOW!
I HAVE DEVISED A WAY TO GET MY BEAR BACK AND GET MY BOOK BACK AND MAKE SOME COIN AND HUMILIATE THE FERRET PUBLICLY, TOO.
OHHHH, MAKE IT STOP... PLEASE JESUS, MAKE IT STOP...
darb
IT WILL BE A WINNER-TAKE-ALL STEEL CRATE MATCH. FIRST THERE WAS THE RUMBLE IN THE JUNGLE, THEN THERE WAS THE THRILLA IN MANILA. AND NOW, LASSIES AND GENTLEMEN, I GIVE YOU...
"THE BRAWL IN THE HALL"?
TICKETS START AT $50.
I'LL WATCH THROUGH THE CAT FLAP.
the BRAWL IN the HALL
TRAINING FOR THE BRAWL IN THE HALL, EH?
FEEL THE BURN, BABY.
darb
OK, YOU'RE PUMPING IRON, I GET THAT, BUT WHY ARE YOU STANDING ON –
LOOK! HE'S ON THE JUICE!
SUN O.J. FLORIDA

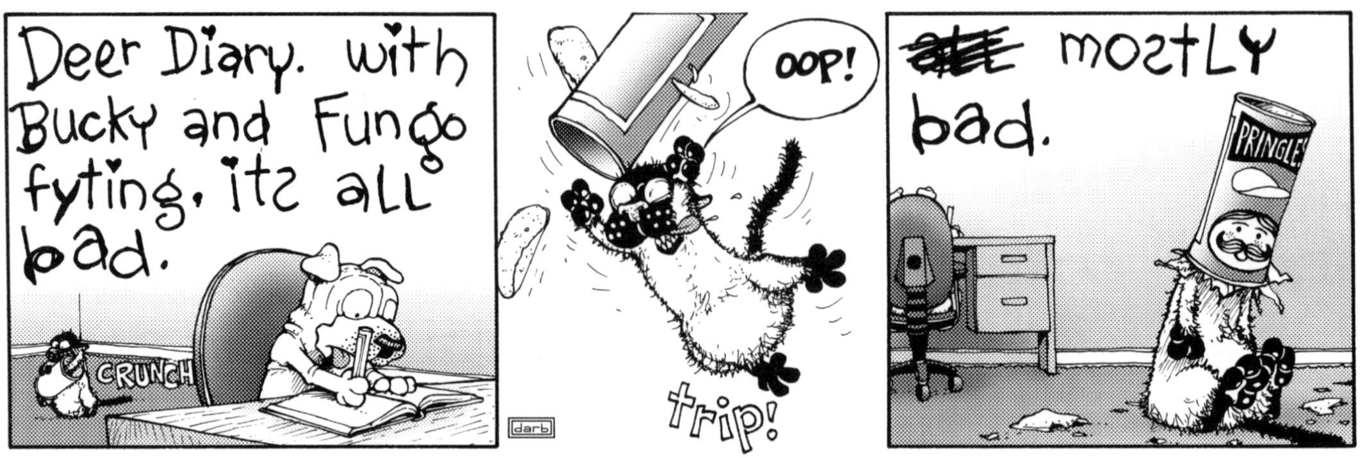
Deer Diary. with Bucky and Fungo fyting. itz all bad.
CRUNCH
darb
OOP!
trip!
mostLy bad.
PRINGLES

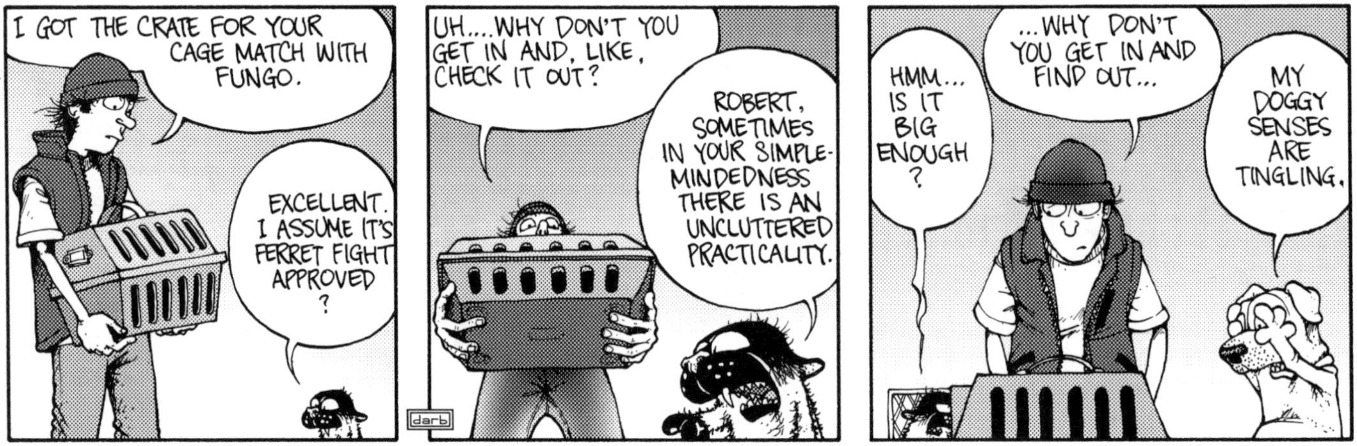
I GOT THE CRATE FOR YOUR CAGE MATCH WITH FUNGO.
EXCELLENT. I ASSUME IT'S FERRET FIGHT APPROVED ?
darb
UH.... WHY DON'T YOU GET IN AND, LIKE, CHECK IT OUT?
ROBERT, SOMETIMES IN YOUR SIMPLE-MINDEDNESS THERE IS AN UNCLUTTERED PRACTICALITY.
HMM... IS IT BIG ENOUGH ?
...WHY DON'T YOU GET IN AND FIND OUT...
MY DOGGY SENSES ARE TINGLING.

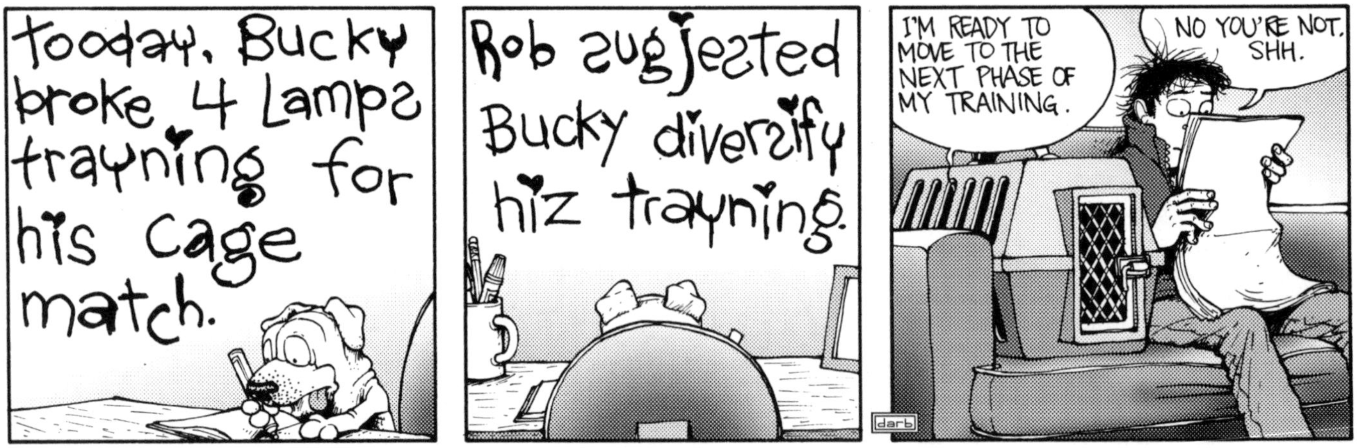
tooday. Bucky broke 4 Lamps trayning for his cage match.
Rob sugjested Bucky diverzify hiz trayning.
darb
I'M READY TO MOVE TO THE NEXT PHASE OF MY TRAINING.
NO YOU'RE NOT. SHH.

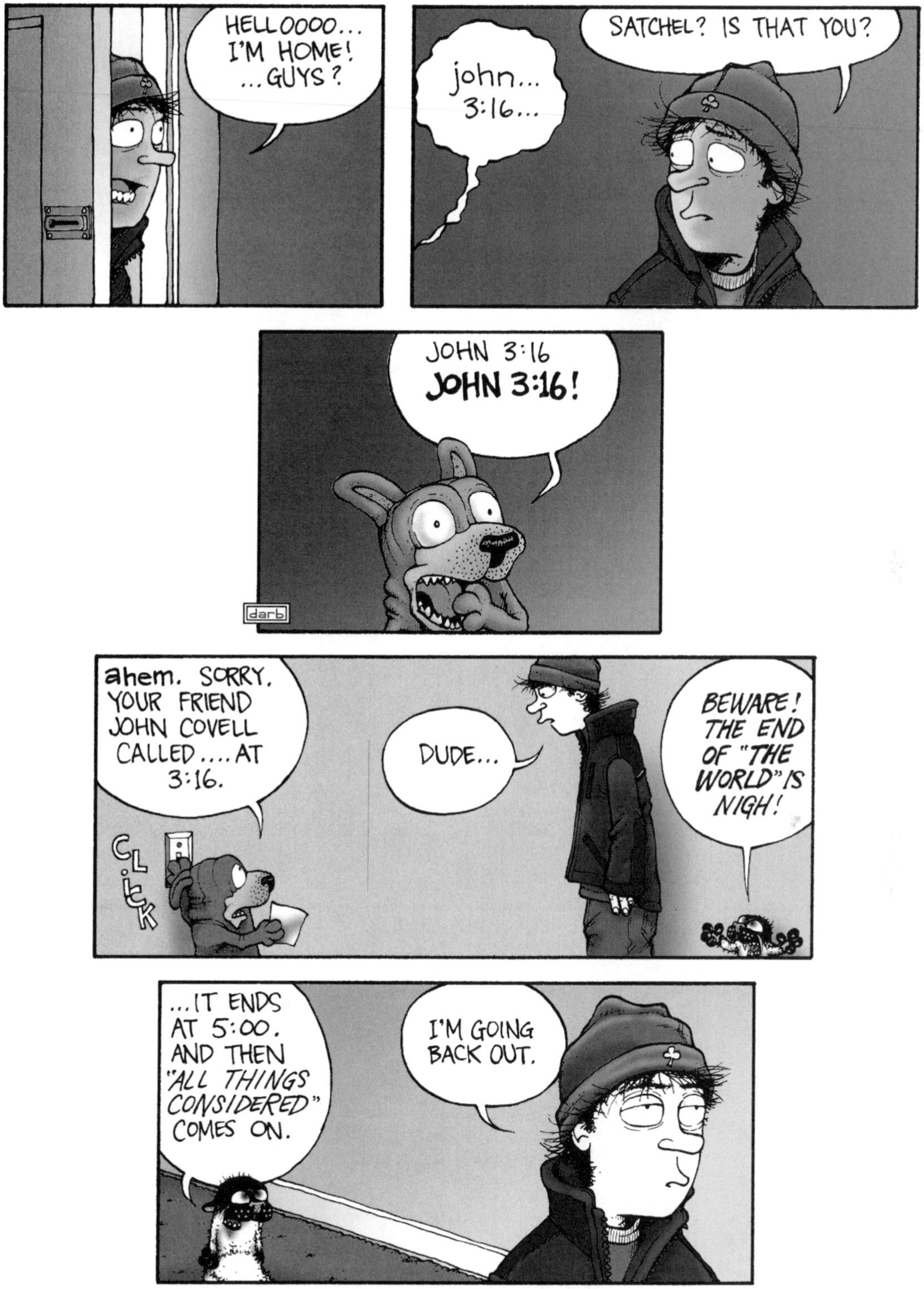
HELLOOOO... I'M HOME! ...GUYS?
john... 3:16...
SATCHEL? IS THAT YOU?
JOHN 3:16
JOHN 3:16!
darb
ahem. SORRY. YOUR FRIEND JOHN COVELL CALLED.... AT 3:16.
CLICK
DUDE...
BEWARE! THE END OF "THE WORLD" IS NIGH!
...IT ENDS AT 5:00. AND THEN "ALL THINGS CONSIDERED" COMES ON.
I'M GOING BACK OUT.

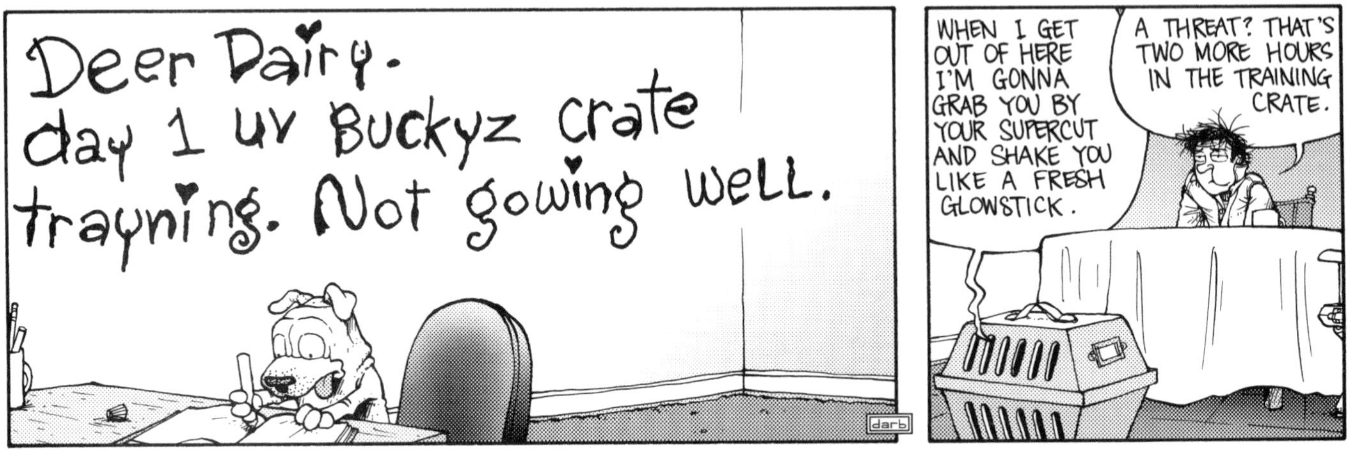
Deer Dairy.
day 1 uv Buckyz crate trayning. Not gowing well.
WHEN I GET OUT OF HERE I'M GONNA GRAB YOU BY YOUR SUPERCUT AND SHAKE YOU LIKE A FRESH GLOWSTICK.
A THREAT? THAT'S TWO MORE HOURS IN THE TRAINING CRATE.
darb

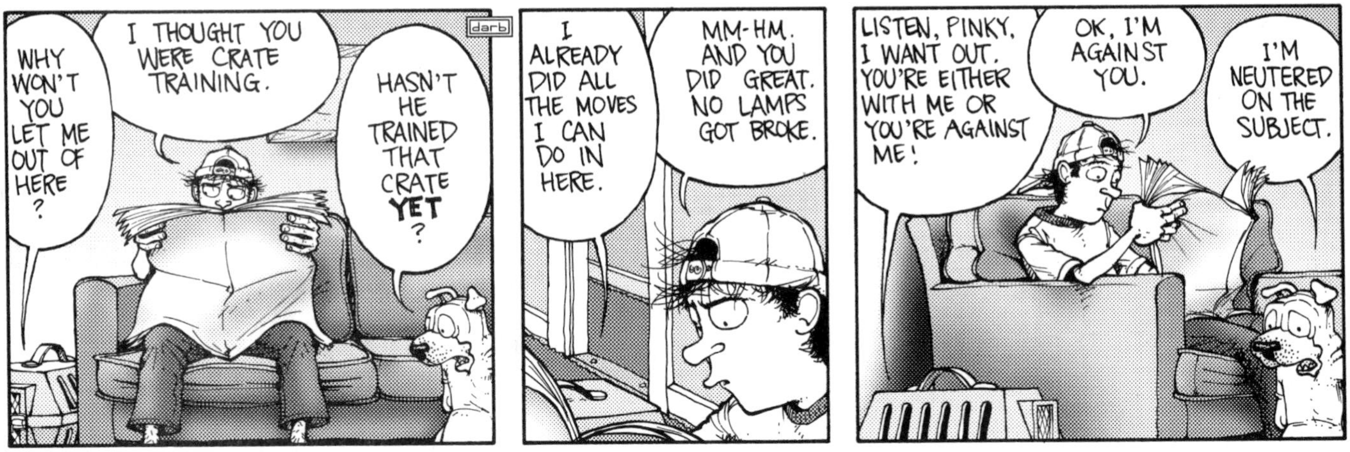
WHY WON'T YOU LET ME OUT OF HERE?
I THOUGHT YOU WERE CRATE TRAINING.
HASN'T HE TRAINED THAT CRATE **YET**?
I ALREADY DID ALL THE MOVES I CAN DO IN HERE.
MM-HM. AND YOU DID GREAT. NO LAMPS GOT BROKE.
LISTEN, PINKY, I WANT OUT. YOU'RE EITHER WITH ME OR YOU'RE AGAINST ME!
OK, I'M AGAINST YOU.
I'M NEUTERED ON THE SUBJECT.
darb

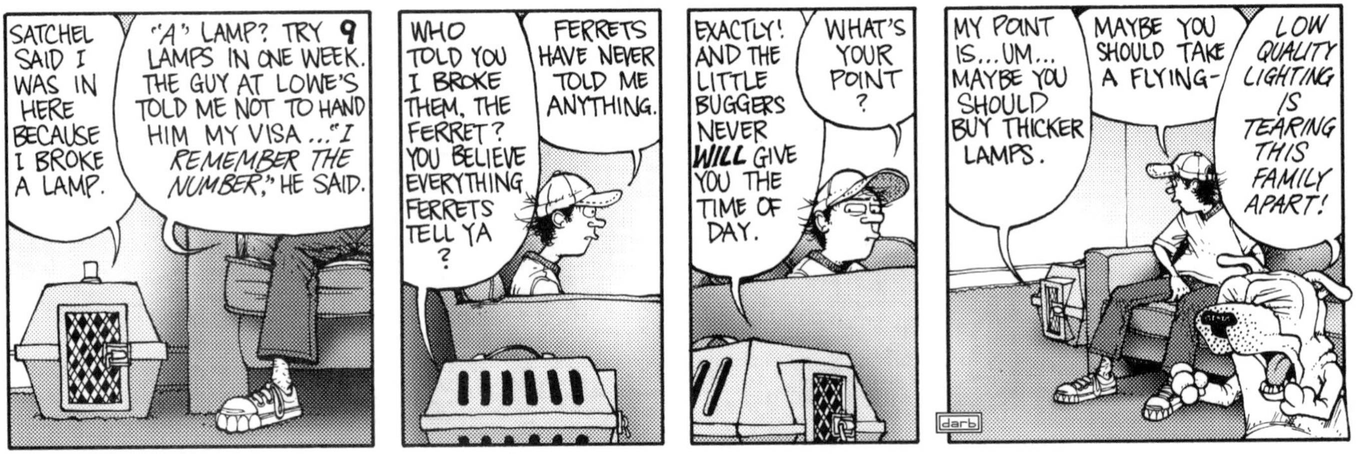
SATCHEL SAID I WAS IN HERE BECAUSE I BROKE A LAMP.
"A" LAMP? TRY 9 LAMPS IN ONE WEEK. THE GUY AT LOWE'S TOLD ME NOT TO HAND HIM MY VISA ... "*I REMEMBER THE NUMBER*," HE SAID.
WHO TOLD YOU I BROKE THEM, THE FERRET? YOU BELIEVE EVERYTHING FERRETS TELL YA?
FERRETS HAVE NEVER TOLD ME ANYTHING.
EXACTLY! AND THE LITTLE BUGGERS NEVER ***WILL*** GIVE YOU THE TIME OF DAY.
WHAT'S YOUR POINT?
MY POINT IS... UM... MAYBE YOU SHOULD BUY THICKER LAMPS.
MAYBE YOU SHOULD TAKE A FLYING-
LOW QUALITY LIGHTING IS TEARING THIS FAMILY APART!
darb

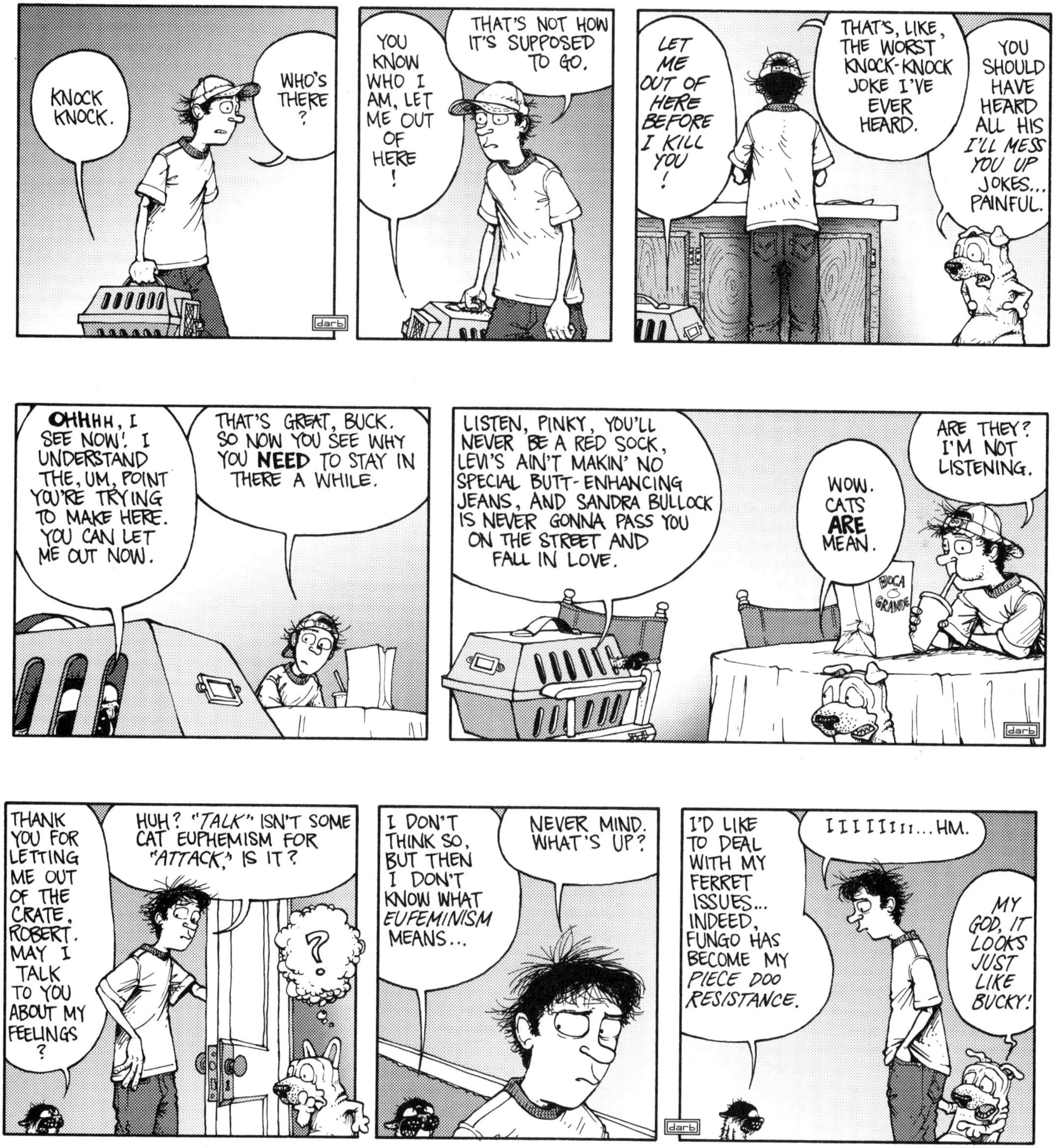
KNOCK KNOCK.
WHO'S THERE?
YOU KNOW WHO I AM, LET ME OUT OF HERE!
THAT'S NOT HOW IT'S SUPPOSED TO GO.
LET ME OUT OF HERE BEFORE I KILL YOU!
THAT'S, LIKE, THE WORST KNOCK-KNOCK JOKE I'VE EVER HEARD.
YOU SHOULD HAVE HEARD ALL HIS I'LL MESS YOU UP JOKES... PAINFUL.
darb
OHHHH, I SEE NOW! I UNDERSTAND THE, UM, POINT YOU'RE TRYING TO MAKE HERE. YOU CAN LET ME OUT NOW.
THAT'S GREAT, BUCK. SO NOW YOU SEE WHY YOU NEED TO STAY IN THERE A WHILE.
LISTEN, PINKY, YOU'LL NEVER BE A RED SOCK, LEVI'S AIN'T MAKIN' NO SPECIAL BUTT-ENHANCING JEANS, AND SANDRA BULLOCK IS NEVER GONNA PASS YOU ON THE STREET AND FALL IN LOVE.
WOW. CATS ARE MEAN.
ARE THEY? I'M NOT LISTENING.
BOCA GRANDE
darb
THANK YOU FOR LETTING ME OUT OF THE CRATE, ROBERT. MAY I TALK TO YOU ABOUT MY FEELINGS?
HUH? "TALK" ISN'T SOME CAT EUPHEMISM FOR "ATTACK," IS IT?
?
I DON'T THINK SO, BUT THEN I DON'T KNOW WHAT EUFEMINISM MEANS...
NEVER MIND. WHAT'S UP?
darb
I'D LIKE TO DEAL WITH MY FERRET ISSUES... INDEED, FUNGO HAS BECOME MY PIECE DOO RESISTANCE.
IIIIIIII... HM.
MY GOD, IT LOOKS JUST LIKE BUCKY!

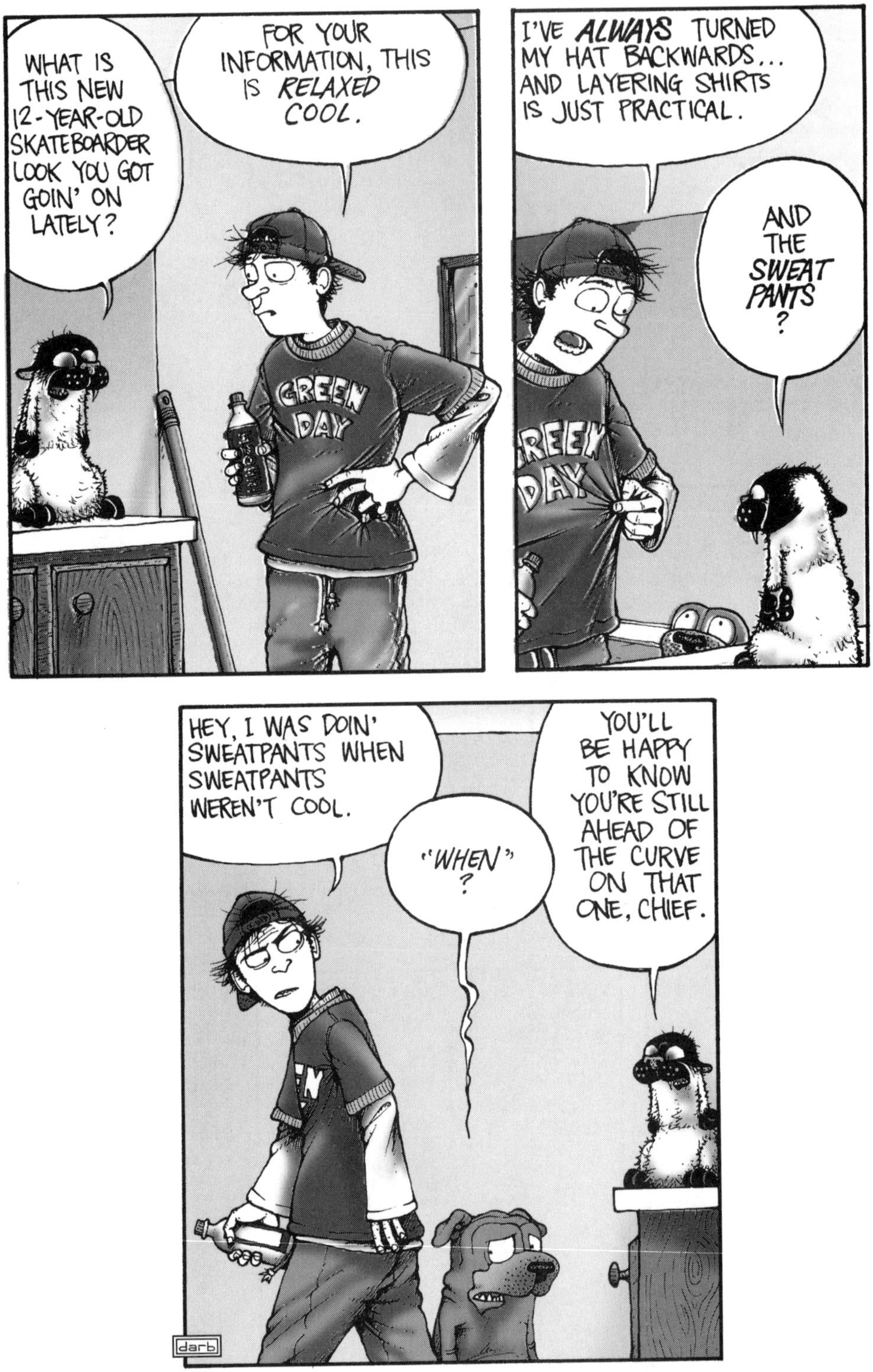
WHAT IS THIS NEW 12-YEAR-OLD SKATEBOARDER LOOK YOU GOT GOIN' ON LATELY?
FOR YOUR INFORMATION, THIS IS *RELAXED* COOL.
GREEN DAY
I'VE ***ALWAYS*** TURNED MY HAT BACKWARDS... AND LAYERING SHIRTS IS JUST PRACTICAL.
AND THE ***SWEAT PANTS***?
HEY, I WAS DOIN' SWEATPANTS WHEN SWEATPANTS WEREN'T COOL.
"*WHEN*"?
YOU'LL BE HAPPY TO KNOW YOU'RE STILL AHEAD OF THE CURVE ON THAT ONE, CHIEF.
darb

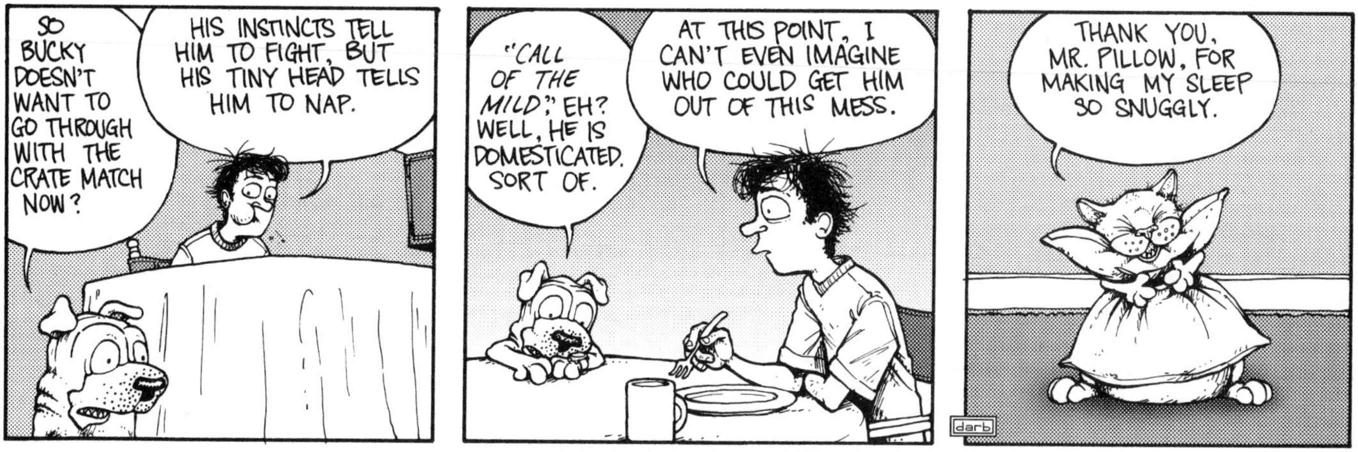
SO BUCKY DOESN'T WANT TO GO THROUGH WITH THE CRATE MATCH NOW?
HIS INSTINCTS TELL HIM TO FIGHT, BUT HIS TINY HEAD TELLS HIM TO NAP.
"CALL OF THE MILD," EH? WELL, HE IS DOMESTICATED. SORT OF.
AT THIS POINT, I CAN'T EVEN IMAGINE WHO COULD GET HIM OUT OF THIS MESS.
THANK YOU, MR. PILLOW, FOR MAKING MY SLEEP SO SNUGGLY.

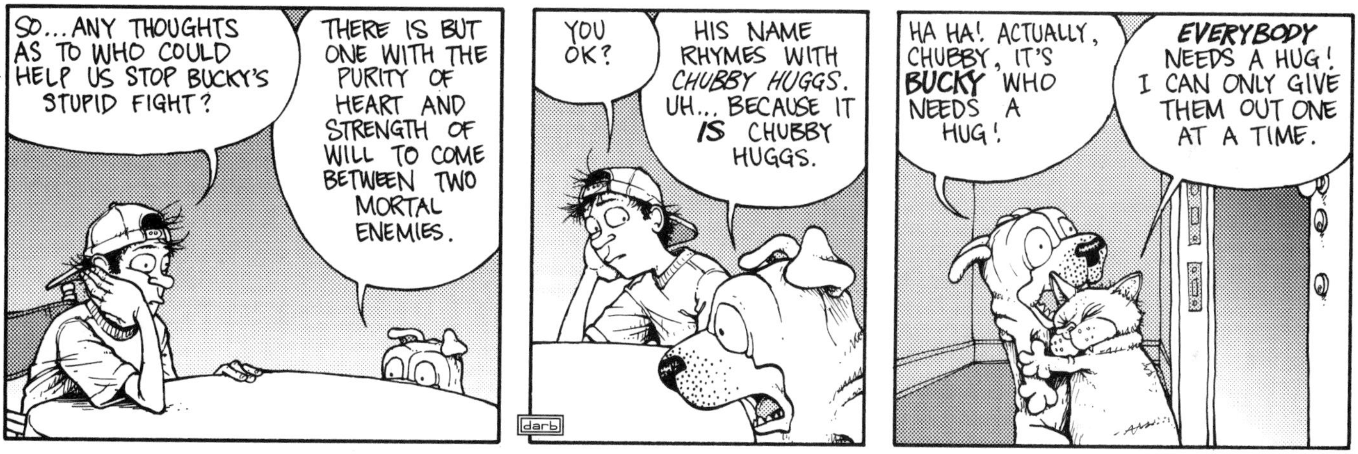
SO... ANY THOUGHTS AS TO WHO COULD HELP US STOP BUCKY'S STUPID FIGHT?
THERE IS BUT ONE WITH THE PURITY OF HEART AND STRENGTH OF WILL TO COME BETWEEN TWO MORTAL ENEMIES.
YOU OK?
HIS NAME RHYMES WITH CHUBBY HUGGS. UH... BECAUSE IT IS CHUBBY HUGGS.
HA HA! ACTUALLY, CHUBBY, IT'S BUCKY WHO NEEDS A HUG!
EVERYBODY NEEDS A HUG! I CAN ONLY GIVE THEM OUT ONE AT A TIME.

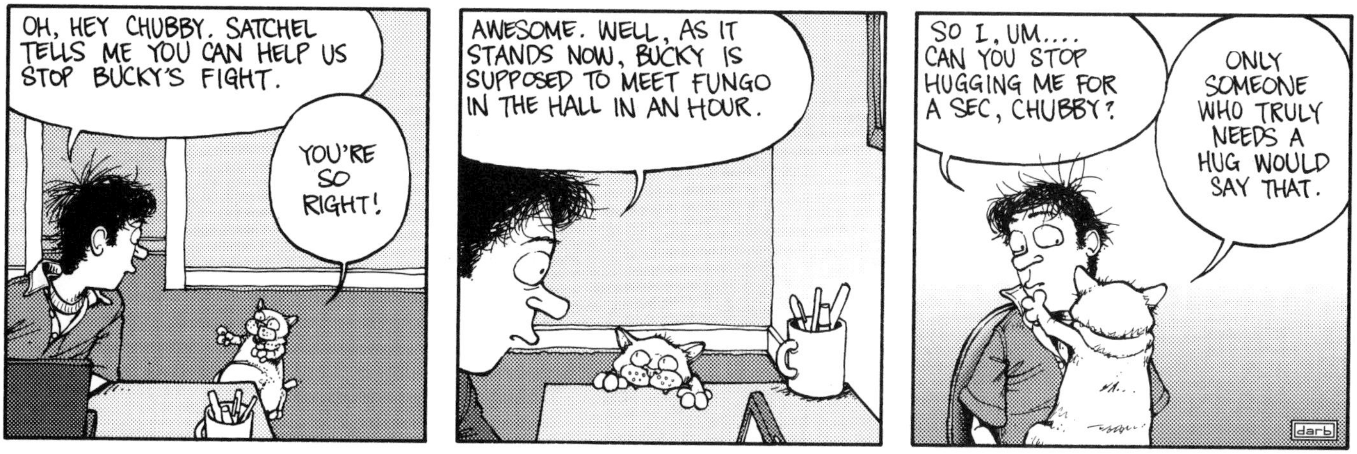
OH, HEY CHUBBY. SATCHEL TELLS ME YOU CAN HELP US STOP BUCKY'S FIGHT.
YOU'RE SO RIGHT!
AWESOME. WELL, AS IT STANDS NOW, BUCKY IS SUPPOSED TO MEET FUNGO IN THE HALL IN AN HOUR.
SO I, UM.... CAN YOU STOP HUGGING ME FOR A SEC, CHUBBY?
ONLY SOMEONE WHO TRULY NEEDS A HUG WOULD SAY THAT.

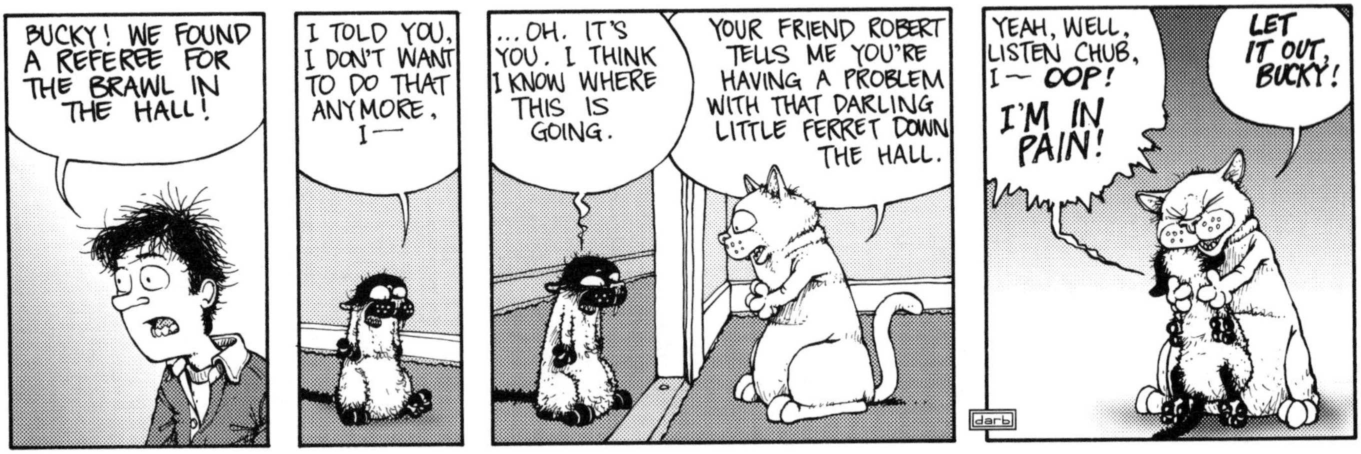
BUCKY! WE FOUND A REFEREE FOR THE BRAWL IN THE HALL!
I TOLD YOU, I DON'T WANT TO DO THAT ANYMORE, I—
...OH. IT'S YOU. I THINK I KNOW WHERE THIS IS GOING.
YOUR FRIEND ROBERT TELLS ME YOU'RE HAVING A PROBLEM WITH THAT DARLING LITTLE FERRET DOWN THE HALL.
YEAH, WELL, LISTEN CHUB, I— **OOP!**
I'M IN PAIN!
LET IT OUT, BUCKY!
darb

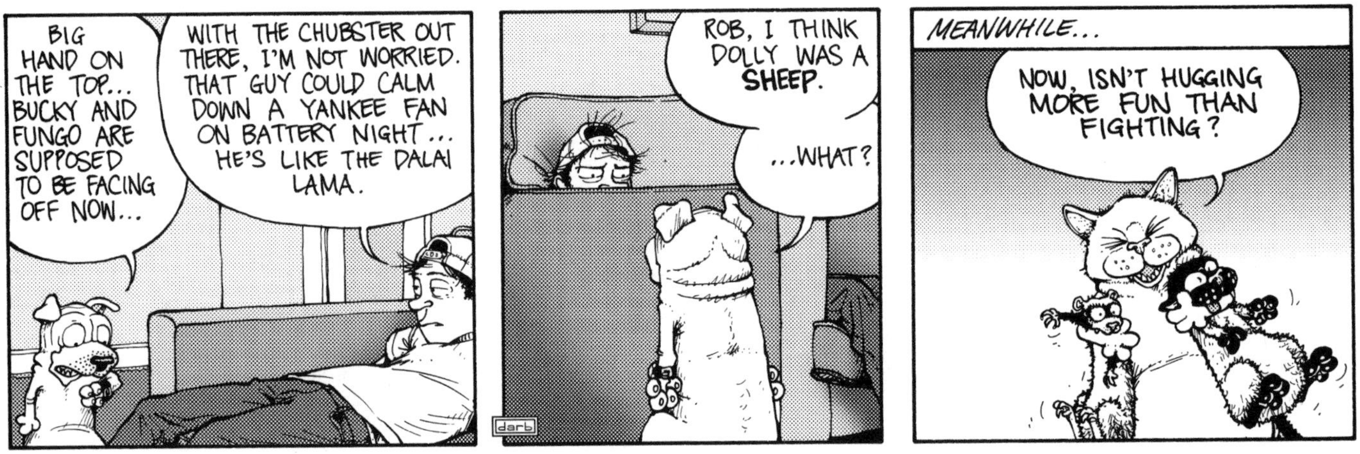
BIG HAND ON THE TOP... BUCKY AND FUNGO ARE SUPPOSED TO BE FACING OFF NOW...
WITH THE CHUBSTER OUT THERE, I'M NOT WORRIED. THAT GUY COULD CALM DOWN A YANKEE FAN ON BATTERY NIGHT... HE'S LIKE THE DALAI LAMA.
darb
ROB, I THINK DOLLY WAS A **SHEEP**.
...WHAT?
MEANWHILE...
NOW, ISN'T HUGGING MORE FUN THAN FIGHTING?

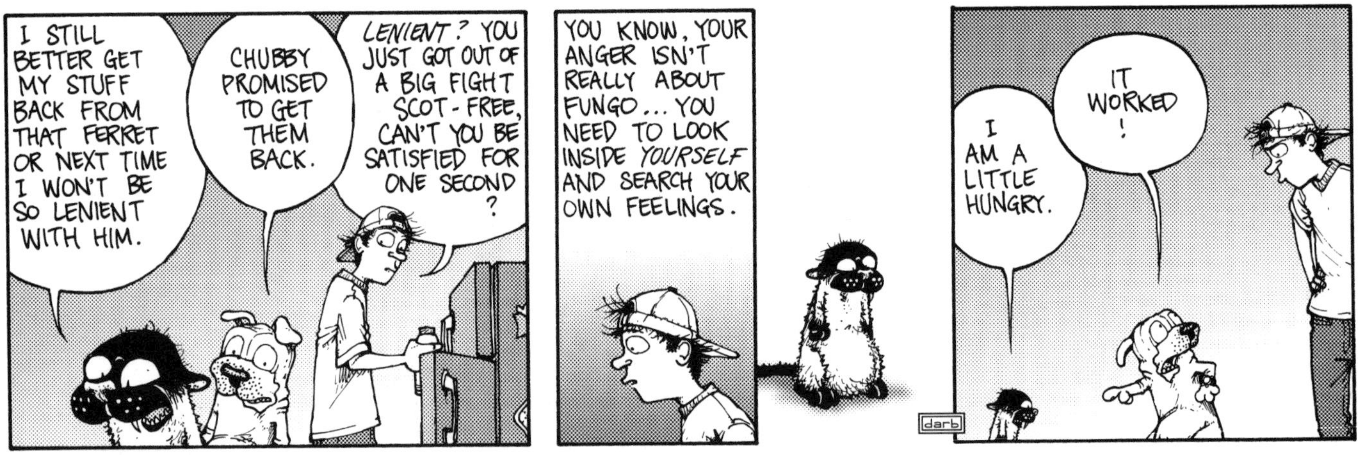
I STILL BETTER GET MY STUFF BACK FROM THAT FERRET OR NEXT TIME I WON'T BE SO LENIENT WITH HIM.
CHUBBY PROMISED TO GET THEM BACK.
LENIENT? YOU JUST GOT OUT OF A BIG FIGHT SCOT-FREE, CAN'T YOU BE SATISFIED FOR ONE SECOND?
YOU KNOW, YOUR ANGER ISN'T REALLY ABOUT FUNGO... YOU NEED TO LOOK INSIDE *YOURSELF* AND SEARCH YOUR OWN FEELINGS.
darb
I AM A LITTLE HUNGRY.
IT WORKED!

OH... SATCHEL... HELLO... HOW LONG HAVE YOU BEEN STANDING THERE?
HI BUCKY! I'VE BEEN HERE MY NORMAL *IN-ONE-PLACE* TIME, THANKS FOR ASKING!
THAT LONG? WELL, IF YOU KNOW WHAT'S GOOD FOR YOU, YOU'LL FORGET THIS EVER HAPPENED.
FORGET WHAT HAPPENED?
WHAT'S GOIN' ON, BOYOS?
EXACTLY.
WELL, BUCKY SAYS NOTHING, BUT WITH YOUR WALLET ON THE FLOOR AND ALL YOUR CREDIT CARD NUMBERS WRITTEN ON THAT PAD, I WOULD HAVE THOUGHT **SOMETHIN'** WAS GOIN' ON! HA HA HA! AHHHH...
darb
ALRIGHT. TO YOUR CLOSET.
YOU BETTER CALL THE WITLESS RELOCATION PROGRAM BEFORE I GET OUT.
OH, I LOVE CALL-IN SHOWS!

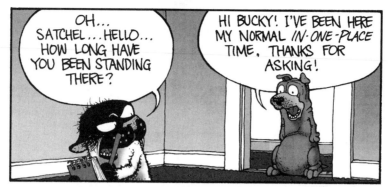

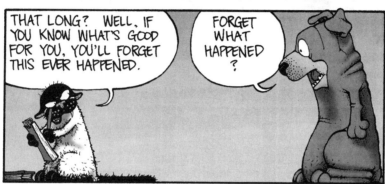

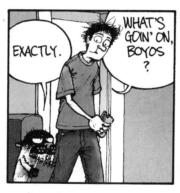

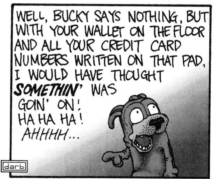

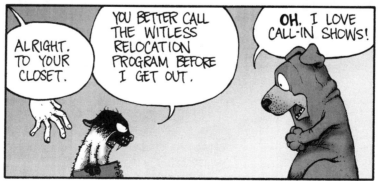

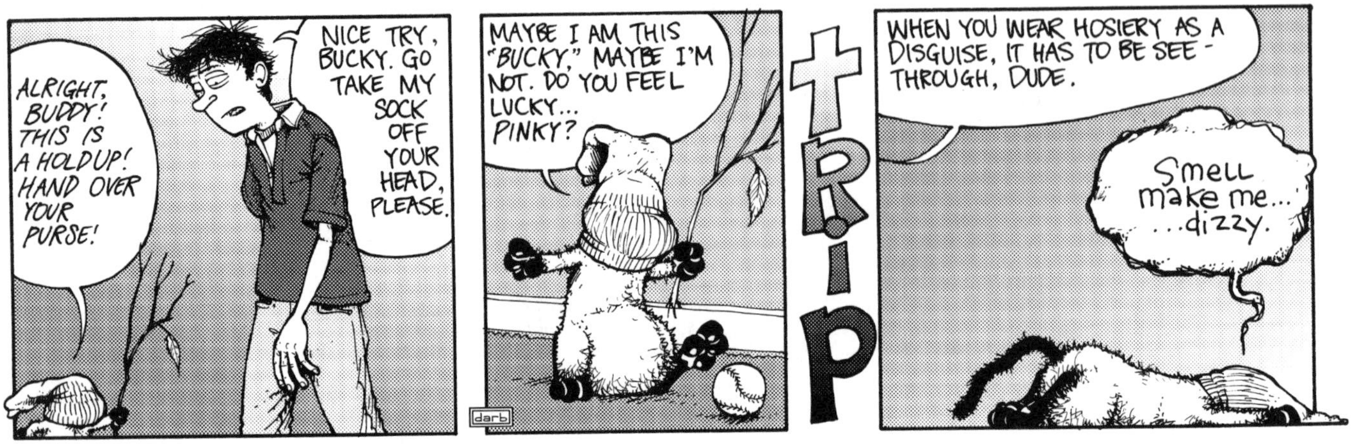
ALRIGHT, BUDDY! THIS IS A HOLDUP! HAND OVER YOUR PURSE!
NICE TRY, BUCKY. GO TAKE MY SOCK OFF YOUR HEAD, PLEASE.
MAYBE I AM THIS "BUCKY," MAYBE I'M NOT. DO YOU FEEL LUCKY... PINKY?
TRIP
WHEN YOU WEAR HOSIERY AS A DISGUISE, IT HAS TO BE SEE-THROUGH, DUDE.
Smell make me... ...dizzy.

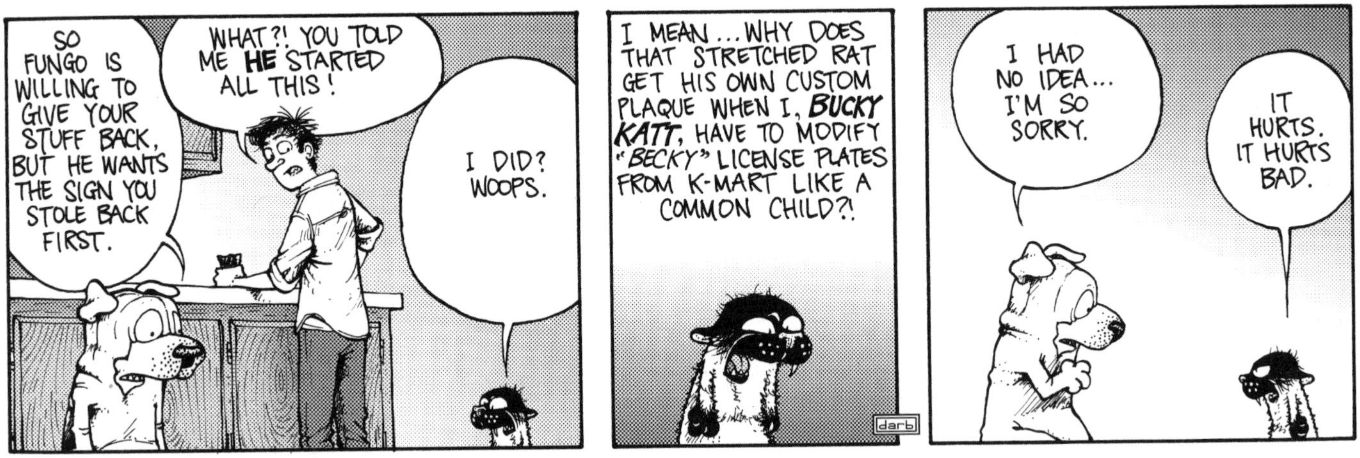
SO FUNGO IS WILLING TO GIVE YOUR STUFF BACK, BUT HE WANTS THE SIGN YOU STOLE BACK FIRST.
WHAT?! YOU TOLD ME HE STARTED ALL THIS!
I DID? WOOPS.
I MEAN... WHY DOES THAT STRETCHED RAT GET HIS OWN CUSTOM PLAQUE WHEN I, BUCKY KATT, HAVE TO MODIFY "BECKY" LICENSE PLATES FROM K-MART LIKE A COMMON CHILD?!
I HAD NO IDEA... I'M SO SORRY.
IT HURTS. IT HURTS BAD.

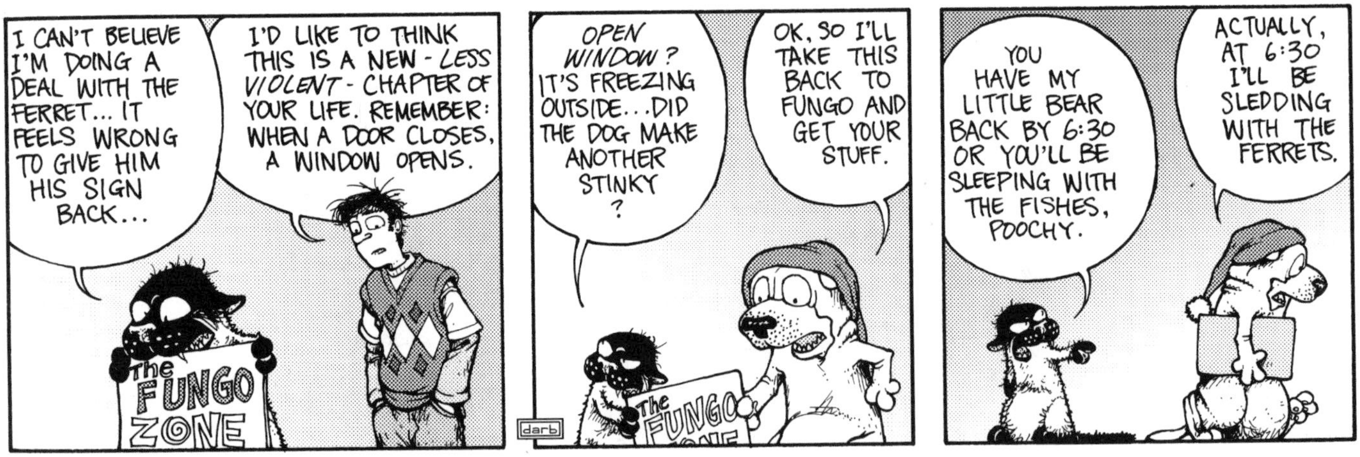
I CAN'T BELIEVE I'M DOING A DEAL WITH THE FERRET... IT FEELS WRONG TO GIVE HIM HIS SIGN BACK...
I'D LIKE TO THINK THIS IS A NEW - LESS VIOLENT - CHAPTER OF YOUR LIFE. REMEMBER: WHEN A DOOR CLOSES, A WINDOW OPENS.
The FUNGO ZONE
OPEN WINDOW? IT'S FREEZING OUTSIDE... DID THE DOG MAKE ANOTHER STINKY?
OK, SO I'LL TAKE THIS BACK TO FUNGO AND GET YOUR STUFF.
YOU HAVE MY LITTLE BEAR BACK BY 6:30 OR YOU'LL BE SLEEPING WITH THE FISHES, POOCHY.
ACTUALLY, AT 6:30 I'LL BE SLEDDING WITH THE FERRETS.

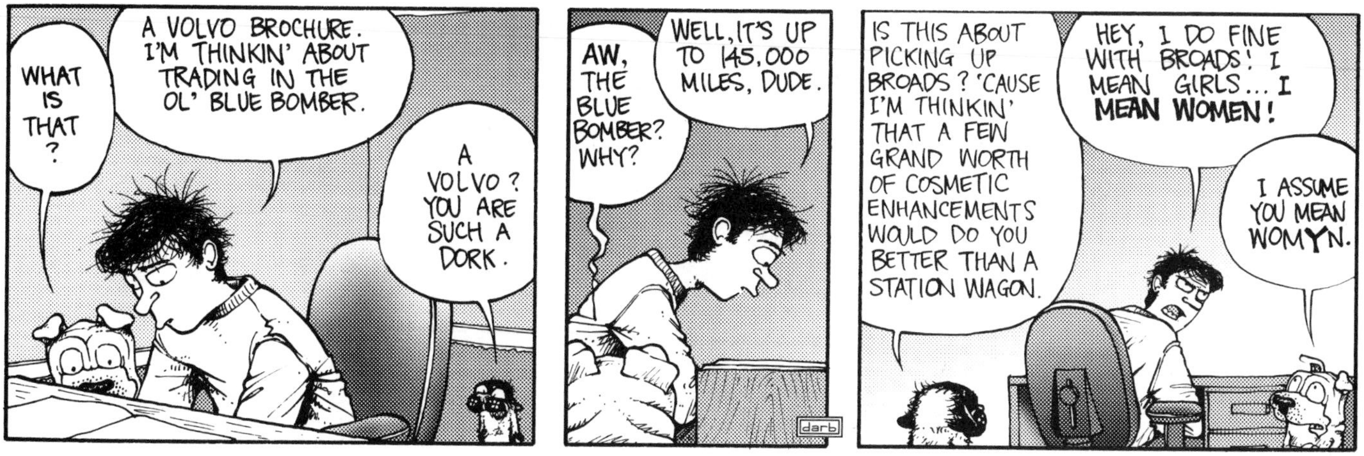
WHAT IS THAT?
A VOLVO BROCHURE. I'M THINKIN' ABOUT TRADING IN THE OL' BLUE BOMBER.
A VOLVO? YOU ARE SUCH A DORK.
AW, THE BLUE BOMBER? WHY?
WELL, IT'S UP TO 145,000 MILES, DUDE.
IS THIS ABOUT PICKING UP BROADS? 'CAUSE I'M THINKIN' THAT A FEW GRAND WORTH OF COSMETIC ENHANCEMENTS WOULD DO YOU BETTER THAN A STATION WAGON.
HEY, I DO FINE WITH BROADS! I MEAN GIRLS... I MEAN WOMEN!
I ASSUME YOU MEAN WOMYN.
darb

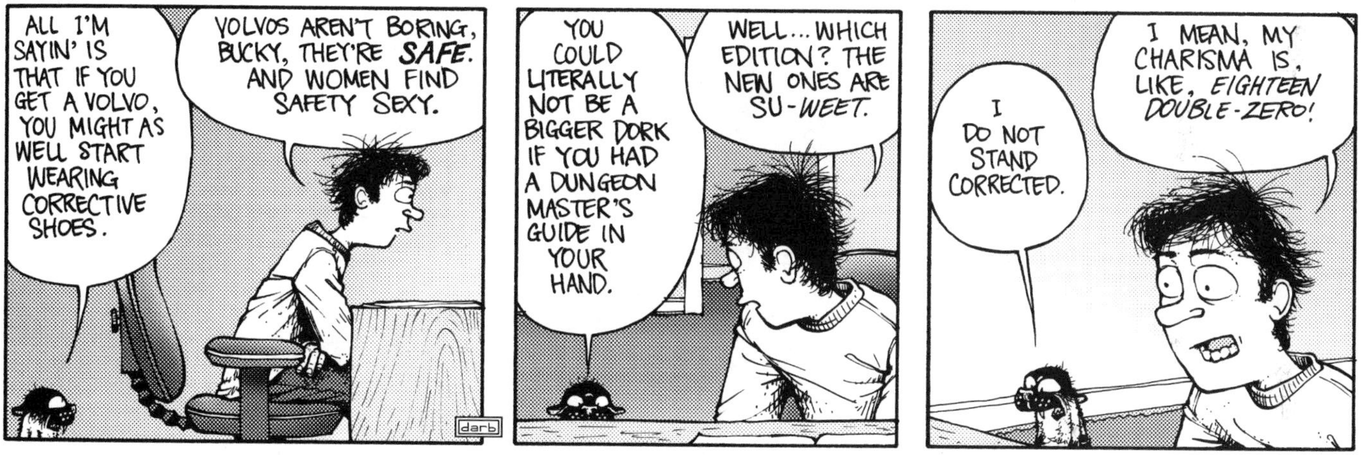
ALL I'M SAYIN' IS THAT IF YOU GET A VOLVO, YOU MIGHT AS WELL START WEARING CORRECTIVE SHOES.
VOLVOS AREN'T BORING, BUCKY, THEY'RE SAFE. AND WOMEN FIND SAFETY SEXY.
YOU COULD LITERALLY NOT BE A BIGGER DORK IF YOU HAD A DUNGEON MASTER'S GUIDE IN YOUR HAND.
WELL... WHICH EDITION? THE NEW ONES ARE SU-WEET.
I DO NOT STAND CORRECTED.
I MEAN, MY CHARISMA IS, LIKE, EIGHTEEN DOUBLE-ZERO!
darb

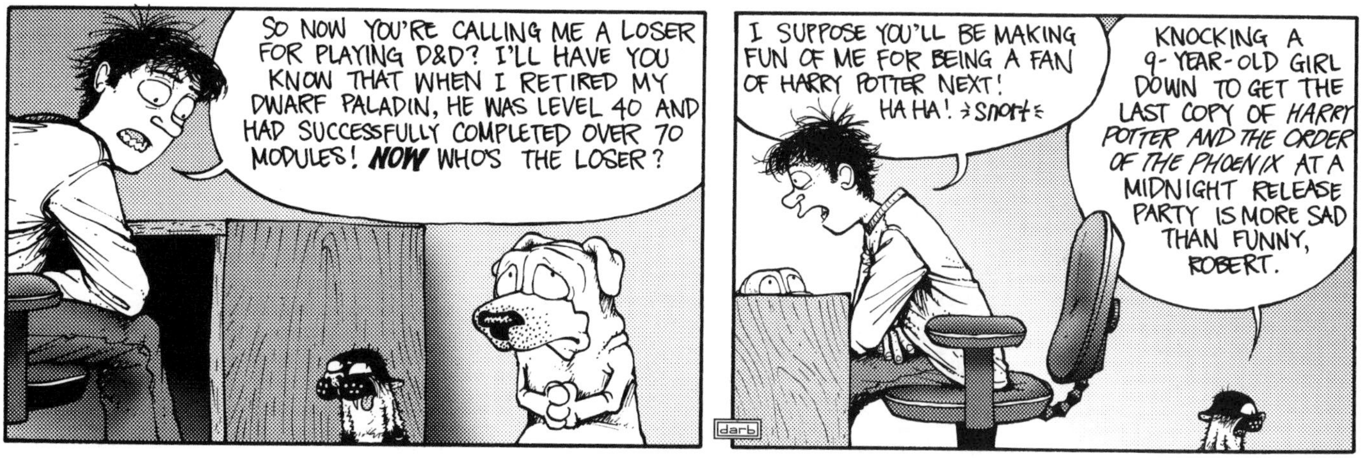
SO NOW YOU'RE CALLING ME A LOSER FOR PLAYING D&D? I'LL HAVE YOU KNOW THAT WHEN I RETIRED MY DWARF PALADIN, HE WAS LEVEL 40 AND HAD SUCCESSFULLY COMPLETED OVER 70 MODULES! NOW WHO'S THE LOSER?
I SUPPOSE YOU'LL BE MAKING FUN OF ME FOR BEING A FAN OF HARRY POTTER NEXT!
HA HA! ≥SNORT≤
KNOCKING A 9-YEAR-OLD GIRL DOWN TO GET THE LAST COPY OF HARRY POTTER AND THE ORDER OF THE PHOENIX AT A MIDNIGHT RELEASE PARTY IS MORE SAD THAN FUNNY, ROBERT.
darb

NOBODY TAKES THE CATNIP MOUSE! NOBODY!
CALM DOWN, DUDE, YOU'RE ACTING LIKE A FREAK.
LET ME TALK TO HIM, ROB.
WHO ARE YOU, THE CAT WHISPERER? I'M DEALING WITH THIS.
I HAVE A BOTTLE! BACK OFF!
BUCKY, THAT BOTTLE IS—
WAP!
BONK
darb
...PLASTIC.
OWWW...
HERE YOU GO.

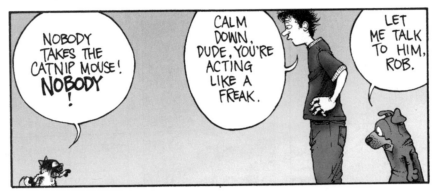

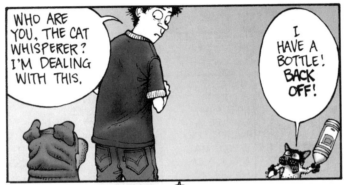

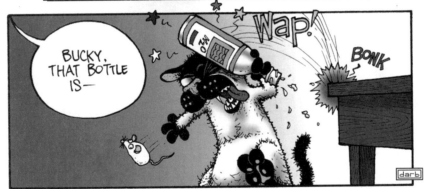

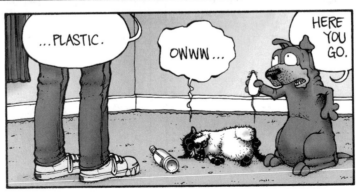

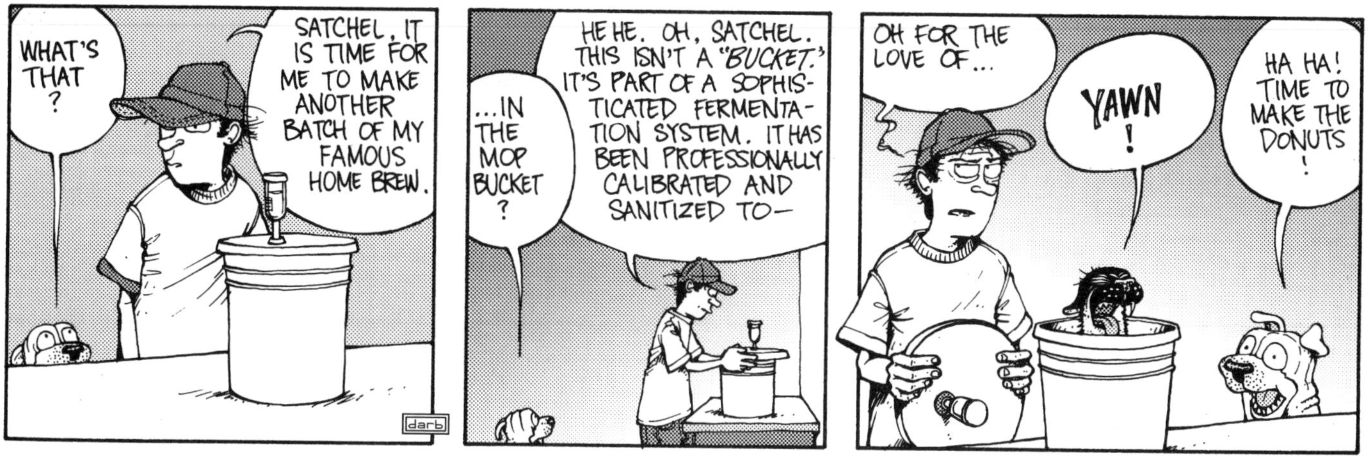
WHAT'S THAT ?
SATCHEL, IT IS TIME FOR ME TO MAKE ANOTHER BATCH OF MY FAMOUS HOME BREW.
...IN THE MOP BUCKET ?
HE HE. OH, SATCHEL. THIS ISN'T A "BUCKET." IT'S PART OF A SOPHISTICATED FERMENTATION SYSTEM. IT HAS BEEN PROFESSIONALLY CALIBRATED AND SANITIZED TO—
OH FOR THE LOVE OF...
YAWN !
HA HA! TIME TO MAKE THE DONUTS !
darb

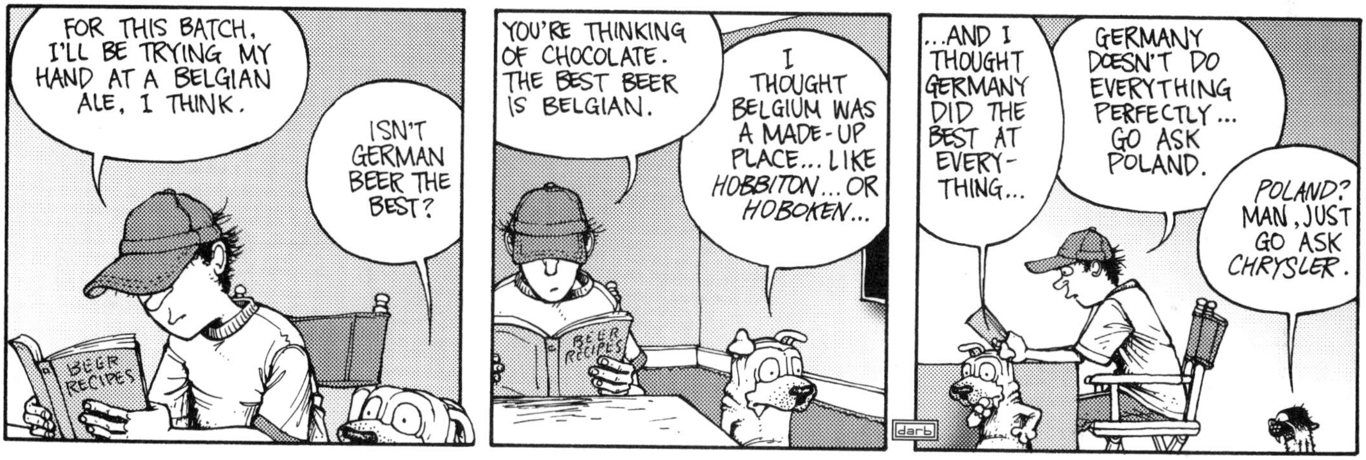
FOR THIS BATCH, I'LL BE TRYING MY HAND AT A BELGIAN ALE, I THINK.
ISN'T GERMAN BEER THE BEST?
BEER RECIPES
YOU'RE THINKING OF CHOCOLATE. THE BEST BEER IS BELGIAN.
I THOUGHT BELGIUM WAS A MADE-UP PLACE... LIKE HOBBITON... OR HOBOKEN...
...AND I THOUGHT GERMANY DID THE BEST AT EVERYTHING...
GERMANY DOESN'T DO EVERYTHING PERFECTLY... GO ASK POLAND.
POLAND? MAN, JUST GO ASK CHRYSLER.
darb

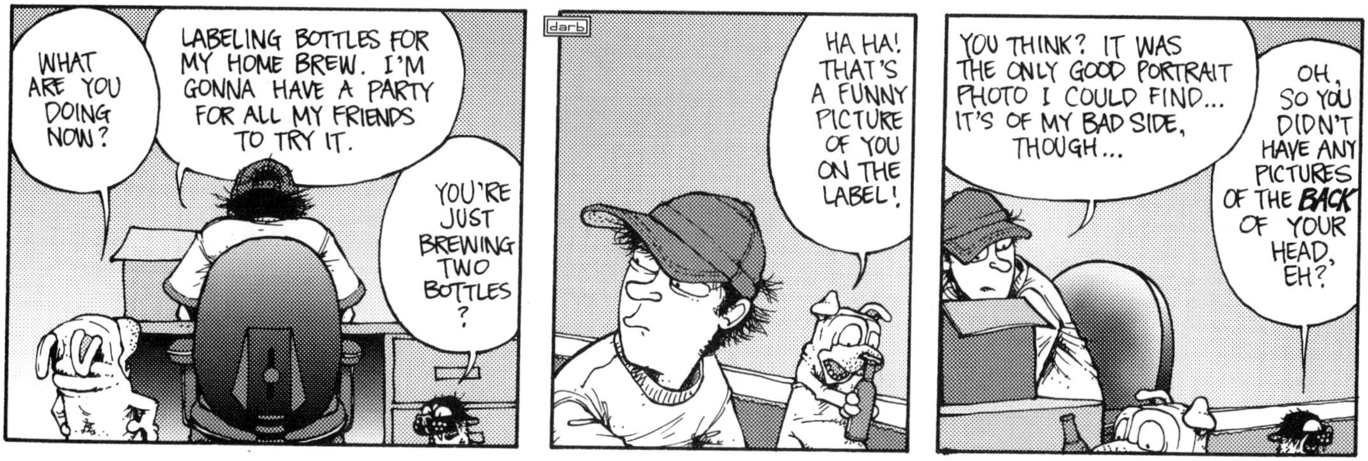
WHAT ARE YOU DOING NOW?
LABELING BOTTLES FOR MY HOME BREW. I'M GONNA HAVE A PARTY FOR ALL MY FRIENDS TO TRY IT.
YOU'RE JUST BREWING TWO BOTTLES ?
HA HA! THAT'S A FUNNY PICTURE OF YOU ON THE LABEL!
YOU THINK? IT WAS THE ONLY GOOD PORTRAIT PHOTO I COULD FIND... IT'S OF MY BAD SIDE, THOUGH...
OH, SO YOU DIDN'T HAVE ANY PICTURES OF THE BACK OF YOUR HEAD, EH?
darb

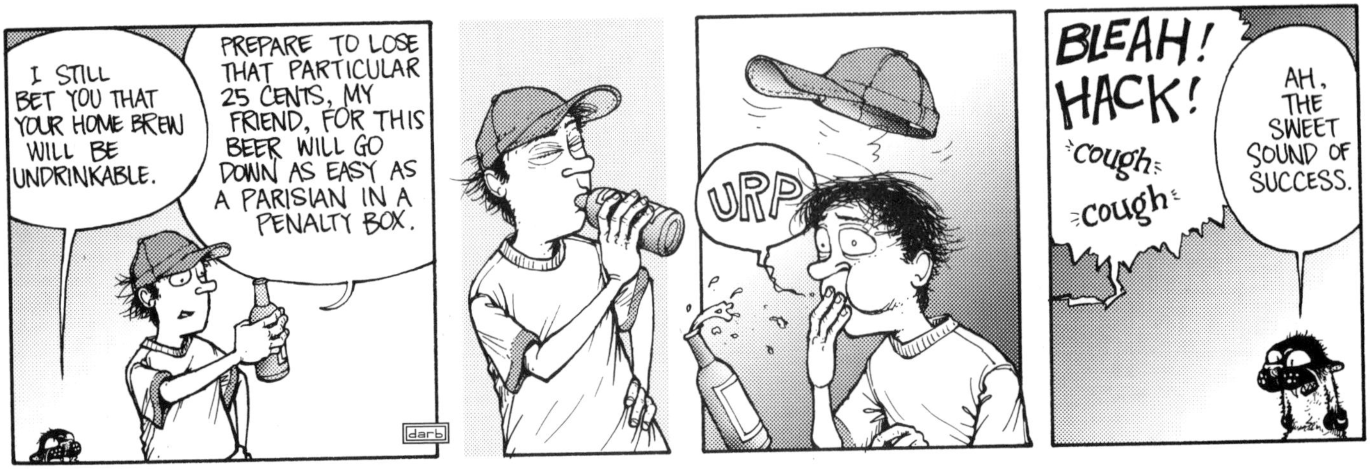
I STILL BET YOU THAT YOUR HOME BREW WILL BE UNDRINKABLE.
PREPARE TO LOSE THAT PARTICULAR 25 CENTS, MY FRIEND, FOR THIS BEER WILL GO DOWN AS EASY AS A PARISIAN IN A PENALTY BOX.
darb
URP
BLEAH! HACK!
cough
cough
AH, THE SWEET SOUND OF SUCCESS.

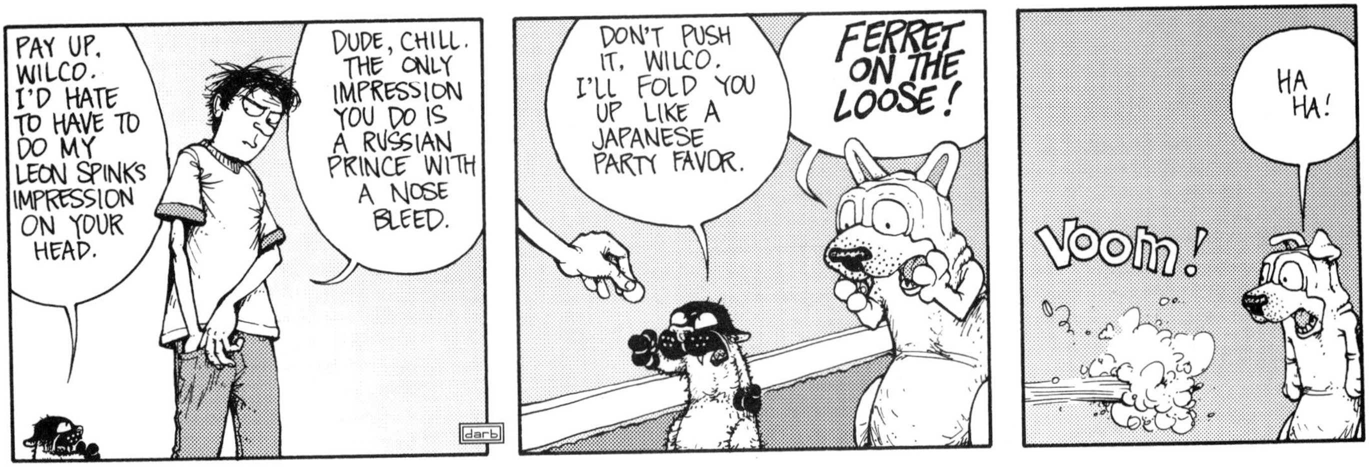
PAY UP, WILCO. I'D HATE TO HAVE TO DO MY LEON SPINKS IMPRESSION ON YOUR HEAD.
DUDE, CHILL. THE ONLY IMPRESSION YOU DO IS A RUSSIAN PRINCE WITH A NOSE BLEED.
darb
DON'T PUSH IT, WILCO. I'LL FOLD YOU UP LIKE A JAPANESE PARTY FAVOR.
FERRET ON THE LOOSE!
VOOM!
HA HA!

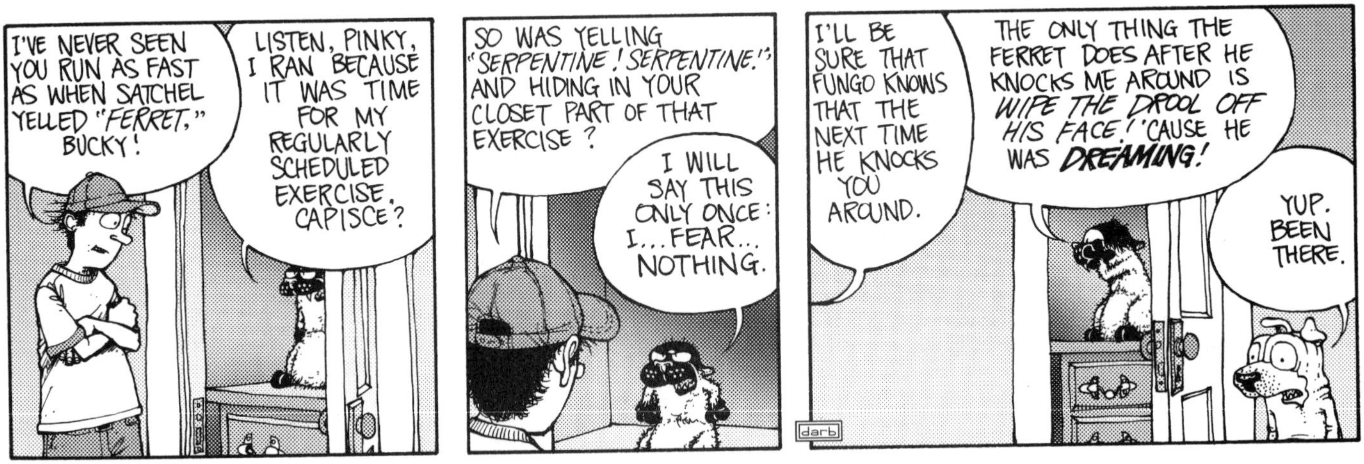
I'VE NEVER SEEN YOU RUN AS FAST AS WHEN SATCHEL YELLED "FERRET," BUCKY!
LISTEN, PINKY, I RAN BECAUSE IT WAS TIME FOR MY REGULARLY SCHEDULED EXERCISE. CAPISCE?
SO WAS YELLING "SERPENTINE! SERPENTINE!" AND HIDING IN YOUR CLOSET PART OF THAT EXERCISE?
I WILL SAY THIS ONLY ONCE: I... FEAR... NOTHING.
darb
I'LL BE SURE THAT FUNGO KNOWS THAT THE NEXT TIME HE KNOCKS YOU AROUND.
THE ONLY THING THE FERRET DOES AFTER HE KNOCKS ME AROUND IS WIPE THE DROOL OFF HIS FACE! 'CAUSE HE WAS DREAMING!
YUP. BEEN THERE.

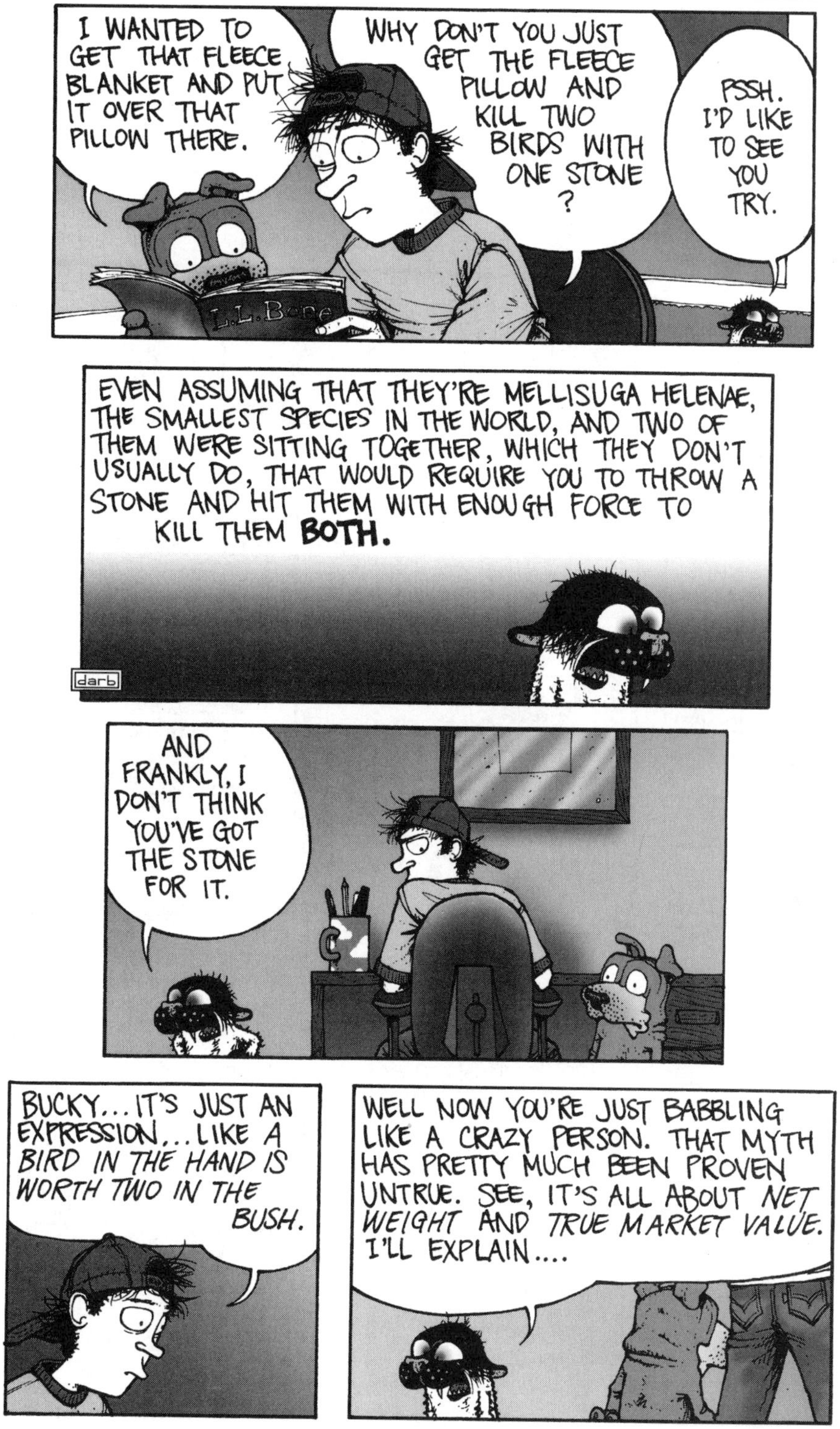
I WANTED TO GET THAT FLEECE BLANKET AND PUT IT OVER THAT PILLOW THERE.
WHY DON'T YOU JUST GET THE FLEECE PILLOW AND KILL TWO BIRDS WITH ONE STONE ?
PSSH. I'D LIKE TO SEE YOU TRY.
L.L.Bone
EVEN ASSUMING THAT THEY'RE MELLISUGA HELENAE, THE SMALLEST SPECIES IN THE WORLD, AND TWO OF THEM WERE SITTING TOGETHER, WHICH THEY DON'T USUALLY DO, THAT WOULD REQUIRE YOU TO THROW A STONE AND HIT THEM WITH ENOUGH FORCE TO KILL THEM **BOTH.**
darb
AND FRANKLY, I DON'T THINK YOU'VE GOT THE STONE FOR IT.
BUCKY... IT'S JUST AN EXPRESSION... LIKE *A BIRD IN THE HAND IS WORTH TWO IN THE BUSH.*
WELL NOW YOU'RE JUST BABBLING LIKE A CRAZY PERSON. THAT MYTH HAS PRETTY MUCH BEEN PROVEN UNTRUE. SEE, IT'S ALL ABOUT *NET WEIGHT* AND *TRUE MARKET VALUE.* I'LL EXPLAIN....

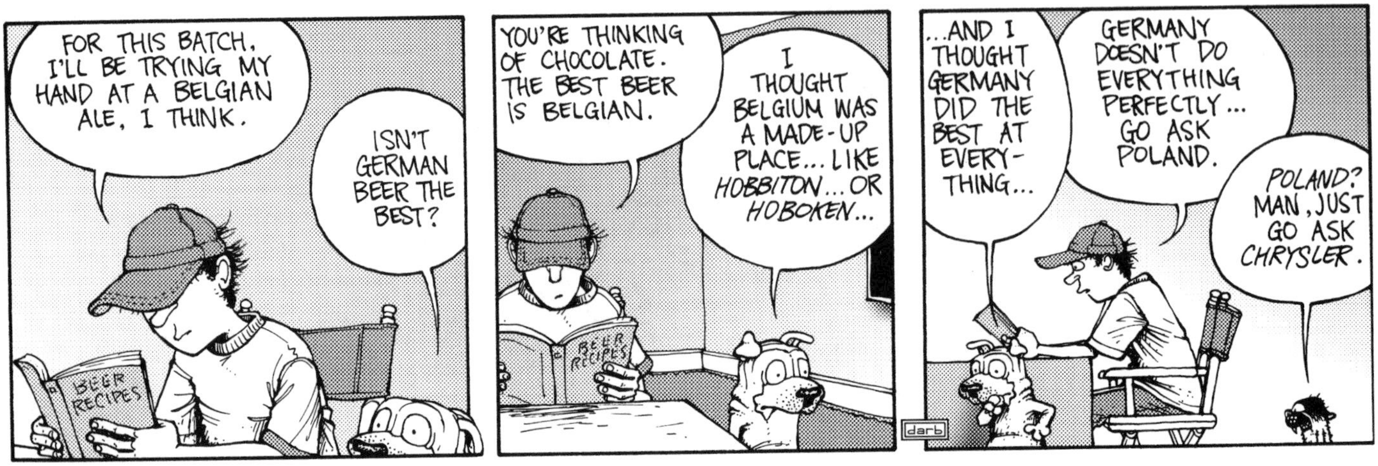
FOR THIS BATCH, I'LL BE TRYING MY HAND AT A BELGIAN ALE, I THINK.
ISN'T GERMAN BEER THE BEST?
BEER RECIPES
YOU'RE THINKING OF CHOCOLATE. THE BEST BEER IS BELGIAN.
I THOUGHT BELGIUM WAS A MADE-UP PLACE... LIKE *HOBBITON*... OR *HOBOKEN*...
...AND I THOUGHT GERMANY DID THE BEST AT EVERYTHING...
GERMANY DOESN'T DO EVERYTHING PERFECTLY... GO ASK POLAND.
POLAND? MAN, JUST GO ASK *CHRYSLER*.
darb

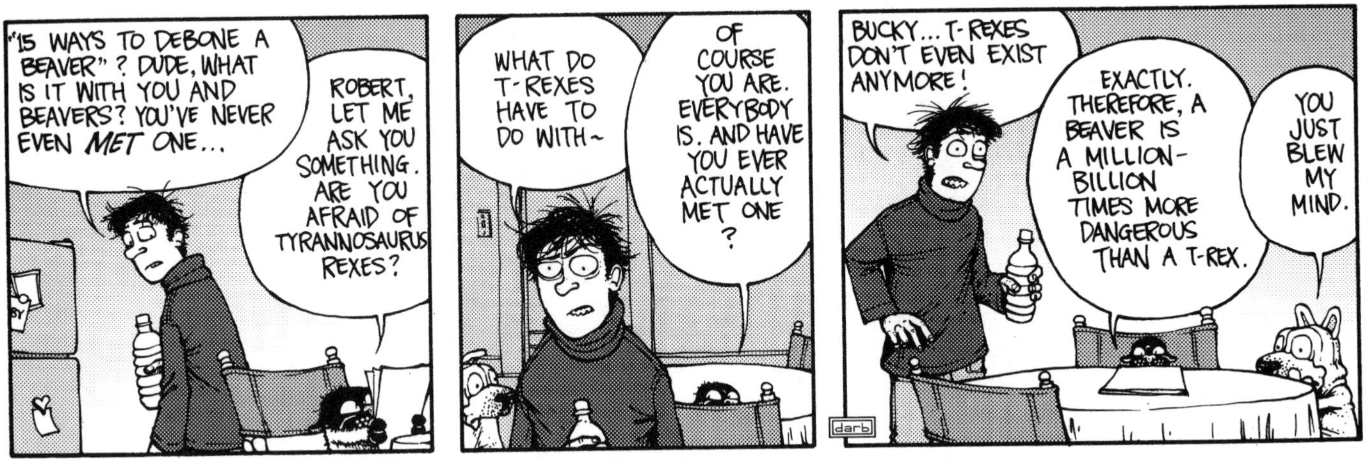
"15 WAYS TO DEBONE A BEAVER"? DUDE, WHAT IS IT WITH YOU AND BEAVERS? YOU'VE NEVER EVEN ***MET*** ONE...
ROBERT, LET ME ASK YOU SOMETHING. ARE YOU AFRAID OF TYRANNOSAURUS REXES?
WHAT DO T-REXES HAVE TO DO WITH~
OF COURSE YOU ARE. EVERYBODY IS. AND HAVE YOU EVER ACTUALLY MET ONE?
BUCKY... T-REXES DON'T EVEN EXIST ANYMORE!
EXACTLY. THEREFORE, A BEAVER IS A MILLION-BILLION TIMES MORE DANGEROUS THAN A T-REX.
YOU JUST BLEW MY MIND.
darb

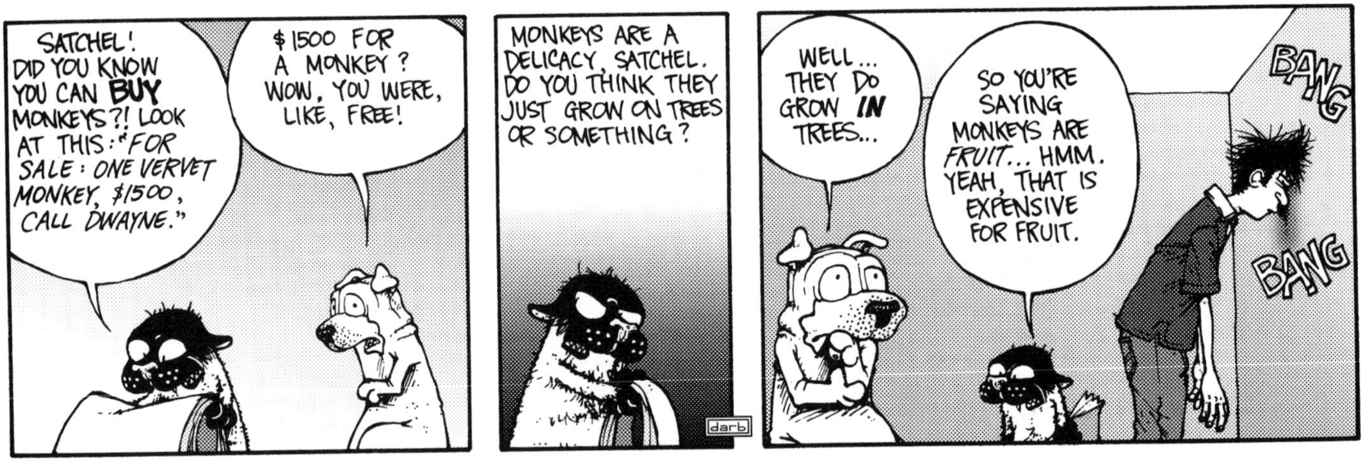
SATCHEL! DID YOU KNOW YOU CAN **BUY** MONKEYS?! LOOK AT THIS: "*FOR SALE: ONE VERVET MONKEY, $1500, CALL DWAYNE.*"
$1500 FOR A MONKEY? WOW, YOU WERE, LIKE, FREE!
MONKEYS ARE A DELICACY, SATCHEL. DO YOU THINK THEY JUST GROW ON TREES OR SOMETHING?
darb
WELL... THEY DO GROW ***IN*** TREES...
SO YOU'RE SAYING MONKEYS ARE *FRUIT*... HMM. YEAH, THAT IS EXPENSIVE FOR FRUIT.
BANG
BANG

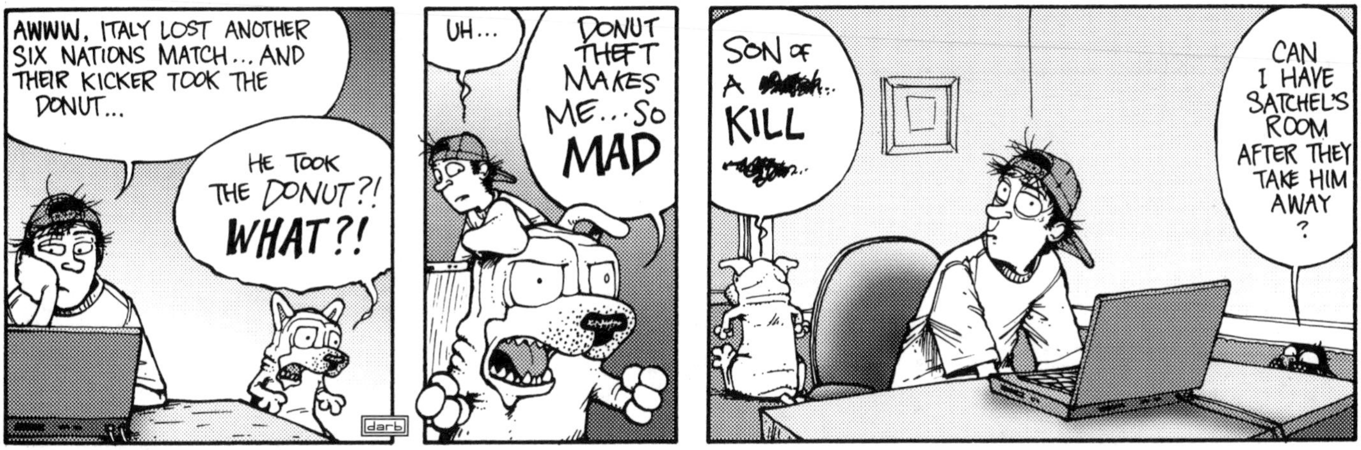
AWWW, ITALY LOST ANOTHER SIX NATIONS MATCH... AND THEIR KICKER TOOK THE DONUT...
HE TOOK THE DONUT?! WHAT?!
darb
UH...
DONUT THEFT MAKES ME... SO MAD
SON OF A ... KILL ...
CAN I HAVE SATCHEL'S ROOM AFTER THEY TAKE HIM AWAY ?

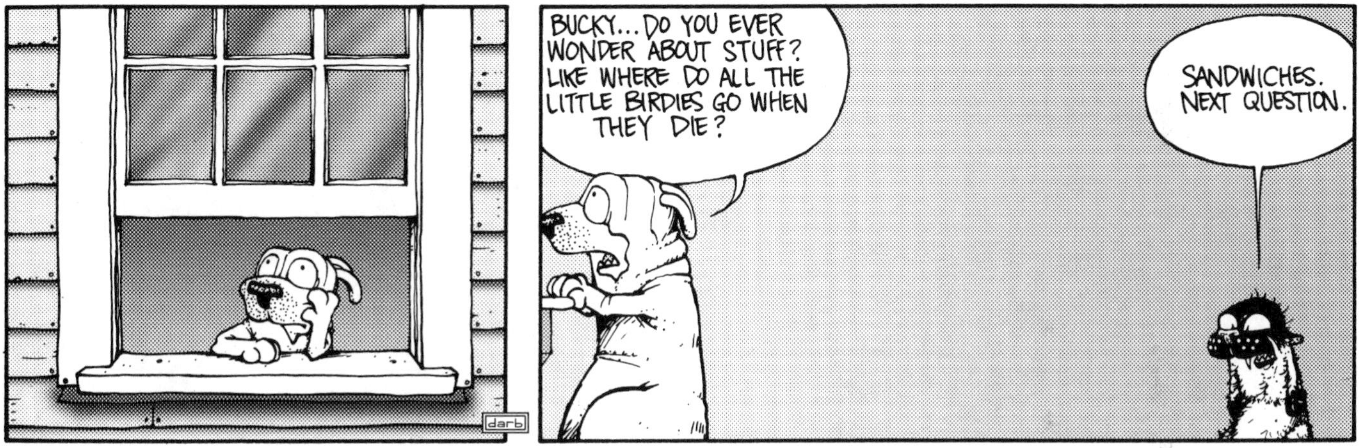
darb
BUCKY... DO YOU EVER WONDER ABOUT STUFF? LIKE WHERE DO ALL THE LITTLE BIRDIES GO WHEN THEY DIE?
SANDWICHES. NEXT QUESTION.

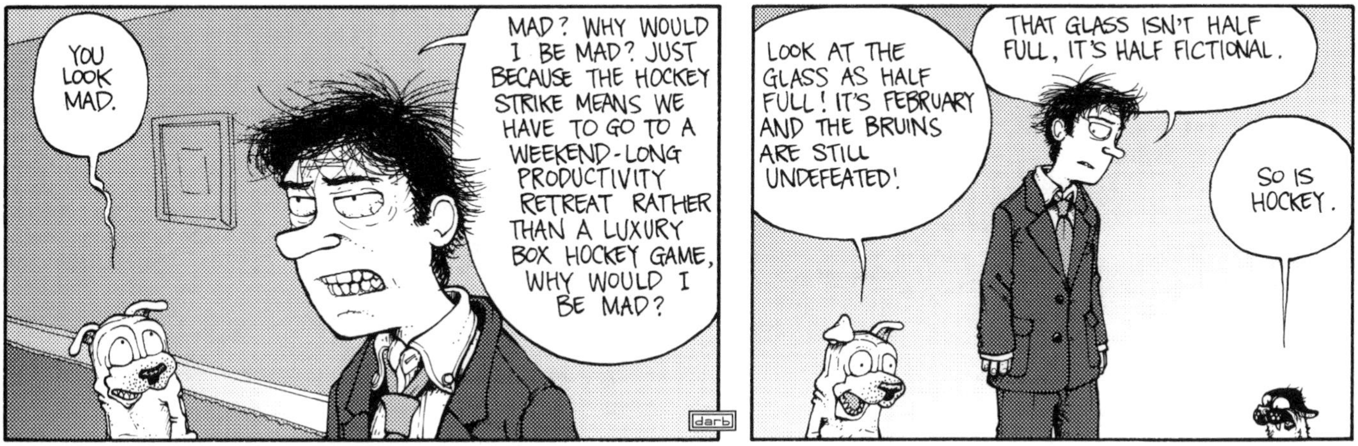
YOU LOOK MAD.
MAD? WHY WOULD I BE MAD? JUST BECAUSE THE HOCKEY STRIKE MEANS WE HAVE TO GO TO A WEEKEND-LONG PRODUCTIVITY RETREAT RATHER THAN A LUXURY BOX HOCKEY GAME, WHY WOULD I BE MAD?
darb
LOOK AT THE GLASS AS HALF FULL! IT'S FEBRUARY AND THE BRUINS ARE STILL UNDEFEATED!
THAT GLASS ISN'T HALF FULL, IT'S HALF FICTIONAL.
SO IS HOCKEY.

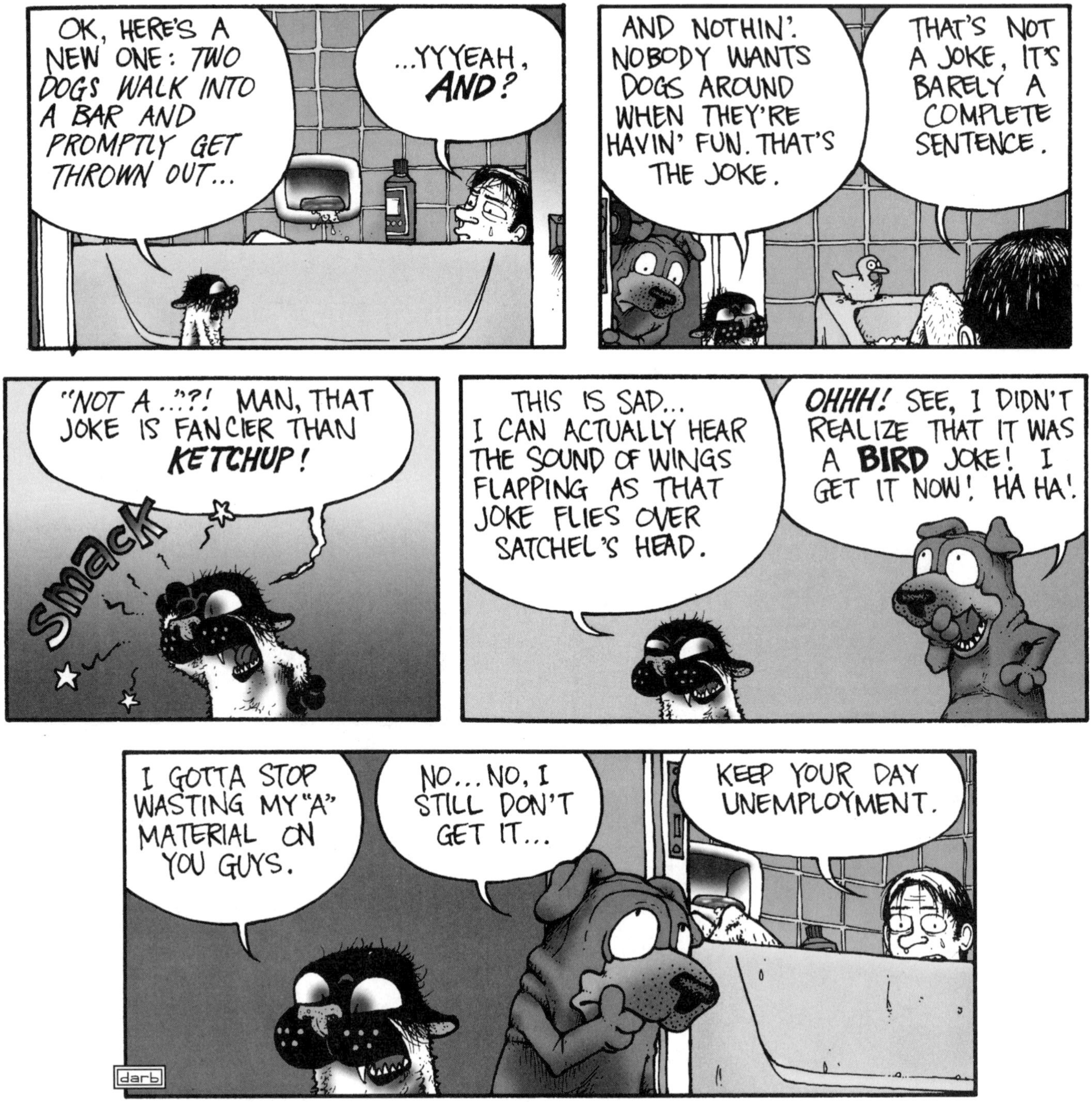
OK, HERE'S A NEW ONE: TWO DOGS WALK INTO A BAR AND PROMPTLY GET THROWN OUT...
...YYYEAH, AND?
AND NOTHIN'. NOBODY WANTS DOGS AROUND WHEN THEY'RE HAVIN' FUN. THAT'S THE JOKE.
THAT'S NOT A JOKE, IT'S BARELY A COMPLETE SENTENCE.
"NOT A..."?! MAN, THAT JOKE IS FANCIER THAN KETCHUP!
SMACK
THIS IS SAD... I CAN ACTUALLY HEAR THE SOUND OF WINGS FLAPPING AS THAT JOKE FLIES OVER SATCHEL'S HEAD.
OHHH! SEE, I DIDN'T REALIZE THAT IT WAS A BIRD JOKE! I GET IT NOW! HA HA!
I GOTTA STOP WASTING MY "A" MATERIAL ON YOU GUYS.
NO... NO, I STILL DON'T GET IT...
KEEP YOUR DAY UNEMPLOYMENT.
darb

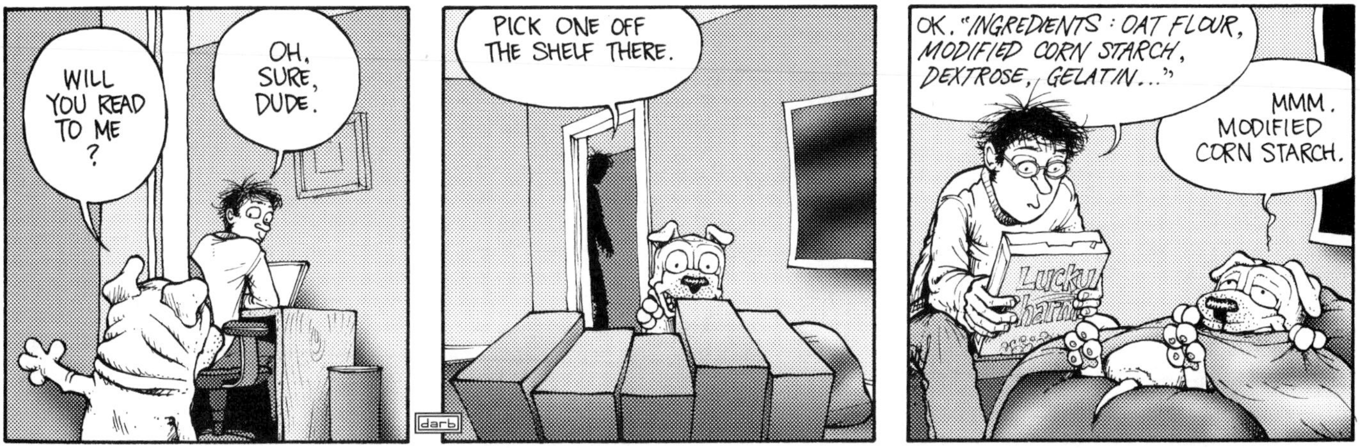
WILL YOU READ TO ME ?
OH, SURE, DUDE.
PICK ONE OFF THE SHELF THERE.
darb
OK. "INGREDIENTS : OAT FLOUR, MODIFIED CORN STARCH, DEXTROSE, GELATIN..."
MMM. MODIFIED CORN STARCH.
Lucky Charms

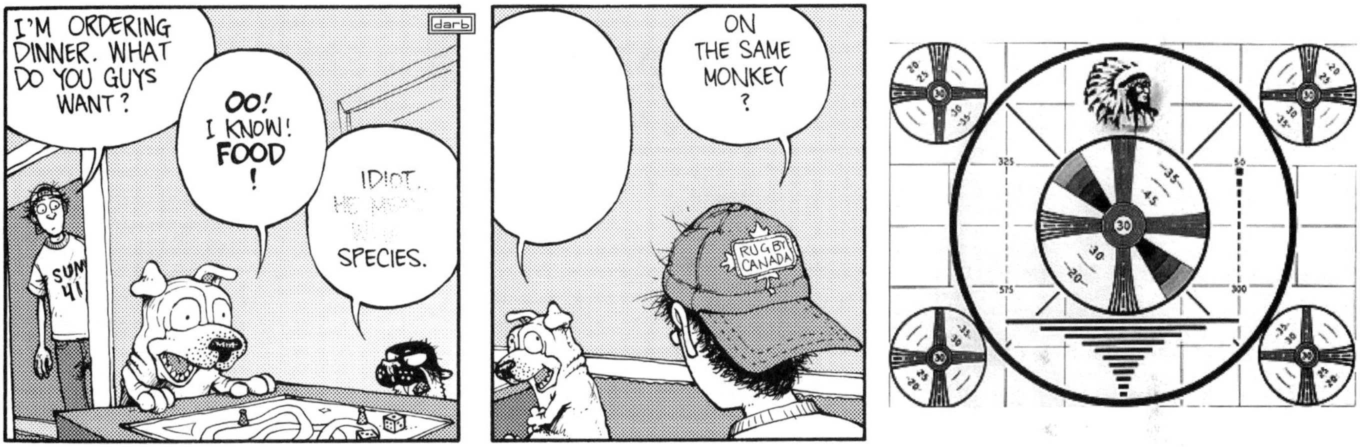
I'M ORDERING DINNER. WHAT DO YOU GUYS WANT?
darb
OO! I KNOW! FOOD !
IDIOT...
SPECIES.
SUM 41
ON THE SAME MONKEY ?
RUGBY CANADA

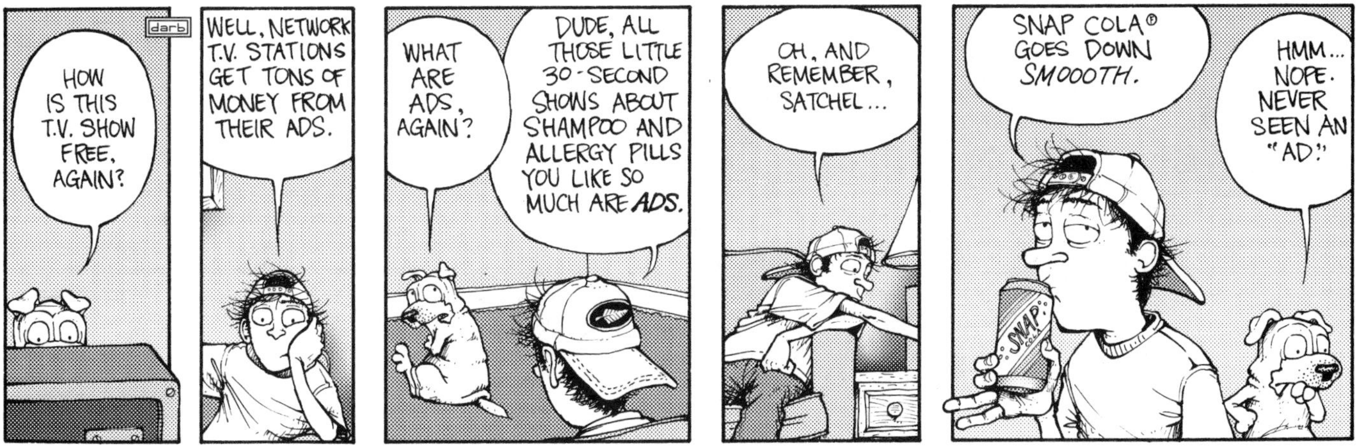
darb
HOW IS THIS T.V. SHOW FREE, AGAIN?
WELL, NETWORK T.V. STATIONS GET TONS OF MONEY FROM THEIR ADS.
WHAT ARE ADS, AGAIN?
DUDE, ALL THOSE LITTLE 30-SECOND SHOWS ABOUT SHAMPOO AND ALLERGY PILLS YOU LIKE SO MUCH ARE ADS.
OH, AND REMEMBER, SATCHEL...
SNAP COLA® GOES DOWN SMOOOTH.
HMM... NOPE. NEVER SEEN AN "AD."
SNAP

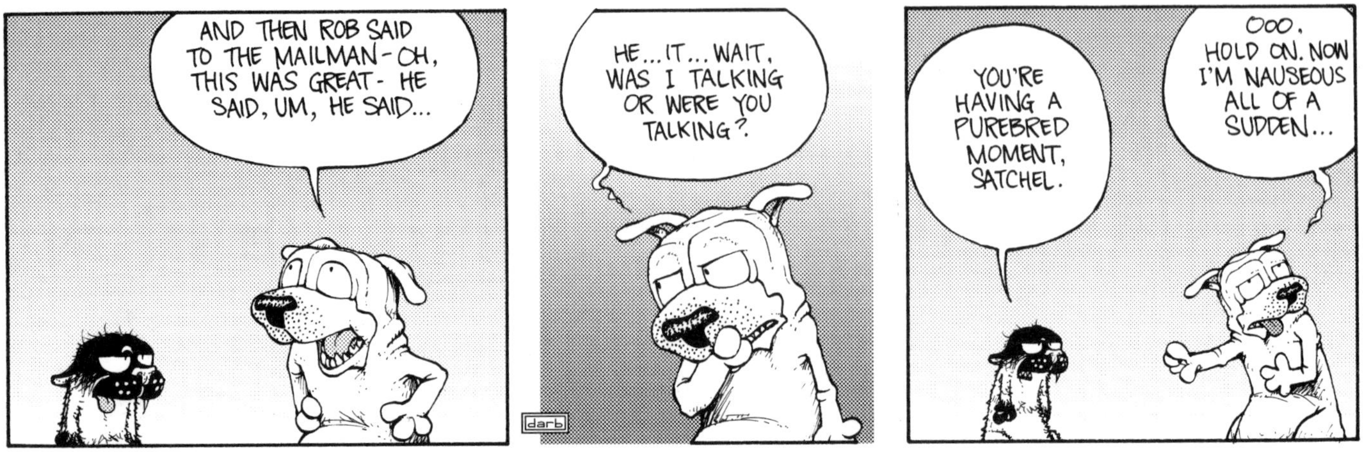
AND THEN ROB SAID TO THE MAILMAN- OH, THIS WAS GREAT- HE SAID, UM, HE SAID...
HE... IT... WAIT, WAS I TALKING OR WERE YOU TALKING?
YOU'RE HAVING A PUREBRED MOMENT, SATCHEL.
OOO. HOLD ON. NOW I'M NAUSEOUS ALL OF A SUDDEN...
darb

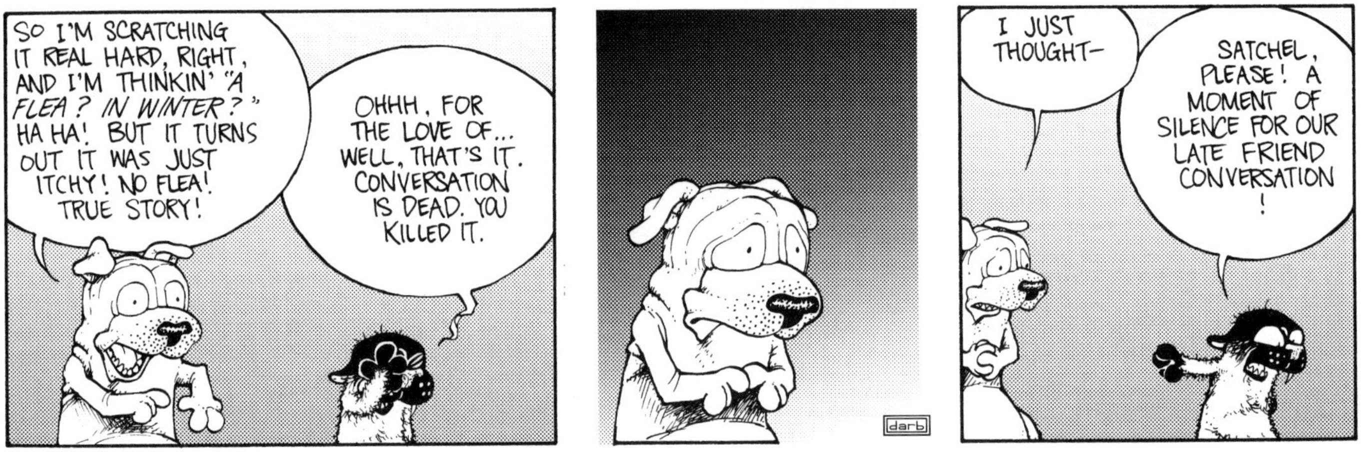
SO I'M SCRATCHING IT REAL HARD, RIGHT, AND I'M THINKIN' "A *FLEA? IN WINTER?*" HA HA! BUT IT TURNS OUT IT WAS JUST ITCHY! NO FLEA! TRUE STORY!
OHHH, FOR THE LOVE OF... WELL, THAT'S IT. CONVERSATION IS DEAD. YOU KILLED IT.
darb
I JUST THOUGHT-
SATCHEL, PLEASE! A MOMENT OF SILENCE FOR OUR LATE FRIEND CONVERSATION!

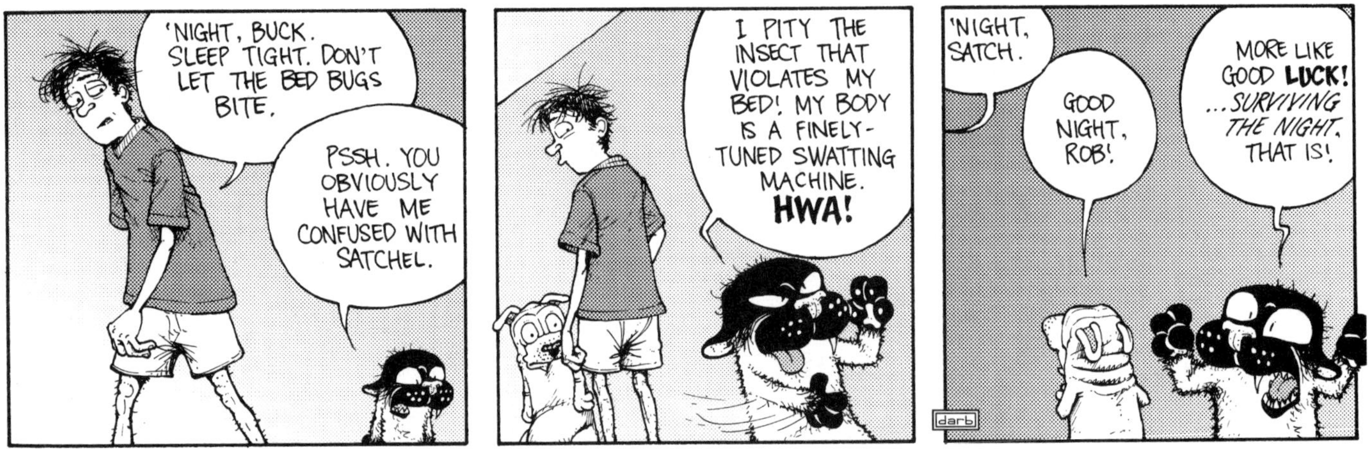
'NIGHT, BUCK. SLEEP TIGHT. DON'T LET THE BED BUGS BITE.
PSSH. YOU OBVIOUSLY HAVE ME CONFUSED WITH SATCHEL.
I PITY THE INSECT THAT VIOLATES MY BED! MY BODY IS A FINELY-TUNED SWATTING MACHINE. **HWA!**
'NIGHT, SATCH.
GOOD NIGHT, ROB!
MORE LIKE GOOD **LUCK!** ...*SURVIVING THE NIGHT*, THAT IS!
darb

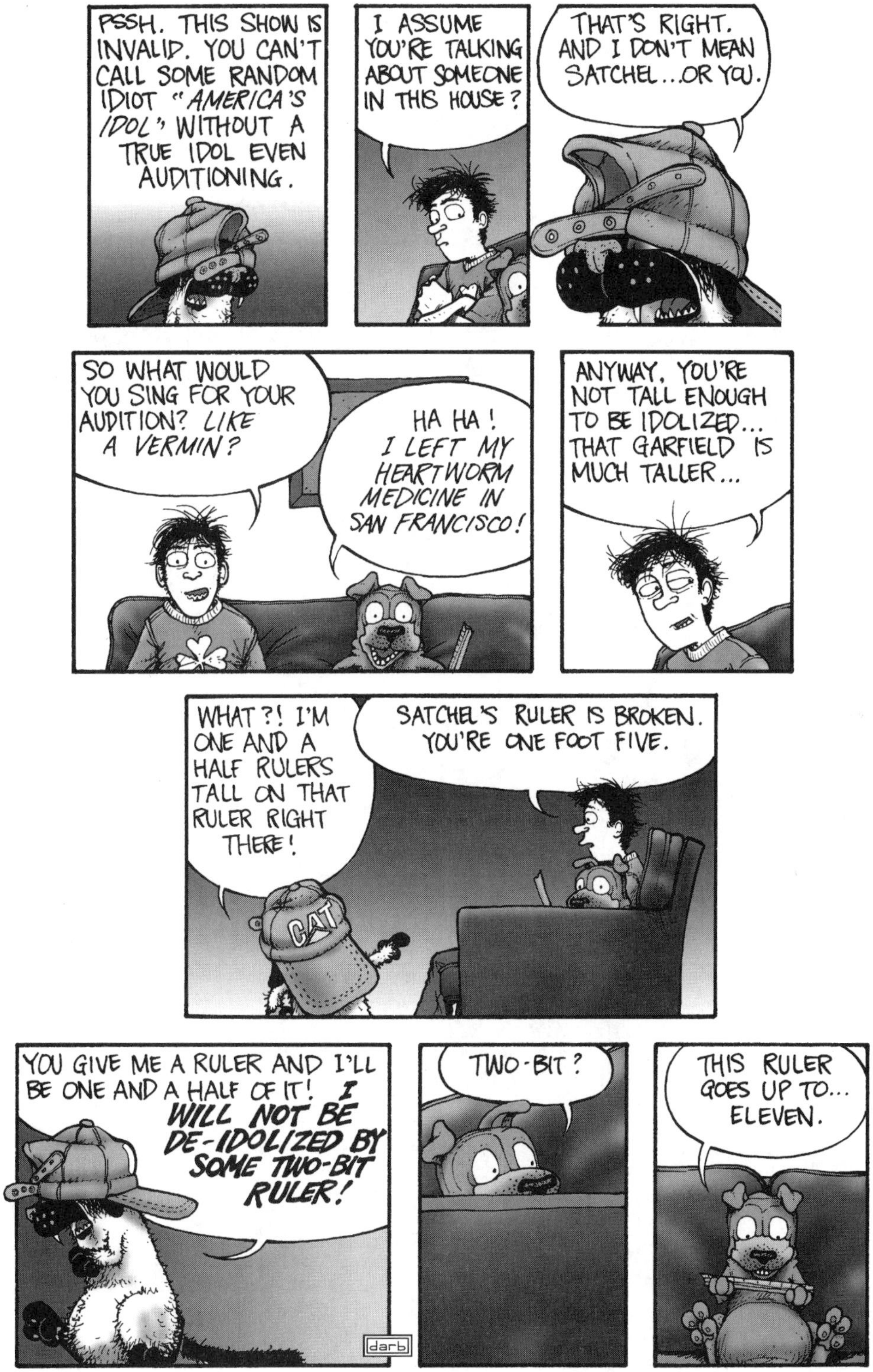
PSSH. THIS SHOW IS INVALID. YOU CAN'T CALL SOME RANDOM IDIOT "AMERICA'S IDOL" WITHOUT A TRUE IDOL EVEN AUDITIONING.
I ASSUME YOU'RE TALKING ABOUT SOMEONE IN THIS HOUSE?
THAT'S RIGHT. AND I DON'T MEAN SATCHEL...OR YOU.
SO WHAT WOULD YOU SING FOR YOUR AUDITION? LIKE A VERMIN?
HA HA! I LEFT MY HEARTWORM MEDICINE IN SAN FRANCISCO!
ANYWAY, YOU'RE NOT TALL ENOUGH TO BE IDOLIZED... THAT GARFIELD IS MUCH TALLER...
WHAT?! I'M ONE AND A HALF RULERS TALL ON THAT RULER RIGHT THERE!
SATCHEL'S RULER IS BROKEN. YOU'RE ONE FOOT FIVE.
CAT
YOU GIVE ME A RULER AND I'LL BE ONE AND A HALF OF IT! I WILL NOT BE DE-IDOLIZED BY SOME TWO-BIT RULER!
darb
TWO-BIT?
THIS RULER GOES UP TO... ELEVEN.

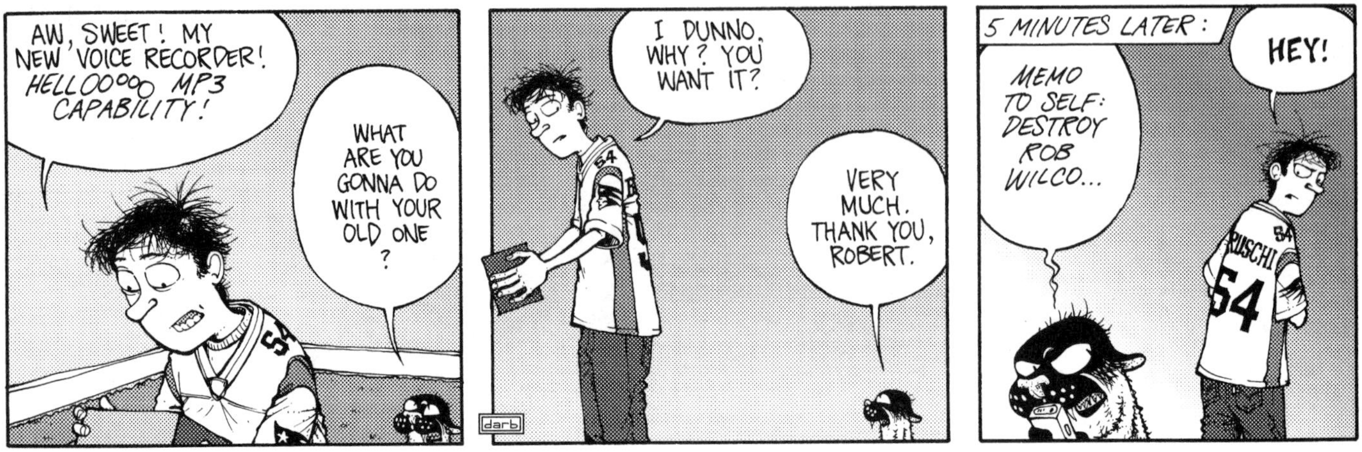
AW, SWEET! MY NEW VOICE RECORDER! HELLOOooo MP3 CAPABILITY!
WHAT ARE YOU GONNA DO WITH YOUR OLD ONE ?
I DUNNO. WHY? YOU WANT IT?
VERY MUCH. THANK YOU, ROBERT.
darb
5 MINUTES LATER:
MEMO TO SELF: DESTROY ROB WILCO...
HEY!
RUSCHI 54

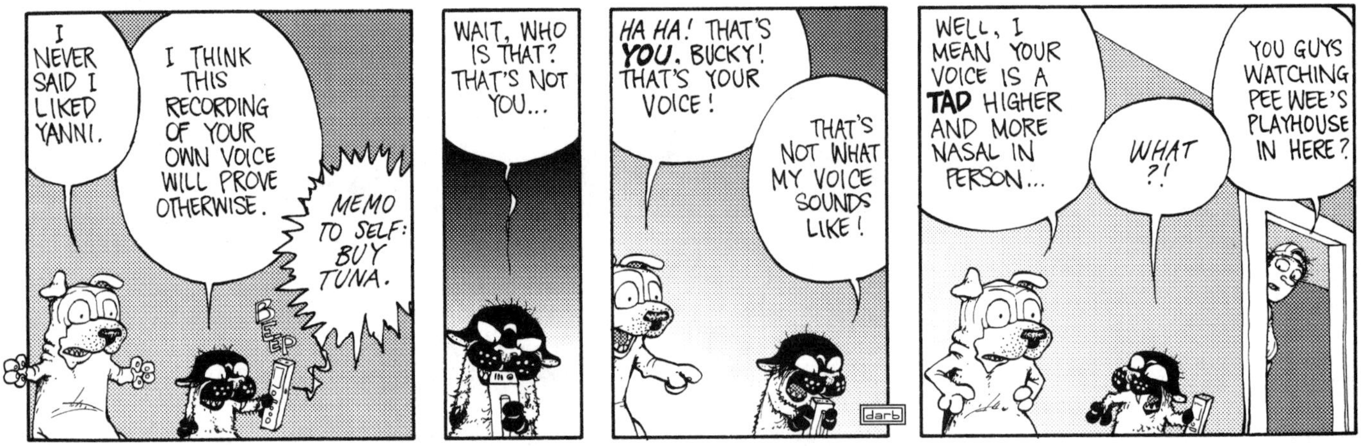
I NEVER SAID I LIKED YANNI.
I THINK THIS RECORDING OF YOUR OWN VOICE WILL PROVE OTHERWISE.
BEEP
MEMO TO SELF: BUY TUNA.
WAIT, WHO IS THAT? THAT'S NOT YOU...
HA HA! THAT'S YOU, BUCKY! THAT'S YOUR VOICE!
THAT'S NOT WHAT MY VOICE SOUNDS LIKE!
darb
WELL, I MEAN YOUR VOICE IS A TAD HIGHER AND MORE NASAL IN PERSON...
WHAT ?!
YOU GUYS WATCHING PEE WEE'S PLAYHOUSE IN HERE?

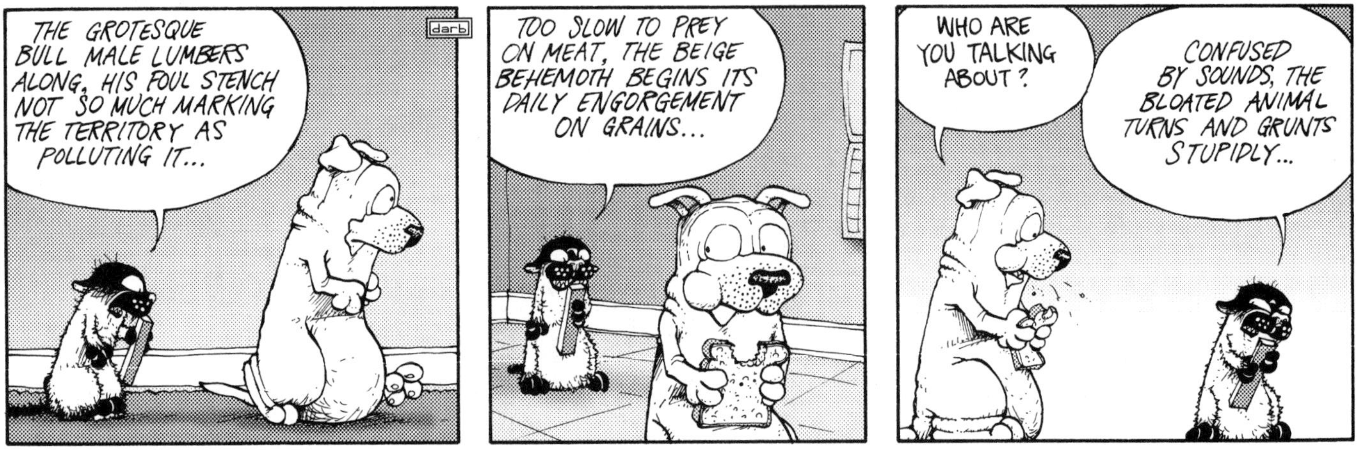
darb
THE GROTESQUE BULL MALE LUMBERS ALONG, HIS FOUL STENCH NOT SO MUCH MARKING THE TERRITORY AS POLLUTING IT...
TOO SLOW TO PREY ON MEAT, THE BEIGE BEHEMOTH BEGINS ITS DAILY ENGORGEMENT ON GRAINS...
WHO ARE YOU TALKING ABOUT?
CONFUSED BY SOUNDS, THE BLOATED ANIMAL TURNS AND GRUNTS STUPIDLY...

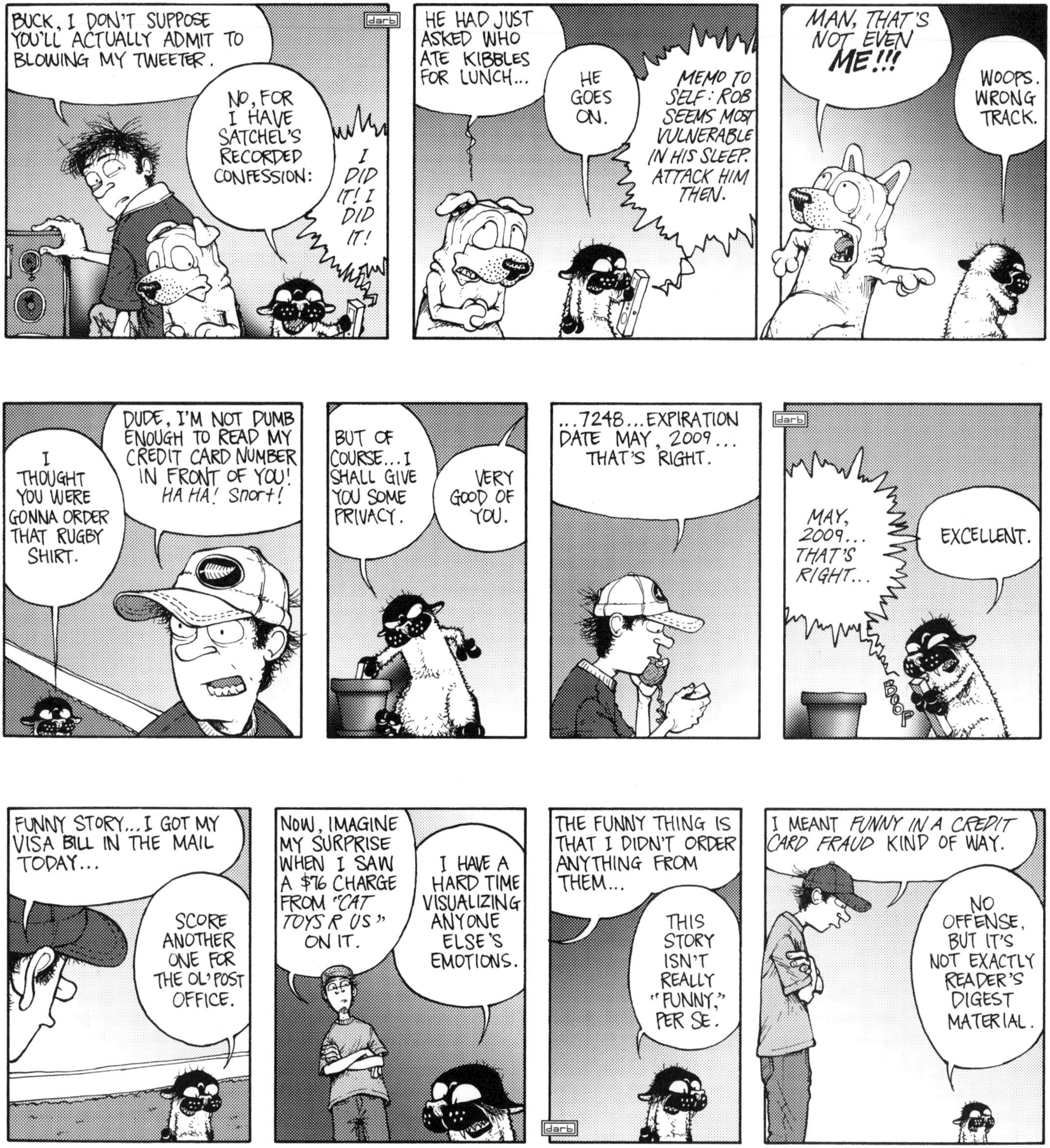
BUCK, I DON'T SUPPOSE YOU'LL ACTUALLY ADMIT TO BLOWING MY TWEETER.
NO, FOR I HAVE SATCHEL'S RECORDED CONFESSION:
I DID IT! I DID IT!
HE HAD JUST ASKED WHO ATE KIBBLES FOR LUNCH...
HE GOES ON.
MEMO TO SELF: ROB SEEMS MOST VULNERABLE IN HIS SLEEP. ATTACK HIM THEN.
MAN, THAT'S NOT EVEN ME!!!
WOOPS. WRONG TRACK.
I THOUGHT YOU WERE GONNA ORDER THAT RUGBY SHIRT.
DUDE, I'M NOT DUMB ENOUGH TO READ MY CREDIT CARD NUMBER IN FRONT OF YOU! HA HA! Snort!
BUT OF COURSE... I SHALL GIVE YOU SOME PRIVACY.
VERY GOOD OF YOU.
...7248...EXPIRATION DATE MAY, 2009... THAT'S RIGHT.
MAY, 2009... THAT'S RIGHT...
EXCELLENT.
BOOP
FUNNY STORY... I GOT MY VISA BILL IN THE MAIL TODAY...
SCORE ANOTHER ONE FOR THE OL' POST OFFICE.
NOW, IMAGINE MY SURPRISE WHEN I SAW A $76 CHARGE FROM "CAT TOYS R US" ON IT.
I HAVE A HARD TIME VISUALIZING ANYONE ELSE'S EMOTIONS.
THE FUNNY THING IS THAT I DIDN'T ORDER ANYTHING FROM THEM...
THIS STORY ISN'T REALLY "FUNNY," PER SE.
I MEANT FUNNY IN A CREDIT CARD FRAUD KIND OF WAY.
NO OFFENSE, BUT IT'S NOT EXACTLY READER'S DIGEST MATERIAL.

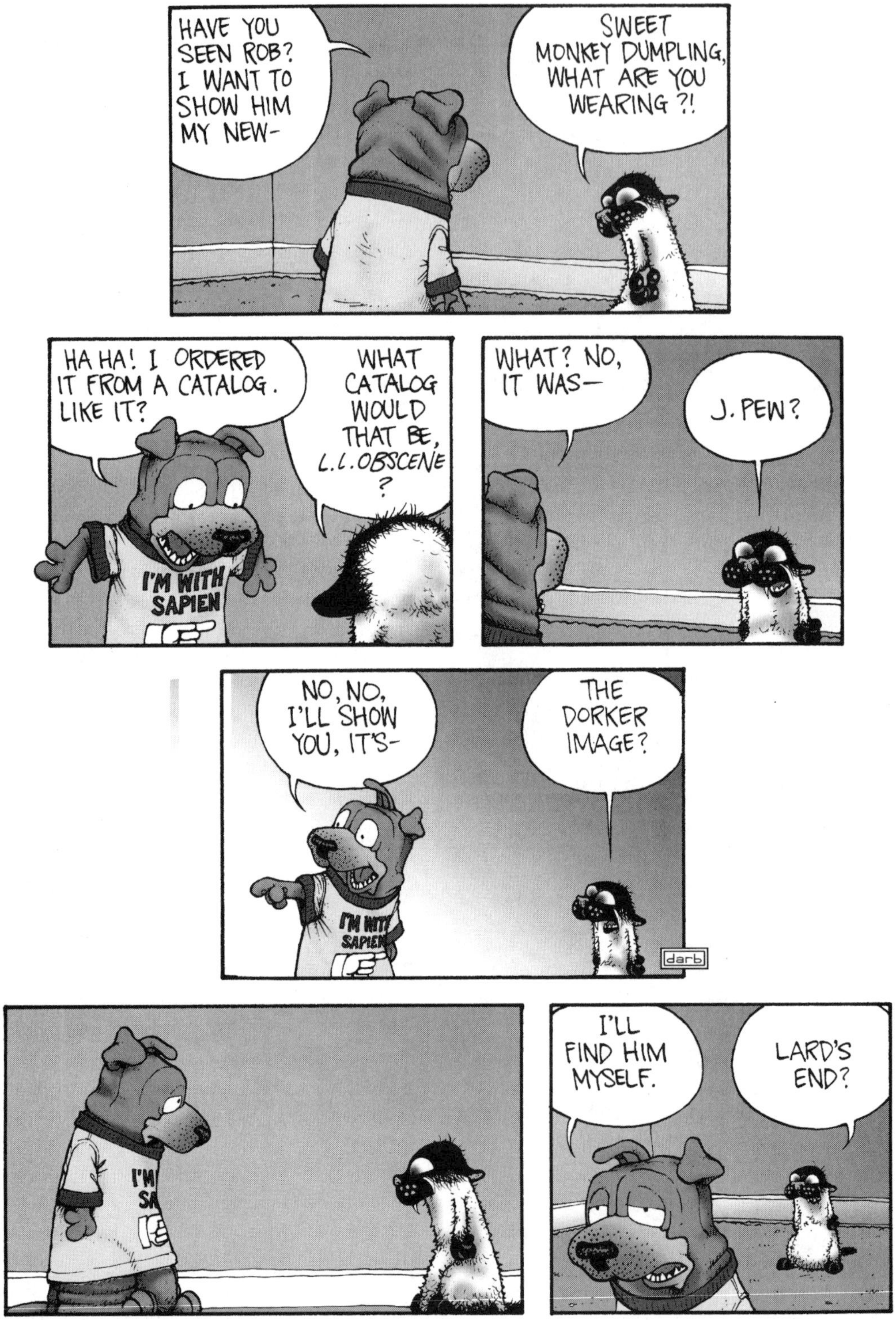
HAVE YOU SEEN ROB? I WANT TO SHOW HIM MY NEW-
SWEET MONKEY DUMPLING, WHAT ARE YOU WEARING ?!
HA HA! I ORDERED IT FROM A CATALOG. LIKE IT?
I'M WITH SAPIEN
WHAT CATALOG WOULD THAT BE, L.L. OBSCENE ?
WHAT? NO, IT WAS—
J. PEW?
NO, NO, I'LL SHOW YOU, IT'S-
THE DORKER IMAGE?
I'M WITH SAPIEN
darb
I'LL FIND HIM MYSELF.
LARD'S END?

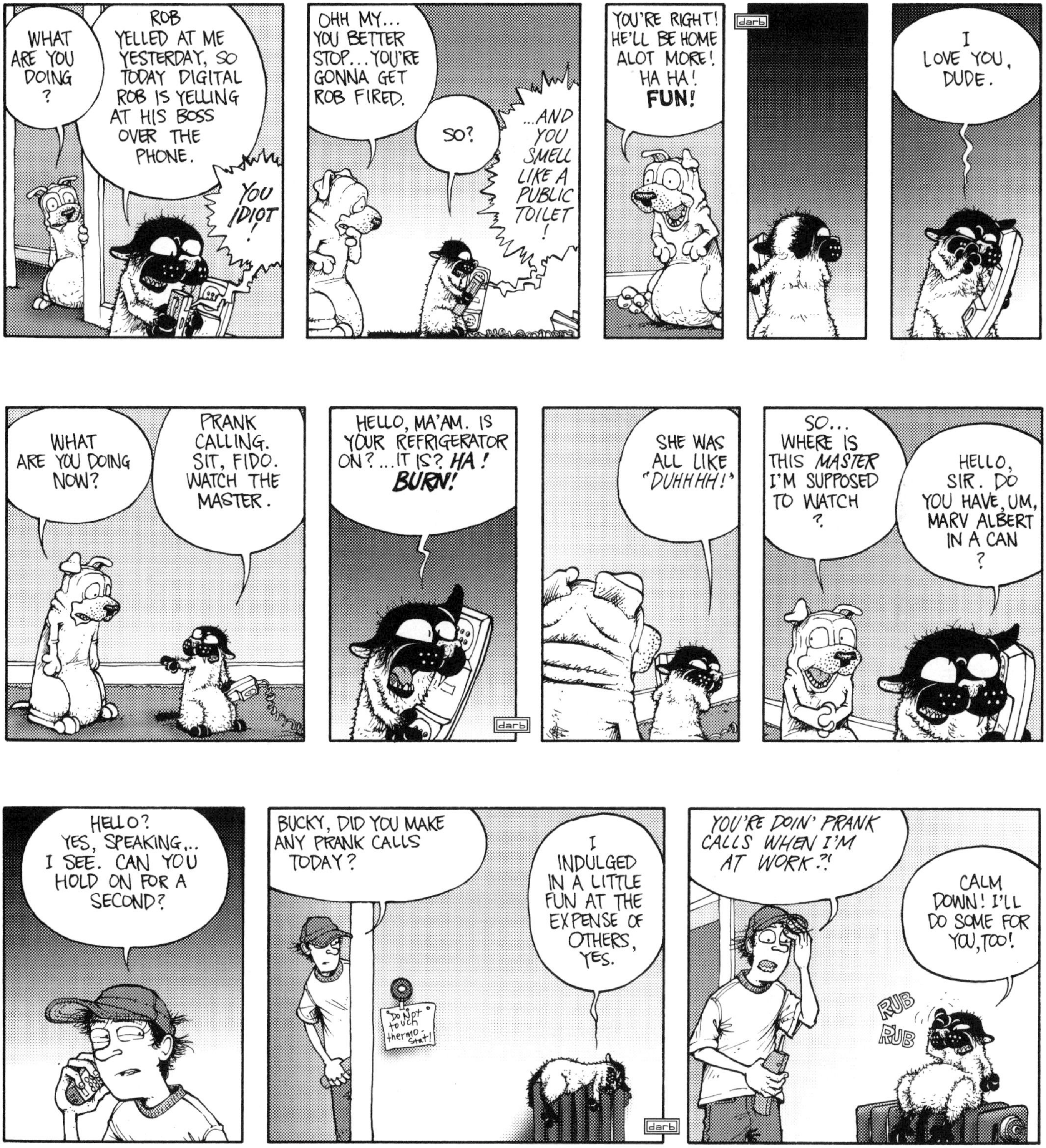
WHAT ARE YOU DOING?
ROB YELLED AT ME YESTERDAY, SO TODAY DIGITAL ROB IS YELLING AT HIS BOSS OVER THE PHONE.
YOU IDIOT!
OHH MY... YOU BETTER STOP... YOU'RE GONNA GET ROB FIRED.
SO?
...AND YOU SMELL LIKE A PUBLIC TOILET!
YOU'RE RIGHT! HE'LL BE HOME ALOT MORE! HA HA! FUN!
darb
I LOVE YOU, DUDE.
WHAT ARE YOU DOING NOW?
PRANK CALLING. SIT, FIDO. WATCH THE MASTER.
HELLO, MA'AM. IS YOUR REFRIGERATOR ON?... IT IS? HA! BURN!
darb
SHE WAS ALL LIKE "DUHHHH!"
SO... WHERE IS THIS MASTER I'M SUPPOSED TO WATCH?
HELLO, SIR. DO YOU HAVE, UM, MARV ALBERT IN A CAN?
HELLO? YES, SPEAKING... I SEE. CAN YOU HOLD ON FOR A SECOND?
BUCKY, DID YOU MAKE ANY PRANK CALLS TODAY?
Do Not touch thermo-stat!
I INDULGED IN A LITTLE FUN AT THE EXPENSE OF OTHERS, YES.
darb
YOU'RE DOIN' PRANK CALLS WHEN I'M AT WORK?!
CALM DOWN! I'LL DO SOME FOR YOU, TOO!
RUB RUB

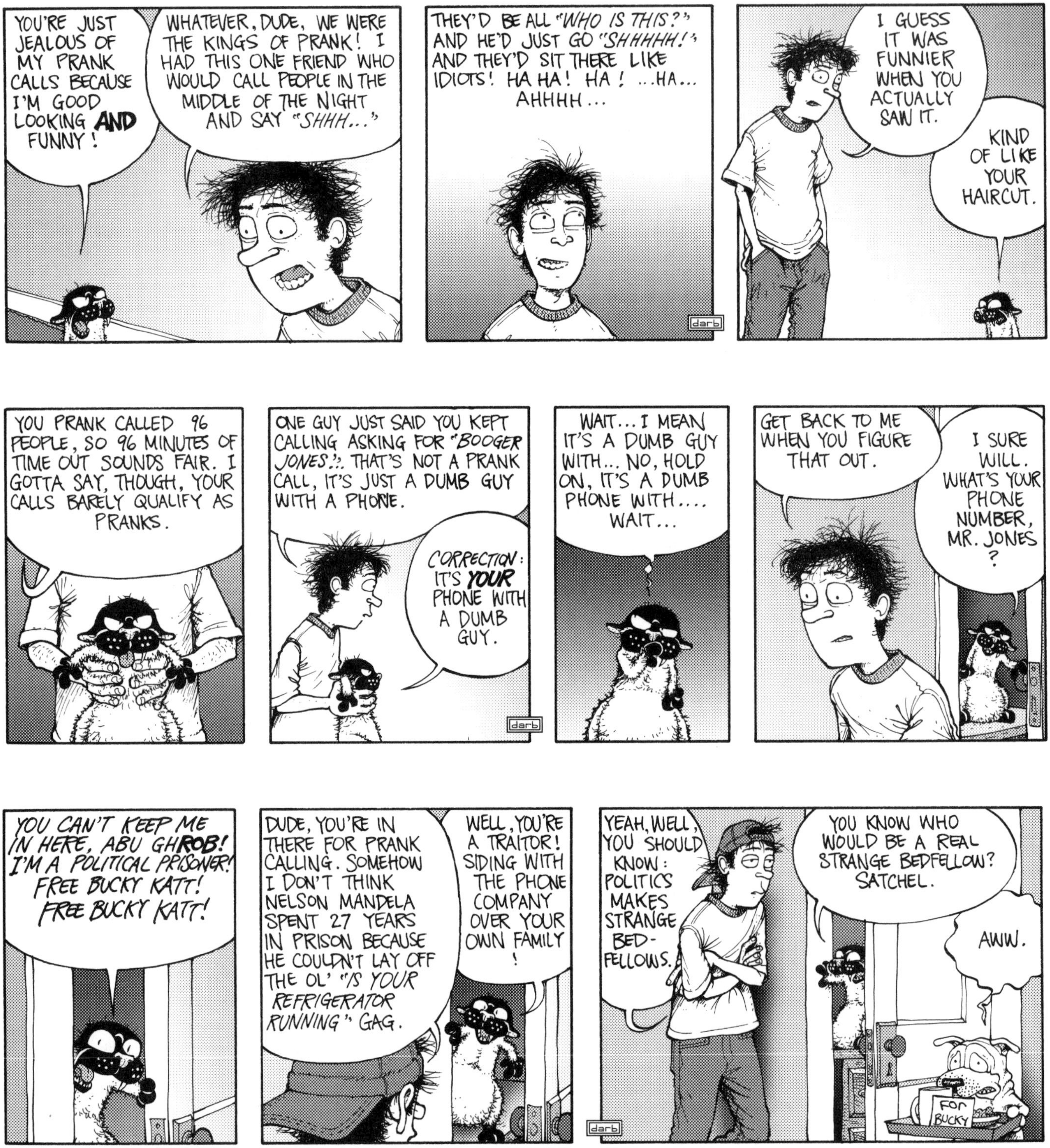
YOU'RE JUST JEALOUS OF MY PRANK CALLS BECAUSE I'M GOOD LOOKING AND FUNNY!
WHATEVER, DUDE, WE WERE THE KINGS OF PRANK! I HAD THIS ONE FRIEND WHO WOULD CALL PEOPLE IN THE MIDDLE OF THE NIGHT AND SAY "SHHH..."
THEY'D BE ALL "WHO IS THIS?" AND HE'D JUST GO "SHHHHH!", AND THEY'D SIT THERE LIKE IDIOTS! HA HA! HA! ...HA... AHHHH...
I GUESS IT WAS FUNNIER WHEN YOU ACTUALLY SAW IT.
KIND OF LIKE YOUR HAIRCUT.
darb
YOU PRANK CALLED 96 PEOPLE, SO 96 MINUTES OF TIME OUT SOUNDS FAIR. I GOTTA SAY, THOUGH, YOUR CALLS BARELY QUALIFY AS PRANKS.
ONE GUY JUST SAID YOU KEPT CALLING ASKING FOR "BOOGER JONES". THAT'S NOT A PRANK CALL, IT'S JUST A DUMB GUY WITH A PHONE.
CORRECTION: IT'S YOUR PHONE WITH A DUMB GUY.
WAIT... I MEAN IT'S A DUMB GUY WITH... NO, HOLD ON, IT'S A DUMB PHONE WITH.... WAIT...
GET BACK TO ME WHEN YOU FIGURE THAT OUT.
I SURE WILL. WHAT'S YOUR PHONE NUMBER, MR. JONES?
darb
YOU CAN'T KEEP ME IN HERE, ABU GHROB! I'M A POLITICAL PRISONER! FREE BUCKY KATT! FREE BUCKY KATT!
DUDE, YOU'RE IN THERE FOR PRANK CALLING. SOMEHOW I DON'T THINK NELSON MANDELA SPENT 27 YEARS IN PRISON BECAUSE HE COULDN'T LAY OFF THE OL' "IS YOUR REFRIGERATOR RUNNING" GAG.
WELL, YOU'RE A TRAITOR! SIDING WITH THE PHONE COMPANY OVER YOUR OWN FAMILY!
YEAH, WELL, YOU SHOULD KNOW: POLITICS MAKES STRANGE BED-FELLOWS.
YOU KNOW WHO WOULD BE A REAL STRANGE BEDFELLOW? SATCHEL.
AWW.
FOR BUCKY
darb

WHAT UP, FLASHDANCE ?
ROB TOOK ME TO THE DOGLYMPICS! AND I GOT THE M.V.D. IN THE ROPE PULL!
MVD
LOOK, YOU TAKE THE TOP OFF AND THERE ARE TREATS INSIDE! HA HA! *BRILLIANT!*
ROB TOOK YOU, YOU SAY? WERE THERE MANY PEOPLE THERE?
OH, YEAH! I GOT SO MANY SCRITCHES MY HEAD HURTS! I GOT A SANDWICH FROM-
SHUT YOUR KIBBLE HOLE FOR A SECOND! DON'T YOU REALIZE YOU'RE JUST JUMPING THROUGH HOOPS FOR THE **MAN**?!
NO, NO, HOOPS ARE TUESDAY.
MVD
darb
THERE IS A PRICE FOR DIGNITY... FORTUNATELY THERE ARE ALSO COUPONS FOR IT.
OOO, THE RED ONES ARE CHEWY !
MVD

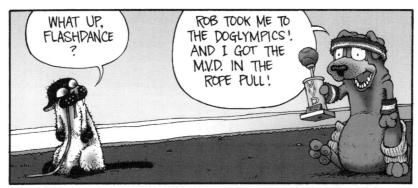

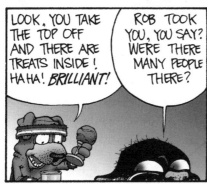

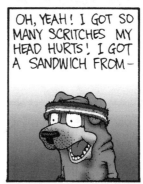

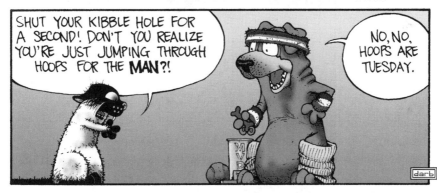

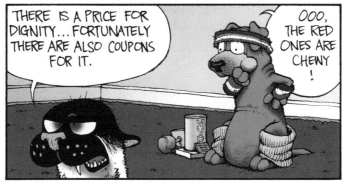

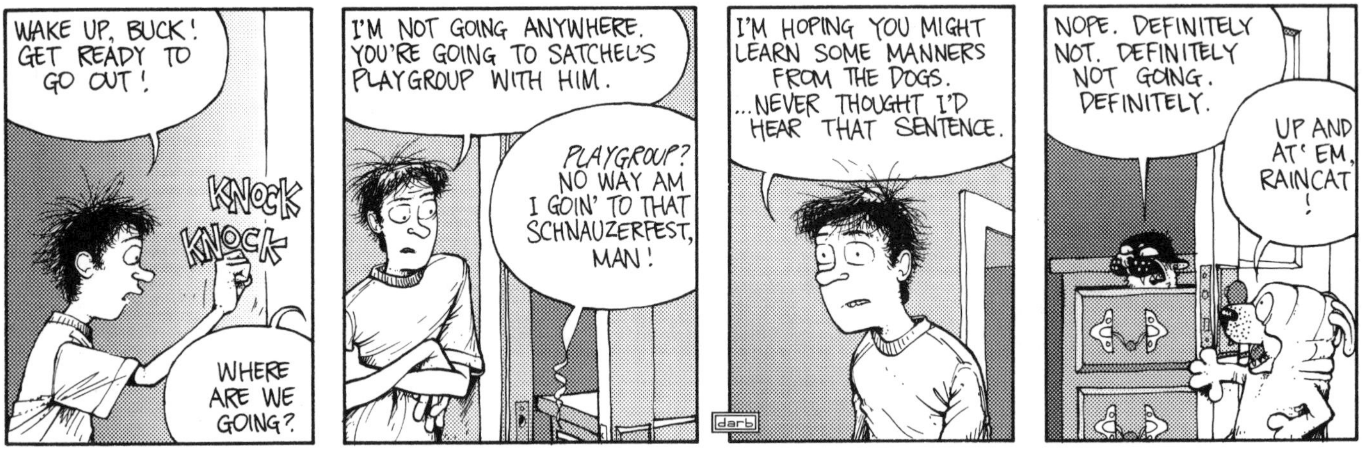
WAKE UP, BUCK! GET READY TO GO OUT!
KNOCK KNOCK
WHERE ARE WE GOING?
I'M NOT GOING ANYWHERE. YOU'RE GOING TO SATCHEL'S PLAYGROUP WITH HIM.
PLAYGROUP? NO WAY AM I GOIN' TO THAT SCHNAUZERFEST, MAN!
I'M HOPING YOU MIGHT LEARN SOME MANNERS FROM THE DOGS. ...NEVER THOUGHT I'D HEAR THAT SENTENCE.
darb
NOPE. DEFINITELY NOT. DEFINITELY NOT GOING. DEFINITELY.
UP AND AT 'EM, RAINCAT!

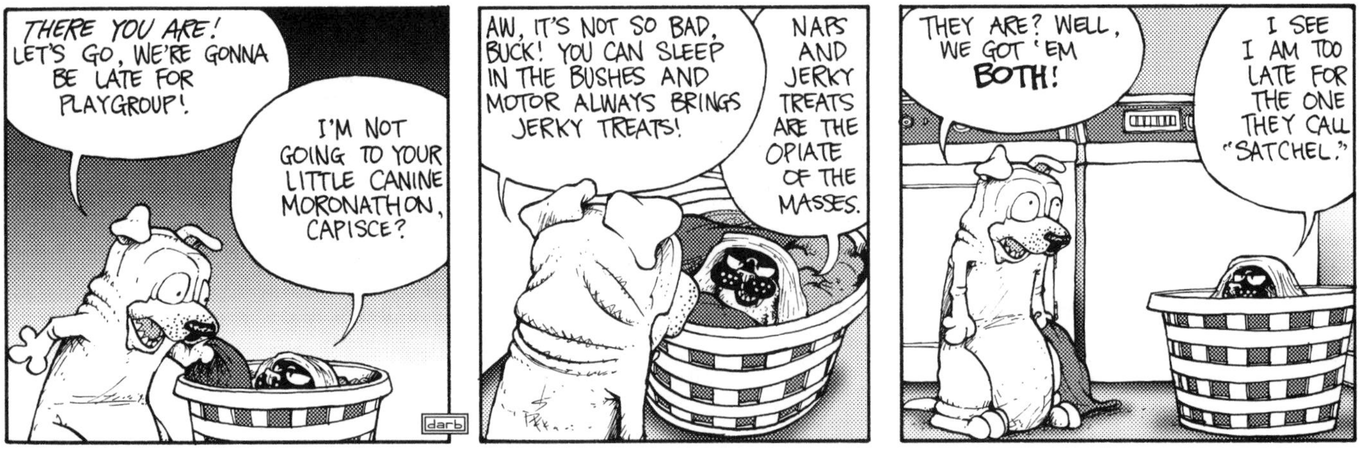
THERE YOU ARE! LET'S GO, WE'RE GONNA BE LATE FOR PLAYGROUP!
I'M NOT GOING TO YOUR LITTLE CANINE MORONATHON, CAPISCE?
darb
AW, IT'S NOT SO BAD, BUCK! YOU CAN SLEEP IN THE BUSHES AND MOTOR ALWAYS BRINGS JERKY TREATS!
NAPS AND JERKY TREATS ARE THE OPIATE OF THE MASSES.
THEY ARE? WELL, WE GOT 'EM BOTH!
I SEE I AM TOO LATE FOR THE ONE THEY CALL "SATCHEL."

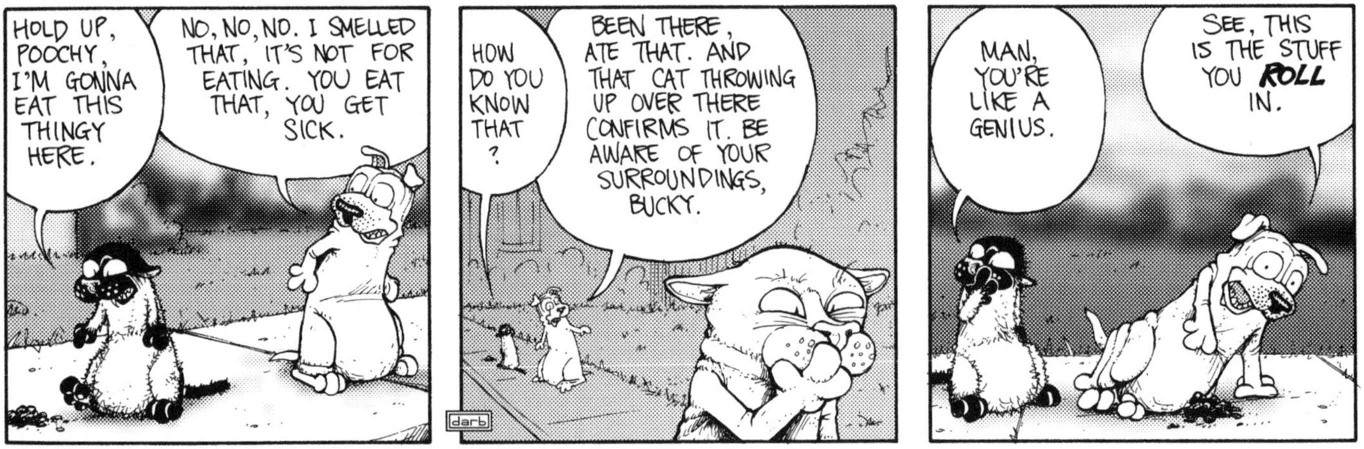
HOLD UP, POOCHY, I'M GONNA EAT THIS THINGY HERE.
NO, NO, NO. I SMELLED THAT, IT'S NOT FOR EATING. YOU EAT THAT, YOU GET SICK.
HOW DO YOU KNOW THAT?
BEEN THERE, ATE THAT. AND THAT CAT THROWING UP OVER THERE CONFIRMS IT. BE AWARE OF YOUR SURROUNDINGS, BUCKY.
darb
MAN, YOU'RE LIKE A GENIUS.
SEE, THIS IS THE STUFF YOU ROLL IN.

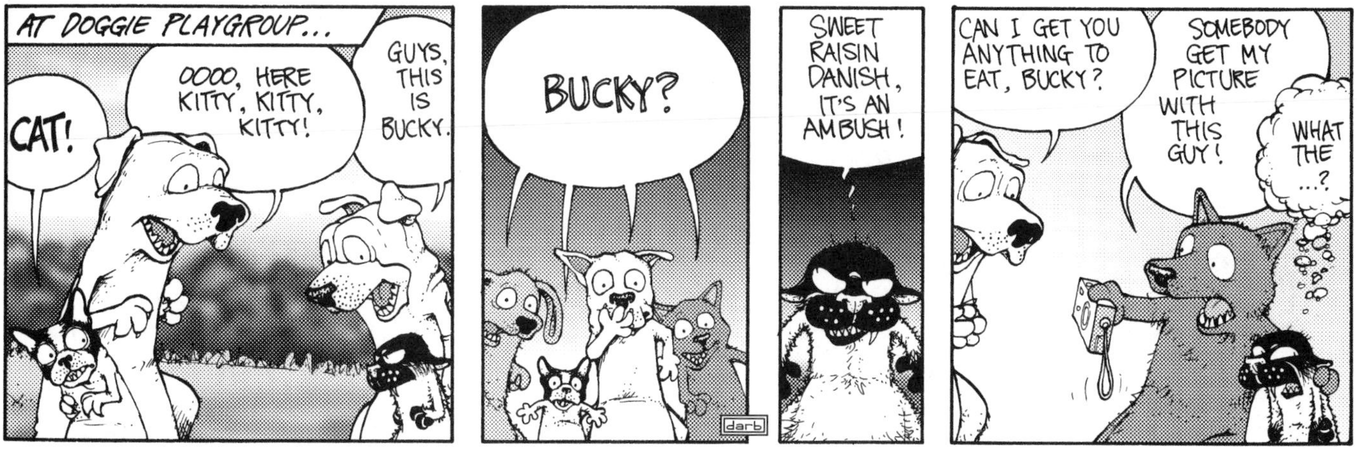
AT DOGGIE PLAYGROUP...
CAT!
OOOO, HERE KITTY, KITTY, KITTY!
GUYS, THIS IS BUCKY.
BUCKY?
SWEET RAISIN DANISH, IT'S AN AMBUSH!
CAN I GET YOU ANYTHING TO EAT, BUCKY?
SOMEBODY GET MY PICTURE WITH THIS GUY!
WHAT THE ...?
darb

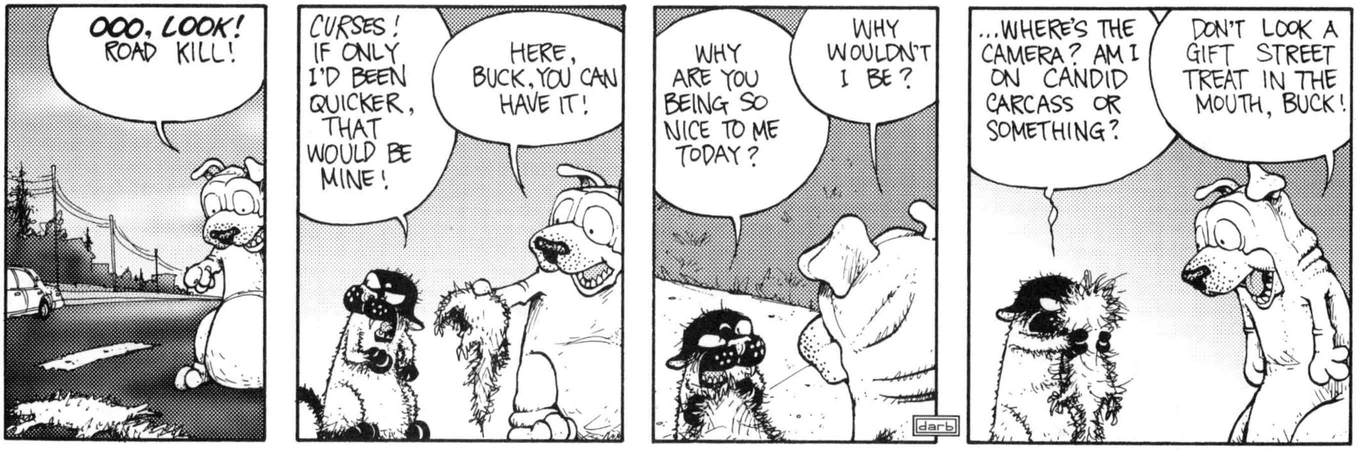
OOO, LOOK! ROAD KILL!
CURSES! IF ONLY I'D BEEN QUICKER, THAT WOULD BE MINE!
HERE, BUCK, YOU CAN HAVE IT!
WHY ARE YOU BEING SO NICE TO ME TODAY?
WHY WOULDN'T I BE?
darb
...WHERE'S THE CAMERA? AM I ON CANDID CARCASS OR SOMETHING?
DON'T LOOK A GIFT STREET TREAT IN THE MOUTH, BUCK!

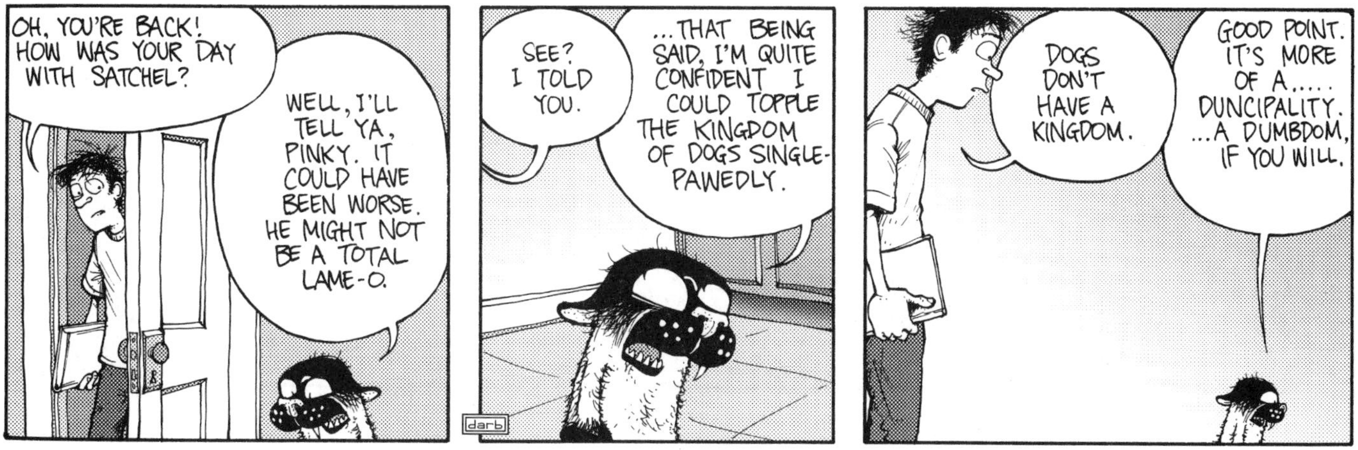
OH, YOU'RE BACK! HOW WAS YOUR DAY WITH SATCHEL?
WELL, I'LL TELL YA, PINKY. IT COULD HAVE BEEN WORSE. HE MIGHT NOT BE A TOTAL LAME-O.
darb
SEE? I TOLD YOU.
...THAT BEING SAID, I'M QUITE CONFIDENT I COULD TOPPLE THE KINGDOM OF DOGS SINGLE-PAWEDLY.
DOGS DON'T HAVE A KINGDOM.
GOOD POINT. IT'S MORE OF A..... DUNCIPALITY. ...A DUMBDOM, IF YOU WILL.

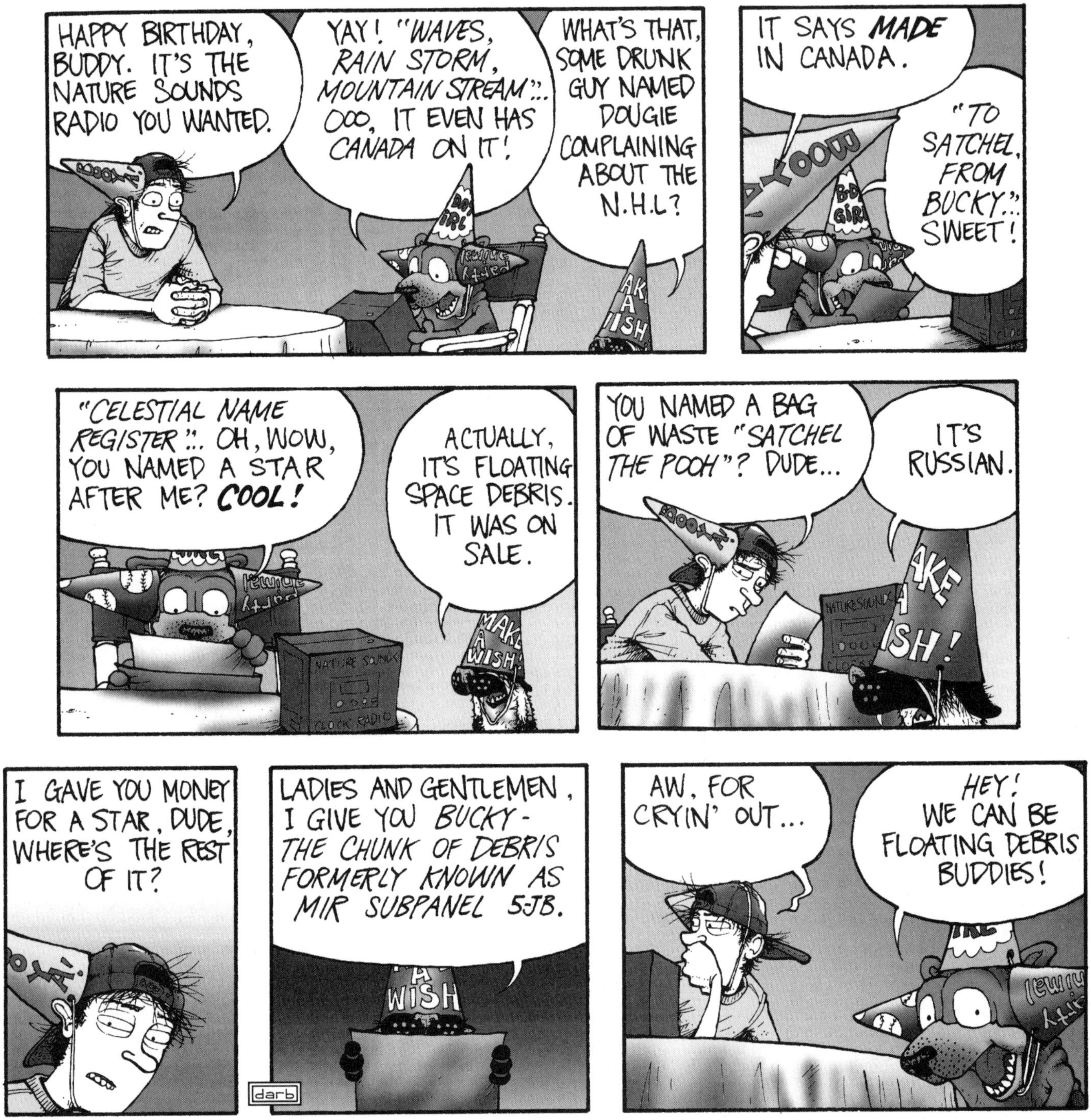

HAPPY BIRTHDAY, BUDDY. IT'S THE NATURE SOUNDS RADIO YOU WANTED.
YAY! "WAVES, RAIN STORM, MOUNTAIN STREAM"... OOO, IT EVEN HAS CANADA ON IT!
WHAT'S THAT, SOME DRUNK GUY NAMED DOUGIE COMPLAINING ABOUT THE N.H.L?
IT SAYS MADE IN CANADA.
"TO SATCHEL, FROM BUCKY."... SWEET!
"CELESTIAL NAME REGISTER"... OH, WOW, YOU NAMED A STAR AFTER ME? COOL!
ACTUALLY, IT'S FLOATING SPACE DEBRIS. IT WAS ON SALE.
NATURE SOUNDS
CLOCK RADIO
YOU NAMED A BAG OF WASTE "SATCHEL THE POOH"? DUDE...
IT'S RUSSIAN.
I GAVE YOU MONEY FOR A STAR, DUDE, WHERE'S THE REST OF IT?
LADIES AND GENTLEMEN, I GIVE YOU BUCKY - THE CHUNK OF DEBRIS FORMERLY KNOWN AS MIR SUBPANEL 5-JB.
darb
AW, FOR CRYIN' OUT...
HEY! WE CAN BE FLOATING DEBRIS BUDDIES!

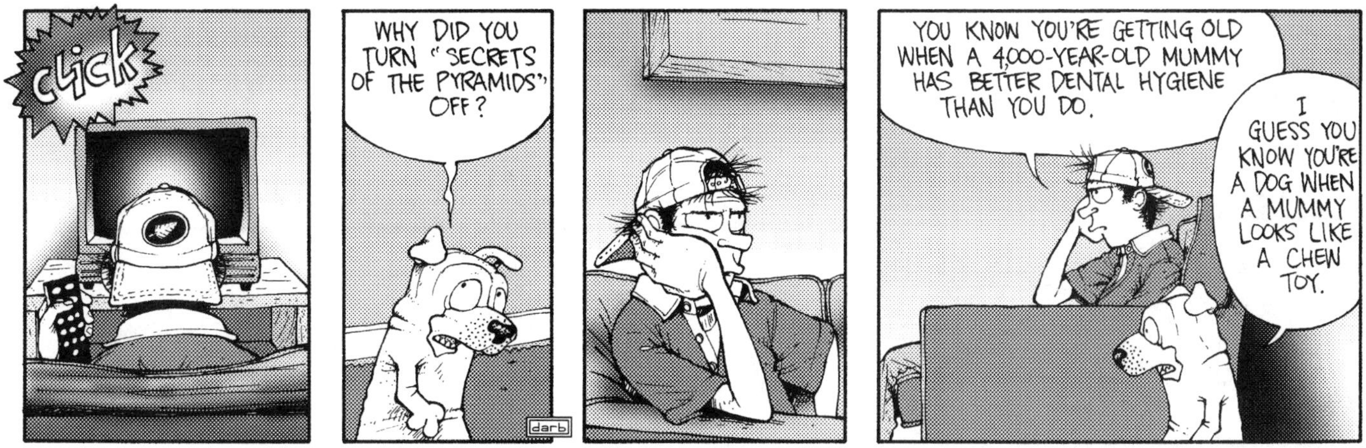
CLICK
WHY DID YOU TURN "SECRETS OF THE PYRAMIDS" OFF?
YOU KNOW YOU'RE GETTING OLD WHEN A 4,000-YEAR-OLD MUMMY HAS BETTER DENTAL HYGIENE THAN YOU DO.
I GUESS YOU KNOW YOU'RE A DOG WHEN A MUMMY LOOKS LIKE A CHEW TOY.
darb

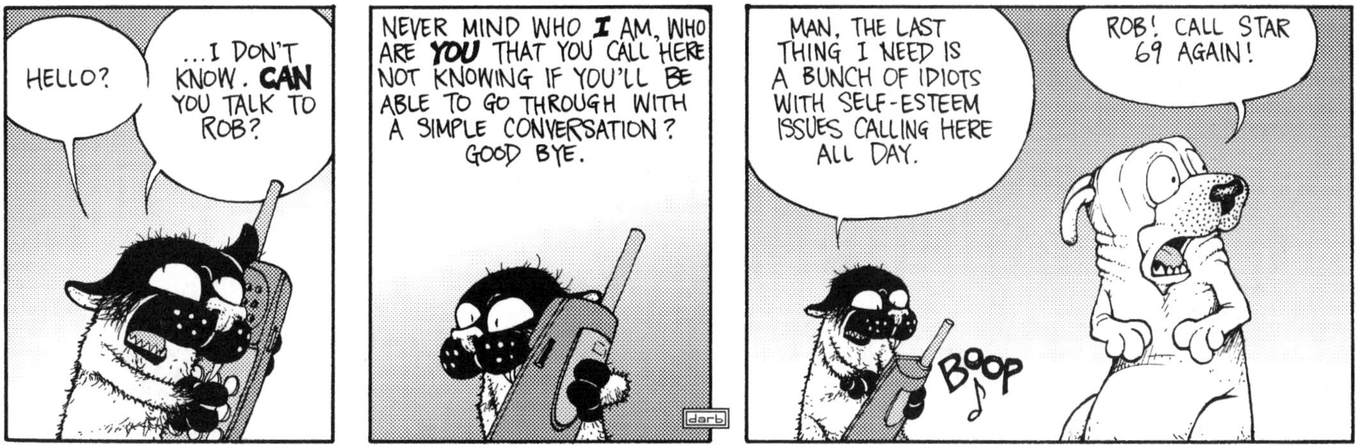
HELLO?
...I DON'T KNOW. CAN YOU TALK TO ROB?
NEVER MIND WHO I AM, WHO ARE YOU THAT YOU CALL HERE NOT KNOWING IF YOU'LL BE ABLE TO GO THROUGH WITH A SIMPLE CONVERSATION? GOOD BYE.
darb
MAN, THE LAST THING I NEED IS A BUNCH OF IDIOTS WITH SELF-ESTEEM ISSUES CALLING HERE ALL DAY.
BOOP
ROB! CALL STAR 69 AGAIN!

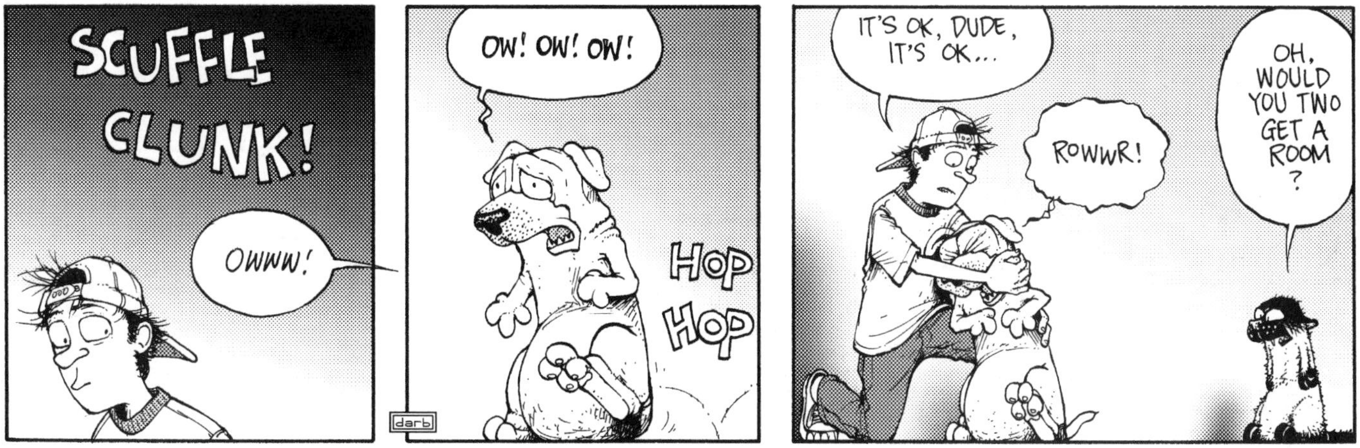
SCUFFLE
CLUNK!
OWWW!
darb
OW! OW! OW!
HOP
HOP
IT'S OK, DUDE, IT'S OK...
ROWWR!
OH, WOULD YOU TWO GET A ROOM?

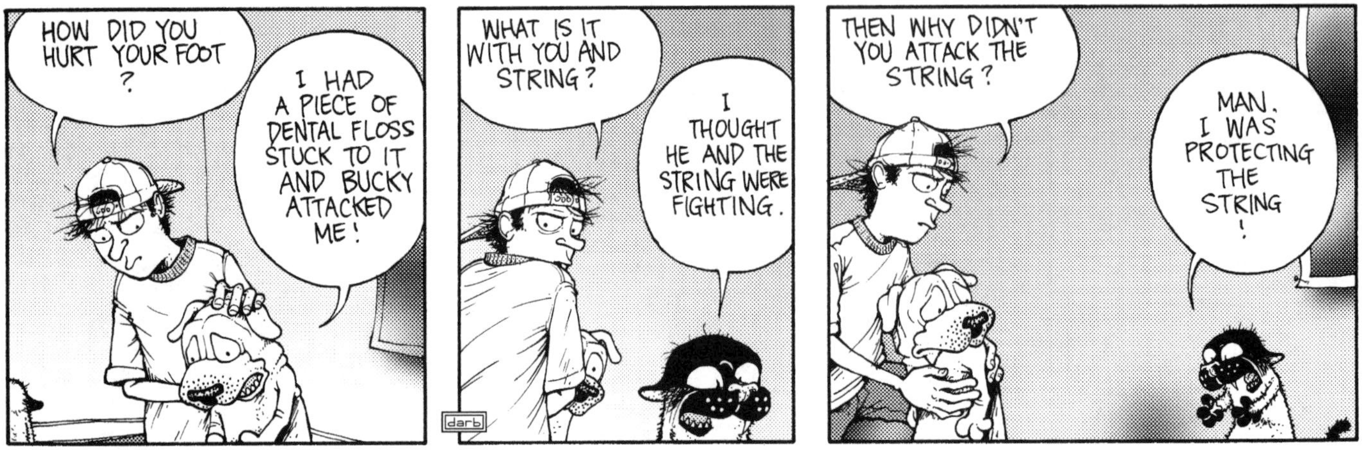
HOW DID YOU HURT YOUR FOOT ?
I HAD A PIECE OF DENTAL FLOSS STUCK TO IT AND BUCKY ATTACKED ME!
WHAT IS IT WITH YOU AND STRING?
I THOUGHT HE AND THE STRING WERE FIGHTING.
THEN WHY DIDN'T YOU ATTACK THE STRING?
MAN. I WAS PROTECTING THE STRING!

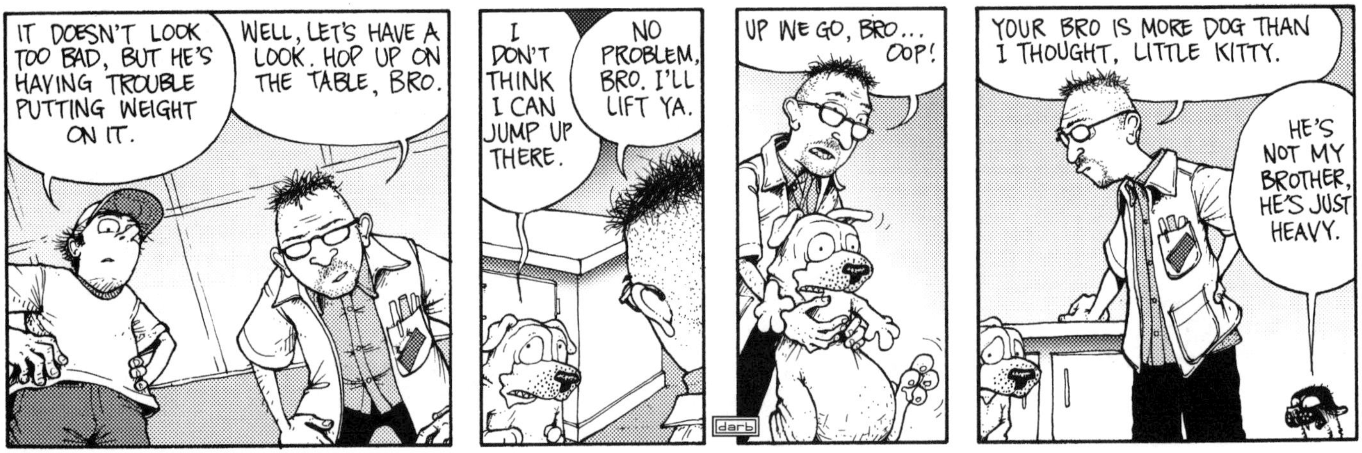
IT DOESN'T LOOK TOO BAD, BUT HE'S HAVING TROUBLE PUTTING WEIGHT ON IT.
WELL, LET'S HAVE A LOOK. HOP UP ON THE TABLE, BRO.
I DON'T THINK I CAN JUMP UP THERE.
NO PROBLEM, BRO. I'LL LIFT YA.
UP WE GO, BRO... OOP!
YOUR BRO IS MORE DOG THAN I THOUGHT, LITTLE KITTY.
HE'S NOT MY BROTHER, HE'S JUST HEAVY.

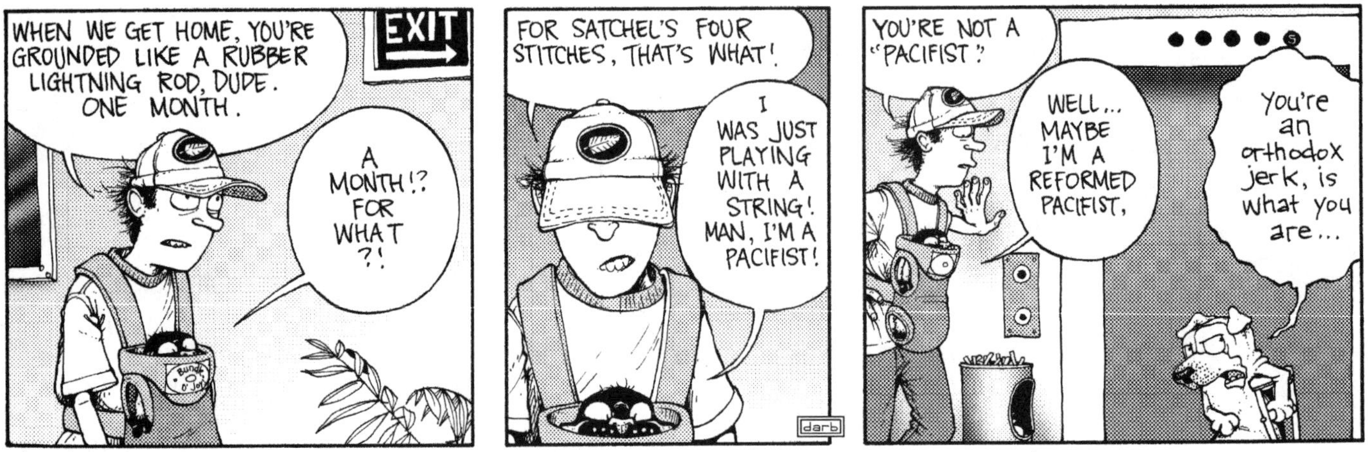
WHEN WE GET HOME, YOU'RE GROUNDED LIKE A RUBBER LIGHTNING ROD, DUDE. ONE MONTH.
EXIT
A MONTH!? FOR WHAT?!
FOR SATCHEL'S FOUR STITCHES, THAT'S WHAT!
I WAS JUST PLAYING WITH A STRING! MAN, I'M A PACIFIST!
YOU'RE NOT A "PACIFIST."
WELL... MAYBE I'M A REFORMED PACIFIST,
You're an orthodox jerk, is what you are...